Pointers in C Programming

A Modern Approach to Memory Management, Recursive Data Structures, Strings, and Arrays

Thomas Mailund

Apress®

Pointers in C Programming: A Modern Approach to Memory Management, Recursive Data Structures, Strings, and Arrays

Thomas Mailund
Aarhus N, Denmark

ISBN-13 (pbk): 978-1-4842-6926-8   ISBN-13 (electronic): 978-1-4842-6927-5
https://doi.org/10.1007/978-1-4842-6927-5

Managing Director, Apress Media LLC: Welmoed Spahr
Acquisitions Editor: Steve Anglin
Development Editor: Matthew Moodie
Coordinating Editor: Mark Powers

Cover designed by eStudioCalamar

Cover image by Engin Akyurt on Unsplash (www.unsplash.com)

Distributed to the book trade worldwide by Apress Media, LLC, 1 New York Plaza, New York, NY 10004, U.S.A. Phone 1-800-SPRINGER, fax (201) 348-4505, e-mail orders-ny@springer-sbm.com, or visit www.springeronline.com. Apress Media, LLC is a California LLC and the sole member (owner) is Springer Science + Business Media Finance Inc (SSBM Finance Inc). SSBM Finance Inc is a **Delaware** corporation.

For information on translations, please e-mail booktranslations@springernature.com; for reprint, paperback, or audio rights, please e-mail bookpermissions@springernature.com.

Apress titles may be purchased in bulk for academic, corporate, or promotional use. eBook versions and licenses are also available for most titles. For more information, reference our Print and eBook Bulk Sales web page at http://www.apress.com/bulk-sales.

Any source code or other supplementary material referenced by the author in this book is available to readers on GitHub via the book's product page, located at www.apress.com/9781484269268. For more detailed information, please visit http://www.apress.com/source-code.

Printed on acid-free paper

Table of Contents

About the Author

Thomas Mailund is an associate professor in bioinformatics at Aarhus University, Denmark. He has a background in math and computer science. For the past decade, his main focus has been on genetics and evolutionary studies, particularly comparative genomics, speciation, and gene flow between emerging species. He has published *String Algorithms in C, R Data Science Quick Reference, The Joys of Hashing, Domain-Specific Languages in R, Beginning Data Science in R, Functional Programming in R,* and *Metaprogramming in R*, all from Apress, as well as other books.

About the Technical Reviewer

Juturi Narsimha Rao has 9 years of experience as a software developer, lead engineer, project engineer, and individual contributor. His current focus is on advanced supply chain planning between the manufacturing industries and vendors.

Acknowledgments

I am grateful to Helge Jensen, Anders E. Halager, Irfansha Shaik, and Kristian Ozol for discussions and comments on earlier drafts of this book.

CHAPTER 1

Introduction

Pointers and memory management are considered among the most challenging issues to deal with in low-level programming languages such as C. It is not that pointers are conceptually difficult to understand, nor is it difficult to comprehend how we can obtain memory from the operating system and how we return the memory again so it can be reused. The difficulty stems from the flexibility with which pointers let us manipulate the entire state of a running program. With pointers, every object anywhere in a program's memory is available to us—at least in principle. We can change any bit to our heart's desire. No data are safe from our pointers, not even the program that we run—a running program is nothing but data in the computer's memory, and in theory, we can modify our own code as we run it.

With such a power tool, it should hardly surprise that mistakes can be fatal for a program, and unfortunately, mistakes are easy to make when it comes to pointers. While pointers do have type information, type safety is minimal when you use them. If you point somewhere in memory and pronounce that you want "that integer over there," you get an integer, no matter what the object "over there" really is. Treat it like an integer, and it behaves like an integer. Assign a value to it, and may the gods have mercy on your soul if it was supposed to be something else and something you need later. You have just destroyed the real object you pointed at.

If you are not careful, any small mistake can crash your program—or worse. If you accidentally modify the incorrect data in your program, all your output is tainted. If you are lucky, it is easily detectable, and you are in for a fun few days of debugging. If you are less fortunate, you can make business decisions based on incorrect output for years to come, never realizing that the code you wrote is fooling you every time it runs—or maybe not every time, just on infrequent occasions, so rare that you can never chase down the problem. When you have bugs caused by pointers (or uninitialized memory),

© Thomas Mailund 2021
T. Mailund, *Pointers in C Programming*, https://doi.org/10.1007/978-1-4842-6927-5_1

they are not always reproducible. Your program's behavior might depend on which other programs are running concurrently on the computer. If you start debugging it, any code you add to the program to examine it will affect its behavior. Loading the program into a debugger will definitely change the behavior as well. I hope that you will never run into such bugs—known as Heisenbugs after Heisenberg's uncertainty principle—but if you mess around with pointers long enough, you likely will.

It sounds like pointers are something we should stay away from, and many high-level programming languages do try to avoid them. Instead, they provide alternative language constructions that are safer to use but provide much of the same functionality that we need pointers for in C. They are not as powerful but alleviate many of the dangers that raw memory pointers pose. In low-level languages such as C, we are programming much closer to the machine. The computer doesn't understand high-level constructions; it understands memory and chunks of bits, and in low-level languages, we can manipulate the computer at this fundamental level. We very rarely need to, nor do we want to, but when we choose to program in low-level languages, it is to get close to the machine, where we can write more efficient programs, measured in both speed and memory usage. And at this level, we get pointers—more efficient, more fundamental, and more dangerous. If, however, we approach using pointers in a structured manner, we can achieve the safety of high-level languages *and* the efficiency of low-level languages. The burden is on the programmer, rather than the language designer, but we can get the best of both worlds for anything that you can do in a high-level language—while maintaining the real power of pointers in the rare cases where you need more.

In this book, I will explain the basic memory model that C programs assume about the computer they run on and how pointers let us access data anywhere in memory. I will explain how you get safe access to memory, by allocating blocks of memory you need, so they are yours to manipulate, and how you can release memory when you no longer need it, so you do not run out of memory before your computations are done. I will explain how pointers are essential for building complex data structures and how you can approach this in a structured way, so they are safe to use. And I will show you how you can use pointers to functions to implement higher-order functions and polymorphic data structures.

I will not cover basic C programming. This is not an introduction to programming or the language. I will assume that you already know the basics and will jump directly into memory and pointers. I will not cover issues related to concurrency and interruptions and such either. That would lengthen the book substantially, and there are already excellent books where you can explore this further.

CHAPTER 2

Memory, Objects, and Addresses

Everything you manipulate when you run a computer program, and the program itself, has to reside somewhere in your computer's memory—on a disk, in its RAM circuits, in various levels of cache, or in a CPU's or GPU's registers. It is not something we necessarily think about when we write programs, but it is an obvious truth: if objects aren't found *somewhere*, we cannot work with them. The reason we can get away with not worrying about memory is that our programming language handles most of the bookkeeping.

Consider the classical "Hello, world!" program:

```c
#include <stdio.h>

int main(void)
{
  printf("Hello, world\n");
  return 0;
}
```

We don't need to think about the computer's memory when we write it (or execute it). Still, many objects must necessarily be represented in memory before we can run the program—the program itself, including the main() function we write ourselves and the printf() function we get from the runtime system. The two arguments we give to main(), argc and argv, are stored somewhere, as is the constant string "Hello, world!\n".

© Thomas Mailund 2021
T. Mailund, *Pointers in C Programming*, https://doi.org/10.1007/978-1-4842-6927-5_2

Or consider a simple function for computing the factorial of a number:

```
int factorial(int n)
{
  if (n <= 1) return 1;
  else return n * factorial(n - 1);
}
```

When we call the function, we must store the argument, n, somewhere. In the recursive case, we call the function again, and in the second call, we need another parameter n. We need another one because we need to remember the current n so we can multiply it to the result of the recursion. Each recursive call must have its own n stored somewhere in memory.

We don't have to worry about where the functions, variables, and constants live in memory when we write this code because the C compiler will generate the necessary machine code to handle it for us. It will allocate the space for constants and variables, and it handles writing function parameters and assignments to variables into the correct memory locations. When we read the value in a variable, it handles getting it from the right memory location for us as well.

However, when we choose to program in a low-level language, like C, the raw memory is never too far away. It is possible to hide memory entirely from the programmer, to pretend that objects are floating around somewhere and never wonder about where that is. However, it comes at a computational overhead, and it limits what we can do with a program in some ways. Low-level languages do not do this. They let us get the memory of objects and manipulate the memory directly. We do not do this willy-nilly because if we did, we would write unmaintainable software. Still, we have the power, and when we use this power carefully, and in a structured way, we can build the features that high-level languages provide using a single mental framework and with little computational overhead.

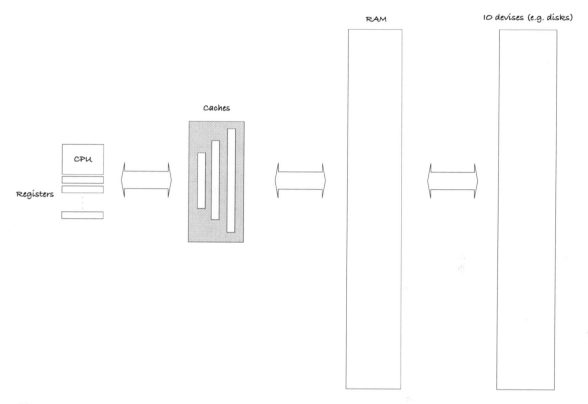

Figure 2-1. *Computer memory hierarchy*

Even though we work with low-level languages, we work with an abstraction of the computer's memory. A modern computer's memory is an immensely complex system, where data lives at different locations, and the time it takes to access it varies widely. A simplified model of a modern computer can look like that in Figure 2-1.

Objects that reside in a CPU's or GPU's registers are incredibly fast to access and manipulate. In comparison, accessing an object on a RAM chip takes geological ages. We cannot hold all the data we operate on in registers, there are too few of them, so we need to move data in and out of the CPU. To alleviate the long delay you get when the CPU has to access objects, the computer moves data you are currently working on into a cache, which the CPU can access faster than the main memory. When you switch to working on some other data, that goes into the cache, and the previous data goes back to main memory. When we need data from files, we usually write code that explicitly gets it from there, but if the computer runs out of main memory, it might also use the file system to swap data you are not using out of and data you are using into RAM.

Your hardware, operating system, and compiler work together to optimize the computational cost of memory access. Your compiler will analyze your programs and put objects in registers when possible. The computer's hardware will move objects from RAM into different levels of cache for faster access. If you are so unlucky that data needs to move to a disk, the operating system will handle that for you. We do not usually write programs that work on memory at this level of detail. It would be incredibly tedious to do, and we would write programs optimized for specific platforms. If you change the hardware, you have different levels of cache, with different performance trade-offs. Writing programs with an abstract memory model is hard enough; writing programs with the full complexity in mind would be close to impossible. We write programs with a simpler conceptual model of computer memory and let the compiler and hardware map from the simple model to the more complex.

In this book, we will pretend that there is only one level of memory, RAM. All data manipulation happens in the CPU, but the compiler will generate the necessary code to move data in and out of the CPU. We will not worry about this, but trust that it does this efficiently. An optimizing compiler is likely better at it than we are anyway, and it certainly is more efficient to write code if we do not worry about such low-level programming. So we will only worry about what our data is doing in that big block of RAM. This is close to how C's memory model work. If you write portable C, the language standard does not make many promises about what the memory looks like. Still, all objects sit in some memory, they have addresses that you can get, and if you have the address of an object, then you can manipulate that object. What you can actually do with the object depends on how you define it, but whatever you can do with an object, you can also do through its address.

The Memory of a Generic Process

The C standard doesn't specify how memory should be organized for running programs, but a typical process, that is, a running program, can look like Figure 2-2. At the lowest memory addresses, at the bottom, you have the code that the process runs. Code is data as well, it is the instructions that the CPU should follow, and it is part of the process' memory. Above that, you have the data that exists throughout the process' lifetime. When you declare global variables, they live as long as the program runs, and this is where they sit in memory. Some of this data will be read-only. There are constants defined in a program that you cannot change. String literals, those you define with " . . . ", are usually immutable, they live in read-only memory, and your program might crash if you try to write to them. Global variables you define yourself, if not declared const, are mutable, and you can write to them. In the figure, I do not make a distinction between the two, but your data usually comes as both read-only and read-write.

On top of that, you have the memory that the program allocates (and deallocates) while it runs. We call this memory area the *heap*, and in Chapter 9 we see how you can allocate memory from it in C. When the process needs more memory, the heap grows upward. When it gets rid of memory, the situation is more complicated. We do not remove a block in the middle and move all the data above it down, that would be time-consuming, and we cannot move objects we have the address of—then they would have moved away, and so accessing the data through an address would not work. Not to worry, though, it is something that C's runtime system will handle for you. At the top, we have the *stack*. The stack handles function calls, and it is where local variables and function arguments live. It typically grows downward. Between the stack and the heap, there is usually a barrier, a piece of memory that you are not allowed to access. It is there to prevent the stack and heap to grow into each other.

The memory that a process sees is rarely the physical memory the computer has. Between a running process and the physical memory, the CPU creates a "virtual" memory. That is the memory space that the program works with, and each time it needs to access memory, the hardware will map the virtual address to a physical one. In the old days, physical and virtual memory was the same, and any program could read and write data anywhere and execute any code from anywhere. This is, obviously, highly unsafe. The virtual memory protects processes from each other and provides a more straightforward address interface to programs.

Programs need to allocate memory for the stack and heap to use it, which typically involves asking the operating system to get a chunk of memory, which in turn will set up this virtual to physical mapping. That is the addresses that the program can freely access. Even though you could, in theory, address the full address space, in practice, the hardware will cause an interrupt if you access data outside of the memory the program got allocated by the operating system. This will typically result in the OS terminating the process. Thus, if you haven't gotten permission to read or write from somewhere, and you do it anyway, then it can be the death of your program.

Similarly, there is usually protection on which memory you can execute. You should not execute random data, so you are prevented from that. And since there are obvious security problems if you allow a program to write into its code, modifying it potentially based on user input, the executable memory is often read-only.

When you write a C program, you are not given any guarantees for how the data is positioned in memory. You have the `register` keyword to tell the compiler that you would like a given variable stored in a register, but this is an anachronism more than anything else. It is only a suggestion to the compiler, and it is allowed to ignore it. Your compiler is better at allocating registers than most programmers, and it *will* likely ignore the keyword altogether. The only practical consequence of using it is that you are then not allowed to take the address of the variable (that would be inconsistent with wanting to keep it in a register). I suggest you never use this keyword. If you do not take the address of a local variable, then the compiler will put it in a register if that makes the most efficient code. Don't interfere with its register allocation.

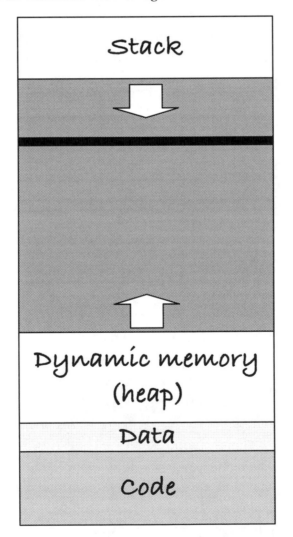

Figure 2-2. *A process' memory layout*

You likely have access to the system calls that lets you manipulate memory at the low levels described, but they are platform dependent, and code you write for one platform will not work on another. The interface to memory that C provides handles the interaction with the operating system, and if you want to write portable code, you should stick with that. Unless you have particular needs, that interface will do everything you need.

In portable C, you cannot assume that your program will run with a memory layout like that described earlier. C is designed to run on practically any hardware and any operating system, and the C standard thus makes few assumptions about the underlying platform. That being said, it is a useful mental model for thinking about your program's memory. You cannot assume that the stack lies at higher memory locations than the heap or that it grows downward instead of upward (and I honestly don't see when that would be relevant for you to worry about).

Even if you write your code in machine code, with full power to access memory as you please, you probably won't see exactly this layout. Addresses are usually scrambled by the architecture, as a defense against hacking attacks (it prevents an attacker from knowing where your code and data are, by randomizing it). If you write multithreaded programs, you need a stack per threat, and they can't all lie at the top of the process' address space. If you dynamically load libraries while executing your program, they need to go somewhere as well. That is code, but the code's location and size are already fixed in this model.

Still, there is a stack, and there is a heap—if not in reality, then conceptually—and I will present memory in this book as if we had processes like these. As long as you don't write your programs with this strong an assumption about the memory layout, it is a useful mental model of the memory you use and manipulate.

Objects, Sizes, and Addresses

While the C language doesn't describe how memory is organized, it does specify that each object has an address and a size. The address is where it sits, conceptually if not in fact, and its size is how many memory locations it takes up. By the C standard, each memory cell takes up one char, and larger objects take up more cells of memory. The C standard doesn't say what size a char actually is; it is just the minimum size of an object that we can put into one block.

You can get the size of an object using the `sizeof` operator. Try running this program:

```
#include <stdio.h>

int main(void)
{
  char c;
  printf("%zu %zu\n", sizeof(char), sizeof c);
  int i;
  printf("%zu %zu\n", sizeof(int), sizeof i);
  double d;
  printf("%zu %zu\n", sizeof(double), sizeof d);
  return 0;
}
```

I got

```
1 1
4 4
8 8
```

but the result will depend on your platform.

When we use `sizeof` on a type or a variable, we get the size of the type/object. Your result might vary from mine (I got size 1 for `char`, 4 for `int`, and 8 for `double`). The size of `char` is always one. That is guaranteed by the C standard. There are no other guarantees about the absolute size of other types, although there are some guarantees about the relative size of objects. For practically all modern hardware, a `char` is 8 bits, but the standard doesn't guarantee it. The constant `CHAR_BIT` will tell you how many bits a `char` contains in your own development environment, but I will be surprised if it isn't 8. If it isn't, then you are working on unusual hardware. If a `char` is 1 byte, that means that for my output, an integer is 32 bits (4 bytes) and a `double` is 64 bits (8 bytes).

All sizes are relative to the minimal size that C works with, and that is the size of a `char`. For the variables, you do not need the parentheses. You can write `sizeof c` instead of `sizeof(c)`. For the types, you do need the parentheses. If you want the size of an object or type related to a variable, that is, the variable itself or something it refers to in cases of structures or arrays, you should prefer to get the size through the variable.

You have specified the type when you declared the variable, and if you use the type once more with `sizeof`, you have two references to it. If you change one and not the other, you can get in trouble. It is better to specify the type once and get it automatically from the variable after that.

If you want to know the address at which a variable sits, you can put an ampersand, &, before the variable:

```
#include <stdio.h>

int main(void)
{
  char c = 1;
  printf("%d %p\n", c, (void *)&c);
  int i = 2;
  printf("%d %p\n", i, (void *)&i);
  double d = 3.0;
  printf("%f %p\n", d, (void *)&d);
  return 0;
}
```

The program prints the (integer) value of a character, the value of an integer, and the value of a `double`, together with the memory addresses where the variables sit. The formatting code `%p` gives us the text representation of the address when we call `printf()`. It will print the memory addresses. The (`void *`) cast is there because the `%p` wants a void pointer. We see more to those in the next chapter.

There are no hard rules for where C should put variables, nor is there any rule that says that you can meaningfully compare the address of objects you haven't allocated together. That being said, if you see that the printed addresses are numbers close together, then the addresses probably are. If your memory addresses are laid out in the process' memory locations as described in the previous section, the preceding program gives you where they sit. I got the result:

```
1 0x7ffee0d888ff
2 0x7ffee0d888f8
3.000000 0x7ffee0d888f0
```

which tells us that the double was put first in memory, then the integer, and then the character; see Figure 2-3. The memory locations are ordered from the bottom and up, so the integer, for example, sits at address 0x7ffee0d888f8 (bottom) to 0x7ffee0d888b (top).

The 8 bytes from 0x7ffee0d88f0 contain the double. Immediately after the double, we have the int. From the sizeof(int) call in the previous program, we know that an int takes up four memory cells on my machine, but there is a gap, the gray area, up to the char, found at address 0x7ffee0d888f0. C can put the variables where it wants, and you have no guarantee that they are consecutive for two separate variables. This layout is what I got on my computer when I translated the program with the compiler and options that I used. If I change any of the options, for example, change the optimization settings, things could look very different. Do not make assumptions about where individual variables are put in memory; the C standard does not make any promises. It only promises that your objects have an address and a size that is determined by its type.

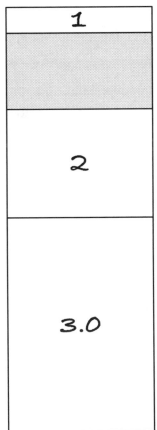

Figure 2-3. *Memory locations for a char, int, and double*

More technically, a block of memory you have allocated in a single operation has an address and a size. From the beginning of the allocated memory and up to its size, you have consecutive addresses, and you can meaningfully compare these addresses and reason about the memory layout. Memory that you have allocated independently, you should not make any assumptions about. Maybe you can use their addresses to work out where the memory sits relative to each other, or maybe you cannot. If you want to compare addresses, stick to looking at addresses within one allocated block.

Memory Allocation

What does it mean to allocate memory? How do we get the memory that our variables sit in? And how do we get more when we need it? Most memory management is automatic in C. When you declare a variable, the compiler generates code for allocating the memory to hold it. For global and static variables, it sets aside memory that will last as long as the program runs. For local variables and function arguments, which you can think of as the same thing, the compiler generates code to get memory for them when you call a function. This memory is allocated on the stack, and it only lives as long as the function call that allocated it. We return to stack-allocated memory later in the chapter.

Although it is a good bet that local variables sit near each other on the stack, you cannot make assumptions if you want your code to run everywhere. Individual variables are independently allocated, and then the language makes no promises about how they relate. But you can allocate more than one value at the same time, and then we get a few more promises.

There are different ways that we can allocate multiple objects at the same time. The simplest is through *arrays* that we will cover in detail in Chapters 5 and 6. An array allocates several objects of the same type and put them, one after another, in consecutive memory locations. In the following program, we allocate an array of five integers and get the addresses of the individual integers:

```
#include <stdio.h>

int main(void)
{
  int array[5];
  printf(" array    == %p\n", (void *)array);
  for (int i = 0; i < 5; i++) {
```

```
    printf("&array[%d] == %p\n", i, (void *)&array[i]);
  }
  printf("sizeof array == %zu\n", sizeof array);
  printf("5 * sizeof(int) == %zu\n", 5 * sizeof(int));

  return 0;
}
```

An integer takes up `sizeof(int)` memory addresses, so five of them takes up 5 * `sizeof(int)`, and that is the size of the array. The integers lie in contiguous memory, with `array[i + 1]` `sizeof(int)` after `array[i]`; see Figure 2-4. The value of an array, the preceding `array`, is the address of the first of the integers.

The integers in the array are part of the same memory allocation, and you are guaranteed that they are structured this way in memory.

With dynamic memory allocation, the topic for Chapter 9, you explicitly allocate memory blocks of the desired size. There, as well, you have a block of memory where the addresses are contiguous. You can use them more freely than you can with arrays, but in practice, you use them either to store array-like data or to store `structs` and `unions`.

Figure 2-4. *Memory layout of an array*

With both `struct` and `union,` you have a single memory allocation when you declare a variable, but a `struct` usually contains more than one data type, and so does a `union` although its purpose is to store different types in the same memory location. When you define a variable of a `struct` or `union` type, you are guaranteed to get a chunk of memory of the relevant type's size that you can index as consecutive memory addresses. For unions, you get a block of memory that is large enough to hold the largest element, and all the elements sit at the first address in the union.

If you run this program

```c
#include <stdio.h>

union data {
  char c;
  int i;
  double d;
};

#define MAX(a,b) (((a)>(b))?(a): (b))
#define MAX3(a,b,c) MAX((a),MAX((b), (c)))

int main(void)
{
  union data data;
  printf("sizeof data == %zu\n", sizeof data);
  printf("max size of components == %zu\n",
         MAX3(sizeof data.c, sizeof data.i, sizeof data.d));

  printf("data at   %p\n", (void *)&data);
  printf("data.c at %p\n", (void *)&data.c);
  printf("data.i at %p\n", (void *)&data.i);
  printf("data.d at %p\n", (void *)&data.d);

  return 0;
}
```

you might get something like

```
sizeof data == 8
max size of components == 8
data at   0x7ffeebd2c900
data.c at 0x7ffeebd2c900
data.i at 0x7ffeebd2c900
data.d at 0x7ffeebd2c900
```

A double is the largest of the three types (on my machine), and the union gets that size—but see the next section for more details about union sizes. All the elements in the union sit at the same address, the address of the union itself, but of course you cannot use them all at the same time. That is not the purpose of unions. You can treat the memory block that the union holds as all three of the types, but a union only holds one of the types at any given time. Therefore, they can store their data in the same memory block and at the same address.

For structures, you get the memory to hold all of the components at the same time, so their size is at least enough to hold all of them. The elements come, one after another, in the order you define them, and the first element is at the first address of the structure. However, between the elements in the struct, there might be unused memory.

When I run this program

```c
#include <stdio.h>

struct data {
  char c;
  int i;
  double d;
};

int main(void)
{
  struct data data;
  printf("sizeof data == %zu\n", sizeof data);
  printf("size of components == %zu\n",
         sizeof data.c + sizeof data.i + sizeof data.d);

  printf("data at    %p\n", (void *)&data);
  printf("data.c at %p\n", (void *)&data.c);
  printf("data.i at %p\n", (void *)&data.i);
  printf("data.d at %p\n", (void *)&data.d);

  return 0;
}
```

I get the output

```
sizeof data == 16
size of components == 13
data at    0x7ffeec6988f8
data.c at 0x7ffeec6988f8
data.i at 0x7ffeec6988fc
data.d at 0x7ffeec698900
```

So the struct variable data takes up 16 memory addresses, even though the data in it only take up 13 bytes (or technically 13 sizeof(char)). The components come in order; first we have c, then i, and then d with c at the same address as the struct, but there is some padding between c and i; see Figure 2-5. If you rearrange the order of the elements, you get them in a different order in memory, but there is likely always some padding.

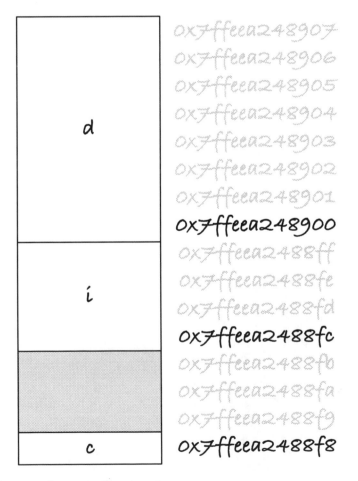

Figure 2-5. *Memory layout of a struct*

The padding might not only be between the components of the struct. You are guaranteed that the first address is where the first component sits, but there can be padding after the last components. If I move c to the bottom of the struct

```
struct data {
  int i;
  double d;
  char c;
};
```

I get the output

```
sizeof data == 24
size of components == 13
data at    0x7ffeef73a8f0
data.c at 0x7ffeef73a900
data.i at 0x7ffeef73a8f0
data.d at 0x7ffeef73a8f8
```

shown in Figure 2-6. The structure is now 24 long, with a gap between i and d and a segment of unused memory after c.

C does not give you many promises about how struct memory should look. The first element at the first address, the elements in order, and that is it. Why does it add this padding? It is not to be malicious. It has to do with memory *alignment*.

Alignment

In the abstract memory model, an address is just an address, and we can put any object there. An object takes up a certain amount of memory, say 4 bytes for a 32-bit integer, so if we put an integer at address *a*, then that address and the following three bytes is where the integer lives. However, on actual hardware, there is more structure to a computer's memory. The memory is not a sequence of bytes, but rather computer words of some given size, for example, 64 bits. The bus that carries data from memory to the CPU works with words of certain sizes. If you ask to get an integer from memory, and it sits in a single word, the computer needs to fetch that single word. If you put an integer at a location that spans more than one word, the computer has to fetch both words and then do some bit manipulation to put it into a register. And even if you ask for a 32-bit integer that sits inside a 64-bit integer, there might be more work for the computer to represent it as an integer in the CPU, if it doesn't sit at a certain offset in its word.

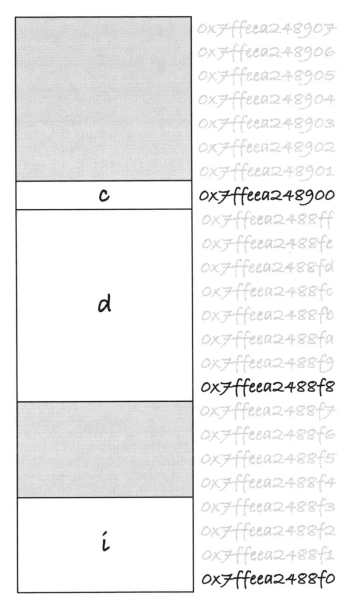

0x7ffeea248907
0x7ffeea248906
0x7ffeea248905
0x7ffeea248904
0x7ffeea248903
0x7ffeea248902
0x7ffeea248901

c   0x7ffeea248900

0x7ffeea2488ff
0x7ffeea2488fe
0x7ffeea2488fd
0x7ffeea2488fc
0x7ffeea2488fb
0x7ffeea2488fa
0x7ffeea2488f9

d

0x7ffeea2488f8

0x7ffeea2488f7
0x7ffeea2488f6
0x7ffeea2488f5
0x7ffeea2488f4
0x7ffeea2488f3
0x7ffeea2488f2
0x7ffeea2488f1

i   0x7ffeea2488f0

Figure 2-6. Structure memory layout after rearranging

When you put objects at memory locations that match what the hardware can handle or simply finds convenient, we say that they are *aligned*, and *memory alignment* can be critical. Typically, the hardware prefers that you put objects at addresses that are a multiple of the size of the objects, so if you have 4-byte integers, your computer might prefer that you put them on addresses that are multiples of four. On some hardware, you are not allowed to put objects at random addresses. You must align them correctly. On other platforms, you can put objects anywhere, but you pay a runtime penalty if they are not aligned. And then there is hardware that doesn't care.

If your compiler is C11 standard compliant, you can use the `alignof()` macro to get the alignment constraints of a type. It will tell you what an address must be a multiple of to correctly align the type. You can try this:

```c
#include <stdio.h>
#include <stdalign.h>

int main(void)
{
  printf("chars align at %zu and have size %zu.\n",
         alignof(char), sizeof(char));
  printf("ints align at %zu and have size %zu.\n",
         alignof(int), sizeof(int));
  printf("doubles align at %zu and have size %zu.\n",
         alignof(double), sizeof(double));

  return 0;
}
```

On my computer, it tells me that `char` can align anywhere (it has alignment 1). This will always be the case and is a property of character types. My `int` objects align at addresses that are multiples of four, and my `double` objects must sit at addresses that are multiples of eight. Alignments are guaranteed to be integral powers of two, and for these numbers, they are $2^0 = 1$ for `alignof(char)` (this is always a character's alignment), $2^2 = 4$ for integers, and $2^3 = 8$ for `double`. This matches their size, but this doesn't have to be the case. For reasons that I will explain later, if an object can sit at any specific address, it will also align at addresses that are multiples of its `sizeof()` higher, so you can always align there. You might, however, also be able to align objects at smaller offsets. If you do not have `alignof()`, you can use `sizeof()` to work out where objects are allowed to sit, but you might be overshooting.

If you go back to the program that generated Figure 2-3, you see that we first defined a character variable, `c`, and it got address 0x7ffee0d888ff. Then we defined the integer `i`, and if integers can only sit at addresses that are multiples of four, we cannot place it right after `c`. An integer has size four (in the example), so if we could place it anywhere, we could put it at 0x7ffee0d88b (that is the first position where we could place it with four memory addresses up to c). We could have placed it at 0x7ffee0d88fc—the c is hexadecimal for 12, which is a multiple of 4—but then c is in the way. So we have to go all the way down to address 0x7ffee0d88f8 before we can find room for the integer. The double needs to sit at least eight positions lower, so there is room for it, and it has to sit at an index that is a multiple of eight. Here we are lucky, and we find room at the first available aligned address, 0x7ffee0d88f0.

With the first struct we made, we have a character first, then an integer, and then a double. It is only the stack that grows downward, so for all other memory structures, we look at the addresses from the bottom up, and in Figure 2-5 we see the character at address 0x7ffeea2488f8, the integer at 0x7ffeea2488fc, and the double at address 0x7ffeea248900. The rule for struct is that the components must come in order, with the first element at the first address, so there is no wiggle room for where c has to go if the structure starts at address 0x7ffeea2488f8. The integer has to go at an address that is a multiple of four, so we have to leave addresses 0x7ffeea2488f9 to 0x7ffeea2488b alone before we get to 0x7ffeea2488fc. The integer ends at address 0x7ffeea2488ff, and the very next address is a multiple of eight, so we can place the double there.

When we rearranged the struct, Figure 2-6, the integer has to come first, and it must sit at an address that is a multiple of four. It ended up at 0x7ffeea2488f0. The next free address is 0x7ffeea2488f4, but this is not a multiple of eight, so we cannot place the double there. We have to continue up to the first address that is a multiple of eight, and that is 0x7ffeea2488f8. The last element, the character, can sit anywhere, so we can place it right after the double. But if we have all three elements by now, why is the structure still larger? What is the point of having the extra space after c?

The issue is this: if you put one struct after another in memory, for example, in an array, C wants element number two to be at the address that is the struct's sizeof() after the first. This goes for all types; if you put one after another in memory, then the distance between them matches their size. That is, after all, what it means to put one after another; the next one starts where the previous one begins.

So let us imagine that we put two of this struct in an array.

```
struct data array[2];
```

Figure 2-7 shows the memory layout of this array with the terminal padding on the left and without it on the right (but in both cases with the padding between the integer and the double). When you allocate an array (or dynamically allocated memory from the heap), you get an address where you can always align the first element of any type. The figure calls that offset zero. The padding between i and d ensures that those two variables are aligned. If the int needs to sit at addresses that are multiples of four, it is fine at offset zero (because the first address is always correctly aligned), and the double sits at offset eight which matches its alignment. The character can sit anywhere, so it is fine as well. In the second structure, the padding after c ensures that the integer still sits at an address that is a multiple of four, it sits at offset 24, and the padding up to d ensures that it sits correctly aligned. The second struct ends at offset 47, so the next free address is offset 48. If we put another struct there, the integer would be fine; 48 is a multiple of 4. With the padding, the third double would sit at offset 56, which is a multiple of 8, so that would be aligned as well. It will continue with correctly aligned elements for as far as the array goes.

If we didn't have the terminal padding after c, we would be in the situation on the right. The first structure is aligned. The first address always is when we allocate memory, and the padding between i and d ensures that the double is aligned as well. The character, of course, always is. But if we continue with the second struct right after c, we immediately get an alignment problem. The structure has size 17: 4 for the int, then 4 for padding, 8 for the double, and then the char. So the offset after the first struct is 17 (since we start at 0), and 17 is not a multiple of 4. We cannot put an integer there. The double would sit at offset 25, which isn't a multiple of 8, so it cannot sit there either. The second struct ends at offset 33, so the next could potentially start at 34. That is a multiple of 4, so we could place an integer there, but the double would have to sit at offset 42 which isn't a multiple of 8.

To correctly align the elements inside a struct, C might have to insert padding between them. Some terminal padding might be necessary as well to make it possible to put structs into arrays. The size of a struct depends on the size of the individual components, their alignment constraints, and also the order in which they are declared inside the structure since the memory will arrange them in that order. You can, in principle, make a structure more memory efficient by rearranging the components, but it isn't worth it. The size of objects and their alignment constraints vary from platform to platform, so if you optimize the memory for one platform, it won't generalize to all platforms. You might make some general rules of thumb about sizes and likely alignment, and try something based on that, but you will be guessing, and while you might make a more compact structure on one platform, you might also make it worse on another. Arranging the components of a structure with this purpose doesn't give you any guarantees, and it might hurt readability. If you keep components that are related close together in the structure definition, the code is easier to read. Readability is more important than micro-optimization. And in the highly unlikely event that the size of a `struct` matters, you can always go back and optimize it or pack the data in some other way. If this is the case, you are also likely to know the platform or platforms where the issue is, and you can optimize for that. Otherwise, just write your structures the way you want and let C worry about padding and alignment.

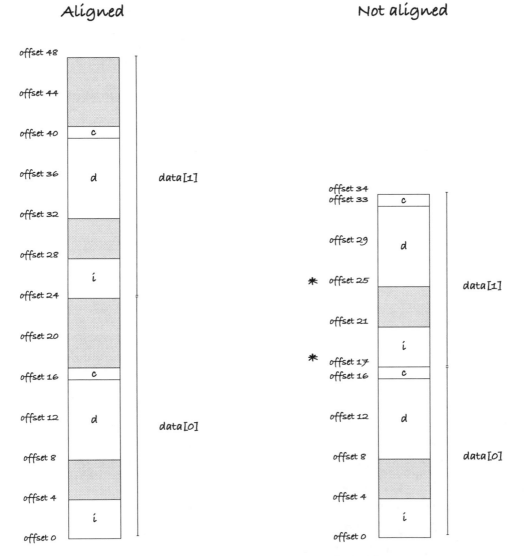

Figure 2-7. *Structure with and without the terminal padding in an array*

What about unions, then? If they are just memory large enough to hold their largest component, can't we get alignment issues there as well? Indeed, we can. Unions must be large enough to hold the largest components, but that is a minimal size. They can be larger, and if there are alignment considerations, they will be. The union in the example in the previous section consisted of a character, an integer, and a double. These can all align to addresses that are multiples of eight; the char can sit anywhere, the int at multiples of eight, and the double at multiples of eight. The union got the same size as the double because that is enough to align the elements. But we can try to put two elements in a union that are not compatible in their alignment. We can take a double that sits at multiples of eight and an object that takes up nine memory locations. We can make such one using a char array of length 9. If the union has size 9, to contain the char array, we cannot put another copy after it. That would be offset 9 which isn't a multiple of 8. We need to put it at the first multiple of 8 address after offset 9 instead, which is 16. So we would expect such a union to have size 16.

You can examine this on your own computer by running this program:

```
#include <stdio.h>

union data {
  char c[9];
  double d;
};

#define MAX(a,b) (((a)>(b))?(a): (b))

int main(void)
{
  union data data;
  printf("sizeof data == %zu\n", sizeof data);
  printf("max size of components == %zu\n",
         MAX(sizeof data.c, sizeof data.d));

  printf("data at   %p\n", (void *)&data);
  printf("data.c at %p\n", (void *)&data.c);
  printf("data.d at %p\n", (void *)&data.d);

  return 0;
}
```

When I run the program, I get

```
sizeof data == 16
max size of components == 9
data at    0x7ffeeae468f0
data.c at 0x7ffeeae468f0
data.d at 0x7ffeeae468f0
```

The elements still sit at the same address as the union (or technically they are such that they can be converted to it), but the size is 16 instead of 9, the size of the largest element. Unions have padding just as structs to match alignment constraints.

As an example of a case where the size of an object and its alignment constraints differ, we can also use a char buffer:

```c
#include <stdio.h>
#include <stdalign.h>

struct data {
  int i;
  char c[9];
};

int main(void)
{
  printf("sizeof components == %zu\n",
         sizeof(char[9]) + sizeof(int));
  printf("sizeof(struct data) == %zu\n",
         sizeof(struct data));
  printf("\n");
  printf("alignof(struct data) == %zu\n",
         alignof(struct data));
  printf("alignment of int == %zu\n",
         alignof(int));
  printf("alignment of char[9] == %zu\n",
         alignof(char[9]));

  return 0;
}
```

If I run it, I get

```
sizeof components == 13
sizeof(struct data) == 16

alignof(struct data) == 4
alignment of int == 4
alignment of char[9] == 1
```

The components, c of size 9 because char has size 1 and i of size 4, fill in total 13 memory locations. The structure is larger; it has size 16. This is because, with alignment 4 for integers, we cannot put another instance of the type before 16 addresses after the first. The structure itself can align at addresses that are multiples of four, however, and not only addresses that are multiples of its size. We can put the structure at such addresses because the initial integer will align there (and the char buffer will align anywhere). If the integer aligns there, it will also align at the first address after the structure. If the first address is a multiple of 4, then addresses that are multiples of 16 following it will be as well.

Alignment might sound frightfully complicated at this point, and you might worry that it is something you need to consider every time you work with addresses. But the truth is that you rarely have to think about it at all. If you declare a variable, its data will sit at an address that is correctly aligned to its type. If you declare an array, the memory will be correctly aligned for each element in it (with the appropriate padding for structs and unions that C handles automatically). If you dynamically allocate memory, then it is correctly aligned for all types. The only way that you can get into trouble is if you take the address of an object and pretend that it is a pointer to an object of a different type. The solution to that problem is simple: don't do that. There are a few safe exceptions, but generally it is not a meaningful thing to do. You do not know how the data of any given type is represented; it will vary from platform to platform, so trying to treat one type as if it was another is not a meaningful thing to do. You can do it on a particular platform, where you know the representation of different types, but there you can also know the alignment constraints of those types. Once you decide to only support one, or a fixed number of platforms, you can specialize your code for that and then deal with alignment issues. If you want to write platform-independent code, you can almost only get into trouble with alignment if you do something you shouldn't be doing in the first place. I can think of a few legitimate cases where you would need to consider alignment, but they are exceedingly rare, certainly not something you would encounter daily. Alignment is important for the hardware, but in day-to-day programming, C takes care of it.

Call Stacks and the Lifetime of Local Variables

To wrap up the chapter, we will look at local variables, when their memory is allocated, and how long they stick around. Dynamically allocated memory, the topic of Chapter 9, we wait with until that chapter, and global variables live forever, so they are simple to understand.

When we declare a variable, C will set aside space for it in memory—in principle, at least. When you use variables in expressions, the compiler might work out that it can eliminate variables by simplifying the expressions they are used in, substituting variables for the values it knows they have. Or it might work out that it can generate faster code by using a register on the CPU rather than a memory cell. But in principle, it sets aside one or more memory cells to hold the value in the variable, and if you ask for the address using an ampersand, you will get it. But not all variables stick around forever. Global variables exist as long as your program runs, yes, but local variables and the parameters of the functions you write do not. They only live as long as a function call is active.

What do I mean by "active"? The conceptual model of function calls you need to have is the *call stack*. We saw it in the generic memory model of processes, but we didn't discuss what it does. C is free to implement function calls anyway it wants, but modern computers use stacks, and so do all C implementations I know of, so it is likely to be more than a conceptual framework to think about functions with. The idea is this: when you call a function, C will push a so-called *stack frame* unto a stack, a first-in-first-out data structure. This stack frame contains the space for all parameters and local variables and some bookkeeping information about how to return from the function call. If you call another function from inside the first function, that function call does the same thing—it pushes a stack frame on the stack with room for its local variables and its bookkeeping. When you return from a function, C removes the stack frame from the stack and uses the bookkeeping to return the program to the state it was in before the function call. When the stack frame is gone, so are the local variables.

This is how it is often implemented in practice; although it doesn't match any particular platform, the explanation should only be used to understand the basic ideas. Your computer uses at least two pointers: one that keeps track of where in your code you are—an *instruction pointer*—and one that keeps track of the stack, the *stack pointer*. As your program runs, the computer takes the instruction that the instruction pointer indicates, executes it, and increments the pointer. The increment is usually to the next instruction, but when you have if-statements or loops, it will jump somewhere else. When you call a function, the computer should move the instruction pointer to the code in the function and execute what is there. When the function returns, it needs to move the instruction pointer back to just after the function call. It needs to store the instruction pointer it should return to somewhere; it cannot use a global location because then you couldn't call another function from the first without overwriting it, so it goes on the stack, which means that it writes it where the stack pointer sits. In the simplest form, the computer could save the instruction pointer at the memory location where the stack pointer is and then decrement the stack pointer. (I use decrement here since our stack moves from high to low addresses, but it could just as well move from low to high and increment instead). If there are further function calls, the instructions are saved, one after another, as the stack pointer moves. When the computer needs to return from a function, it can increment the stack pointer, and it will find the saved instruction pointer there.

However, we also need to allocate memory for local variables, and other temporary values if required, and the stack is an obvious place to put this memory. In that case, the location of the stored instruction pointer is not as simple, and when we need to move the stack pointer, we need to know how much memory we have allocated in a function to move it the right amount. In the following description, I will use three pointers instead, and I assume that all three are stored in registers, so I don't need to worry about how to find them. The pointers are the instruction pointer, ip; the stack pointer, sp, that points at the next address where we can allocate memory on the stack; and then the *frame pointer*, fp, which points at the memory address where the stack pointer was when a function call started. When we allocate memory on the stack, the stack pointer moves, but the frame pointer remains constant unless we call a function or return from one, and we can use it to access local variables. They will be at a fixed offset from the frame pointer.

```
int foo(int x, int y)
{
  return x + y;
}

int main(void)
{
  /* 1 */ int a = 13, b = 42;
  /* 2 */ int c = foo(a, b);
  /* 3 */ return 0;
}
```

The numbers in main() are there so I can refer to them. I will pretend that the instruction pointer points at lines in the code, instead of the machine code the compiler generates. It will be simpler for everyone.

Now, look at Figure 2-8. We start the example at line 2 in main(). Since main() is also a function, there is some stack above it, but we do not know what happens with our program before main() is called, so we ignore it. In main(), we have allocated two variables, a and b; they are local variables and went on the stack. The stack pointer points at the next free address, below a and b, and the frame pointer points at the beginning of main()'s data.

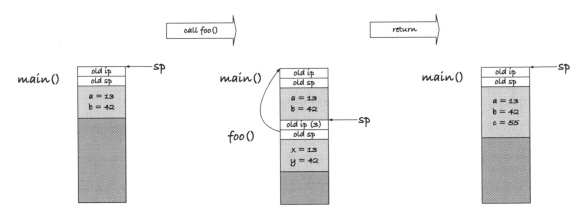

Figure 2-8. *The stack in action*

The next action we must take is calling foo(). There are different ways a computer uses to pass arguments to functions, but a stack is a common approach, and I will assume that this is the case in the example. It is my example, and I get to decide. In reality, arguments are passed through registers where possible.

To call foo(a,b), we must put the values of a and b on the stack. Arguments are passed as values in C, so it is the values and not, for example, the location of the variables we need. So we push those two values on the stack, decrementing sp, so it points past them, and then we are ready for the function call.

When we call foo(), our computer saves the frame pointer, so we can restore it after the call, and it saves the instruction pointer so it knows where it should return to after the call. In our example, that is line 3 in main(). Now the stack pointer points to the first free memory location on the stack, which is where foo() can put its data. The frame pointer should go to that location as well, so foo() knows where its memory starts.

Inside foo(), the function needs to get its input into its variables. If you go two locations back from the frame pointer, you get the memory locations where the arguments are. Technically, it can just get them from that location when it needs them, but if it modified them, and the calling function planned to do something with them after, it would be unpopular, so it copies them. It does its addition and is ready to return. When it does, we need to restore the previous stack frame, and we need to return the instruction pointer to the next instruction in main(). We can get the instruction pointer by looking at the address one above fp, we can restore the stack pointer moving it two addresses higher than fp, and then we can restore fp from the saved value.

After the call, the stack still holds the function arguments. They are not in variables in the C program, but they are there in the running code, and some assembly program might find a way to exploit that. We don't, so we get rid of them. Deallocating memory at the top of the stack is easy. Increment the stack pointer, so they fall below it, and we can consider them gone. The actual data is still there; we don't erase it in any way, but next time we put data on the stack, we overwrite it. The last thing we do in the example is to save the return value of foo() in a new local variable, c. We allocate the memory for it, by decrementing the stack pointer, and put the value there.

We didn't see the return value of the function anywhere in the example. It could have gone on the stack, so the caller could get it from there, but return values usually go in a register, so I decided not to put them on the stack here.

If you look at any specific hardware, function calls are almost certainly implemented in a different way than I just described. The registers will be different, some setup before function calls and cleanup after will be automatic, and some are the responsibility of the caller or callee. There will be many differences in details. But the overall description will match. You have a stack, and local variables are put on that stack as needed. When a function returns, the memory the local variables contained is freed for other purposes, and you should consider the objects gone forever.

The C standard does not guarantee that function calls are implemented by a stack at all, so use the description here as a mental model only. It is highly likely that function calls are implemented as a variant of this, but they could be implemented in other ways. The rules for how long a local variable stick around is the same, however. The standard does guarantee this.

CHAPTER 3

Pointers

You can store the address of an object in another object, and this is where we get to *pointers*. A pointer is a variable that stores memory addresses of other objects. You declare a variable to be a pointer by adding an asterisk, *, after the type it points to. If we declare

```
int i = 1;
int *pi = &i;
int **ppi = &pi;
```

then i is an integer, pi is a pointer to an integer (it has type int *), and ppi is a pointer to a pointer to an integer (it has type int **, so it is a pointer to int *, which is a pointer to an integer). The pi variable stores the address for i (because we assign pi = &i), and the ppi variable stores the address for pi.

If we run the code

```
printf("i = %d, &i = %p\n", i, &i);
printf("pi = %p, &pi = %p\n", pi, &pi);
printf("ppi = %p, &ppi = %p\n", ppi, &ppi);
```

we can see the values the variables hold, and the addresses they sit in. On my computer, I got

```
i = 1, &i = 0x7ffee283d8fc
pi = 0x7ffee283d8fc, &pi = 0x7ffee283d8f0
ppi = 0x7ffee283d8f0, &ppi = 0x7ffee283d8e8
```

This means that the integer in variable i sits at memory address 0x7ffee283d8fc. When we assigned &i to pi earlier, it got this address as its value. The value sits at address &pi, which is 0x7ffee283d8f0. The ppi variable holds pi's address, 0x7ffee283d8f0, and sits itself at address 0x7ffee283d8e8; see Figure 3-1.

© Thomas Mailund 2021

T. Mailund, *Pointers in C Programming*, https://doi.org/10.1007/978-1-4842-6927-5_3

On my machine, the pointers take up 8 bytes (you can check how large they are on your machine using, e.g., `sizeof pi`), so that is what I have put in the figure. The arrows pointing from `pi` to `i` and `ppi` to `pi` is the way we typically draw pointers. Later on, it becomes cumbersome to explicitly position values and pointers in memory, and we will represent pointers as arrows to objects instead.

For full disclosure, I have to say that you should not reason the way I just did about the memory layout. There are no guarantees in the C standard about where independent objects sit in memory, and even if the addresses look like they do here would be arranged in this way. Regardless of what the pointer values are, the variables could be arranged in other ways. On my machine, they are arranged this way, but you cannot make assumptions in portable code. It is not important for the example where exactly they sit in memory; however, the structure will be the same. The `ppi` pointer contains the memory address of the `pi` pointer that in turn holds the address of the integer `i`.

Knowing the address of an object is of little use if we cannot also access the object and manipulate the object through the pointer. We can do both by *dereferencing* pointers. If you put an asterisk in front of a pointer, you get the object that it points to. For example, this `printf()` call will print the value in `i` because we get what `pi` points to when we write *pi, and we print the value in `pi` (`i`'s address) when we get *ppi:

```
printf("i = %d, pi = %p\n", *pi, *ppi);
```

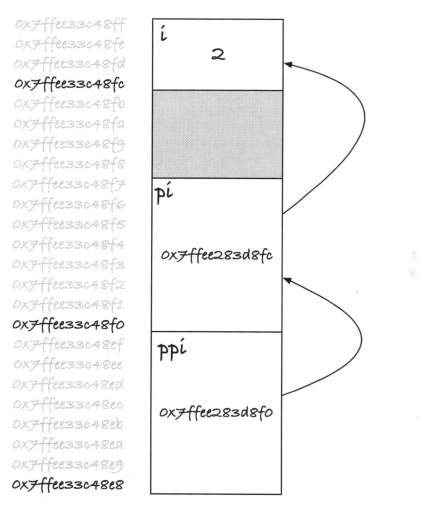

Figure 3-1. *Memory location and values of i, pi, and ppi*

If you want the value in i from ppi, you must dereference twice. Writing *ppi gives you the value in pi, which is i's address, and dereferencing that gives you i, so **ppi refers to i.

If you assign to a dereferenced pointer, you change the object that it is pointing at. If you run this code:

```
*pi = 2;
printf("i = %d, pi = %p, ppi = %p\n", i, pi, ppi);
**ppi = 3;
printf("i = %d, pi = %p, ppi = %p\n", i, pi, ppi);
```

you should get output that looks like this (except for the exact addresses):

```
i = 2, pi = 0x7ffee283d8fc, ppi = 0x7ffee283d8f0
i = 3, pi = 0x7ffee283d8fc, ppi = 0x7ffee283d8f0
```

In both assignments, we change i because that is what both *pi and **ppi refer to. We do not change pi or ppi. You do not modify a pointer when you modify what it points at. If you want to change the pointer, you must assign to the pointer itself. Here, for example, we point pi to another integer's address:

```
int i2 = 42;
pi = &i2;
```

Now, pi holds the address of i2 instead of i. The assignment doesn't change i or any of the other variables, but it changes the value of pi such that it now points elsewhere to the address of i2.

Pointers give us the possibility to refer to the same value through more than one variable. That is one of the purposes of them. When this happens, we call it *aliasing*. First, *pi was an alias for i, and when we assigned &i2 to *pi, it became an alias for i2.

Call by Reference

What is the point of having pointers if they only let you alias variables you already have? Not much, but that is not what we use them for. If it were, this would be the end of the book. There are, of course, other uses in contexts that we will cover in detail in the remainder of the book. In this section, I will motivate pointers via so-called call-by-reference function calls, something you cannot do without pointers in C. Then, for the remaining sections in the chapter, I will go through more technical aspects of pointers and pointer types.

In C, functions are call by value. What this means is that when you provide an argument to a function call, that value goes into the local variable that the corresponding function parameter holds. Consider this function:

```
void doesnt_mutate(int i)
{
  i += 42;
}
```

It takes an integer as its single parameter, the argument will be held in the local variable i, and the function then adds 42 to it. This modifies the value stored in i. Now let us imagine that we call the function like this:

```
int j = 0;
doesnt_mutate(j);
```

What then happens to j? If you have written C functions before, and I assume that you have, then you know that j doesn't change because we call doesnt_mutate() with it. The variable j holds an integer, it is zero since we initialize it as such, and it remains zero after the function call. What we pass to the function is the *value* that j holds, zero, but not the variable itself. Inside the function call, i will get the value zero when we call the function, and then it is updated. But the two integer variables are stored in different places in memory, and nothing connects them; see Figure 3-2 A).

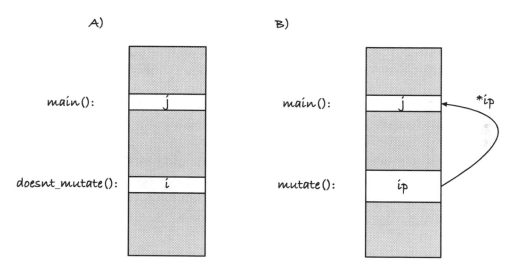

Figure 3-2. *Pointer arguments to functions*

The function call copies the bytes that variable j holds into the memory that contains the parameter i, and it is only the memory in the second location that we modify inside the function call.

If we have a pointer to the address of the function argument, however, we can write values into it; see B). If our function looked like this

```
void mutate(int *ip)
{
  *ip += 42;
}
```

and we called it like this

```
mutate(&j);
```

then the `ip` variable inside the function call holds the *address* of `j`, not its value. It is still a local variable; there is still an object sitting on the stack that contains its memory, but the local variable is a pointer to `j`. If we dereference `ip`, we look at the memory where `j` sits, and if we modify the memory there, then we modify the memory that `j` holds. So with this function, we *are* changing `j`. With the pointer, you have access to the memory in the calling function, not just the memory of the variable in the callee. You get a *reference* to an object instead of its value—that is *call by reference*.

The function argument, `ip`, is still a local variable. It resides on the stack in the `mutates()` call's stack frame. If you change the memory it sits in, say

```
void foo(int *ip)
{
  ip = 0;
}
```

then you have changed the local variable, and you have not affected the caller. If you want to change a pointer, then you need a pointer to a pointer:

```
void bar(int **ipp)
{
  *ipp = 0;
}
```

To change an object, you need a reference to it, which means that you need a pointer to it. A pointer isn't different from other types in this regard; if you want a function to change an argument pointer, then it needs a reference to it, that is, it needs a pointer to it.

If possible, you should avoid writing functions that have side effects through references, but they do have their uses in many places, where they can simplify your code. Mostly, however, you want to use them when you operate on structures that represent more complex types of objects. This is particularly relevant when you build data structures where you want to update different elements throughout your program. We will dig into that in Chapters 11 to 12, but here I will show a small example.

Say we need to write a program that manipulates points and rectangles. This could, for example, be part of a GUI application. It is natural to define a type for points and rectangles and functions for moving them around. The following is an example with somewhat limited functionality that doesn't use pointers:

```c
#include <stdio.h>

typedef struct point {
  double x, y;
} point;

point move_point_horizontally(point p, double amount)
{
  p.x += amount;
  return p;
}

point move_point_vertically(point p, double amount)
{
  p.y += amount;
  return p;
}

point move_point(point p, double delta_x, double delta_y)
{
  p = move_point_horizontally(p, delta_x);
  p = move_point_vertically(p, delta_y);
  return p;
}
```

```c
void print_point(point p)
{
  printf("point <%.2f, %.2f>\n", p.x, p.y);
}

typedef struct rectangle {
  point upper_left;
  point lower_right;
} rectangle;

rectangle move_rectangle(rectangle rect,
                         double delta_x,
                         double delta_y)
{
  rect.upper_left =
    move_point(rect.upper_left, delta_x, delta_y);
  rect.lower_right =
    move_point(rect.lower_right, delta_x, delta_y);
  return rect;
}

void print_rectangle(rectangle rect)
{
  printf("rectangle:\n");
  print_point(rect.upper_left);
  print_point(rect.lower_right);
  printf("\n");
}

int main(void)
{
  point p = { .x = 0.0, .y = 0.0 };
  print_point(p);
  p = move_point(p, 10, 10);
  print_point(p);
  printf("\n");
```

```
  rectangle rect = {
    .upper_left = { .x =  0.0, .y = 10.0 },
    .lower_right = { .x = 10.0, .y =  0.0 }
  };
  print_rectangle(rect);

  rect = move_rectangle(rect, 10, 10);
  print_rectangle(rect);

  return 0;
}
```

It might not be the most realistic code. I probably wouldn't have written functions `move_point_horizontally()` and `move_point_vertically()`, or if I did I would not implement `move_point()` based on them but instead go the other way, but the code illustrates a point (no pun intended). In the code, since we cannot modify our input beyond the local variable for a point or a rectangle we get as an argument, we must return a new object every time we want to modify one, and we need to overwrite the old one. If we assume that both passing an argument and returning one require copying the object—the compiler might be able to optimize something away, but it could be two copies—then the `move_point()` function results in multiple unnecessary copies.

The `move_point()` function potentially copies a point into the parameter, and it has to return a point, that is, two copies. I say potentially because the compiler might inline functions and save copying, but in the worst case, it needs to copy everything. Each of the function calls in the function body might also copy the object twice. So we could end up with copying the point six times.

```
point move_point(point p /* 1 */, double delta_x, double delta_y)
{
  p = move_point_horizontally(p, delta_x); /* 2 copies */
  p = move_point_vertically(p, delta_y); /* 2 copies */
  return p; /* another copy */
}
```

There is nothing wrong with copying structures as input and output, and for smaller structures, you do not pay much of a performance penalty, but it is wasteful. Sometimes, it is worthwhile because you get cleaner code. For large objects, however, you should prefer to pass a pointer to the object instead of copying it.

With move_rectangle(), it gets worse. Here, we might need to copy two points in and out of the function, and the calls to move_point() inside the function involve the six copies we counted earlier, each.

```
rectangle move_rectangle(rectangle rect, /* 2 */
                         double delta_x,
                         double delta_y)
{
  rect.upper_left = /* 6 */
    move_point(rect.upper_left, delta_x, delta_y);
  rect.lower_right = /* 6 */
    move_point(rect.lower_right, delta_x, delta_y);
  return rect; /* 2 */
}
```

The larger the object, and the more components it has, the more you have to copy.

If you want to modify an object, you have to overwrite it every time you call a function. If we write

```
point p = { .x = 0.0, .y = 0.0 };
p = move_point(p, 10, 10);
print_point(p);
```

it is easy to forget the assignment and end up with

```
point p = { .x = 0.0, .y = 0.0 };
move_point(p, 10, 10);
print_point(p);
```

This is valid C code; the compiler won't complain, but you do not get what you want.

If you pass the objects to the functions as pointers, you can modify them without copying them. You still have to copy data, the input pointer, but that is always a relatively small object that is quickly copied (and will be copied in a register in practice which makes it *very* fast).

A pointer version of move_point_horizontally() will look like this:

```
void move_point_horizontally(point *p, double amount)
```

```
{
  p->x += amount;
}
```

The p->x syntax gets the component x from the point structure through a pointer. It is syntactic sugar for (*p).x. It is a question of taste which of the syntaxes you prefer. I always use the arrow operator, but I know friends who swear to the dereference syntax. If you are consistent, and your choice matches your collaborators, then you are fine.

The complete rewrite is listed in the following. The main difference, except for passing the points and rectangles as references, is that we do not return an updated object from any of the functions. We do not need to, as we modify the input object where it is.

```
#include <stdio.h>

typedef struct point {
  double x, y;
} point;

void move_point_horizontally(point *p, double amount)
{
  p->x += amount;
}

void move_point_vertically(point *p, double amount)
{
  p->y += amount;
}

void move_point(point *p, double delta_x, double delta_y)
{
  move_point_horizontally(p, delta_x);
  move_point_vertically(p, delta_y);
}
```

```c
void print_point(point *p)
{
  printf("point <%.2f, %.2f>\n", p->x, p->y);
}

typedef struct rectangle {
  point upper_left;
  point lower_right;
} rectangle;

void move_rectangle(rectangle *rect,
                    double delta_x,
                    double delta_y)
{
  move_point(&rect->upper_left, delta_x, delta_y);
  move_point(&rect->lower_right, delta_x, delta_y);
}

void print_rectangle(rectangle *rect)
{
  printf("rectangle:\n");
  print_point(&rect->upper_left);
  print_point(&rect->lower_right);
  printf("\n");
}

int main(void)
{
  point p = { .x = 0.0, .y = 0.0 };
  print_point(&p);

  move_point(&p, 10, 10);
  print_point(&p);
  printf("\n");

  rectangle rect = {
    .upper_left =  { .x =  0.0, .y = 10.0 },
    .lower_right = { .x = 10.0, .y =  0.0 }
  };
```

```
print_rectangle(&rect);

move_rectangle(&rect, 10, 10);
print_rectangle(&rect);

return 0;
}
```

A separate issue to taking pointers as arguments is returning pointers. You can return pointers from a function as you can return any other type, but you have to be careful with what that pointer contains!

Here is a small example that might not appear dangerous at first sight, except for the BOOOM!!! comment.

```
#include <math.h>
#include <float.h>
#include <stdio.h>

typedef struct vector {
  double x;
  double y;
  double z;
} vector;

void print_vector(vector const *v)
{
  double x = v->x, y = v->y, z = v->z;
  printf("<%.2f, %.2f, %.2f>\n", x, y, z);
}

double vector_length(vector *v)
{
  double x = v->x, y = v->y, z = v->z;
  return sqrt(x*x + y*y * z*z);
}
```

```
vector *shortest(int n, vector *vectors[n])
{
  vector *shortest = &(vector){
    .x = DBL_MAX, .y = DBL_MAX, .z = DBL_MAX
  };
  double shortest_length = vector_length(shortest);
  for (int i = 0; i < n; ++i) {
    vector *v = vectors[i];
    double length = vector_length(v);
    if (length < shortest_length) {
      shortest = v;
      shortest_length = length;
    }
  }

  return shortest;
}

int main(void)
{
  vector *vectors[] = {
    &(vector){ .x = 10.0, .y = 13.0, .z = 42.0 },
    &(vector){ .x = -1.0, .y = 32.0, .z = 15.0 },
    &(vector){ .x =  0.0, .y =  3.0, .z =  1.0 }
  };

  print_vector(shortest(3, vectors));
  print_vector(shortest(2, vectors));
  print_vector(shortest(1, vectors));
  print_vector(shortest(0, vectors)); // BOOOM!!!

  return 0;
}
```

We have a 3D vector type, and we have a function, shortest(), that finds the shortest vector in an array (for array details, I once again refer you to Chapter 5). When finding the shortest vector, to avoid a special case when the input is an empty sequence, we say that if there are no vectors, then the shortest vector is one with maximal values for all three coordinates. That is the DBL_MAX defined in <float.h>. The

```
        (vector){
  .x = DBL_MAX, .y = DBL_MAX, .z = DBL_MAX
};
```

creates a vector with the initialization from inside the curly brackets, and adding & to it

```
vector *shortest = &(vector){
  .x = DBL_MAX, .y = DBL_MAX, .z = DBL_MAX
};
```

gives us its address. We put that address in the shortest pointer to use as the default value. It will be replaced as soon as we find a smaller value.

However, in the BOOOM!!! line, where we do have an empty sequence, things go sideways. Potentially, anyway, it will depend on your architecture how bad it goes. The shortest() function returns a pointer to the default value we created, but that is a variable *allocated on the stack*, and we have just returned from the function that allocated it. The address for it is still there, and presumably the data is as well, but as soon as we call another function, the data could be overwritten.

The error is especially nefarious in this program because there is a good chance that you do *not* see it in this code. When we call print_vector(), the compiler might not allocate space for its local variables, it can optimize them away and get the values from v, and v might not overwrite the stack location where longest sits. The printf() call might not overwrite it either. And as long as the function calls leave the object alone, you will not see that it doesn't exist any longer. The data is still there, after all. As long as you do not overwrite it, you will not see any problems. So you could test it and observe that everything goes according to plan. And then, one day, you use the function, call a function that overwrites the object, and now you are in trouble. Weeks, months, or years after you tested that everything worked.

We can try to fake this situation with a function that writes to a large part of the stack:

```
void trash_stack(void)
{
  volatile char x[1000];
  for (int i = 0; i < 1000; i++) {
    x[i] = 0;
  }
}
```

The `volatile` is there to prevent the optimizer from removing the loop. Without it, it can conclude that we never use x and eliminate it. By making x `volatile`, we tell the compiler that someone else might be looking at it, so it won't optimize it away.

Now call it between getting the longest object and printing it:

```
vector *v = shortest(0, vectors);
print_vector(v);
trash_stack();
print_vector(v);
```

The first call to `print_vector()` might give you the expected output, but the second call probably won't. In the second call, you are likely to see that the longest vector is now the shortest: (0,0,0). This is not something that your compiler will catch—not unless it caught that you returned the address of a local variable in the first place—but it will likely break your program. And it could be hard to track down this bug.

Worse, it could still work fine for you, with your compiler and on your development machine, but someday someone else will compile it when your code is rolled out in production, and then BOOOM!!! is too mild a word.

It is safe to pass an address of an object on the stack along to further function calls. The object is alive while those functions execute, and it will not be deallocated until they, and the calling function, return. But you should never point to a local variable that is no longer alive. If you never return the address of a local variable, you will be fine, so be careful when you return pointers to ensure that they cannot point at local variables. If you need to return a pointer from a function, do not allocate it on the stack. If you need to create an object to return the address of, you must use dynamic memory allocation; see Chapter 9.

We could try to get around the problem by making the default vector `static`. Then it wouldn't be destroyed when we return from `shortest()`, but we would get another problem: if we get a pointer to the `static` default, we can change it, and that would modify the behavior of all future calls to `shortest()`.

We would be better off to choose a different default to return from `shortest()` when we do not have any elements to choose the shortest from. We need to return an address because that is the return type, but it must be something we cannot confuse for a valid `vector`. There is a special kind of pointer for this, the *NULL pointer*.

NULL Pointers

NULL pointers are pointers that hold a unique value that sets them apart from other pointers and indicate that they do not point at anything. This is different from not *actually* pointing at anything. A pointer that isn't initialized, or points at a variable that no longer exists, does not point at anything either. We just cannot recognize that such a pointer refers to memory that it is no longer valid to access. With a NULL pointer, we know that it doesn't refer to anything, and we know that we should refrain from dereferencing it. Most likely, dereferencing a NULL pointer will crash your program, but it is up to the underlying platform, so you cannot rely on it. Nothing good will come of dereferencing a NULL pointer, though you can safely assume that.

You set a pointer of any type to a NULL pointer using the literal 0 or the macro NULL from <stddef.h>.

```
int *i_null = 0; // integer NULL pointer
double *d_null = NULL; // double NULL pointer
```

It is a question of taste whether you use 0 or NULL. I will use 0 in this book.

In the comments here, I specified which type of NULL pointer they were, because the standard allows for different NULL pointers for different types. However, if you assign a NULL pointer of one type to another type, you get that type's NULL pointer:

```
i_null = (int *)d_null; // Still an integer NULL pointer
```

and NULL pointers compare equal

```
if (i_null == (int *)d_null)    printf("Yep!\n");
if (d_null == (double *)i_null) printf("Also yep!\n");
```

Comparing any NULL pointer to NULL or 0 also evaluates to true.

```
if (i_null == NULL) printf("Yep!\n");
if (d_null == 0)    printf("Also yep!\n");
```

NULL pointers, however, do not compare equal to any other pointer. So

```
int *ip = ...; // any value that is not a NULL pointer
if (i_null == ip) printf("This doesn't happen.\n");
if (ip == 0)      printf("Also doesn't happen.\n");
```

So there is not much use in thinking about NULL pointers of different types as being different. They are simply allowed to be represented differently, but as the standard does not specify how they must be represented, merely how they should behave, it makes no practical difference.

However, the representation can matter if you try to assign zero to a pointer in some other way.

```
int zero = 0;
int *ip = (int *)zero;
```

Here, you assign an integer to `ip`, and you are allowed to do this. You can use it to point to a specific address. For embedded systems, for example, this is useful. It is highly platform dependent, and thus not portable, so it is not something we do in this book, but it is allowed. However, you have given `ip` the address zero, and NULL is not defined to be zero. The literal 0, when you assign it to a pointer, means the NULL pointer. The compiler has to give `ip` the bit pattern it uses for NULL pointers, and it has to implement the rules for NULL pointers. Since NULL pointers typically *are* the zero address, it will likely work, but this potentially has a different semantics than assigning the literal 0. You should not get up to such shenanigan; use 0 or NULL.

If you use a pointer as a Boolean:

```
if (p) {
  // Do something...
}
```

then p evaluates to false if p is a NULL pointer, and otherwise it evaluates to true.

```
if (!p) {
  // We have a NULL pointer
} else {
  // p is not NULL. It points at *something*
  // but it might point at something invalid
}
```

Again, don't rely on any particular representation of a pointer. It is when you use a pointer as a truth value that the NULL pointer rules apply. This might not be the same as testing if p is NULL:

```
int null = 0;
int *p = NULL;
if (p == (int *)null) // do stuff
```

Here, you should compare with NULL:

```
if (p == NULL) // do stuff
```

or with the literal 0

```
if (p == 0) // do stuff
```

(this will work because both NULL and 0 are NULL pointers here; they have that type
when we compare with a pointer), or you should use simply p as a truth value:

```
if (p) // do stuff
```

Those are the ways you should check if a pointer is NULL. Otherwise, you are
entering undefined behavior by relying on the bit representation of NULL pointers.

Pointers are not automatically NULL when they do not point at a valid object. It
would require C to keep track of all addresses that you have assigned any pointer to,
which would incur appreciable overhead in your programs, nor does C automatically
initialize pointers to be NULL. C doesn't initialize automatic, that is, stack-allocated
variables in general, and the same holds for pointers. You have to explicitly state that a
pointer doesn't point at anything by assigning it 0 or NULL. It is good practice to initialize
pointers to be NULL if you do not have a better value, but it is a question of taste whether
you do it if the control flow is simple enough to make it clear that the pointer will be
assigned to shortly. I tend to always start out with a NULL pointer unless I have a value to
assign it right away.

In the example from the previous section, where we returned a pointer to a stack-
allocated object, we can use a NULL pointer instead. If the input to shortest doesn't
have at least one element, we return a NULL pointer, and then we let the caller work out
what to do about it.

```
vector *shortest(int n, vector *vectors[n])
{
  if (n < 1) return 0; // Return a NULL pointer

  vector *shortest = vectors[0];
  double shortest_length = vector_length(shortest);
  for (int i = 1; i < n; ++i) {
    vector *v = vectors[i];
    double length = vector_length(v);
```

```
    if (length < shortest_length) {
      shortest = v;
      shortest_length = length;
    }
  }

  return shortest;
}
```

If the caller wants a default, they are responsible for choosing it.

```
vector const longest = {
  .x = DBL_MAX, .y = DBL_MAX, .z = DBL_MAX
};
vector const *v = shortest(0, vectors);
v = v ? v : &longest;
print_vector((vector *)v);
```

In v ? v : &longest, we use the return value from shortest() as a truth value. The expression says that if v is not NULL, then we use it, and otherwise we use the longest vector.

This code is far from safe. We create a const object because we do not want to change longest, but we cast the const away. If we wanted a constant longest object, we could have defined a global variable in the first place, but we discarded that solution earlier. We shouldn't use one in shortest() because that makes assumptions about what the caller wants with the shortest vector. Leaving the decision about what to do if there isn't a shortest vector to the caller is better, because they know what they want to do with the vector they get, and they can decide what the appropriate action is.

If we start allowing NULL pointers in our code—and generally we should—then it is a design choice which functions should handle them. Some we might allow assuming that they never get NULL input, while others must be able to handle them. If we leave the vector_length() function as it is:

```
double vector_length(vector *v)
{
  double x = v->x, y = v->y, z = v->z;
  return sqrt(x*x + y*y * z*z);
}
```

then it cannot handle NULL. The `v->` operation dereferences the pointer, and dereferencing NULL pointers is undefined behavior, typically crashing your program. It is reasonable to require that this function cannot handle `NULL` pointers. It should return the length of a vector, and `NULL` means we do not have a vector, so what would a natural return value be in that case?

There is nothing in `print_vector()`'s responsibility that says that it cannot print a NULL vector, so we can update it to do this:

```
void print_vector(vector const *v)
{
  if (!v) {
    printf("NULL\n");
  } else {
    double x = v->x, y = v->y, z = v->z;
    printf("<%.2f, %.2f, %.2f>\n", x, y, z);
  }
}
```

With dynamic memory management, Chapter 9, we use NULL pointers to handle allocation errors, and when we build recursive data structures, Chapters 11 to 12, they are the go-to value for the base cases in the recursion.

Const and Pointers

If you declare a variable using the `const` keyword, it tells the compiler that you are declaring a constant, a variable that shouldn't change. It does two things: it will make the compiler complain if you try to change the value of a constant, and it gives the compiler the option of optimizing references to the value because it knows that you promised not to change that value. If you declare an integer, you can make it constant by putting the `const` keyword before or after the type:

```
const int i = 42;
```

or

```
int const i = 42;
```

You can read the first as "a constant integer i" and the second as "an integer constant i." Either formulation works, and both declarations do the same thing. They make it a compilation error to change the value of i.

Early on, I got used to the first variant, and it is the one I instinctively use, but if you are just learning C, I urge you to use the second instead, and I have done my best to only use that variant in this book. If I have messed up in places, I beg your forgiveness. It is hard to change an old habit. The reason that I think the second is better is that it makes it easier to combine pointers and qualifiers such as const, as we shall see in this section. If we didn't have the first variant, we would have a consistent rule for how to specify which types are constants and which are not; with the first rule, we have a special case for the base type. Special cases too often mess things up, so avoid them if you can. If you get started with the first variant, it is as hard to switch to the second as it is quitting smoking, so don't get started. You should only ever use the second variant.

Back to const variables! If you declare a variable const, then you cannot assign a new value to it later, and that rule is easy to remember. But if you add pointers to the mix, things get muddier. A const variable sits somewhere in memory, at least if the compiler hasn't optimized that away, so you can get a reference to that address. If you get a pointer to that address that you *are* allowed to write through, you could change the "constant." What happens, however, is where it can get complicated.

If you declare a pointer, the type before the * is the type you point at. So if you declare

```
const int *ip;
```

(the first variant), you get a pointer to const int. The same, of course, is the case if you declare

```
int const *ip;
```

(the second variant), which gives you a pointer to int const which is the same qualified integer.

This pointer can point to our int const variable i from before because we have declared that we shouldn't be allowed to change what it points at. We have declared that we don't want to change i, so we shouldn't be able to do it indirectly either. If we say that ip points to a constant, then the compiler will check that we do not change the object we point to, and so we get the same type safety through *ip and i when we do

```
int const i = 42;
int const *ip = &i;
```

54

Both variables say that they will not change the value in i. So here, all is well. But you could also write

```
int const i = 42;
int *ip = (int *)&i;
```

Now you have a pointer through which you can change i, even though you have declared i to be const! You are allowed to do this. You are allowed to cast a qualified type, but are you then allowed to change what ip points at? The compiler will not complain; you have told it that ip points to a non-const integer, but what will happen at runtime?

The answer is an unsatisfactory "we don't know." The standard says that it is undefined behavior to change a variable we defined as const. In practice, however, compilers usually exploit undefined behavior for optimization purposes. If you allow it to do what it wants in a given situation, it might as well try to make the code more efficient.

If you run this:

```
int const i = 42;
int *ip = (int *)&i;
*ip = 13; // i == 42 or i == 13?
printf("i == %d, *ip == %d\n", i, *ip);
```

chances are that i and *ip have different values after you assign to ip. Even though we have declared i as const, it doesn't quite mean that it is a constant the way compile-time constants are. It has an address when you use &, so *ip will point at an address that can contain an integer. This is safe because int const and int are the same underlying type, and they only differ in the qualifier const. So you can write to *ip, and it gets the value 13, so that is what we will print for that variable in the last line. However, the compiler might recognize that i is the constant 42 and use that in the call to printf(). So although we are talking about the same memory address, we get two different values after the compiler has optimized the code. Or then again, you might get something completely different. You have invoked undefined behavior, after all.

To make things more complicated (because why not?), it is not undefined behavior when you modify a variable that wasn't declared const, even if the code goes through a pointer to const at some point before modifying it.

Imagine that we have a function such as this:

```
void foo(int const *cip)
{
  int *ip = (int *)cip;
  *ip = 5;
}
```

We take a pointer to int const, we cast it, and then we modify what it points to. We are allowed to do this. Then we run code like this elsewhere in our program:

```
int const i = 42;
int j = 13;
foo(&i);
foo(&j);
printf("i == %d, j == %d\n", i, j);
```

The compiler will likely optimize the generated code, so i remains a 42 after we call foo(&i), but it will *not* optimize for j, even though foo() promised not to change what its input points at. What foo() does is valid, and it should change what its argument points to. You are allowed to change const values this way.

It is confusing, but it is the way it is. It would be easier if it was always illegal to modify a const value. Still, there are many applications where we want to do so, where the const value isn't truly const, for example, because we change some meta-information but conceptually have a const. When you declare a pointer to const, you ask the compiler to help you with remembering that you shouldn't change what it points to, but you are allowed to—you just need to make your intent explicit through a type-cast.

When you define a variable you allocate the memory for it and you specify whether it can change. If it is const, you shouldn't expect it to change, and the compiler probably won't expect it either. If you do not define it as const, then you are allowed to change it, even if you have a const pointer to it. You can cast the pointer and change the value. If you call a function that promises not to change its input, the compiler doesn't trust it, and neither should you. Because const doesn't actually mean *constant*, it means that you want the type-checker to remind you to be explicit about your intent before you change the value.

If you declare a pointer to a constant integer, either as

```
const int *ip;
```

or

```
int const *ip;
```

you have not declared the *pointer* to be constant. It is the type that the pointer points *at* that is constant—not the pointer. Here is the rule for `const` (and other qualifiers) and why the second variant is easier to work with:

> For any type `T`, `T const` is a constant of that type.

Understand "constant" in the context of what we just saw earlier. It might not be constant, but it is something the compiler will yell at you for writing to unless you use an explicit cast. If you also use the first variant for `const` declaration, you have a special case because a `const` before the first type makes that type `const`. Stick with using the second variant. If you do, you have the same rule for pointers:

> For any type `T`, `T *` is a pointer to that type.

With these two rules, you can work out that

```
int const *icp;
```

is a pointer to type `T` (because it has the form `T *`) and that the type `T` is a constant type; it has the form `U const` where the type `U` is `int`. So we have a pointer to a constant `int`. When you apply these two rules, you will find it easier to read the type declaration from the right and to the left. The `*` and `const` in the rules affect the type to the left of them, and we apply the rules recursively—so read it backward.

If we want the *pointer* to be constant, so it always points to the same address, but we want to be able to change what it points at, then we can work out the type declaration from the rules as well. We want a constant, so write `const` to the right of the type we are declaring. Now the type has the form `T const`. What do we want `T` to be? It should be a pointer, so we update `T` to a pointer `U *`, and then our type is `U * const`. We have reached the end of our declaration now if we want a constant pointer to `int`, because then `U` must be `int`, and thus we declare

```
int i;
int * const cip = &i;
```

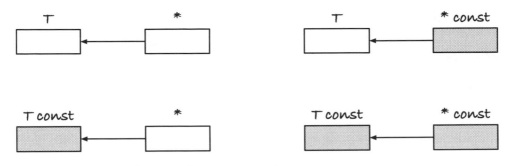

Figure 3-3. *Constant data and constant pointers*

We must initialize the pointer here because it is constant, so we cannot point an address at it later. Here, it points to the variable i, and it always will. We cannot give it another address. But we can change i and *cip to our heart's content.

The four combinations of const/non-const underlying type and const/non-const pointers look like this:

```
int *              i_p   = 0;
int const *        ic_p  = 0;
int * const        i_pc  = 0;
int const * const  ic_pc = 0;
```

and I have tried to illustrate the types in Figure 3-3 where white boxes mean a variable is mutable and gray means that they are const.

You can change both i_p and what it points to because none of those are const. For ic_p, you can change the pointer, but not what it points at. With i_pc, you cannot change the pointer, but you can modify what it points at, and with ic_pc you can modify neither of the two.

We have seen many times by now, and probably earlier in our lives, that we can assign from a const variable to a non-const. Nothing can go wrong with that because we only modify the memory of the non-const variable. The same is, obviously, also true for pointers. You can assign a const pointer to a non-const pointer. Naturally, you can also assign a non-const pointer to a non-const pointer, but there is nothing particularly surprising in that. With pointers, though, we also have to consider what we point *at*. We could make a rule that you can only assign between pointers to the exact same type, but there is nothing wrong with letting a pointer, which promises not to change its pointed-at value, look at a non-const address. It is not changing anything, so there is no reason to restrict it from doing so. And indeed, we are allowed to assign a pointer to non-const to a pointer to const.

In Figure 3-4, I have summarized these two rules in a graphical form. The squiggly boxes mean any type and qualifier as long as the two are the same before and after the assignment. Rule A) is the one we have used many times and rule B) is the same rule, just for pointers. If two pointers point to the same type, then there are no differences between pointer types and other variable types. We can assign a `const` value to a non-`const` variable because it cannot change anything except the variable we assign to. The new rule is in C) and says that we can add `const`-ness to the pointed-at type, but we are not allowed to go the other way and remove `const` from what we point at. That rule, in a more concise form, is shown in Figure 3-5. In the figure, it says "qualifier" because the rule applies to all qualifiers and not just `const`. The section is about `const` because we tend to use it more than the other qualifiers. Still, everything in this section about specifying types and assigning between them also applies to, for example, `volatile`. You can remove qualifiers from the pointer and add them to the type you point at, but not the reverse.

The rules for declaring types and assigning between pointers are the same as we add more levels of indirection, so I will not go on about it for much longer, but there is a point I want to make so I will take us one more level up and add pointers to the four types we have seen so far.

```
int **              i_p_p   = 0;
int const **        ic_p_p  = 0;
int * const *       i_pc_p  = 0;
int const * const * ic_pc_p = 0;
```

Figure 3-4. *Rules for const and pointers in assignments*

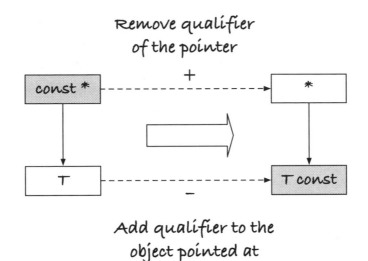

Figure 3-5. *Adding and removing qualifiers for pointer assignment*

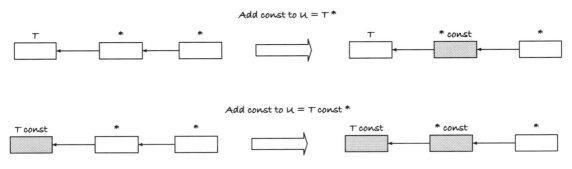

Figure 3-6. *Assignments between pointers to pointers with and without const*

I won't include the corresponding const variables; they will tell us nothing except that we cannot assign to them. In Figure 3-6, I have illustrated these four pointers as well, including the two legal assignments between them. You can assign from the unqualified int ** pointer to int * const * and from int const ** to int const * const *, but not between any of the others.

Why? Because that is what the rules say. You can assign from T * to T const * (and other qualifiers besides const), but not between T * and U * for different types T and U. If we peel away the last pointer in the preceding types, we have the two non-const types T = int * and U = int const *.

```
typedef int * T;
typedef int const * U;
```

```
T *          i_p_p   = 0;
U *          ic_p_p  = 0;
T const *    i_pc_p  = 0;
U const *    ic_pc_p = 0;
```

We can assign from i_p_p to i_pc_p because they have type T * and T const *, and we can assign from ic_p_p to ic_pc_p because they have type U * and U const *, respectively.

You might now object that surely there shouldn't be a problem with assigning from, for example, i_p_p to ic_p_p, because you make a non-const value const, so you won't change anything you shouldn't. You restrict what you can do, and that cannot cause problems. The thing is that it can—because you can create a non-const alias to a const object if you were allowed to do this. Say I have variables

```
int *p = 0;
int const ** q = 0;
int const i = 42;
```

and follow along in Figure 3-7. In the figure, boxes and arrows that are dashed do not represent actual objects. We start with p and q as NULL pointers, so they do not point at any existing objects. The dashed boxes are there to show their type and nothing more. Actual data will be shown in fully drawn boxes.

I can take the address of p, it has type int **, and assign it to q. This is the assignment that isn't allowed, but we do it anyway (and in code, you can explicitly cast it, so you can always do it, even if you shouldn't).

```
q = (int const **)&p;
```

Now I have created an alias for p in *q. In the figure, boxes that touch are aliases; they are the same object but represented as different boxes to indicate their types. The pointer q points at the object p, so p and *q are the same objects, and unless we direct q somewhere else, they remain so. This means that anything they might end up pointing at later will be accessible through both of them.

Then we assign &i to *q:

```
*q = &i;
```

61

Both the address of i and *q have type int const *, so this is a perfectly valid assignment. We expect to be able to assign one pointer type to another, so we are not doing anything wrong when doing that.

However, it creates more aliases. Since q points to p and *q now points to i, all three of *p, **q, and i refer to the same object. They differ in type; *p is not const, but the other two are. But because *p is not const, we can change the value of the object through it. The *actual* object is const; we declared that memory location to be int const, so if we change *p, we enter undefined behavior.

You can try it out yourself with this program. The questionable part is the assignment from &p to q, where the code needs an explicit cast to compile. When I run the program, I get different values for i and *p in the last printf(), because the compiler has optimized reading the const integer. What you get is up to your compiler. The behavior is undefined.

```c
#include <stdio.h>

int main(void)
{
  int *p = 0;
  int const **q = 0;
  int const i = 42;

  q = (int const **)&p;
  *q = &i;

  // Now I have an int alias to an int const!
  printf("&i == %p, *p == %p\n", (void *)&i, (void *)p);

  *p = 5; // DANGER: We are trying to change const int
  // This may or may not actually change i.
  // It is up to the C compiler
  printf("i == %d / %d\n", i, *p);

  return 0;
}
```

```
int *p = 0;
int const **q = 0;
int const i = 42;
```

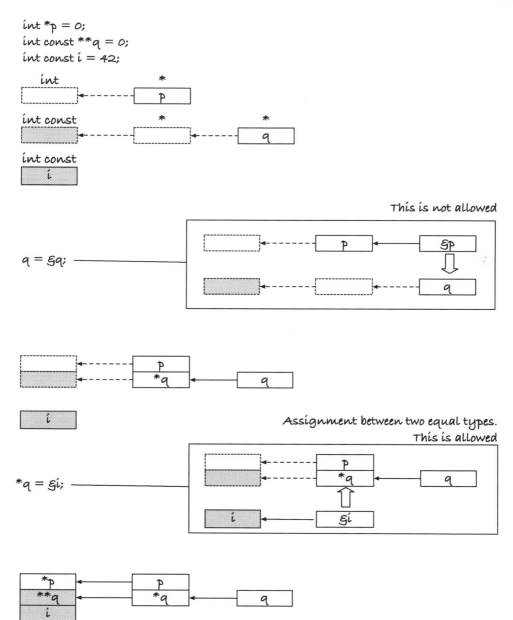

Figure 3-7. *Creating a non-const alias to a const object*

```
int **p = 0;
int const * const **q = 0;
int const i = 42;
int const * const r  = &i;
```

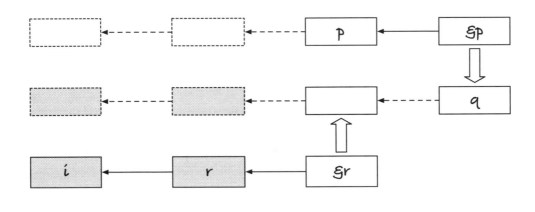

```
q = &p;
*q = r;
```

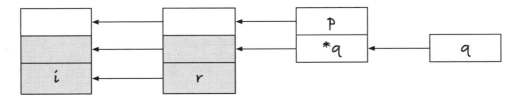

Figure 3-8. *Creating yet another illegal alias*

What about the other types? Do I run into the same problem if I assign from int **
to int const * const? No, here I cannot do the same trick to create an invalid alias, but
that is because I consider the types in isolation. If we allow ourselves to add another level
of pointers, we are back in the same situation. Consider Figure 3-8. Here, we have an int
** pointer p, we assign its address to an int const * const ** pointer u, and when we
then assign the address of an int const * const object, r, into *q, we have created not
just one but two illegal aliases.

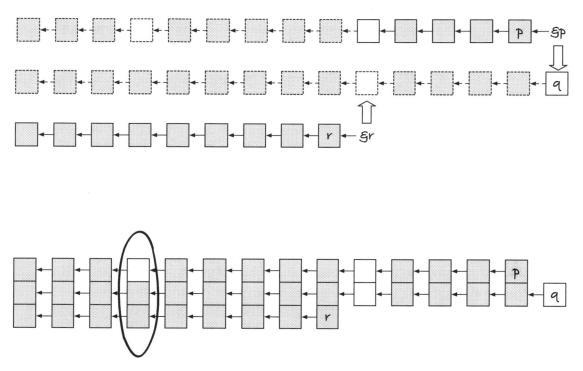

Figure 3-9. *General setup for smuggling in an illegal alias*

Admittedly, here we are not assigning an int ** to an int const * const * when we assign from &p to q. The types are int *** and int const * const **. We do not create a problem if we allowed assignments from int ** to int const * const *, but then we would have to disallow assignments for some cases with more levels of pointers.

In the examples, we have exploited that we can write &p into q and then an object we shouldn't modify into *q, but there can be several levels of references between the two places where we write pointers to create an illegal alias. All it takes is that we have a place where we can write p into a pointer structure that allows us to write another, more restricted type, r, somewhere further down the chain. By "more restricted" I mean that r has an immutable object in its chain of pointers that is allowed to be modified through p. Figure 3-9 shows the general case of this.

If there is a non-const link in the type we assign from, to the left of a non-const link in the type we assign to, then we can create an illegal alias this way. This is what the type-checker prevents. If the first link in the first assignment is non-const for p but const for q, we cannot smuggle in the extra assignment to make an illegal alias. That is why we can add a const to the type we point at. If the type except for the const at the immediate level is the same, then we cannot have alias issues either—if the type is the same, then what we can modify with one alias we can also modify through another.

The assignment rules are stricter than they need to be. They prevent entirely safe assignments, like `int **` to `int const * const`, where you cannot smuggle in any false alias—if you tried to put a `const` object into a chain with the `int **` alias, you would have to go through the `int const * const` type, which doesn't allow you any assignments. You could allow such assignments but at the cost of complicating the type rules. Or make a special case for links of pointers that are all `const`. C takes the simpler approach and allows you to add `const` to the object you point to, but otherwise the type must be the same.

Restricted Pointers

When the compiler sees a `const` variable (but not a pointer to `const`), it knows that its value doesn't change, so it can optimize the code it generates to exploit this. If it reads the value of a `const` variable, it can generate code that remembers the constant value instead of fetching it from a variable. Getting a constant is orders of magnitude faster than fetching a value from cache or main memory, so there is much to gain here. The `restrict` keyword provides a similar optimization opportunity. It is a qualifier to a pointer type (so like with `const`, you need to put it after the * to modify the pointer and not the underlying type). It tells the compiler that this pointer is not an alias of anything else; the memory it points at is only referenced through the pointer itself. Writing to other pointers will not change the value it points at, and writing through the pointer will not affect what other pointers read.

Before the compiler generates code, it will analyze it to find the optimal machine code. If it can work out where you get data from, and maybe remember it for later instead of fetching it from memory every time you use it, it can generate faster code. The promise you make when you write `restrict` helps it eliminate the case where it would otherwise have to assume that a value you access could have chanced since it fetched data from it last and force it to fetch the data once more. Beware, though, that current compilers are not really good at warning you if you break that promise! If you *actually* modify data through a different pointer, the optimized code will be incorrect.

The following program illustrates the difference:

```
#include <stdio.h>

void abc(int *a, int *b, int *c)
{
  *a += *c;
  *b += *c;
}

void abc_restrict(int *a, int *b, int * restrict c)
{
  *a += *c;
  *b += *c;
}

int main(void)
{
  int x, y;
  x = y = 13;
  // No problem here. We haven't made any restrict
  // promises
  abc(&x, &y, &x);
  printf("%d %d\n", x, y);

  // We break the promise here by passing
  // using &a both as argument a and c in
  // in the function
  x = y = 13;
  abc_restrict(&x, &y, &x);
  printf("%d %d\n", x, y);

  return 0;
}
```

In the function abc(), we add the value that c points at to the integers that a and b point to, and we dereference c twice to do this. We call abc() as abc(&x,&y,&x), so c points to the same integer as x. Consequently, when we update *a, we change the value at *c before we add it to *b.

With abc_restrict(), we have told the compiler that *c doesn't change (unless we write to *c, which we don't). It is, therefore, free to remember *c from the first access, so when it needs *c to add it to *b, it can use the saved value. In this code, I *lied* to the compiler when I told it that *c wouldn't change through other pointers, because both a and c point at the same integer, x, but the compiler is gullible and believed me, and it might have optimized the code accordingly. It is usually not a good idea to lie to your compiler. You will be the one to suffer; it really couldn't care less.

When I run the code without compiler optimization, the result of both function calls is the same:

```
26 39
26 39
```

If I turn on optimization, however, I get

```
26 39
26 26
```

In the second function, the compiler didn't fetch the value at *c a second time to add it to *b. I have told it that it doesn't change, and it believed me.

The optimization that the compiler can do with restrict is similar to what it can do with const, but you are allowed to change what c points at. The compiler will change the value there, and it will recognize that the value has changed if you dereference the pointer again. The optimization is only there to tell the compiler that the value doesn't change through some other pointer. Then the code that the compiler generates can remember values instead of fetching them again each time you look at the memory at the other end of a restricted pointer.

CHAPTER 4

Pointers and Types

If pointers simply hold memory addresses, why do they have different types? Isn't a memory address just a memory address? Usually, yes, an address is simply an address on a modern architecture, but the language standard doesn't guarantee it. Pointers to different types are allowed to have different representations if the underlying hardware requires it (with a few rules for how you can convert between them), and you should be careful with assuming that they hold the same kinds of addresses.

Even if a pointer merely holds an address, and all addresses are equal, there are still at least three reasons that we want them to have types. First is type-checking. In statically typed languages such as C, the type-checker seeks to eliminate programming errors by analyzing your program and checking if all variables are used in a way consistent with their intended purpose, as specified by their type. Many operations are nonsensical on most types. What does it mean to turn a floating-point number into uppercase? Or divide a string by four? If you attempted to do it in a running program, it would either crash or completely garble up its computation. The type-checker is there to prevent such errors. It is not perfect at catching all errors, which is provably impossible for a program to do, but it identifies many errors that want to catch as early as possible—before your program is running in any critical setting.

Second, types do more than check that you use objects as you intended. They specify how bit patterns and chunks of computer memory should be interpreted. A 64-bit integer and a 64-bit floating-point number are both 64-bit binary words, but we interpret the bit patterns differently. We also interpret a 64-bit and a 32-bit integer differently, when we look at the memory location where we find it. If we are looking for a 64-bit (or 8-byte) integer, we need to look at 8 bytes to get the number; if we are looking at a 32-bit (4-byte) integer, we only need to look at the next 4 bytes at the address. When you dereference a pointer, you want C to interpret what it finds at the address the correct way. The pointer type ensures this. If we only worked with (untyped) addresses, we would need to explicitly specify the interpretation we want of what we point at, each time we dereference.

© Thomas Mailund 2021
69
T. Mailund, *Pointers in C Programming*, https://doi.org/10.1007/978-1-4842-6927-5_4

Pointers, Types, and Data Interpretation

In the following, I will do some things that you shouldn't ever do. I do it to illustrate a point, but I enter a territory that the C standard says the behavior is undefined. The standard uses the term "undefined behavior" frequently. It means that you are allowed to do it, but you won't know what will happen in general. It is not laziness that leaves things undefined; instead, it is giving compilers freedom to optimize their code to the hardware the code will run on. Suppose you specify the behavior of a program too tightly. In that case, the compiler has to generate extra code to adjust the behavior when it deviates from what the underlying hardware would do. Leaving it undefined frees the compiler to generate optimal code for any platform. The side effect is, of course, that you cannot write portable code if you rely on the behavior that the standard leaves undefined. The following example is not portable to all platforms, because I cast between pointer types that I might not be allowed to. It will probably work for you as well, as most desktop architectures will allow it, but if it doesn't work, read the example and move on to the next section where I explain why that might be.

But back to the example. If pointers are just addresses, we can cast one pointer type to another and make them point to the same address. If we then dereference them, they will look at the same data—it is the data at the same address, after all—but they will interpret the data differently. Consider this program:

```c
#include <stdio.h>

int main(void)
{
  printf("sizes: double = %zu, long = %zu, int = %zu, char = %zu\n",
         sizeof(double), sizeof(long), sizeof(int), sizeof(char));

  double d;
  double *dp = &d;
  long   *lp = (long *)&d;
  int    *ip = (int *)&d;
  char   *cp = (char *)&d;
  printf("dp == %p, lp = %p\nip == %p, cp == %p\n\n", dp, lp, ip, cp);

  d = 42.0;
  printf("*dp == %.20f, *lp == %ld,\n*ip == %d, *cp == %d\n",
         *dp, *lp, *ip, *cp);
```

```
  *ip = 4200;
  printf("*dp == %.20f, *lp == %ld,\n*ip == %d, *cp == %d\n",
         *dp, *lp, *ip, *cp);

  *cp = 42;
  printf("*dp == %.20f, *lp == %ld,\n*ip == %d, *cp == %d\n",
         *dp, *lp, *ip, *cp);

  return 0;
}
```

If you run it, you might get this output:

```
sizes: double = 8, long = 8, int = 4, char = 1
dp == 0x7ffee0d88f0, lp == 0x7ffee0d88f0,
ip == 0x7ffee0d88f0, cp == 0x7ffee0d88f0
*dp == 42.00000000000000000000, *lp == 4631107791820423168,
*ip == 0, *cp == 0
*dp == 42.00000000002984279490, *lp == 4631107791820427368,
*ip == 4200, *cp == 104
*dp == 42.00000000002940225841, *lp == 4631107791820427306,
*ip == 4138, *cp == 42
```

It is unlikely that you get the same addresses; you might not get the exact same sizes, but if you are using an x86-64 architecture, as most personal computers do these days, then the dereferenced values will be the same.

The four pointers all see the same address (Figure 4-1), and dp and lp know they should look at 8 bytes (their sizeof is 8 sizeof(char) and char on this architecture is a byte). The pointer ip should look at 4 and cp at 1 byte. Thus, it should not surprise that we get different values for ip and cp than we do for the others. That lp and dp interpret what they point at differently is a consequence of how we represent floating-point numbers. I will not go into it in this book but suffice to say that the bits in those 8 bytes are interpreted differently, and that is reflected in the output.

When we assign 42.0 to the double, we set the bit pattern in its 8 bytes such that we have the floating-point representation of 42. This looks very different if we interpret the same bits as a long integer, as we can see. The integer and character pointers see 0, which we can conclude means that the low 4 bytes in the double are all 0 bits.

When we assign to *ip, we change the 4 lower bytes. We go through an integer
pointer, so C knows (even though we lied to it) that it is looking at a memory object of
4 bytes, and it overwrites the existing data with the bits that represent the integer 4200.
It changes both the double and the long—it changes half their bits, after all—but it is
the lower bits, and we do not see a large change. The change is there, though. We also
change the char at the first byte because the lower byte in the 4-byte 4200 is no longer 0.
We can get the lower byte of a number by taking the division remainder of 256 (think of
bytes as base 256, i.e., 2 to the power of 8), and that is the 104 we see. When we assign 42
to *cp, we change the char to 42, and we replace the 104 in the integer with 42.

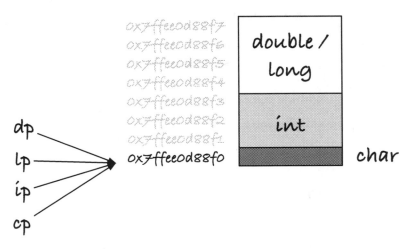

Figure 4-1. *The same memory, interpreted as a char, an int, and a double*

The type we give a pointer tells C how it should handle dereferenced values, that is,
how it should treat the memory at the address we point at and how many memory cells
starting at that address are part of the object. Since C will look beyond the first address
whenever sizeof is greater than one, you also have to be careful here. If you cast the
address of a small object to a pointer of a larger type, you can quickly get into trouble.
You can always cast integer values to a larger type, for example:

```
int i = 42;
long l = (long)i;
```

(you do not even need the type-cast here). This is safe because C already has memory set aside for the variables, and you are merely copying bits. This, however, is not safe:

```
int i = 42;
long *lp = (long *)&i;
```

If you dereference `lp`, C will pick 8 bytes from the memory address where `i` sits, but there are only four allocated for the integer (on my machine, at least). What happens is anyone's guess, but it probably will be bad.

If you want to put a `char`, an `int`, and a `double` at the same position, then you should use a `union`. That is what unions are for, after all. You can achieve the same thing with a `union`, and that is the safe way to do it. You can even get pointers of the different types to the union's address.

The point of the example is not that you cannot put different objects in the same memory, you can, but you need type information to treat the size and the data in the memory correctly. If pointers didn't have types, we would need to provide the type in some other way.

The third reason we want to give pointers types might be less apparent but has to do with how we handle arrays of objects (see Chapter 5) and array-like objects, that is, memory where we have laid out objects of the same type contiguously. The next object's address is exactly one past previous object's last address. Here, the types tell us how far apart two consecutive objects are—objects of type T are `sizeof(T)` apart—and because the pointers know how large the objects they point at are, we can use so-called *pointer arithmetic* when we work with arrays, as we shall see in Chapter 5. Here, I will give you a taste of how it works.

In the following program, I have defined a to be a sequence of five integers, one to five. This gives me `5 * sizeof(int)` consecutive memory addresses. The first integer sits at index 0, the second at offset `sizeof(int)`, and number i sits at offset `(i - 1) * sizeof(int)`. The address just past the array is `5 * sizeof(int)`.

```
#include <stdio.h>

int main(void)
{
  int a[] = { 1, 2, 3, 4, 5 };
  int n = sizeof a / sizeof *a;
```

```
// get a pointer to the beginning of a
int *ip = a;
char *cp = (char *)a;

for (int i = 0; i < n; i++) {
  printf("a[%d] sits at %p / %p / %p\n",
         i, (void *)&a[i], (void *)(ip + i),
         (void *)(cp + i * sizeof *a));
}

return 0;
}
```

The line

```
int n = sizeof a / sizeof *a;
```

is an idiom for getting the correct number of elements in an array. The first sizeof gives us the size of the array, and the second provides us with the size of one element, what the array "points to," so dividing the first by the second gives us the number of elements. Here, of course, we know that it is five, but we might change the size later and forget to update n. We don't use sizeof(int) for the second number for a similar reason. We don't want to count the wrong number of elements if we change the type of the array later.

When running the program, I got

```
a[0] sits at 0x7ffeeaa468f0 / 0x7ffeeaa468f0 / 0x7ffeeaa468f0
a[1] sits at 0x7ffeeaa468f4 / 0x7ffeeaa468f4 / 0x7ffeeaa468f4
a[2] sits at 0x7ffeeaa468f8 / 0x7ffeeaa468f8 / 0x7ffeeaa468f8
a[3] sits at 0x7ffeeaa468fc / 0x7ffeeaa468fc / 0x7ffeeaa468fc
a[4] sits at 0x7ffeeaa46900 / 0x7ffeeaa46900 / 0x7ffeeaa46900
```

but you can check for yourself. As you can see, the addresses match. Notice that to get to index i from the integer pointer, we use ip + i. Because of the type, we know that we need to move in jumps of sizeof(int). With the char pointer, we have to explicitly include the size; a character pointer jumps in quantities of the size of char which is always 1. This might look like a fringe case where types are important, but pointer arithmetic is used throughout C programs.

Generally, you do not want to index into the middle of an object, because you do not know how C chooses to represent objects. But it can have its uses. For example, we might want to pick out the individual bytes of an integer. In Chapter 6, we see how we can sort integers in linear time if we do this, although there we do so without pointing into the integers. Here is a program that runs through the array from before and prints the individual bytes in the elements:

```c
#include <stdio.h>

int main(void)
{
  int a[] = { 1, 2, 3, 4, 5 };
  int n = sizeof a / sizeof *a;

  for (int i = 0; i < n; i++) {
    printf("%d = [", a[i]);
    char *cp = (char *)(a + i);
    for (int j = 0; j < sizeof *a; j++) {
      printf(" %d ", cp[j]);
    }
    printf("]\n");
  }

  return 0;
}
```

We iterate through the integers, and for each integer, we set a char pointer to point to the address of the first byte in that integer. When we write a + i, we use a as a pointer, and we get the address of a[i] (with no ampersand needed because we already get the address from a + i). Now we go through the number of bytes in an integer. If cp is a char pointer, then cp + j is the char that is j addresses higher than it. We can dereference it with *(cp + j), but cp[j] is syntactic sugar for doing exactly this. The types matter for the correct indexing. For the array, a + i is i *integers* past a, but cp + j is j *characters* past cp. The type of the pointer/array determines what the step size is when we add a number to them.

Although I will tell you in the next section that you should be careful with casting from one pointer type to another, this program is actually standard compliant. You can always cast to a character pointer and use it to run through the bytes in an allocated object.

When I run the program, I get the output:

```
1 = [ 1 0 0 0 ]
2 = [ 2 0 0 0 ]
3 = [ 3 0 0 0 ]
4 = [ 4 0 0 0 ]
5 = [ 5 0 0 0 ]
```

There are 4 bytes per int (because sizeof(int) is 4 with the compiler I use), and the numbers 0 to 5 sit in the first byte of the integers, with the remaining 3 bytes set to 0. This will not always be the case. C does not guarantee how integers are represented; that is defined by your hardware architecture. In principle, any kind of bit pattern can be used, but in practice, there are two integer representations: *big-endian* and *little-endian*. They differ in which direction the most to least significant bytes sit. Consider a 32-bit integer; see Figure 4-2. Do we put the first (least significant) 8 bits into the first byte in memory and then the rest in the following bytes? Or do we put the eight most significant bits in the first byte? Different architectures (and various file formats and network protocols) make different choices, but if you use an x86-64 chip, like me, then you will have a little-endian architecture, and you will get the same results as I got earlier.

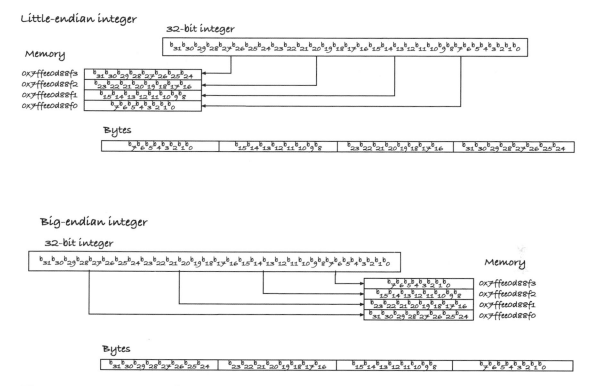

Figure 4-2. *Integer endianness*

You can try this program to check if your integers are one or the other. It computes an integer from its bytes by considering them as base 256 numbers (base 256 because that is the number of digits we have with 8 bits). You already know how the pointer arithmetic for the cp pointer works, and the only difference between the two functions is the order in which we go through the bytes.

```c
#include <stdio.h>

int little_endianess(int i)
{
  char *cp = (char *)&i;
  int result = 0, coef = 1;
  for (int j = 0; j < sizeof i; j++) {
    result += coef * cp[j];
    coef *= 256;
  }
```

```c
  return result;
}

int big_endianess(int i)
{
  char *cp = (char *)&i;
  int result = 0, coef = 1;
  for (int j = sizeof i - 1; j >= 0; j--) {
    result += coef * cp[j];
    coef *= 256;
  }
  return result;
}

int main(void)
{
  for (int i = 0; i < 10; i++) {
    printf("%d: little = %d, big = %d\n",
           i, little_endianess(i), big_endianess(i));
  }

  return 0;
}
```

In the interest of honesty, I must admit that the program only works for non-negative integers, but the failure has nothing to do with endianness. The two-complement representation of negative numbers, used on practically all hardware, doesn't allow us to consider a 32-bit integer as a four-digit base 256 integer. Looking into the guts of an object only takes us so far, and while we can examine the individual bytes in an integer using a char pointer, there are limits to what we can do with it.

The way our programs interpret data, stored in its raw bit format, depends on the type we give our objects, and the same goes for pointers. At their heart, they are nothing but addresses into the computer's memory, but the type we give them tells the program how to interpret what it finds at the address they store (and what we mean when we want an address a specific offset from the address we point to).

Although I did it myself in this section, I don't want you to cast pointers of one type into another. Do as I say, and not as I do. Casting a pointer of one type to a pointer of another, or addressing the same memory as different types, as I have done, was for educational purposes. If you do it, you easily enter undefined behavior territory. In the next section, I will explain some of the main reasons for this.

Casting Between Pointers of Different Types

A pointer holds an address, but pointers of different types hold pointers to different types—obviously. Does that mean that they are represented the same way, and the type information is only used by the compiler to check that you use them correctly? Often, yes, but this is not guaranteed by the C standard.

Void Pointers

What you are guaranteed is that you can assign a pointer to an object of any type to a void pointer (see later), and if you cast it back, you get the original pointer.

```
int *ip = 0x12345;
void *p = ip;
int *ip2 = p;
assert(ip == ip2);
```

A void pointer is a generic pointer with no underlying type—void is an incomplete type that you cannot otherwise use. You can assign to any data pointer from a void pointer without type-casts. This is an easy way to slip past type-checking, so be careful.

These rules only apply to pointers to data objects. The C standard does not require that pointers to functions and pointers to data are compatible, so assigning a function pointer to a void pointer is not necessarily supported. You can convert between function pointers of different types, though. In the POSIX standard, you can store function pointers in void *, but the C standard leaves the behavior undefined. We return to function pointers in Chapter 13.

Qualified Types

If you have pointers to the same underlying type, for example, int, but one is qualified,[1] it could be volatile int, and the other is not, then you can assign the nonqualified to the qualified and get the same representation.

```
int i;
int *ip = &i;
volatile int *ip2 = ip;
assert(ip == ip2);
```

You don't need an explicit cast to add a qualifier, but you do need one to remove it if you want to get back to the original type.

You can cast away the const qualifier. This is legal, and you get a pointer to the same object. Be careful, though, because if the object you point to is const, then modifying it invokes undefined behavior.

```
int i = 42;
int const *ip = &i;    // Adding qualified, fine
int *ip2 = (int *)ip; // Removing it again, fine
*ip2 = 13;             // Changing i, no problem, i isn't const

int const i2 = 13;
ip2 = (int *)&i2;      // Removing qualifier, but ok
*ip2 = 42;             // UNDEFINED BEHAVIOUR, i2 is const
```

Unions

You are allowed to cast a union to the types that its members have:

```
union U {
  int i;
  double d;
};

union U u;
int *ip = (int *)&u;
double *dp = (double *)&u;
```

---

[1]The qualifiers are const, restrict, and volatile and combinations thereof.

and you will get the correct pointer if you cast them back again.

```
assert((union U *)ip == &u);
assert((union U *)dp == &u);
```

You are not guaranteed that you can safely cast in the other direction, though, for example, cast an int pointer to a union pointer, just because the union has an int member.

```
int i;
union U *up = (union U *)&i;
```

You do not have the guarantee that you can do this, only that if the original address holds the union, then it will be correct. A union U pointer might not be allowed to point to an arbitrary integer. There could be alignment issues, for one thing, and even if not, if you use up to access the double member, the integer object at the address is likely too small to hold the data you write into it. For me, with sizeof(int) == 4 and sizeof(double) == 8, something very bad might happen if I tried.

Struct Pointers

You can assign a pointer to a struct of any type to a pointer to a struct of any type.

```
struct S *s = ...;
struct T *t = (struct T *)s;
assert((struct S *)t == s);
```

If you cast a pointer to one type of structure to a pointer to another kind of structure, and back again, you get the original pointer. This does not mean that it is safe to dereference such a pointer, of course, because the structures can look very different—but one struct pointer can hold the value that another struct pointer can hold.

Character Pointers

You can always cast any pointer to an object to a character type, for example, char or unsigned char, and you get a pointer to the first address of where that object sits.

```
int i;
char *x = (char *)&i;
assert((char *)&i == x);
```

The following `sizeof(T)` addresses for the type T object we look at, we can access the data, and we can modify the data if the object we are pointing at is mutable, that is, not `const`.

Arbitrary Types

You are also guaranteed that you can cast from a T * to a U * for any types T and U, but here you are *not* guaranteed that you get the same pointer if you go back again. That depends on the alignment of the referenced type, the type of what you point to. If the types have the same alignment, then you are guaranteed that you get the same object back, but otherwise the behavior is undefined.

```
int i = 42;
int *ip = &i;
double *dp = (double *)ip;
int *ip2 = (int *)dp;
// Maybe ip == ip2, or maybe not.
```

This generally means that if you cast to a type that has stricter alignment constraints, like from an `int` with alignment 4 on my computer to `double` with alignment 8, then the behavior is undefined. I could get away with casting in the other direction, but when we write code, we do not know what the alignment constraints will be for other architectures, so this is dangerous to make assumptions about.

Don't cast between arbitrary types. You have no idea about what will happen, the standard gives you no guarantees, and in any case, it might be meaningless to dereference a pointer you got this way. Because what happens if you dereference pointers after you have converted them? You cannot dereference a `void` pointer, so we don't need to worry about that. You can safely dereference a pointer to an object of the pointer's underlying type, even with other qualifiers, but what happens might involve undefined behavior. For example, changing a `const` object is undefined.

If you cast between some arbitrary types, and their alignment matches so this is a well-defined operation, dereferencing them can still go arbitrarily wrong. We have two aliases to the same object, but with different types, and while there are a few exceptions, this generally involves undefined behavior. This means that the compiler is free to do what it wants with that code. Obviously, if you have an object of one size, and write to it through a pointer to a larger type, you will write outside of the bounds of its memory. Your program might crash, or most likely you will overwrite other variables. That is an obvious problem. But you are not out of the woods if you write to a large object through a smaller type. The bit patterns used to represent different values mean that writing the smaller object into the larger doesn't necessarily match what you want. A float is typically smaller than a double, and it is always valid to write

```
float f = 1.34;
double d = f;
```

but go through pointers and you can get into trouble:

```
double d;
float *f = &d;
*f = 1.34;
```

We write the value 1.34 to the address *f as a float. What that looks like to a double is up to the compiler (and the computer architecture, of course).

If you aim a pointer of the wrong type at an object, you have an *invalid alias*, and the C standard doesn't give you any guarantees about what happens. It does, however, give the compiler some freedom to optimize. There is a rule, called the *strict alias* rule, that says that whatever pointers of different types point at, it is different objects. Turn on your compiler's optimization, and it will exploit this.

Consider this program:

```
#include <stdio.h>

int f(int *i, long *l)
{
  *i = -1;
  *l = 0;
  return *i;
}

int main(void)
{
  long x;
  int i = f((int *)&x, &x);
  printf("%ld %d\n", x, i);
  return 0;
}
```

In f(), we have a pointer to an int and to a long. We write -1 to the integer, which sets all its bits to 1 in the two-complement representation. Then we write 0 to the long, which sets all its bits to 0 (for all integer representations that I have ever heard about). In main(), we call f() with two pointers to the same object. So we would expect that *i = -1 wrote 1 bit in some of the bits in the long object x. With the compiler I am using, an int is half the size of a long, so it would set the first half of the bits to 1 and leave the rest the way they were. Not that it matters, because we then write zero bits into the entire object. Finally, we return the integer that i points to. If we have just set the entire x to zeros, it should point to an integer where all the bits are zero as well, so we expect that f() returns zero. If I compile the program without optimization, that is indeed what I see. If I turn optimization on, however, f() returns -1. Why?

The strict alias rule says that i and l cannot point to the same object, because they do not have compatible types. So when the compiler works out what to return from f(), it can see that we just assigned -1 to *i, and the rule tells it that the assignment to *l cannot have changed that, so it concludes that it can return -1 and that it does not need to fetch *i once more from memory. We lied to the compiler when we pointed an int * at a long, and we shouldn't have done that.

The general rule is that you should never alias objects of different types—you might be able to store the pointer to one type in another, but you shouldn't *use* the object you point to then. The actual rules in the language standard are slightly more complex, but if you do not do this, then you are safe.

With a char pointer, the strict aliasing rule does not apply. Character pointers are special in that they are always allowed to point to any other object, and if the object is mutable, we are allowed to modify the object we point to. In the following program, j gets the value 0 regardless of optimization:

```
#include <stdio.h>

int f(int *i, long *l)
{
    *i = -1;
    *l = 0;
    return *i;
}

int g(char *c, long *l)
```

```
{
  *c = -1;
  *l = 0;
  return *c;
}

int main(void)
{
  long x;
  int i = f((int *)&x, &x);
  int j = g((char *)&x, &x);
  printf("%ld %d %d\n", x, i, j);

  return 0;
}
```

Void Pointers

There are cases where we want pointers to "something," where "something" means that we do not care (right now) what it is. The type you use for such pointers is void. If you declare a void pointer, you can point it at anything at all.

```
int i;
char c;
void *p = &i;
p = &c;
```

Here, we point p at an integer and then at a char, and we do so without casting the type. That is acceptable because a void pointer just holds an address. We cannot do much with void pointers. If you dereference them, you get the type void, which isn't a type as such and C will not interpret it in any way. The only thing you can do with a void pointer is to store an address. That sounds pretty useless, but it is how C can implement generic functionality, that is, functionality that works for more than one type.

The `qsort()` function from the standard library is an example of a generic function. You can use it to sort arrays of any type that you can define an order on—integers, strings, floating points—anything at all that can be ordered. It can sort anything because it is oblivious to the type of the objects it sorts. For `qsort()`, the data is just a chunk of memory. It knows how many data elements are in the chunk, and it knows how large they are (so it knows how many addresses go between one element and the next), but that is all it knows. It is up to the caller of the function to make sense of the data; you do this by providing the call with a function for comparing elements.

When `qsort()` sorts the element, and it wants to know if one element is larger than another, all it has is the addresses where the elements are found in memory, referenced by `void` pointers. It will call the comparison function with these, and the comparison function must then (1) assign the `void const *` pointers into pointers of the correct type, so it can use them for something, and (2) compare the elements. The function should return a negative integer if the first element is smaller than the second, zero if the two elements are equal, and a positive number if the second element is larger than the first. If you want to sort an array of integers, for example, you must convert the `void` pointers into `int` pointers and compare what they point at. That comparison could be subtracting the second element from the first; it will be negative if the second element is larger, positive if it is smaller, and zero if the two values are equal, exactly as it should be. The following function does this; see also Figure 4-3.

```
int int_compare(void const *x, void const *y)
{
  // Get the objects, and interpret them as integers
  int const *a = x;
  int const *b = y;
  return *a - *b;
}
```

Functions such as `qsort()` can operate on any data by delegating the part of the algorithm that requires data knowledge to a parameter function. We will revisit using `void` pointers as generic data and using functions as arguments—function pointers, as it turns out—several places in the book. For now, I will leave you with the following program that shows how you can use `qsort()` to sort both integers and strings, by providing the correct comparison function:

qsort():

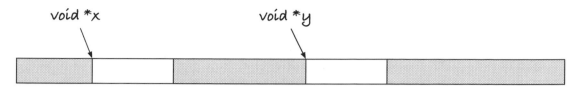

int_compare(void *x, void *y):

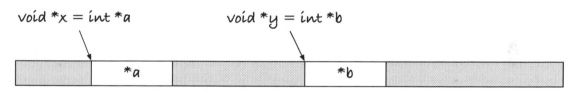

Figure 4-3.   *Comparison in qsort()*

```c
#include <stdio.h>
#include <string.h>

int int_compare(void const *x, void const *y)
{
  // Get the objects, and interpret them as integers
  int const *a = x;
  int const *b = y;
  return *a - *b;
}

int string_compare(void const *x, void const *y)
{
  // Get the objects and interpet them as strings
  char * const *a = x;
  char * const *b = y;
  return strcmp(*a, *b);
}
```

```
int main(void)
{
  int int_array[] = { 10, 5, 30, 15, 20, 30 };
  int int_array_length =
    sizeof int_array / sizeof *int_array;

  qsort(int_array, int_array_length,
        sizeof *int_array, int_compare);
  printf("int_array = ");
  for (int i = 0; i < int_array_length; i++) {
    printf("%d, ", int_array[i]);
  }
  printf("\n");

  char *string_array[] = { "foo", "bar", "baz" };
  int string_array_length =
    sizeof string_array / sizeof *string_array;

  qsort(string_array, string_array_length,
        sizeof *string_array, string_compare);
  printf("string_array = ");
  for (int i = 0; i < string_array_length; i++) {
    printf("%s, ", string_array[i]);
  }
  printf("\n");

  return 0;
}
```

For the `string_compare()` function, remember that we get the *address* of the elements in the array. The array consists of strings, that is, `char *`, but that is not what the function is called with. That is the values in the array. The function is called with pointers to the values, so pointers to strings or pointers to pointers to `char`, that is, `char **`. And because it is a `const` in the parameter, we need to get that added somewhere as well. The easiest way to work out the type, and get `const` at the right place, I think is this: In the algorithm, `qsort()` thinks that we have an array of `void`—conceptually at least, since it is impossible to have anything of `void`. We know that we have an array of `char *`, so we should get the correct type by substituting `void` for `char *` everywhere. So `void const *`, with `void -> char *`, becomes `char * const *`.

It is no different from the integer case, where we have an array of `int` that `qsort()` thinks is an array of `void`, so we get the type by `void -> int` which gives us `void const *` to `int const *`. Still, I have often seen students cast the `void` pointers to `char` pointers (or `char const *`) perhaps because they reason that they are both pointers. With the pointer to pointer, you also get three places to put the `const`, `char const **` (wrong), `char * const *` (correct), `char ** const` (wrong). If you always substitute `void` with the correct type, you will get the correct pointer type.

The arguments to `qsort()`, besides the comparison function, are the array, which it obviously needs, the number of elements—it needs to know the length of the array—and the size of the data objects. It needs to know how large objects are to know where individual objects are. It needs to know how many bytes two objects are apart, and that is a multiple of the object size in bytes. We return to indexing into arrays in Chapter 5.

It is not necessary to use an explicit cast to convert `void` pointers from and to other types.

```
int i = 42;
int *ip = &i;
void *vp = ip;
char *cp = vp;
```

You do not need an explicit cast to convert to and from `void` and data pointers. This is potentially dangerous since we are implicitly casting between pointer types. However, in many cases, it is convenient that you do not need to cast `void` pointers because we use them with generic functions. We do not need to cast the preceding input to `qsort()` to `(void *)`. Similarly, when we have functions that return `void` pointers—such as those we will use in Chapter 2—we do not need casts either. Beware of the dangerous, though. The preceding example circumvents the type-checker and casts an integer pointer to a character pointer without errors or warnings. It is easy to see that this is happening in simple code like this, but it is obviously more challenging in more complicated code. If we want to change the type of a pointer, we should be explicit about it. It should never be by accident. Do be careful when going to and from `void` pointers.

CHAPTER 5

Arrays

Arrays are collections of objects of the same type, laid out in memory as a sequence of contiguous objects. There is a close relationship between arrays and pointers to the first element in an array; you can use an array as if it is a pointer to its first element, and it degrades to that type automatically if you use it that way. If you pass arrays as arguments to functions, they are always implicitly passed by reference, as a pointer to the first element. They are still different types, however. You cannot assign to an array, so in that way arrays resemble `const` pointers, and the size of an array is the total size of all the objects it contains, where the size of a pointer to the first element is just the size of the pointer. Still, as we shall see, when we work with arrays, we rarely distinguish between having a pointer and an array.

You define an array of type `T` with the syntax `T array[]`, in some variant of the following examples for integers:

```
int a1[5];
int a2[5] = { 1, 2, 3 }; // only init first three
int a3[] = { 1, 2, 3, 4, 5 };
```

The first array contains five integers, but we have not initialized them—they can have any value whatsoever at this point. The second also contains five integers, but we have defined the first three of them. After declaring the integer, you can specify the array's values afterward in curly braces. You do not have to set all of them—here, we only define the first three of five—but it is an error to provide more values than you say that the array contains. In the last case, we do not specify how many values the array should hold, but we provide initial values. When we do this, the array will hold the values we provide, and the size will match the number of values exactly.

© Thomas Mailund 2021

T. Mailund, *Pointers in C Programming*, https://doi.org/10.1007/978-1-4842-6927-5_5

It might also be possible to declare an array whose length depends on a variable, such as

```
int n = strlen(s);
char buffer[n + 1];
```

The buffer is allocated on the function call stack when we write buffer[n + 1], and it is a so-called *variable length array* because it depends on a runtime variable. These were introduced in the C99 standard, but in the C11 standard, they turned optional because memory allocation problems on the stack are practically impossible to catch by the programmer, and variable length arrays were judged to be a security issue as well. It is likely that your compiler still supports them, but if not, you would need to allocate the buffer on the heap, as we will explore in Chapter 9. I will use variable length arrays until we get to that chapter because we haven't gotten to dynamic allocation yet, but if the code doesn't compile for you, add large enough constants for their length until you read the next chapter.

C knows the size of an array because it knows the size of the underlying type and how many elements the array holds, so sizeof() will give you the number of bytes the array takes up in memory. This size is the number of elements times the size of the underlying type, so an int array of length 5

```
int A[5]; has sizeof A == 5 * sizeof(int).
```

If you take the value of an array, you get the address of the first element in the array. Thus, we get a pointer to the beginning of the array if we write something like int *ap = array. If you take the *address* of the array, you get a pointer to the array, of course, but on all compilers I know, this is the same address. The value of an array equals the address of its first values (and we will see why later in the chapter). The address of the array is a different type, but practically guaranteed to be the same address as the array's value.

There is a close correspondence between pointers and arrays, and in any expression, you can use an array as if it was a pointer to the underlying type. Thus, we do not need a cast to assign an array to a pointer of the underlying type; we are free to pretend that the array *is* such a pointer. They are not the same type, however. The sizeof() an array is not the size of a pointer to its elements, you cannot assign to an array, and the address of an array is a pointer to an array and not a pointer to a pointer of the underlying array. If ip is an integer pointer, &ip has type int **. If array is an integer array, &array is a pointer to an array, and the two are different and incompatible types. That being said, in many places, we use pointers and arrays interchangeably, and there are places that the C standard will always implicitly translate an array into a pointer. This happens, for example, every time you use an array as a function argument, as we shall see in the next section.

Consider this program:

```c
#include <stdio.h>
#include <assert.h>

int main(void)
{
  int array[] = { 1, 2, 3, 4, 5 };
  int *ap = array;
  printf("sizeof array == %zu, sizeof ap == %zu\n",
          sizeof array, sizeof ap);
  printf("%p %p %p %p\n", array, &array, ap, &ap);

  int n = sizeof array / sizeof *array;
  for (int i = 0; i < n; i++) {
    assert(array[i] == ap[i]);
    assert(array + i == ap + i);
    assert(*(array + i) == *(ap + i));
  }

  return 0;
}
```

We define an array of integers of length 5, and we point an integer pointer at it, which means that it points at the first integer in the array. The size of the array will be 5 * sizeof(int) because that is how many bytes it takes up in memory. The size of the pointer, however, will be sizeof(int *), which is likely substantially less. On my setup, an int is 4 bytes (and the array is therefore 20 bytes), while a pointer is 8 bytes. The address of the array is a pointer, so it is 8 bytes, and so is the address of the pointer—the address of a pointer is itself a pointer, so when ap has type int *, &ap has type int **.

When we compute the length of the array in the program, we used

```c
int n = sizeof array / sizeof *array;
```

The first `sizeof array` gives us the number of bytes in the array, and the second `sizeof *array` gives us the number of bytes in the first element in the array. Since `array` is an integer array, `sizeof *array == sizeof(int)`. If you change the type of the array later, you need to update the size calculation as well, if you had used `sizeof(int)`. If you use `sizeof *array` (or alternatively `sizeof array[0]`), you get the new type for free.

When we run through the loop, we use the array as a pointer in different expressions, and because arrays decay into pointers when you use them as such, the behavior is the same for `array` and `ap`.

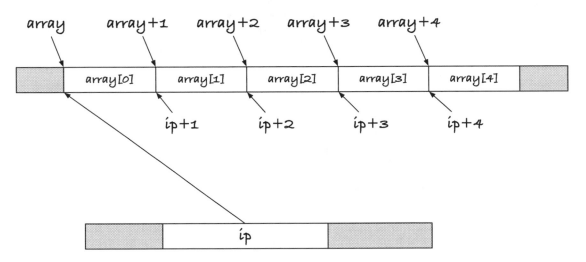

Figure 5-1. *Memory layout of an array and a pointer to the array*

Arrays, Indices, and Pointer Arithmetic

Before we can explore how arrays and pointers fit together, we must examine the memory layout of arrays. Assume that we have defined an array of five integers and pointed an integer pointer to the array, like this:

```
int array[5];
int *ip = array;
```

In Figure 5-1, I have illustrated how the array and the pointer sit in memory. The array consists of five consecutive memory blocks, each of `sizeof(int)` bytes, and `array` is the address of the first integer. C considers both `array` and `&array` the same value, but you cannot point `array` somewhere else, so you should not consider it a pointer, even if it holds an address. The integer pointer, `ip`, also points to the address where the array begins. This *is* a pointer, and it sits somewhere in memory, so in the figure, I have shown it as taking up memory. The value at that memory location is the address of the array. Unlike `array`, we can change `ip` to make it point somewhere else.

The five integers in `array` are found at `array[0]`, `array[1]`, `array[2]`, `array[3]`, and `array[4]`. Since these are consecutive integers in memory, the integers sit at the location where `array` points, one integer further down, two integers further down, and so on.

For any pointer `p` and integer `i`, you can add the integer and pointer, `p + i` or `i + p`, and you can subtract the integer from the pointer `p - i`. Notice that subtraction is not symmetric; you cannot subtract a pointer from an integer. The interpretation for such *pointer arithmetic* relates to arrays. If `p` points into an array, then `i + p` and `p + i` point to the element `i` higher than where `p` points, as long as `p + i` does not point more than one element past the last element. For subtraction, `p - i` points to the element that is `i` indices lower, provided that `p - i` does not point before the first element; see Figure 5-2. The type of pointer subtraction is `ptrdiff_t` and is signed.

The part about not pointing before or after the array objects is to get strict compliance with the language standard. You will most likely get a valid address even if you use an expression that would index outside of the array—although this would be an address that you should be very careful about dereferencing since you do not know what it holds. But the standard only guarantees it when you stay within an allocated array or array-like object. The latter refers to a single allocated chunk of memory where you layout objects the same way as an array, one after another of the same type. In such cases, you get valid pointers when you add or subtract an integer. Otherwise, you could, for example, risk an under- or overflow or whatever else your architecture can throw at you. The behavior is undefined unless you stay within the bounds of the array—except that you are allowed to point at the address right after the last element. In the figure, `p + 3` points one past the last element, and that is also guaranteed to be a valid address. Pointing one past the last element is a useful pattern for looping through a range:

```
T * range_begin = array;
T * range_end = array + n; // n is the length of the array
for (T *p = range_begin; p < range_end; p++) {
  // do something
}
```

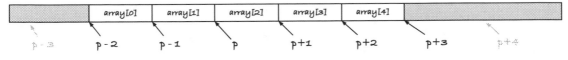

Figure 5-2. *Adding and subtracting integers and pointers*

So pointing one object past the end is explicitly guaranteed by the standard.

The comparison p < range_end between two pointers is also part of pointer arithmetic. If you have pointers p and q into the same array-like object, you can compare them: p < q, p <= q, p > q, and p >= q. You can always compare them with == and !=, regardless of where they point, but less than and greater than only have a defined interpretation in a range spanned by an array.

Going back to our int array and int * pointer in Figure 5-1, we have a pointer that points to the first element in the array. The five integers in the array lie at addresses ip + 0, ip + 1, ip + 2, ip + 3, and ip + 4 (and ip + 5 points one past the last element). The array itself works just like a pointer in this regard, so you get the same addresses at array + 0, array + 1, array + 2, and so on.[1]

The notation array[i] is syntactic sugar, a more convenient notation, for *(array + i), and similar for ip[i] and *(ip + i). The subscript operation we do with the square brackets means that we compute the address of the element we want by adding the offset to the pointer to the array, and then we extract the value we find at that address. The two notations do exactly the same; the compiler translates the subscript notation into the pointer notation blindly this way. The following program shows you the equivalent notations and that arrays and pointers work exactly the same way:

```c
#include <stdio.h>
#include <assert.h>

int main(void)
{
  int array[5] = { 0, 1, 2, 3, 4 };
```

---

[1]There is one slight difference between indexing into an array and though a pointer, but the effect is the same. When you write array[i], the compiler generates code that goes to the address array + i and gets whatever is at that memory location. If you use p[i], the compiler first has to get the value at p's memory location, it needs to get the value of p first, and then it does the same as for the array. This is because you can change the value of a pointer, you can make it point somewhere else, but you cannot change the value of an array. It always points to the same memory location. Therefore, the code needs to do a little more work with a pointer. The effect of the operation is the same, however. As seen from the programmer, there is no difference.

```
  int *ip = array;

  for (int i = 0; i < 5; i++) {
    assert(array + i == ip + i);

    assert(array[i] == ip[i]);
    assert(array[i] == *(array + i));
    assert(ip[i] == *(ip + i));
  }

  return 0;
}
```

The size of an int is sizeof(int), so the distance from one element to the next is that number of addresses. Therefore, if ip points to the first element in the array, then ip + i must lie at address ip + I * sizeof(int) if we looked at the memory through a char pointer. With a character pointer, we see each addressable memory block; typically, this means each byte. From a char * point of view, the first int is sizeof(int) locations; then the next int is the next sizeof(int) locations. To move a pointer from pointing at the first integer to pointing at the second, the char pointer must move sizeof(int) locations.

So you can think of adding to an int pointer as moving in jumps of sizeof(int).

We can explore this by running through the array using both an index computed from the array and integer pointer and one using a char pointer. For the integer pointer, adding i to it will give us the element at index i, and the same is the case for the array because it becomes a pointer when we use it this way. For the char pointer, however, we have to adjust the size of the jumps. If you run the following code, you will see that you get the same addresses from the three different ways of addressing the array's integers:

```
int *ip = array;
char *p = (char *)array;
for (int i = 0; i < n; i++) {
  printf("%p %p %p\n",
          // int array has the right offset
          (void *)(array + i),
          // int * has the right offset
          (void *)(ip + i),
          // char * jumps in bytes...
          (void *)(p + i * sizeof(int)));
}
```

97

To hammer the point home, we can try iterating through the array with a different, but similar, kind of pointer arithmetic. We can get the address one past the last element by casting the array to a char pointer and adding sizeof array. The cast means that when we add the size, we do so as char, so we get the address that is sizeof array after array, which is the first address after the array. We can run a for-loop from the beginning of the array to this point, incrementing an integer pointer by one in each iteration and moving a char pointer by sizeof(int) each time:

```
char *end = (char *)array + sizeof array;
for (ip = array, p = (char *)array;
     p != end;
     ip++, p += sizeof *ip) {
  printf("%p %p\n", (void *)ip, (void *)p);
}
```

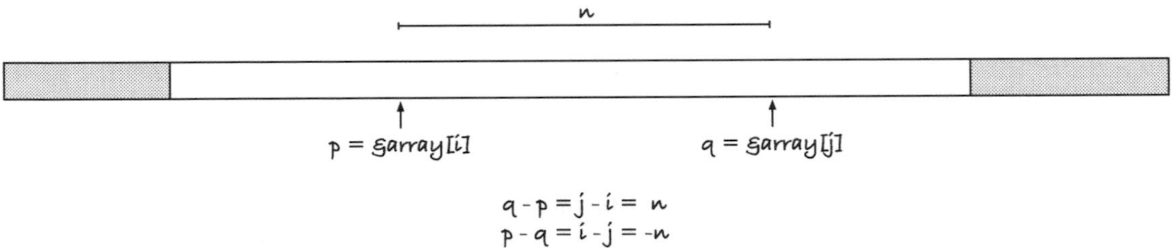

$$q - p = j - i = n$$
$$p - q = i - j = -n$$

Figure 5-3. *Subtracting a pointer from a pointer*

In the increment, I wrote sizeof *ip instead of sizeof(int). The size is the same here, but it is defensive programming to use variables instead of types when you write code like this. If the type of ip changes, the sizeof *ip is updated automatically, while sizeof(int) would not be. The type-checker would not warn you about this, since it is valid code to write sizeof(int), even if you meant the size of some other type.

For any type T, adding or subtracting an integer i to a T * pointer into an array will give you an address that is i * sizeof(int) higher or lower in the array from the perspective of a char *.

If you have two pointers into an array or array-like object, then you can also subtract them. If, for example, p points to the value at index i and q points to the value at index j in an array, then p - q gives you the value i - j, and q - p gives you j - i; see Figure 5-3. If q points at a larger index than p, then q - p thus gives you the number of elements between *p and *q.

In the following code, we use this pointer arithmetic to find the middle element in a range for a binary search. A binary search locates an element in a sorted array by checking the value in the middle of the range. If that element is too small, we know that we have to search in the upper half of the range—because the elements in the array are sorted—and if it is too large, we must search in the lower half. Thus, we can cut the search space in half in each iteration.

```c
int *bin_search(int *left, int *right, int x)
{
  while (left < right) {
    int *mid = (right - left) / 2 + left;
    if (*mid == x) return mid;
    if (*mid < x) {
      left = mid + 1;
    } else {
      right = mid;
    }
  }
  return 0;
}
```

The function uses two pointers to specify the range it should search in, and it uses the expression (right - left) / 2 + left to get a pointer to the middle of the interval. If the middle value is the one we are searching for, we return it, and if we do not find the element in the entire search, we return a NULL pointer. There are smarter interfaces, but this suffices for showing the use of pointer subtraction. Do not try to get the middle element using (left + right) / 2; you are not allowed to add pointers.

You can use the function like this:

```c
int a[] = { 1, 2, 4 };
int n = sizeof a / sizeof *a;
int *res = bin_search(a, a + n, 2);
```

Representing a range of an array using two pointers, one to the first element in the range and the second that points one past the last, is an idiom in C. With a full array, we know the beginning and the size of the data. For a subrange, we need a start and an end index. The pointers representation of a range gives you the same interface to full and sub-arrays and is one of the reasons that the standard always allows you to point one past the last element.

Out-of-Bounds Errors

If you somehow make a pointer that references something outside the bounds of an array, before the first element or more than one past the last element, you risk overflows or underflows, depending on how pointers are represented. This can make your pointers end up pointing anywhere, at least as far as the language standard is concerned—in practice, it is much less likely. But even if nothing untoward happens when computing an address, it most likely will if you try to dereference the said pointer. You might access memory that your process does not have permission to see, in which case your program will crash. Worse, you can mess up the state of your program, so it gives faulty output—if you are particularly unlucky, output that is sufficiently like the expected that you do not notice. Out-of-bounds errors, when you access data outside the range of an array you are working with, are frequent, and you should program defensively to avoid them.

Unfortunately, I do not have much general advice for avoiding these problems. When you decide to work with a block of memory with room for n objects, of whatever size, you need to keep track of where it starts and where it ends. If you do not know what n is, you cannot allocate the right amount of memory, and if you do not know where the memory block begins and ends, you cannot safely access it. You need to know where all arrays begin and end, and there is no easy way around that.

Consistency goes a long way to help you, though. If you work on a range of objects, decide how to represent the range, and use the same representation unless there are excellent reasons not to. With indices, we typically say that the range (i, j) will include the first number but not the last, so for an array, the range would be the elements x[i],x[i+1],...,x[j-1] (but not including x[j]). For pointers, you can do the same. If you run through the range [from,to), then you run as long as from < to, but you do not go to from <= to. These are not hard rules, and if you have good reasons for breaking them, then do so, but consistency makes it easier to write correct code.

Accessing data beyond the bounds of an array is a common and often severe error, and the only way to prevent such errors is to be careful. To the best of my knowledge, there is no easy trick here. Be careful when you design your code; that is the only way to go.

Pointers to Arrays

I mentioned at the beginning of the chapter that for an array `array`, `&array` is typically the same address as the array itself. The type, however, differs. Since `&array` is the address of an array, naturally the type should be a pointer to an array. Specifying that type, however, requires a slightly off-putting syntax. In Chapter 3, I said that you create a pointer to type T by putting an * behind the type, T *, but for arrays (and for functions as we shall see in Chapter 13), this isn't quite as simple. When we define an array, we put the type of the items in the array before the variable name and then the length of the array in square brackets after the variable. We cannot put * after the [ ] to get a pointer to an array. You need to put an * followed by the variable you define in parentheses, preceded by the type of the array and followed by [ ] like this:

```
int (*a1)[];
int (*a2)[10];
```

The number in the brackets, if any, is part of the type and is used by the compiler to determine `sizeof()`—regardless of where the pointer actually points. Consider this program:

```
#include <stdio.h>

int main(void)
{
  int array[10];
  int (*ap1)[] = &array;
  int (*ap2)[10] = &array;
  int (*ap3)[5] = &array; // Warning
  int (*ap4)[20] = &array; // Warning
  int *ip = array;

  printf("%p, sizeof array == %zu\n", (void *)array, sizeof array);
  // We cannot get sizeof *ap1, it is an incomplete type.
  printf("%p\n", (void *)*ap1);
  printf("%p, sizeof *ap2 == %zu (%zu)\n",
        (void *)*ap2, sizeof *ap2, 10 * sizeof(int));
  printf("%p, sizeof *ap3 == %zu (%zu)\n",
        (void *)*ap3, sizeof *ap3, 5 * sizeof(int));
```

```
printf("%p, sizeof *ap4 == %zu (%zu)\n",
        (void *)*ap4, sizeof *ap4, 20 * sizeof(int));
printf("%p, sizeof *ip == %zu (%zu)\n",
        (void *)ip, sizeof ip, sizeof(int *));

return 0;
}
```

The output might look like this:

```
0x7ffeeb6fe860, sizeof array == 40
0x7ffeeb6fe860
0x7ffeeb6fe860, sizeof *ap2 == 40 (40)
0x7ffeeb6fe860, sizeof *ap3 == 20 (20)
0x7ffeeb6fe860, sizeof *ap4 == 80 (80)
```

All the pointers contain the same address, the address where the first element in the array sits. The ap1 pointer has a type that allows us to assign any integer array to it, but since it hasn't specified the underlying array's size, the type is considered "incomplete," and we cannot get its size using sizeof(). With ap2, we have specified that it points to an array of length 10, which matches array, so the type-checker accepts the assignment. The size of *ap2 is the same as sizeof array because the type of ap2 says that it points at an array of length 10. The remaining two array pointers have different length. We assign array to both, but since array's length is neither 5 nor 20, we get warnings. When we compute their sizes, we get the value assuming that the type specification was correct, and not the true size of array.

Arrays and Function Arguments

The differences between pointers and arrays quickly go away when you move away from where arrays are declared. If you use arrays as function parameters, you get pointers. The syntax is the same as for arrays, but both sizeof() and & will treat the parameter as a pointer. When you call a function with an array argument, it decays into a pointer, and the function will treat it as such.

```
void not_what_you_want(int array[])
{
  // sizeof array is sizeof(int *) here!
  printf("%zu\n", sizeof array);
  // Here, the array and the address of the array
  // are different. array is a local variable
  // that holds a pointer to the array!
  printf("%p %p\n", (void *)array, (void *)&array);
}
```

There is syntax for specifying the size of an array when it is a function argument. You can tell C that an argument is an array, without specifying the size:

```
void array(int a[])
{
  printf("array: %zu %zu\n", sizeof a, sizeof *a);
}
```

You can specify a constant size:

```
void array_with_size(int a[50])
{
  printf("array[50]: %zu %zu\n", sizeof a, sizeof *a);
}
```

or a size you provide when you call the function:

```
void array_with_parameter_size(int n, int a[n])
{
  printf("array[n]: %zu %zu\n", sizeof a, sizeof *a);
}
```

but for this syntax, you must put the argument n before the array a[n]—you will get a compile time error otherwise. That is a little unfortunate, since many functions in the standard library put the length after the array argument, but that is how it is.

It doesn't matter what you do here, however, because C will still treat the array as a pointer regardless of the syntax you use. The different syntax lets you clarify the intended data for function calls, but the type-checker will not do anything with it. At best, you will get warnings when you compile this code because the compiler knows that the arrays are turned into pointers and that this might not be what you want.

It is not an error to call a function that wants an array of a given size with a parameter of a different size. Not even if the argument is shorter than the function expects, and the function then might access memory beyond the last element in its input. You might get the compiler to give you a warning in some limited cases. If you put `static` before a constant in the argument declaration, you tell the compiler that arguments should have at least the specified size. For example, with this declaration:

```
void size_constrained(int a[static 4])
{
  // Do stuff
}
```

you say that the argument to the function should be at least four integers long. If you give it an argument that is shorter, and if you have enabled the right warnings, your compiler will tell you that you are doing something wrong.[2]

```
int b[2];
size_constrained(b); // Warning
```

However, there is no check if you give the same function a pointer.

```
int *p = b;
size_constrained(p); // No warning
```

If you call such a constrained function through another function, you do not necessarily get any help either—even if that function also specifies a minimal size.

```
void indirect_size_constrained(int a[static 2])
{
  size_constrained(a); // No warning
}
```

If we write a function that takes *pointer* to an array as argument, rather than the array itself or a pointer to the first element, then the type information *is* kept to some extent. For example, with this function:

```
void pointer_to_array(int (*a)[3])
```

---

[2]I stress might, here, because the compiler might not support this, and some compilers will even consider the static specification a syntax error.

```
{
  printf("*a: %zu = %zu x %zu\n",
         sizeof *a, sizeof *a / sizeof **a, sizeof **a);
}
```

you will get a warning if the argument is a pointer to an array shorter than 3, and `sizeof` `*a` will still be `3 * sizeof(int)`, because that is the size of an integer array of length 3. It also works if the length is a parameter:

```
void pointer_to_array_n(int n, int (*a)[n])
{
  printf("*a with n = %d: %zu = %zu x %zu\n",
         n, sizeof *a,
         sizeof *a / sizeof **a, sizeof **a);
}
```

and if you call the function through another function:

```
void indirect_pointer_to_array(int n, int (*array)[1])
{
  pointer_to_array(array); // Warning, because 1 != 3
}
```

The type-checking for array arguments is so limited that it is close to useless, and you shouldn't rely on it. The checking is better if you use pointers to arrays. There, the type-checker will require that you use the right size. The reason for this is more natural to explain after we look at multidimensional arrays, so I will delay the explanation to the last section of the chapter where we do that.

If your function has an array argument, consider the length specifications as comments rather than type declarations. As a rule of thumb, you should treat arrays as pointers every time they are function arguments. At the point in the code where you define an array, the value of an array is an address to the first element, and the size of the array is the number of bytes it takes up in memory. Practically everywhere else, an array is synonymous with a pointer to the first element in the array, and C doesn't distinguish between pointers and arrays there. Still, comments are useful when they show the intent of code, and if you want to be explicit that you use a parameter as an array, and that it has a given size, then use the array notation for the function argument.

Multidimensional Arrays

All the arrays we have seen so far are one-dimensional. Whether we work on them as arrays with indices, or we access them through pointers, they represent a sequence of elements of one dimension. But you can also define multidimensional arrays; you just need to add more dimensions when you define a variable. For example, you can define a two-by-two array using

```
int A[2][2];
```

or a three-dimensional array as

```
double B[4][2][6];
```

If your compiler supports variable length arrays, you can also use runtime values:

```
int n = f();
int m = 2 * n;
long table[n][m];
```

If you want to provide initial values, the syntax resembles the one you use for one-dimensional arrays, but you can provide arrays as the elements:

```
double A[2][3] = {
  { 1, 2, 3 },
  { 4, 5, 6 }
};
```

You can leave out the size of the first dimension:

```
double A[][3] = {
  { 1, 2, 3 },
  { 4, 5, 6 }
};
```

and C will infer it from how many elements you use in the initialization, but it will not infer the size of following dimensions. Even though we provide three in both rows of this table, C will not infer that the second dimension is three elements long.

The initialization can be incomplete, as it can for one-dimensional arrays. If you only provide some of the values, then only those values are set. Here, the braces are important. For the following two arrays:

```
double A[3][2] = {
  { 1 }, { 3 }
};
double B[3][2] = {
  1, 3
};
```

we initialize the first two columns in A's first two rows. We provide two rows, wrapped in braces, and one value for each. For B, we set the first two columns in the first row. The values are filled in row-wise (they are grouped by the second dimension, the columns, but this means that we have defined a row here and not a column). If the compiler initialized the memory that holds the variables to zero, A would now be

```
1 0
3 0
0 0
```

while B would be

```
1 3
0 0
0 0
```

C needs to know all except the first dimension to work out the size of the full table, so it can initialize it correctly. Since the deepest dimension could have all incomplete initializations, C cannot work out the dimensional size by itself. That is why you must specify it, even if you can leave out the first dimension. For the first dimension, C will assume that the array is large enough to hold all the specified values, but nothing more, if you do not provide a dimension size.

You do not need to provide the same number of initial values per dimension, so it is valid to write code such as

```
char x[4][3] = {
  { 'a', 'b', 'c' }, // complete row
  { 'd', 'e'      }, // first 2 columns
  { 'f'           } // on the first column
  // the fourth row is not initialised
};
```

You index into a multidimensional array using the same syntax for one-dimensional arrays; you just need to use more indices, one per dimension. If we index into the preceding array D, D[1] gives us the row

```
{ { 5, 6 }, { 7, 8 } },
```

and in this row, we can pick the first column, D[1][0]:

```
{ 5, 6 }
```

and then, for example, get the second element there, D[1][0][1], which is 6.

An obvious application of multidimensional arrays is matrices; you can see two-dimensional arrays used as such in this little program:

```c
#include <stdio.h>

void mult(int n, int m, int l,
          double C[n][m],
          double const A[n][l],
          double const B[l][m])
{
  for (int i = 0; i < n; i++) {
    for (int j = 0; j < m; j++) {
      double x = 0.0;
      for (int k = 0; k < l; k++) {
        x += A[i][k] * B[k][j];
      }
      C[i][j] = x;
    }
  }
}

void print_matrix(int n, int m, double const A[n][m])
{
  for (int i = 0; i < n; i++) {
    for (int j = 0; j < m; j++) {
      printf("%2.2f ", A[i][j]);
    }
```

```
    printf("\n");
  }
}

int main(void)
{
  double A[2][3] = {
    { 1, 2, 3 },
    { 4, 5, 6 }
  };
  double B[3][2] = {
    { 1, 2 },
    { 3, 4 },
    { 5, 6 }
  };
  double C[2][2];
  mult(2, 2, 3, C, A, B);

  print_matrix(2, 2, C);

  return 0;
}
```

It is not the most exciting program, but it should give you an idea about how we can work with multidimensional arrays.

But let us dig into how such arrays are represented in memory and how we can work with them through pointers. Take this two-by-three matrix A:

```
int A[2][3] = {
  { 1, 2, 3 },
  { 4, 5, 6 }
};
```

It is two-dimensional; the first dimension has length 2, and the second has length 3. But the computer's memory is not two-dimensional, so the representation must be linearized somehow. The way I like to think about the memory layout is recursive. A one-dimensional array is a sequence of the underlying type, so an `int` array is a sequence of `int`, and if the array is used as a pointer, it points at the first element. A two-dimensional array is a sequence of the underlying type, which is a one-dimensional array. If used as a pointer, it points to the first one-dimensional array. So, if we define a two-dimensional array as

```
int A[2][3] = {
  { 1, 2, 3 },
  { 4, 5, 6 }
};
```

you get a sequence of one-dimensional arrays of integers. The one-dimensional arrays have length 3, and the two-dimensional array contains two of those. The memory layout of this matrix is shown in Figure 5-4, A).

A three-dimensional array, likewise, is a sequence of the underlying type, which is two-dimensional arrays (that are then sequences of one-dimensional arrays and so on). The array

```
int B[2][2][3] = {
  { { 1, 2, 3 }, {  4,  5,  6 } },
  { { 7, 8, 9 }, { 10, 11, 12 } }
};
```

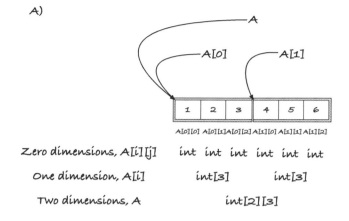

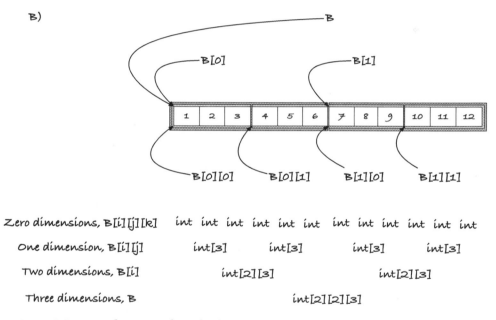

Figure 5-4. *Memory layout of multidimensional array*

is shown in Figure 5-4, B). The general case is that an n-dimensional array is a sequence of $(n - 1)$-dimensional arrays of the right size. The last part is essential. C needs to know the size of the $(n - 1)$-dimensional arrays both to arrange the memory and to allow pointer arithmetic. Remember, if you have a pointer p of a given type, T, then adding i to it, p + i, it gives you an address that is sizeof(T) * i after p. For this pointer arithmetic to work, all the objects must have the same size, and that size must be known. You can throw away the first dimension and work with an array as a pointer, but the remaining dimensions are essential to know.

When you leave out the groupings in the initialization and give the array sequence of the underlying objects:

```
double A[][3] = {
  1, 2, 3, 4, 5, 6
};
```

then knowing the memory layout of arrays makes it easier to reason about what happens with incomplete array initialization. For a one-dimensional array, you initialize the initial elements when you do not provide all of them.

```
int array[5] = { 1, 2, 3 }; // only first three
```

With a multidimensional array, you fill in from the left as well:

```
int A[2][2] = { 1, 2, 3 };
```

Here, the first row gets 1 and 2 because the first row is first in memory, and then the second row gets a 3, and the last element is not initialized.

If you use more braces, you fill out the first parts of the arrays at the deeper dimensions.

```
int B[2][2] = { { 1 }, { 2, 3 } };
```

Here, the first row gets 1 and an uninitialized value, and the second row gets 2 and 3.

You can explore the memory layout of A and B with this program:

```
#include <assert.h>

int main(void)
{
  int A[2][3] = {
    { 1, 2, 3 },
    { 4, 5, 6 }
  };

  assert(sizeof A == 2 * 3 * sizeof(int));
  assert(sizeof *A == 3 * sizeof(int));
  assert(sizeof A[0] == 3 * sizeof(int));
  assert(sizeof A[0][0] == sizeof(int));

  int *p = (int *)A;
  for (int i = 0; i < 2; i++) {
    // p now points to the first element in row i
```

```c
      assert(p == A[i]);
      for (int j = 0; j < 3; j++) {
        // p points to column j in row i
        assert(A[i] + j == p);
        assert(&A[i][j] == p);
        assert(A[i][j] == *p);
        p++;
      }
    }

    int B[2][2][3] = {
      { { 1, 2, 3 }, {  4,  5,  6 } },
      { { 7, 8, 9 }, { 10, 11, 12 } }
    };

    assert(sizeof B == 2 * 2 * 3 * sizeof(int));
    assert(sizeof B[0] == 2 * 3 * sizeof(int));
    assert(sizeof B[0][0] == 3 * sizeof(int));
    assert(sizeof B[0][0][0] == sizeof(int));

    p = (int *)B;
    for (int i = 0; i < 2; i++) {
      // p now points to row i
      assert(p == (int *)B[i]);
      for (int j = 0; j < 2; j++) {
        // p now points to column j in row i
        assert(p == (int *)(B[i] + j));
        for (int k = 0; k < 3; k++) {
          // p now points to the k'th element in B[i][j]
          assert(B[i][j] + k == p);
          assert(&B[i][j][k] == p);
          assert(B[i][j][k] == *p);
           p++;
        }
      }
    }

    return 0;
}
```

You will find that the sizes of the objects match what you would expect, for example, since B is a two-by-two-by-three integer matrix, its size is 2 * 2 * 3 * sizeof(int). Likewise, A[0] is a one-dimensional integer array of length 3, so its size is 3 * sizeof(int). When we run through the arrays, incrementing the later dimensions fastest, we move through addresses integers apart. The cast to int * before those loops is necessary because two-dimensional arrays do not become pointers to the underlying type automatically. The type of A is an array, and if you use it as a pointer, it is a pointer to the first element in the array, and it has the corresponding type. If A was a one-dimensional array of int, we could use it as an int pointer. It would decay to an integer pointer at any time we use it as such. But the underlying type is *not* an integer. In the program, A is a length 2 array of *integer arrays of length 3*. That is its type, and if you want a pointer to it, it must be a pointer to this type, not int *. We are still safe to point an int * at A, though. The array holds the address of its first element, and that is also the address of the first integer in the memory layout. The types just differ.

We know how to define pointers to arrays, we saw it at the beginning of the chapter, so we can make pointers that can move through the underlying array types. Consider this program:

```c
#include <stdio.h>

int main(void)
{
  int C[2][2][3] = {
    { { 1, 2, 3 }, {  4,  5,  6 } },
    { { 7, 8, 9 }, { 10, 11, 12 } }
  };
  int dim1 = sizeof C / sizeof C[0];
  int dim2 = sizeof C[0] / sizeof C[0][0];
  int dim3 = sizeof C[0][0] / sizeof C[0][0][0];

  printf("C dimensions %d x %d x %d\n", dim1, dim2, dim3);

  printf("First element in each row: ");
  int (*first_dim_p)[2][3] = C;
  int (*first_end)[2][3] = C + dim1;
  for ( ; first_dim_p < first_end; first_dim_p++) {
    printf("%d ", *(int*)first_dim_p);
```

```
  }
  printf("\n");

  printf("First element in each column: ");
  int (*second_dim_p)[3] = (int (*)[3])C;
  int (*second_end)[3] = (int (*)[3])C + dim1 * dim2;
  for ( ; second_dim_p < second_end; second_dim_p++) {
    printf("%d ", *(int*)second_dim_p);
  }
  printf("\n");

  return 0;
}
```

Your output should be

```
C dimensions 2 x 2 x 3
First element in each row: 1 7
First element in each column: 1 4 7 10
```

In the first half of the program, we compute the size of the dimensions for the array C. We can, of course, see that where we define the array C, but computing them this way illustrates that the size of C and the underlying types gives us the sizes we expect. C's size is `2 * 2 * 3 * sizeof(int)` because it is a two-by-two-by-three integer array. Its underlying type, which we can get by looking at its first element, `C[0]`, is a two-by-three integer array, so `2 * 3 * sizeof(int)`, and dividing the first by the second gives us 2, the length of the first dimension—similar for the other two dimensions.

After that, we have two loops. For the first, we define a pointer to C's underlying type, which is two-by-three integer arrays. We can use C as a pointer, it will decay to one if we do, so we can assign C to this pointer to make it point at the first element. Then we can go through the rows by increments of it. Its increment size is the number of bytes that the underlying type has, `2 * 3 * sizeof(int)`, so it will go through them, all two of them, and point at the beginning of each. At that position, we extract the first integer. We need to cast the pointer to `(int *)` before we dereference it because C will not automatically cast a multidimensional array to a pointer to the base type. Arrays only decay to pointers to their immediate underlying type, in this case, a two-dimensional array. You need to explicitly go all the way down to integers here.

The second loop does much the same. Here, we want a pointer to the elements in the second dimension of C, which are length 3 arrays. We will loop through all the columns, and we could do that by first looping over all the rows, and in an inner loop handle the columns, but if we consider the memory layout of C, we know that we can also see C as a sequence of second-dimension objects. Jumping through these, rather than the first dimension, just requires smaller jumps. If we define a pointer to length 3 arrays, we get the jump size we want. Then we simply need to work out the interval we should jump through. Obviously, we should start at the first element, which is the address we get from C. There are two columns per row and two rows, so we should jump four times, and we can compute the end address from that. We need to cast C in these computations because the pointer arithmetic must be on pointers to objects of the right size. So we cast C to the type of the second dimension, arrays of length 3, set the beginning and end pointers, and then we get going with the loop.

What happens when we use multidimensional arrays as function arguments? Remember that for one-dimensional arrays, they decayed to pointers to their underlying type, and the type-checker ignores the size information we provide. It turns out that multidimensional arrays work the same way as one-dimensional arrays. With these, arrays also decay to pointers, but in their case, it is pointers to arrays. When you have an array argument, it decays to the underlying type, the type it is a sequence of, and for multidimensional arrays, that is a lower-dimensional array.

Consider this program:

```
#include <assert.h>

void array_full_size(int A[10][10])
{
  // A becomes a pointer to length 10 arrays
  assert(sizeof A == sizeof(int (*)[10]));
  assert(sizeof *A == 10 * sizeof(int));
}

void array_incomplete_size(int A[][10])
{
  // A becomes a pointer to length 10 arrays
  assert(sizeof A == sizeof(int (*)[10]));
  assert(sizeof *A == 10 * sizeof(int));
}
```

```c
void pointer(int (*A)[10])
{
  // A is explicitly a pointer to length 10 arrays
  assert(sizeof A == sizeof(int (*)[10]));
  assert(sizeof *A == 10 * sizeof(int));
}

int main(void)
{
  int A[10][10];
  assert(sizeof A == 10 * 10 * sizeof(int));
  array_full_size(A);
  array_incomplete_size(A);
  pointer(A);

  int B[5][10];
  assert(sizeof B == 5 * 10 * sizeof(int));
  // B's first dimension is wrong, but no warnings
  array_full_size(B);
  array_incomplete_size(B);
  pointer(B);

  int C[10][5];
  assert(sizeof C == 10 * 5 * sizeof(int));
  // You get warnings here, because the
  // second dimension doesn't match
  array_full_size(C);
  array_incomplete_size(C);
  pointer(C);

  return 0;
}
```

The three functions are equivalent in what they do and how they treat their first argument. The sizeof() will tell you that the argument is a pointer, and if there are warnings about sizeof(), they will probably tell you that the argument is interpreted as type int (*)[10]. That is because the argument *is* a pointer to one-dimensional arrays of length 10. In the second function, we do not specify the first dimension, but C would ignore it anyway. The argument in both of the first two functions is a pointer rather than an array and indistinguishable from the explicit pointer we use in the third function.

C will also ignore that the B array doesn't have the correct first dimension. This is entirely equivalent to it ignoring the length of one-dimensional arrays. But it does not overlook the length of the second dimension. That one, you have to get right, or you will get warnings. The arguments are turned into pointers to arrays, but such pointers need to know the size of the objects they point at, and to do that, they must know how many objects they hold. So when you call a function with a multidimensional array, you throw away information about the first dimension, but you keep the remaining. This also explains why using pointers to arrays as function arguments is more stringently type-checked than using arrays. That is because they must know what they point at. We do not need to know the size of the first dimension, so C doesn't care about the first dimension. But with pointers to arrays, it must know them, and since a multidimensional array argument gets turned into a pointer to arrays of the lower dimensions, the type-checker will check those. So all three functions will complain that C doesn't have the correct second dimension. None of the function arguments are arrays themselves, so the sizeof() of them is the size of a pointer. That is, after all, all that they are.

There are times where we want to work with arrays where the rows have different length. For example, we might want to represent a lower triangular matrix without putting zeros in the upper triangle. We can define one like this:

```
double *A[] = {
  (double[]){1},
  (double[]){2, 3},
  (double[]){4, 5, 6}
};
```

We could print the matrix like this:

```
int n = sizeof A / sizeof *A;
for (int i = 0; i < n; i++) {
  for (int j = 0; j <= i; j++) {
```

```
    printf("%2.2f ", A[i][j]);
  }
  printf("\n");
}
```

This looks array-like (and we do have arrays in play here), but it is a little more complicated.

The type of A is an array to pointers to double. The underlying type to the left of A is double *, and the [] means that we are defining an array. We only have a single [] so it is a one-dimensional array, not a two-dimensional one. The rows in A also look like arrays, but they are not quite. The (double[]) is a type-cast that tells C that the expression on the left should be translated into a one-dimensional double array. The expression creates an array, where the first array is a one-dimensional array of length 1— there is one element in the initial value—the second is a double array of length 2, and the third is an array of length 3. So we do create three arrays, of different length, but they do not go directly into A. They cannot because A is an array of double pointers, and arrays are not pointers. They just decay to them when we use them as such. And that is what we are doing here. We define the rows as arrays, but we define A as an array of pointers, so what we get is pointers to the three arrays we use as rows. The memory layout is as shown in Figure 5-5.

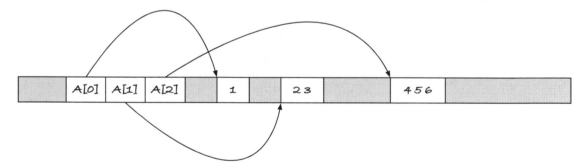

Figure 5-5. *Representation of a lower triangular matrix*

A contains three arrays in the sense that it contains three pointers to arrays, and we can mostly use pointers as we use arrays. But these three arrays decayed into pointers when we defined A, so it is really three pointers we have in the array, and if you get the size of the array, you will find that it is the size of three double *.

```
assert(sizeof A == 3 * sizeof(double *));
```

The size of an array is the number of bytes it takes up in memory, and if it held the six double we put into it, the size should be 6 * sizeof(double):

```
assert(sizeof A == 6 * sizeof(double)); // FAILS
```

which it only is if a double is half the size of double *, which it probably isn't. The elements in A are double * (because that is what A is an array of), so their size are all sizeof(double *).

```
assert(sizeof A[0] == sizeof(double *));
assert(sizeof A[1] == sizeof(double *));
assert(sizeof A[2] == sizeof(double *));
```

If they were really arrays, the first should be sizeof(double), the second 2 * sizeof(double), and the third 3 * sizeof(double). But they are not arrays. They are pointers to the first element in the arrays we created when we initialized A.

If we add a little more code to the definition, we could define A as

```
double row0[] = {1};
double row1[] = {2, 3};
double row2[] = {4, 5, 6};
double *A[] = { row0, row1, row2 };
```

The first definition didn't name the rows, but otherwise we have done exactly the same.

When we use A as a pointer, it decays to one. It is an array of double *, so it decays to a pointer to that type, so it becomes a double **.

```
double **p = A;
assert(p[0] == A[0]);
assert(p[1] == A[1]);
```

The syntax for accessing elements in an array and at a certain offset of an array is the same, so we can just as well use the pointer as we can use the array:

```
assert(p[0][0] == A[0][0]);
```

This is what is happening anyway when we use index into an array.

The arrays of pointers work the same way as multidimensional arrays, except that the memory layout is different. If A was a two-dimensional array, then it would decay to a pointer to its first element when we used it as a pointer. It does the same when it is a one-dimensional array of pointers. In the first case, the pointer is to an array of one-dimensional arrays, and in the second it is a pointer to double. In either case, if we take the pointer and index once more, we get the position that is at the index's offset from that address. For a multidimensional array, all the elements are laid out contiguously in memory. For the array of pointers, the rows lie somewhere separate from the first dimension. You use the two types in exactly the same way.

CHAPTER 6

Working with Arrays

Enough about general considerations for arrays and pointers—it is time we see how we use both in practice. I will start by showing a few examples of how we can solve some selected problems using both arrays and pointers and illustrate how closely related the two things are. Quite often, the code you write to operate on an array is the same as the code you write to operate on pointers, even when you do not use pointers plus offsets (which is, after all, exactly what we do when we use the array syntax). In an attempt to make it at least appear that we are working with two different types of objects, I will use different conventions for the functions in this section. Functions with array arguments will have the type

```
rettype function(int n, type array[n]);
```

while functions with pointer arguments will have the type

```
rettype function(type *begin, type *end);
```

The idea is that we know an array and its length in the first case, and in the second case, we have pointers to where the array begins and ends. This is exactly the same information (see Figure 6-1), but for arrays, knowing their length is more natural than knowing a pointer to where it ends, while for pointers it is often more convenient to know the beginning and end of a sequence of objects.

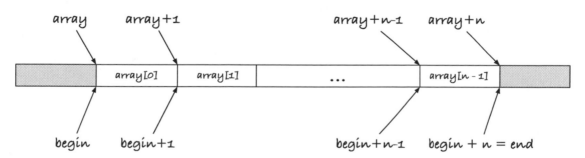

Figure 6-1. *The length of an array, n, and the pointer range (begin,end)*

123

© Thomas Mailund 2021
T. Mailund, *Pointers in C Programming*, https://doi.org/10.1007/978-1-4842-6927-5_6

If you want to run through every element in an array, you start at zero and continue as long as your index is less than the length of the array. For example, if you want to add a number to each element in an integer array, you can write a function that looks like this:

```
void add_array(int n, int array[n], int x)
{
  for (int i = 0; i < n; i++) {
    array[i] += x;
  }
}
```

If you have a range for the array elements through a pointer pair, you do the same thing, except that you do not test if the index is less than n, but you test that the pointer you run through the array is less than the end address.

```
void add_pointers(int *begin, int *end, int x)
{
  for (int *ip = begin; ip < end; ip++) {
    *ip += x;
  }
}
```

The for-loop looks similar, and the body only differs in how we update the integer we point to. With an array index, you get the integer like this array[i], which, recall, is the same as *(array + i). When you already have a pointer, that in increment through the elements in the range, you just dereference it.

With functions such as this, you usually do not introduce the extra pointer ip. You can use begin. Although it is a pointer, you do not change anything in the calling scope by moving it. For that, you need a pointer to a pointer. Here, begin is just a local variable, and we can run it up to end without any issues, as long as we do not need the beginning of the range later in the function.

```
void add_pointers(int *begin, int *end, int x)
{
  for ( ; begin < end; begin++) {
    *begin += x;
  }
}
```

I used a for-loop because it shows how closely related the two solutions are, but it is also common to use a while (begin < end) loop. For this particular problem, however, the natural solution

```
void add_pointers(int *begin, int *end, int x)
{
  while (begin < end) {
    *begin++ += x;
  }
}
```

is ugly. It is normal to update the pointer in the while-loop's body, but combining the increment and addition does not make the code easy to understand.

Since the functions take different arguments, you must, of course, call them with different parameters. If you have an array and a size, it is easy to call add_array(), but it is equally easy to get the beginning of the interval, array, and the end of the interval, array + n.

```
int array[] = { 1, 2, 3, 4, 5 };
int n = sizeof array / sizeof *array;
add_array(n, array, 2);
add_pointers(array, array + n, -2);
```

Another equally simple problem is adding all the elements in an array. The straightforward solutions, using either an array or a range of pointers, look like this:

```
int sum_array(int n, int array[n])
{
  int sum = 0;
  for (int i = 0; i < n; i++) {
    sum += array[i];
  }
  return sum;
}
```

```
int sum_pointers(int *begin, int *end)
{
  int sum = 0;
  for ( ; begin < end; begin++) {
    sum += *begin;
  }
  return sum;
}
```

Somehow, I like the while-loop solution for this problem better than the one for adding a constant to all elements:

```
int sum_pointers(int *begin, int *end)
{
  int sum = 0;
  while (begin < end) {
    sum += *begin++;
  }
  return sum;
}
```

but I think I still prefer the for-loop solution.

In the next example, we will reverse the elements in an array, and here the natural solution differs between an array approach and a pointer approach. For the array, we can run an index up to the middle of the array, at each index swapping with the element at the same index counting from the back of the array, that is, we swap the value at index i with that at index n-i-1, where n is the length of the array:

```
void swap_array(int array[], int i, int j)
{
  int tmp = array[j];
  array[j] = array[i];
  array[i] = tmp;
}

void reverse_array(int n, int array[n])
{
  for (int i = 0; i < n/2; i++) {
```

```
    swap_array(array, i, n - i - 1);
  }
}
```

With pointers, we can move one pointer from the beginning of the range and another from the end of the array, swapping the integers they point to until they meet.

```
void swap_pointers(int *i, int *j)
{
  int tmp = *i;
  *i = *j;
  *j = tmp;
}

void reverse_pointers(int *begin, int *end)
{
  if (end <= begin) return;
  end--; // point to last element
  while (begin < end) {
    swap_pointers(begin++, end--);
  }
}
```

When we swap, we need to point to the integers we wish to exchange, so here we cannot use the rule that begin points to the first element in the range and end points one element past it. The interface that reverse_pointers() provides to the caller, however, uses that convention. There are times when you need both the beginning and end of an interval to point into the array, but you should always provide a consistent interface to users of your code, and the usual convention is that the end pointer doesn't point at the last element but one past it.

The first line in the function seems superfluous. If end is less than or equal to begin, then we would never enter the while-loop, and everything would still work. This is correct, and I cannot imagine a case where it wouldn't work. However, the C standard guarantees us that we can point at any item in an array and one past the last item, but it does not guarantee that we can point one element before the first element. If both begin and end point to the first element in the array, because we attempt to reverse an empty interval, we would move end to point to an invalid item when we decrement it. This could theoretically give us an underflow.

Sieve of Eratosthenes

For a slightly more interesting example, we turn to the Sieve of Eratosthenes. This is an algorithm that computes all primes less than some number n. It works as follows: you create a list of candidate primes, initially all the numbers from 2 to $n - 1$. The smallest candidate is a prime (it is 2), and we move it to a list of primes. Then we remove all the numbers that it divides. The smallest that remains is also a prime (it is 3). Each time we have removed candidates divisible by the smallest element, the smallest element that remains is a prime. If we repeat this procedure until there are no candidates left, we have identified all the primes.

We will see a simple array solution and an equally simple pointer version. Both methods follow the same idea but take different approaches, and of the two versions, the array solution is faster. The efficiency of the implementation, however, is not the purpose of the example. If we wanted better algorithms, there are smarter approaches to solving the problem. Our goal here is learning about arrays and pointers.

Array Solution

In the array solution, we will eliminate candidates by setting them to zero—we can use any number that we know is not prime to indicate that a number is eliminated, and zero is as good as any. We will go through the candidates in an outer loop, and when we get an index with a non-zero element, we know that we have a prime p. When we then remove candidates divisible by p in an inner loop, we will go through the array in jumps of size p and set the numbers we encounter to zero. We obviously do not want to eliminate p itself, so we start the inner loop after p. We could choose $2p$, but any number m between p and p^2 that is divisible by p is also divisible by a smaller prime. We will already have eliminated them. So we can start the inner loop at p^2. By the same reasoning, we can terminate the outer loop at $\sqrt{n}$ instead of n.

When we have finished this procedure, all the composite numbers in the candidates array are zero, and what remains are primes. We can then run through the array and compact it, so we have primes at the beginning of the array. The user of the algorithm needs to know how many primes we found, so they can know how many numbers are in the array after we are done, so we will make the algorithm return this number.

The implementation looks like this:

```
int compact0(int n, int array[n])
```

```
{
  int m = 0;
  for (int i = 0; i < n; i++) {
    if (array[i] > 0)
      array[m++] = array[i];
  }
  return m;
}

int eratosthenes(int n, int buf[n - 2])
{
  // Init
  for (int i = 2; i < n; i++) {
    buf[i - 2] = i;
  }

  // Sieve
  for (int i = 0; i*i < n - 2; i++) {
    if (buf[i] == 0) continue;
    int p = buf[i];
    for (int j = p*p; j < n; j += p) {
      buf[j - 2] = 0;
    }
  }

  // Compact
  return compact0(n - 2, buf);
}
```

The compact0() function is the simplest of the two. We run the index i through the array while keeping track of how many non-zero integers we have put at the front of it. If we have inserted m non-zero elements at the front, then the next place we should insert one, if there are more, is at index m. So when we see a non-zero index, we put it in array[m] and increment the counter m. When we have made it through the array, m already holds the number of non-zero elements, so we return it.

In eratosthenes(), we initialize the buf array with the numbers from 2 to n. After that, we run the algorithm as described earlier. When we index into buf, we subtract 2. In the algorithm, we work on the numbers from 2 to n, so we don't have 0 and 1 as prime candidates. Because we don't put them at the beginning of the buf array, we must compensate for it by subtracting two when we index into it.

When we call compact0() as the last step, we give it a buffer with n-2 elements, so that is the first argument to the function. Inside compact0(), the argument n is the length of the array, while inside erathosthenes() it is n-2, but as long as we remember to give compact0() the correct length, all is well.

Pointer Solution

In the second solution, the eratosthenes() function will also take an array as input. We can easily change it to take a begin and end range, but an array is a more natural argument to the function. You can, of course, do the same with pointers as you can with arrays—the two are the same when you pass an array to a function—but we will take a different approach to try something else.

It is when we sieve the primes that the two approaches differ. In the array version, we jump through the candidates in jump sizes given by the current prime, and we tag those numbers we want to remove. Then we compact the array at the end. With the pointers, we will compact the output simultaneously with removing numbers divisible by the current prime. We will have the following invariants. The primes we have identified will sit in the interval from buf (the input array) to a pointer, candidates. From candidates to another pointer, end, we keep the potential candidates. In a loop, we move the candidates pointer one step forward, in effect moving the smallest candidate to the list of primes, and then we filter the interval between candidates and end; see Figure 6-2. When we are done, all the primes are between buf and candidates, so we can get their number from candidates - buf.

The main function is straightforward. We initialize the buffer, set up the candidates and end pointers, and then loop while there are candidates left, that is, as long as candidates < end. We get the prime and increment the candidates pointer, and then we sieve the candidates.

```c
int eratosthenes(int n, int buf[n - 2])
{
  // Init
  for (int i = 2; i < n; i++) {
    buf[i - 2] = i;
  }

  // Sieve
  int *candidates = buf;
  int *end = buf + n - 2;
  while (candidates < end) {
    int p = *candidates++; // Get prime and move it
    sieve_candidates(&candidates, &end, p);
  }
  return end - buf;
}
```

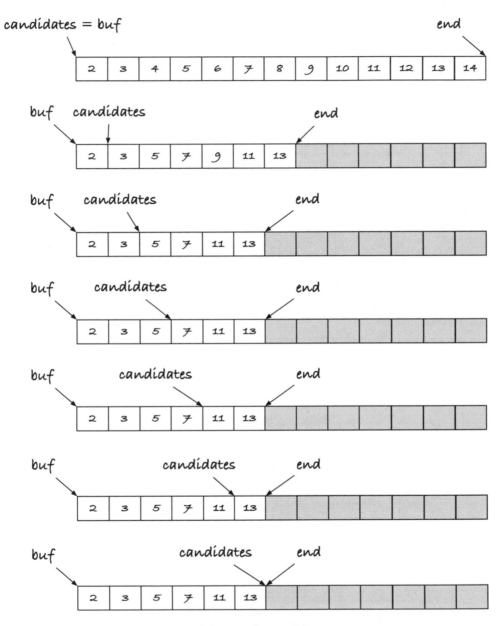

Figure 6-2. *The pointer version of Eratosthenes Sieve*

The sieve_candidates() compacts the candidates by removing those divisible by the prime p. It does that by scanning through all the candidates, moving those that p do not divide to the front. It does this in an analogous way to how we compacted the non-zero numbers in the array version.

```
void sieve_candidates(int **from, int **to, int p)
{
  int *output = *from;
  for (int *input = *from ; input < *to; input++) {
    if (*input % p != 0)
      *output++ = *input;
  }
  *to = output;
}
```

In this function, we take pointers to the range pointers as input, and so we call the function with the pointers' addresses. That way, we can update the interval from within the function. We only update the end pointer, since we have already incremented the candidates pointer before we call the function. So, we could have made the from argument an int * type instead, but I dislike such asymmetry when I call a function with a range, so I prefer that either both or none of the arguments are pointers to pointers.

If you want pointers to integers, instead of their addresses, you can change the implementation so sieve_candidates() return the new end pointer:

```
int *sieve_candidates(int *from, int *to, int p)
{
  int *output = from;
  for (int *input = from ; input < to; input++) {
    if (*input % p != 0)
      *output++ = *input;
  }
  return output;
}

int eratosthenes(int n, int buf[n - 2])
{
  // Init
  for (int i = 2; i < n; i++) {
    buf[i - 2] = i;
  }
```

```
  // Sieve
  int *candidates = buf;
  int *end = buf + n - 2;
  while (candidates < end) {
    int p = *candidates++; // Get prime and move it
    end = sieve_candidates(candidates, end, p);
  }

  return end - buf;
}
```

You could also move both the beginning and end of the candidates interval in the sieve_candidates() function. You could get the prime and increment the input inside the function. In that case, you do need both the beginning and end of the interval to be the addresses of the pointers.

```
void sieve_candidates(int **from, int **to)
{
  int p = *(*from)++; // Get prime and move it
  int *output = *from;
  for (int *input = *from ; input < *to; input++) {
    if (*input % p != 0)
      *output++ = *input;
  }
  *to = output;
}

int eratosthenes(int n, int buf[n - 2])
{
  // Init
  for (int i = 2; i < n; i++) {
    buf[i - 2] = i;
  }

  // Sieve
  int *candidates = buf;
  int *end = buf + n - 2;
  while (candidates < end) {
```

```
  sieve_candidates(&candidates, &end);
}

return end - buf;
}
```

I don't like the third solution much because the `sieve_candidates()` function does more than its name implies, but it is a matter of taste. In any case, you can see how we can solve the same problem through pointers in several ways.

Radix Sorting

The last example I will show, before moving on, is more involved and also more useful. That example is *radix sort*, an algorithm that lets us sort integers in linear time. We will implement it using a mix of arrays and pointers, choosing which is more convenient for each subtask.

Radix sort is based on repeated *bucket sorts*, so let us implement that first, in its simplest form. The simplest variant of bucket sort is known as *count sort*, and the idea is this. If we have elements from some small and ordered set, I will use `unsigned char` later, we can build a table with one entry per possible element in the set. Then, we can scan through our input and count how often we see each element. If we then run through the table in increasing order of keys, we can output each key the number of times we have seen it in the input. Because we go through the table in the correct order, it gives us the elements in sorted order.

We call the entries in the table `buckets` because in the general case we put our elements there, but for count sort, we just count. An implementation can look like this:

```c
#include <stdio.h>

void sort_chars(int n, unsigned char array[n])
{
  int buckets[256];
  for (int i = 0; i < 256; i++) {
    buckets[i] = 0;
  }

  for (int i = 0; i < n; i++) {
```

```
    unsigned int bucket = array[i];
    buckets[bucket]++;
  }

  int k = 0;
  for (int i = 0; i < 256; i++) {
    for (int j = 0; j < buckets[i]; j++) {
      array[k++] = (unsigned char)i;
    }
  }
}

int main(void)
{
  unsigned char array[] = { 'f', 'o', 'o', 'b', 'a', 'r' };
  int n = sizeof array / sizeof *array;

  sort_chars(n, array);
  for (int i = 0; i < n; i++) {
    printf("%c", array[i]);
  }
  printf("\n");

  return 0;
}
```

We initialize the table with zeros—we have seen each element zero time before we start—and then we increment the count for a key each time we see it in the input. After that, we go through the table and fill the array accordingly.

Count sort works well for characters because there are only 256 of them—assuming that a char has 8 bytes. If we tried the same for integers, the buckets table would be too large. If integers are 32 bits, then we have more than 4 billion of them, and since each bucket should contain an integer, that is 4 billion times 4 bytes. Your machine might run out of memory. Even if it doesn't, initializing the table, and running through it in the last step, requires that you run through 4 billion integers. The algorithm is slow, in addition to wasteful in memory. We need a little more work before we can use it to sort integers.

First, we go from count sort to bucket sort. If we are only sorting characters, then counting how often we see one suffices, but if we want to sort something more complex using a key that in the next function is also just a character, then we need to store the objects in the buckets.

We could make a table that contains some data structure where we could store the elements, but since the chapter is on arrays, it might not surprise you that we will use an array instead. It is possible to represent the buckets as sub-segments of an array and move the input to the correct buckets when we scan through the input.

We start by counting how many times each key occurs in the input, just as before. After that, we compute a table that for each key k tells us how many occurrences of keys *smaller* than k there are in the input. This table, let us call it buckets, identifies the buckets. If we have an array output where we wish to write the sorted elements, then all the elements with key k should go between index buckets[k] and buckets[k+1]; see Figure 6-3. For each key, in our example that is all characters but in the figure I have made it the set {0, 1, 2, 3, 4}, we have a count that we then translated into the bucket numbers. For key 0, we have two occurrences in the input, and buckets[0] points to index 0 in the output (because there are no keys smaller than 0). This is the index where the zeros should be inserted. Key 1 also occurs twice, and buckets[1] points to index 2— not because there are two ones in the input, but because there are two zeros; the zeros' bucket goes before the ones' bucket, and it takes up two entries. There are also two twos, and the two bucket starts at index 4 (before it, we have two entries for zeros and two for ones). We do not have any threes in the input, but it is a key, and it gets a bucket value. The threes, if we had any, should go in the bucket starting at index 6 (there are two zeros, two ones, and two twos that go before the zeros). There is one 4 key in the input. The four bucket also starts at six because the threes' bucket is empty.

When we have built the buckets table, we can scan through the input, extract each element's key, and get its bucket. We will put the element at the first index in the bucket, and then we will move the bucket pointer to the next index. That way, every time we see a new key, it goes into its bucket in the next position. Figure 6-4 shows a run of the bucket sort algorithm. In A) we are ready to process the first element; the output is empty, but we have the bucket pointers ready. The first element is two, so we look up the bucket pointer for two and find that it is four. We insert two at that index and update buckets[2] to five. Then, in B), we see a zero. Since buckets[0] is zero, that zero goes into index 0 in the output, and we update buckets[0] to one. We keep following this procedure until we have gone through the entire input, H), at which point we have the sorted elements in the output array.

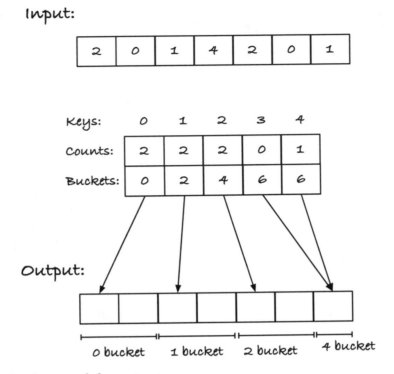

Figure 6-3. *Buckets and the output array*

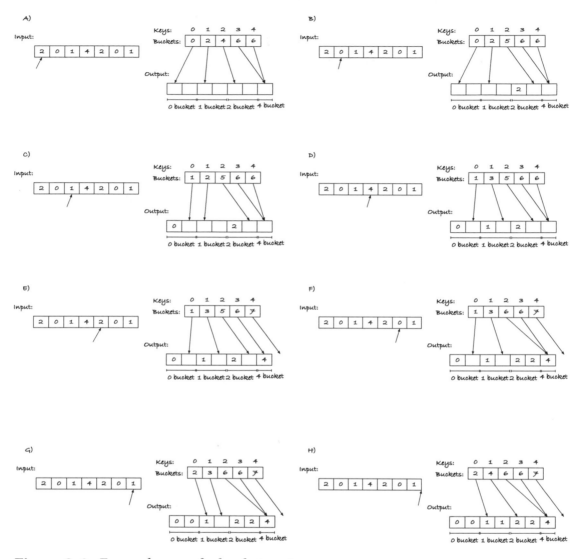

Figure 6-4. *Example run of a bucket sort*

If the keys and the input are the same, the counting sort is a better choice, of course. It is more straightforward, and we only need to know how many times each key occurs. But if the keys are only part of objects, then we keep the full data while sorting the elements when we use this bucket sort.

As an example, we can take strings as our input data and sort them with respect to the first character. We need 256 buckets as before, we can count how many times each character appears as the first character in the input similarly to before, and then we can compute the buckets array. I find it easier to compute that array from the right because I can count how many keys I have seen as I move toward the left and then put the indices at that offset from the right. After we have the table, the scan through the input, with copying the strings to their buckets, is straightforward:

```c
#include <stdio.h>

void compute_buckets(int n, char *array[n], int buckets[256])
{
  for (int i = 0; i < 256; i++) {
    buckets[i] = 0;
  }

  for (int i = 0; i < n; i++) {
    unsigned char bucket = (unsigned char)array[i][0];
    buckets[bucket]++;
  }

  int m = n;
  for (int i = 256 - 1; i >= 0; i--) {
    int count = buckets[i];
    buckets[i] = m - count;
    m -= count;
  }
}

void sort_strings(int n, char *input[n], char *output[n])
{
  int buckets[256];
  compute_buckets(n, input, buckets);
  for (int i = 0; i < n; i++) {
    unsigned char bucket = (unsigned char)input[i][0];
    int index = buckets[bucket]++;
    output[index] = input[i];
  }
}
```

```c
int main(void)
{
  char *array[] = {
    "foo", "boo", "bar", "qoo", "qar", "baz", "qux", "qaz"
  };
  int n = sizeof array / sizeof *array;
  char *output[n];

  sort_strings(n, array, output);

  for (int i = 0; i < n; i++) {
    printf("%s\n", output[i]);
  }

  return 0;
}
```

If you run the program, you will see that we have sorted the strings with respect to their first character, but not the remaining characters. First, we get the strings that start with b, then foo, and then the strings that start with q. Within the bucket, that is, within the part of the array that starts with the same first character, the strings are in the same order as they were in the input. When a sorting algorithm keeps the order of the elements, except for the key we sort with, we say that the algorithm is *stable*, and that is important for the next step—because now we finally get to radix sorting integers.

Because the bucket sort is stable, we can sort a 2-byte integer by first sorting it using the least significant byte as key and then using the most significant byte. The first sort leaves the integers far from sorted, but if we extract integers with the same most significant byte, they are in the correct order. For numbers that agree on the first 8 bits, their relative order is determined by the next 8 bits, and the first bucket sort orders the input with respect to those. Then, if, when we sort with respect to the next byte, we put them in buckets determined by that byte, and within each bucket, they remain ordered because the sort is stable. Thus, if we first sort with the least significant byte and then the next, then we have sorted with respect to both bytes. This argument works for as many bytes as you want, so we can sort all size integers—at least all non-negative integers, but we will handle the negative integers later.

We can implement that idea like this:

```c
void bucket_sort(int n, int offset,
                 int const input[n], int output[n])
{
  int buckets[256];
  for (int i = 0; i < 256; i++) {
    buckets[i] = 0;
  }

  for (int i = 0; i < n; i++) {
    unsigned char bucket = (input[i] >> 8 * offset) & 0xff;
    buckets[bucket]++;
  }

  int m = n;
  for (int i = 256 - 1; i >= 0; i--) {
    int count = buckets[i];
    buckets[i] = m - count;
    m -= count;
  }

  for (int i = 0; i < n; i++) {
    unsigned char bucket = (input[i] >> 8 * offset) & 0xff;
    int index = buckets[bucket]++;
    output[index] = input[i];
  }
}

void radix_sort(int n, int array[n])
{
  // It is *very* unlikely that sizeof an integer is odd, but if
  // it is, you need to move the results from helper
  // to array. I assume that we have an even number of bytes
  // because that is practically always true for int
  static_assert(sizeof *array % 2 == 0,
                "integer sizes must be powers of two");
```

```
// Helper buffer; handle input/output switches
// when bucket sorting
int helper[n];
// For switching between the buffers
int *buffers[] = { array, helper };
int bucket_input = 0;

for (int offset = 0; offset < sizeof *array; offset++) {
  bucket_sort(n, offset,
              buffers[bucket_input],
              buffers[!bucket_input]);
  bucket_input = !bucket_input;
}
}
```

For the bucket sort, the only difference between this version and the previous is how we get the keys from the input. Here, we have an offset that tells us which byte in the integer we want. We extract the byte using shifting and masking out the least significant byte. We could also get the bytes by casting the integer to a char pointer and using offsets, but then we would need to deal with endianness. Shifting and masking get the job done just as well.

In radix_sort(), we iterate through the bytes in an integer and bucket sort with respect to them. The bucket sort needs both an input and an output array—you cannot write the output back into the input array because you might overwrite something you need to scan through later, so this is unavoidable. To deal with that, we allocate a buffer, helper. With repeated calls to bucket sort, we flip between the input array and the helper array. We could use two fixed arrays and then copy the data between them after each call, but flipping between the array is more efficient. In the first call, we sort the data in array into helper. In the second call, they go from helper to array. And we keep switching until we have made it through sizeof *array iterations. We handle the switching by putting both arrays into another array. That makes the array buffers an array of buffers (where the type of the buffers in this case is int *, but that is also what both array and helper are). The variable bucket_input is the one that picks out which array should be used as input and which should be used for output. In each iteration, we flip it.

In the implementation, I have assumed that this is an even number. I am not aware of any architecture where this isn't the case. If you have an odd number, you need to copy the elements from `helper` to `array` after sorting the integers, but I haven't bothered here.[1]

You can now try sorting integers using this function:

```c
int main(void)
{
  int array[] = { -1, -2, 13, 12, 13, 6, 14, -3, 42, 13 };
  int n = sizeof array / sizeof *array;
  radix_sort(n, array);
  for (int i = 0; i < n; i++) {
    printf("%d ", array[i]);
  }
  printf("\n");

  return 0;
}
```

You will, however, likely find that the negative numbers are sorted as larger than the positive numbers, and they are in the reverse order on top of that. If that happens, it is because your computer represents integers as two's complement, and almost all hardware does. I will not bore you with what that is, but merely say that the bit patterns for integers in this format are such that the negative numbers, when seen as unsigned numbers, are larger than the positive numbers and in reverse order. For our purposes, for fixing the problem, that suffices.

If we know that the negative numbers will end up in the wrong end of the output, we can separate the positive and negative numbers before we sort. We can explicitly put the negative numbers at the lower end of the array and the positive integers at the high end.

We will write a function, `split()`, that moves all the negative numbers to the left and all the non-negative numbers to the right and returns the splitting point between the two segments. We use two helper functions here, `scan_right()` that finds the leftmost non-negative number in a range and `scan_left()` that finds the rightmost negative number:

```c
// Both left and right must point to legal addresses
```

---

[1] The `static_assert` macro was introduced in C11, so if your compiler doesn't support it, just delete the line. It is unlikely that your integer type should have an odd size.

```
int *scan_right(int *left, int *right)
{
  while (left < right) {
    if (*left >= 0) break;
    left++;
  }
  return left;
}

// Both left and right must point to legal addresses
int *scan_left(int *left, int *right)
{
  while (left < right) {
    if (*right < 0) break;
    right--;
  }
  return right;
}
```

Unlike the convention we usually use, where left would be the first element in the range and right points one past the last, both point into the range with these functions. It makes the code easier to write if we do it this way, and the functions are never supposed to be called by anyone besides ourselves in this algorithm, so we can get away with breaking conventions in this case.

Segmenting and splitting the interval now works by repeatedly finding the leftmost non-negative and the rightmost negative values and swapping the two, until the left and right pointers meet. When that happens, we are done. We need to know the size of the negative part for later, so we get it as the distance from the beginning of the array to the left pointer and return it.

```
void swap(int *left, int *right)
{
  int i = *left;
  *left = *right;
  *right = i;
}
```

```c
int split(int n, int array[n])
{
  int *left = array, *right = array + n - 1;
  while (left < right) {
    left = scan_right(left, right);
    right = scan_left(left, right);
    swap(left, right);
  }
  return left - array;
}
```

If we split the input into the positive and negative parts, with the positive numbers at the high end, we can sort the two segments independently. That will put the non-negative numbers in their correct locations, but the negative numbers need to be reversed. Reversing an array, however, is not difficult. We have already implemented that a few pages back, and here is another version of that:

```c
void reverse(int n, int array[n])
{
  int *left = array, *right = array + n - 1;
  while (left < right) {
    swap(left++, right--);
  }
}
```

For both `split()` and `reverse()`, there is a potential problem if the array is empty. We compute `right` as the address n - 1 from `array`, which could be `array - 1` if n is zero. If this is a valid address, then the `while`-loops will work correctly—we never enter them—but to be strictly compliant with the C standard, we cannot assume that the address before the first element in an array is valid. We resolve the problem by requiring that you cannot call the functions with empty arrays and ensure it in the main sorting function.

Putting it all together, we can radix sort integers like this:

```c
void sort_int(int n, int array[n])
{
  if (n <= 0) return;
```

```
  int m = split(n, array);
  if (m > 0) {
    radix_sort(m, array);
    reverse(m, array);
  }
  if (m < n) {
    radix_sort(n - m, array + m);
  }
}
```

All the functions we call takes a size and an array as input. When we call split(), it should work on the entire array, so it gets n and array. The first radix_sort() should only sort the negative numbers, so we tell it that the input is of length m. We still give it all of array, though, because we cannot pass parts of an array to a function. In function calls, arrays are always pointers, but when we specify the length as m and give the function array, we are in effect calling the function on the first m elements of array. The same goes for the following reverse() call. For the last radix_sort(), the length is the number of non-negative integers in the input, which is n - m. The array they sit in sits at address array + m, so we call the sorting function with that.

Generic Functions on Arrays

Generic functions are functions that will work on any type (with whatever properties required by the function). In C, generic types mean void pointers. If a function can work on more than one type, it will take one or more void pointers as arguments. In Chapter 4, we saw how qsort() uses void pointers to sort any type of data we can provide an order on via a function. Now it is time to try writing our own array functions that work on any array type.

There is not a huge difference between operating on void pointers and pointers of other types, except that you cannot dereference them, that is, look at what they point to, and you do not know how large the objects they point at are so you cannot do pointer arithmetic—so, actually, a huge difference, since we basically cannot do anything with void pointers instead of pointing.

If you have an array of a certain type, and you want to move from the address of one element to the next, then you need to add one to a pointer of that type. The pointer type tells the compiler how much you need to add to get to the next element. Since void is an incomplete type, it is something we don't know what is, we cannot do the same with void pointers. While some compilers will let you treat them as character pointers, so you can do arithmetic where the assumed size of the objects is one char, this is not guaranteed by the standard. However, the standard says that you are always allowed to cast data to character pointers to get the address of their first byte, so we can cast our void pointers to char pointers and manipulate the underlying data that way. Then, if you want to move to an address at the right distance, you must multiply the number of elements you wish to move with the size of the objects.

If we have to cast void pointers to char to manipulate data anyway, why use void pointers in the first place. You are guaranteed by the standard that you can get a char pointer to the first memory address of any object, and you can use it to scan through to the last memory address in the object. But char pointers have a type; you need a type-cast to point them at other data objects, and you signal with your code that you can use what they point to as characters. That might not be a signal that you want to send. If you work with objects where you know nothing about their type or underlying representation, then you shouldn't pretend that they are blocks of char. If you need to manipulate their raw memory, or more frequently if you need to move from one object to the next in an array, you have to use a character pointer, but the rest of the time, to signal that it is unknown data, use void *.

What if we want to do something with what they point at? We cannot dereference them, and even if we could, we wouldn't know what kind of data they point at. We need to use other generic functions, or we need to ask the caller for information. As an example of the first situation, consider reversing the elements in an array. We have already seen a reversal function for integers in the last section, and it should be obvious that we could write a similar function for other types. We should therefore, one should think, be able to write a function that can reverse arrays of any types.

A couple of the solutions we saw took pointers to either end of the array, one pointing at the first element and one pointing to the last. Then, they swapped the objects they pointed at, and the left pointer increased by one while the right pointer decreased by one. We can do the same with void pointers, except that we have to deal with the size of the objects explicitly, and we need to cast to a char pointer to do this. To get the first element, we do not need to do anything. If we assign the address of an array to a void pointer, it will point at the beginning of the array; in other words, it points at the first element. For the second pointer, we want to point at the last element. If the array has length n, we want to point at index n - 1, but adding n - 1 will only work if the objects have size 1. If they do not, we must multiply by the object size. Adding to a void pointer is not standard compliant (although some compilers allow it), so we need to use char * for that. When we update the pointers, we must increase and decrease with the object size as well because adding or subtracting one only works if the objects have size one.

So, we reach a solution that looks like this:

```
void reverse(void *array, int n, int size)
{
  if (n <= 0) return; // avoid right underflow
  char *left = array;
  char *right = left + size * (n - 1);

  while (left < right) {
    // TODO: swap *left and *right
    left += size; right -= size;
  }
}
```

The swapping part also needs to know about the object sizes. With integers, we could swap with code such as

```
int tmp = *left;
*left = *right;
*right = tmp;
```

but we cannot dereference void pointers, so it won't work. Even if we could, if we do not know the size of the objects, then we don't know how many bytes to copy to move one value into another memory address. If, however, we do know the size of the objects, as we do in our reverse() function, then we can move that many bytes between the objects. For the tmp variable, we can't get the underlying type because we do not know it, but we can use a buffer that can hold the right number of bytes. With that idea, the complete reverse() function can look like this:

```
void reverse(void *array, int n, int size)
{
  if (n <= 0) return; // avoid right underflow
  char *left = array;
  char *right = left + size * (n - 1);
  char tmp[size];

  while (left < right) {
    memcpy(&tmp, left, size);
    memcpy(left, right, size);
    memcpy(right, &tmp, size);
    left += size;
    right -= size;
  }
}
```

The memcpy() function blindly copies size bytes from one address to another, and that is exactly what we need here.

If we know the size of the objects our array contains, there are many algorithms we can generalize from working on one type to all types. But if we need to know more than just the size of the objects, we need the caller to provide that information as well, and that typically involves giving the generic function a pointer. We saw this qsort() in Chapter 2, but let us try to write our own function with this feature. We will write a function that tests if an array is sorted. That way, we can reuse the comparison functions from Chapter 2.

An array is sorted if we can run through it, compare each element to the next, and find that a larger element is never in front of a smaller element. If we have a fixed type, for example, int, we can do this:

```
bool int_is_sorted(int n, int array[n])
{
  for (int i = 1; i < n; i++) {
    if (array[i - 1] > array[i])
      return false;
  }
  return true;
}
```

A generic version requires a function to help us compare array[i - 1] with array[i], and we need to access the elements with a void pointer that increments by the right amount.

If array is a void pointer, and obj_size is the size of the individual elements in the array, then we can get the indices as

```
void const *a = (char *)array + (i - 1) * obj_size;
void const *b = (char *)array + i * obj_size;
```

The type-cast is there, once again, so we can do pointer arithmetic. We don't need to do any arithmetic on a and b, so they can stay void *.

If we then have a function argument, cmp(), that works as the functions for qsort(), we can compare the two elements as cmp(a, b). Combining these two things, a void pointer function for checking if an array is sorted can look like this:

```
typedef int (*compare_function)(void const *,
                                void const *);
bool is_sorted(void const *array,
               size_t len, size_t obj_size,
               compare_function cmp)
{
  for (int i = 1; i < len; i++) {
    void const *a = (char *)array + (i - 1) * obj_size;
    void const *b = (char *)array + i * obj_size;
    if (cmp(a, b) > 0) {
      // a is larger than b, so the array is not sorted
      return false;
    }
  }
  return true;
}
```

The typedef defines a function pointer type. We return to those in Chapter 13, but for now simply accept that it defines a type of functions that take two void const pointers as input and returns an int.

You can try it out in the following program that uses comparison functions for integers and strings both to sort arrays and test whether they are sorted:

```c
#include <stdio.h>
#include <string.h>
#include <stdbool.h>

int int_compare(void const *x, void const *y)
{
  // Get the objects, and interpret them as integers
  int const *a = x;
  int const *b = y;
  return *a - *b;
}

int string_compare(const void *x, const void *y)
{
  // Get the objects and interpret them as strings
  char * const *a = x;
  char * const *b = y;
  return strcmp(*a, *b);
}

typedef int (*compare_function)(void const *, void const *);
bool is_sorted(void const *array,
               size_t len, size_t obj_size,
               compare_function cmp)
{
  for (int i = 1; i < len; i++) {
    void const *a = (char *)array + (i - 1) * obj_size;
    void const *b = (char *)array + i * obj_size;
    if (cmp(a, b) > 0) {
      // a is larger than b, so the array is not sorted
      return false;
    }
  }
  return true;
}

int main(void)
```

```
{
  int int_array[] = { 10, 5, 30, 15, 20, 30 };
  int int_array_length =
    sizeof int_array / sizeof *int_array;

  if (is_sorted(int_array, int_array_length,
                sizeof *int_array, int_compare)) {
    printf("int_array is sorted\n");
  } else {
    printf("int_array is not sorted\n");
  }
  qsort(int_array, int_array_length,
        sizeof *int_array, int_compare);
  if (is_sorted(int_array, int_array_length,
                sizeof *int_array, int_compare)) {
    printf("int_array is sorted\n");
  } else {
    printf("int_array is not sorted\n");
  }

  char *string_array[] = { "foo", "bar", "baz" };
  int string_array_length =
    sizeof string_array / sizeof *string_array;

  if (is_sorted(string_array, string_array_length,
                sizeof *string_array, string_compare)) {
    printf("string_array is sorted\n");
  } else {
    printf("string_array is not sorted\n");
  }
  qsort(string_array, string_array_length,
        sizeof *string_array, string_compare);
  if (is_sorted(string_array, string_array_length,
                sizeof *string_array, string_compare)) {
    printf("string_array is sorted\n");
  } else {
```

```
    printf("string_array is not sorted\n");
  }

  return 0;
}
```

For our final trick, we get slightly more ambitious and implement our own generic sorting algorithm. We have everything we need to put together an insertion sort—we can compare and swap objects—so it will be a simple task.

Insertion sort works by iterating through the input, keeping a sorted list of the elements it has seen so far on the left of the array. In each iteration, it moves the next element to its correct position in the sorted list on the left by swapping with its left neighbor as long as it is larger than the element itself. The swapping code we already have, but we can pull it out into a function to make the code more readable.

```
void swap(void *a, void *b, size_t obj_size)
{
  char tmp[obj_size];
  memcpy(&tmp, a, obj_size);
  memcpy(a, b, obj_size);
  memcpy(b, &tmp, obj_size);
}
```

The main algorithm is equally simple. Go through the elements in the input and swap them down. We can start at index 1 because the first element is already sorted—an array of one element is sorted by default. The swap_down() function should take a pointer to the beginning of the array, so it knows when to stop swapping the object it should swap down—which we must compute the address of—and the object size and comparison function, so we can work with generic data. Computing the address of the element means moving i times the size of the objects to the right of the start of the array.

```
void insertion_sort(void *array,
                    size_t len, size_t obj_size,
                    compare_function cmp)
{
  char *start = array;
  for (int i = 1; i < len; i++) {
    swap_down(start, start + i * obj_size, obj_size, cmp);
```

```
    }
}
```

In the final function, we need a pointer to the current element and the previous element, the one to its left. We get the second by subtracting obj_size from current. We use the comparison function to compare the two elements, and if the current is greater than or equal to the previous, we are done. Then we have found its correct position. Otherwise, we swap the two elements and decrement the current pointer. We can do this by setting it to the previous pointer.

```
void swap_down(char *start, char *current,
               size_t obj_size,
               compare_function cmp)
{

  while (current != start) {
    char *prev = current - obj_size;
    if (cmp(prev, current) <= 0) break; // done swapping
      swap(prev, current, obj_size);
      current = prev;
  }
}
```

Except for explicitly computing the positions in the array, working with generic data through void pointers is not more challenging than working with typed arrays. There is a little more computing, and there is no type-checking of the input when it goes through void pointers, but other than that it is rarely a huge obstacle.

CHAPTER 7

Strings

Strings are little more than pointers to a sequence of characters, which we require is terminated by the zero character `'\0'`. There is even less language support for strings as a type than there is for arrays. You have syntax for creating literal strings, but beyond that, a string is indistinguishable from any other pointer to `char`. That strings are zero-terminated is a protocol, an expectation of functions that work with strings, but it is not enforced by the language in any way or form.

With strings, you can define an immutable string using double quotes (immutable because it is undefined what will happen if you try to change a character in it). Such strings are constants in your program's executable and usually stored in read-only memory. Even if they are not, however, you shouldn't invoke undefined behavior by modifying one—entering undefined behavior territory should never be done lightly.

Once you have defined such a string, however, what you have is merely a pointer to `char` (although if you define it with double quotes, you should use `char const` to be on the safe side). You can treat a string as any other pointer and any `char` pointer as a string if it points to a `char` sequence terminated by `'\0'`. There is absolutely no difference.

```c
#include <stdio.h>
#include <string.h>
#include <assert.h>

int main(void)
{
  char const *string = "hello, world!\n";
  char const *cp = string;
  int n = strlen(string);
  for (int i = 0; i < n; i++) {
    assert(string[i] == cp[i]);
```

© Thomas Mailund 2021
T. Mailund, *Pointers in C Programming*, https://doi.org/10.1007/978-1-4842-6927-5_7

```
    assert(string + i == cp + i);
    assert(*(string + i) == *(cp + i));
  }

  return 0;
}
```

Including `<string.h>` here gives us the function `strlen()`. It doesn't include a "string type" or anything of the sorts.

Strings as Sequences of Bytes

The way that C represents a string is as a pointer to a buffer of `char`s that are terminated by the zero char, `'\0'`.[1] If you create the string `"hello, world\n"` and assign it to the pointer `string`, you get a block of memory that contains the bytes of the strings, one by one, and `string` will point to the first of them; see Figure 7-1. C doesn't store any information about the size of the string, but you can always find the end of the string by searching for the zero bytes. C's standard library already has a function for this, `strlen()`, but we might learn something from implementing our own.

---

[1]This character is sometimes called NUL, but do not confuse it with NULL, which is the null pointer. This is a character that holds the value zero, but has nothing to do with pointers in itself.

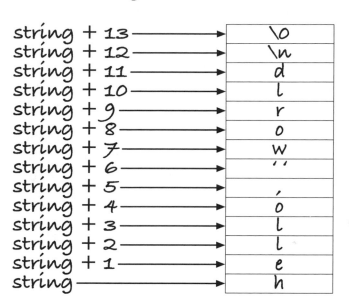

char *string = "hello, world\n";

string + 13 ──────→	\0
string + 12 ──────→	\n
string + 11 ──────→	d
string + 10 ──────→	l
string + 9 ──────→	r
string + 8 ──────→	o
string + 7 ──────→	w
string + 6 ──────→	
string + 5 ──────→	,
string + 4 ──────→	o
string + 3 ──────→	l
string + 2 ──────→	l
string + 1 ──────→	e
string ──────→	h

Figure 7-1. *Memory layout for "hello, world\n"*

A straightforward approach to compute a string's length is to run through the string using an index, until the value at that index is zero. The length of the string is then the index we got to.

```
int strlen_index(char const *s)
{
  int i = 0;
  while (s[i])
    i++;
  return i;
}
```

In the while-loop, we exploit that any non-zero char is considered true and only the zero char is false.

An alternative approach is to run through the string with a pointer into it—which is really just the same thing except that we do not compute the offset +i in each iteration. When we reach a zero char, we point to the end of the string. The length of the string is the number of bytes between the two pointers, and we can get that by subtracting the beginning from the end.

```
int strlen_pointer(char const *s)
{
  char const *x = s;
  while (*x)
    x++;
  return x - s;
}
```

Subtracting one pointer from another is a case of pointer arithmetic, as we discussed in Chapter 5. When you subtract pointers, you ask for the distance in between them in steps of the size of the underlying object. In strlen_pointer(), x points some bytes higher than s—the number of non-zero characters we iterated past, and s - x gives us that number; see Figure 7-2.

Both our functions and the standard library strlen() return the number of bytes up to the null byte, but do not include it. A string always takes up at least one more byte than its length so it can terminate with the '\0' byte. It is a common mistake in C to forget to set aside that one extra byte. Now you know why you have to do this.

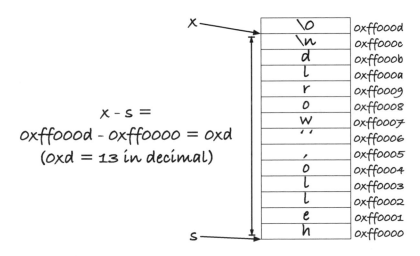

Figure 7-2. *String length via pointer arithmetic*

Let us take another string operation, copying a string. The standard library has strcpy(), but we can write our own. The function, like strcpy(), will take two arguments: a buffer that we copy the string into and a pointer to the string we have to copy from. I call the first argument a buffer, rather than a string, even though they are both char pointers because we do not know if the first one is a string. It is only a string if it points to a sequence of bytes that is terminated by the zero character '\0'. That is not required for the first argument of the function, unlike the second argument. I will generally call a char * pointer a buffer if we do not require that it is zero-terminated and we intend to write into it, but call it a string when we assume that it is zero-terminated. The buffer must be large enough to hold the copied string plus the termination byte. That means that it must have room for the string plus the zero byte. When we use strlen() or our own variants to get the length of a string, we do not include the terminal character, but if we are to store a string in a buffer, we must include it to turn the buffer into a string at the end. The input thus has to look like the top row in Figure 7-3.

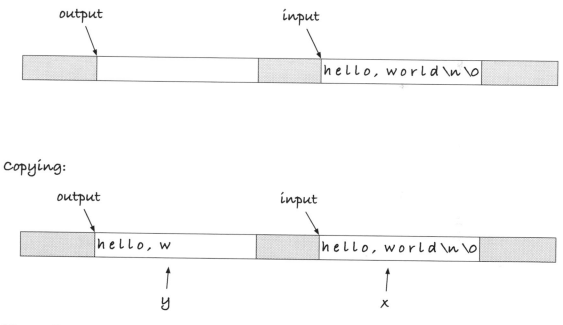

Figure 7-3. Copying a string

The standard library's strcpy() returns a string—the destination (first argument) buffer. I have never been in a situation where that was useful, but often been in the situation where I wanted to know where the copying finished—the point where the terminal zero was inserted. If, for example, I want to concatenate strings, I want to continue copying from the point where the last copy finished. So I suggest that our copying function returns that pointer instead of its first argument.

We can copy the string using this approach. We point a pointer at the beginning of both the input and the output and call the pointers x and y, respectively. We have more input as long as x points at a non-zero byte, and we can test that by testing if *x is true. When we write *x, we get what x points at, and it will be false if and only if that is the zero byte. Then, in a loop, we move both x and y through the sequence of chars. The x pointer runs along the input and the y pointer along the output buffer. At each step, we copy what x points to, *x, into the location that y points to, *y. When *x is the zero byte, we terminate the loop, but we haven't copied the last byte into the output buffer then, so we handle that as the last step of the function. See the bottom half of Figure 7-3.

```
#include <stdio.h>
#include <string.h>

char *string_copy(char *output, char const *input)
{
  char const *x = input;
  char *y = output;
  for ( ; *x ; x++, y++ )
    *y = *x;
  *y = '\0';
  return y;
}

int main(void)
{
  char const *string = "hello, world\n";
  int n = strlen(string);
  char buffer[n + 1];
  string_copy(buffer, string);
  printf("%s", buffer);

  return 0;
}
```

The variable we declare in main() is not a string. It is an array, and it gives us a sequence of n + 1 char values. It functions as a char * pointer, but it is not terminated with the zero character, '\0', and so it is not string. If you put the zero character anywhere in there, you have a string; the buffer is allowed to be longer than where the string terminates, but not shorter.

```
char buffer[n + 1];
```

In this code, we compute the length of `string` and add one to it when we allocate the buffer. This is to make room for both the string and the terminal `char`. Since the buffer length depends on a runtime variable, it is a variable length array, and these, as we saw in Chapter 5, might not be supported by your compiler. If your compiler complains about the preceding code, replace the definition with

```
char buffer[14];
```

The string `"hello, world\n"` has length 13, so it is 14 when we add `'\0'`.

Another and more succinct way to implement the copying is to use the input and output pointers directly. Inside the function, they are just usual arguments. We will not modify the pointers that were arguments to the function any more than we would modify any other argument to a function as seen from the calling side. In this code, you will not expect the `main()` variable x to change just because you change the x in `f()`. Likewise, you should not expect a pointer to change if you modify it inside a function.

```
void f(int x)
{
  x += 1;
}

int main(void)
{
  int x = 2;
  f(x);
  // x is still 2
  return 0;
}
```

So, we can move `output` and `input` along the buffer/string and copy the bytes that way. In the following `while`-loop, we increment the pointers and copy the byte in the same statement. When you write `*input++`, you read the byte at the address first, to get its value, and then you move the pointer one step forward. Likewise, when you write `*output++` on the left-hand side of the assignment, you assign the byte to the current address before you move the pointer. This code does a lot on a few lines, and to the novice, it might be hard to read, but it is a very C-like way to write this function. With a little experience, it becomes second nature to both read and write code such as this:

```
char *string_copy(char *output, char const *input)
{
  while (*input) {
    *output++ = *input++;
  }
  *output = '\0';
  return output;
}
```

We still have to assign the zero byte at the end of the output as a separate statement, but we can avoid this with a slight change. If we first do the copy and then the test for the zero byte, we have already handled it when we leave the loop. Such a solution could look like this:

```
char *string_copy(char *output, char const *input)
{
  while ( (*output = *input) ) {
    output++; input++;
  }
  return output;
}
```

In the while-loop test, we do an assignment. If you take an assignment and look at its value, it is the object that you assigned, in this case, the byte we copied. So the assignment is true until we copied the zero byte, where it becomes false. That is what we want. The body of the while-loop just increments the pointers.

You could also use the do-while construction to achieve the same:

```
char *string_copy(char *output, char const *input)
{
  do {
    *output++ = *input;
  } while (*input++);
  return output;
}
```

Here, we always assign before we test and increment the input, so we will have assigned the termination character before we terminate the loop.

If you want to go completely bananas, you can compact the function into this:

```
char *string_copy(char *output, char const *input)
{
  while ( (*output++ = *input++) ) ;
  return output;
}
```

Here, we combine the "assign and increment" approach from two versions ago with the "test the assignment" from the previous version. This is a very C way to write the function and something you are likely to see in the wild. To me, though, it is a little too much, but your mileage might vary.

Integers to Strings

For the next example, we will try to run backward through a string. We will write a function that creates the string representation of an integer. The idea is this: if you have an integer n, you can get the last digit as n % 10, the remainder when you divide by ten. This is not surprising; this is exactly what the last digit is. Then you can integer-divide n by ten, so the second last digit, the "tens" in the number, moves down to the last digit, the "ones." Now you can get that digit by taking the remainder again. You can repeat taking remainders and dividing until you have gone through all of n's digits, when the number you have left is zero, and then you are done.

See Figure 7-4 for an example. There, we start with the number 314, and we want to write it into the string pointed to by string. With the strategy we have chosen, we have to do this starting from the last digit, so we put a pointer to the position in the string where that should go (after putting a zero byte at the position one after to terminate the string). We will handle zero, negative, and positive numbers as different cases. The figure only describes the case for positive numbers, but see later for the other cases. For a positive integer n, the number of digits to represent it is $\lfloor \log_{10} n \rfloor + 1$. It is also $\lceil \log_{10} (n + 1) \rceil$, and that will also work for $n = 0$, but our algorithm won't work for zero; we need to handle zero explicitly, so I will stick with the first calculation. In C, it is the expression (int) log10(n) + 1. When we start, we move a pointer, s, so it points (int)log10(n) + 1 + 1 past the string pointer; we insert the zero byte there and move it one to the left. Then we start the algorithm. We compute n % 10, insert it at *s, divide n by 10, and move s one step to the left. We repeat this until we are done.

We do not want to insert n % 10 directly into *s. That is an integer, and *s is a character, and the characters for the digits are unlikely to have the same integer values—they do not in any encoding I am aware of. We need to translate the number into a character, but fortunately that turns out very easy. If you have a string `digits = "0123456789"`, then you find digit `'i'` and index `digits[i]`, for example, `digits[0] == '0'` and `digits[5] == '5'`.

Figure 7-4. *Translating the integer 314 into a string*

If you are using the ASCII character encoding, which you most likely are, then the digits have values such that digit '1' has integer value 0+ 1, digit '2' has integer value 0+ 2, digit '3' has integer value 0+ 3, and so on. So you can also get the digit as

```
'0' + (n % 10);
```

but I find an expression such as

```
digits[n % 10];
```

easier to read myself.

We can implement it like this:

```
int no_digits(int n)
{
  assert(n > 0);
  return (int)log10(n) + 1;
}

void pos_int_to_string(int n, char *s)
{
  assert(n > 0);

  // Go to the last position and zero-terminate
  s += no_digits(n);
  *s-- = '\0';
```

```
  // Move backwards and insert digits
  char const *digits = "0123456789";
  while (n) {
    *s-- = digits[n % 10];
    n /= 10;
  }
}
```

As the name `pos_int_to_string()` suggests, however, it only works for positive integers. For zero, we will never enter the `while`-loop, and for negative numbers, we will need to add a minus at the beginning of the string.

This is easily fixed; we simply handle the three different cases:

```
void int_to_string(int n, char *s)
{
  // If n is zero, write zero and we are done
  if (n == 0) {
    s[0] = '0'; s[1] = '\0';
    return;
  }

  // If it negative, write a minus at the front of the
  // string and translate the problem into the case
  // for positive nubers.
  if (n < 0) {
    *s++ = '-'; n = -n;
  }
  pos_int_to_string(n, s);
}
```

There is one more special case, however, and it relates to how numbers are likely represented on your computer. Unless you work on very exotic hardware, negative numbers are represented in the so-called two's complement, and there you do not have the same number of positive and negative numbers. There is one more negative number, the smallest you can represent, and if n is that number, then -n cannot be held in an int. We can add that as yet another special case or simply observe that the algorithm we have works just fine for negative numbers as well and change `pos_int_to_string()` into neg_int_to_string(). If we change the sign for positive numbers, we know that we can hold the value of -n. For each positive number, we can hold the corresponding negative number (and one more).

This, unfortunately, gives us yet another problem. Will our troubles never end? If n is negative, then no_digits() doesn't work. And of course, we cannot simply call no_digits() with -n because that will take us right back to the problem we just had!

It isn't hard to compute the number of digits, though. In the algorithm, we insert digits as long as n is non-zero, so we can compute the number of digits the same way, without spending substantially longer time than we do on creating the string.

```
int no_digits(int n)
{
  int digits = 0;
  for ( ; n ; n /= 10)
    digits++;
  return digits;
}

void neg_int_to_string(int n, char *s)
{
  assert(n < 0);
  char const *digits = "0123456789";
  for ( ; n ; n /= 10) {
    *s-- = digits[-(n % 10)];
  }
}

void int_to_string(int n, char *s)
{
  if (n == 0) {
    s[0] = '0'; s[1] = '\0';
    return;
  }

  if (n < 0) *s++ = '-';
  if (n > 0) n = -n;
  s += no_digits(n);
```

```
  *s-- = '\0';
  neg_int_to_string(n, s);
}
```

Of course, if we don't know the length of the string we construct, and we do not want to spend time computing it, we can just create the string in the wrong order. We know how to reverse a string because we have implemented reversal of arrays before, and strings behave the same way:

```
void reverse_string(char *s)
{
  if (*s == 0) return;
  char *left = s;
  char *right = s + strlen(s) - 1;
  for ( ; left < right; left++, right--) {
    char c = *left;
    *left = *right;
    *right = c;
  }
}

void neg_int_to_string_rev(int n, char *s)
{
  assert(n < 0);
  // We need to remember the beginning for reversal
  char *front = s;
  char const *digits = "0123456789";
  for ( ; n ; n /= 10) {
    *s++ = digits[-(n % 10)];
  }
  // Reverse the string to get the right order
  *s = '\0';
  reverse_string(front);
}
```

The if (*s == 0) check in reverse is to avoid empty strings. If we have one, we would point one to the left of the first address, and we are not allowed to do that. It is easy and quick to test, so we might as well avoid a problem that, although highly unlikely to ever be an issue, is nevertheless there.

Since we already have a pointer to both the beginning and the end of the string of decimals, we might as well exploit this and not use strlen() to get the end of the string we reverse, so you could also write it as

```c
void reverse_string(char *left, char *right)
{
  if (right <= left) return; // avoid rigth underflow
  right--; // move to the first included character
  for ( ; left < right; left++, right--) {
    char c = *left;
    *left = *right;
    *right = c;
  }
}

void neg_int_to_string_rev(int n, char *s)
{
  assert(n < 0);
  // we need to remember the beginning for reversal
  char *front = s;
  char const *digits = "0123456789";
  for ( ; n ; n /= 10) {
    *s++ = digits[-(n % 10)];
  }
  *s = '\0';
  reverse_string(front, s);
}
```

But let us now attempt a different approach, where we also do not compute the number of digits beforehand. If we do not know the number of digits we end up with, we don't know where the last digit should go when we start, but we know where a single-digit number should go—precisely at the position our string points at. So we can deal with integers greater than -10 (and smaller than zero; recall that we are now working on negative numbers). We can get the digit that we want by looking up in `digits` at index `-(n % 10)`. The integer `n % 10` is numerically smaller than the smallest integer—it is a single-digit integer, after all, so we know that we can also represent the corresponding positive integer, `-(n % 10)`, so we have no risk of overflow here. But if n is smaller than or equal to -10, we *first* need to insert all the digits in n / 10 before we can insert the last. If we implement the algorithm recursively, and require that the recursive calls give us the position in the string where the next digit should be inserted, then we can insert all the preceding digits recursively and insert `-(n % 10)` at the position the recursion gives us. That solution can look like the following code, and an execution is shown in Figure 7-5:

```c
char *neg_int_to_string(int n, char *s)
{
  assert(n < 0);
  char const *digits = "0123456789";
  if (n <= -10) {
    s = neg_int_to_string(n / 10, s);
  }
  *s = digits[-(n % 10)];
  return s + 1;
}
```

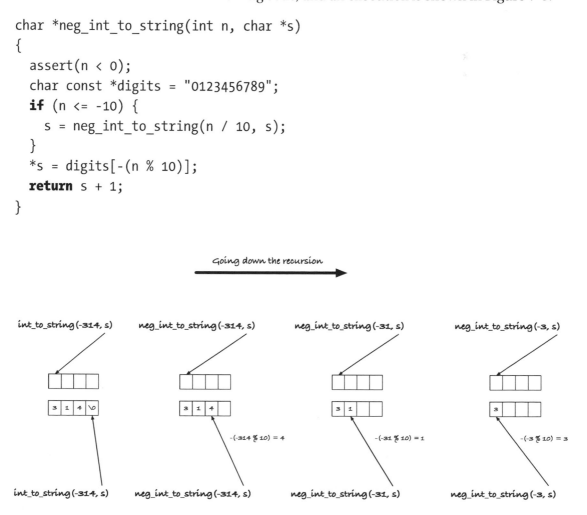

Figure 7-5. *Inserting digits with the recursive algorithm*

In int_to_string(), we handle zero explicitly, insert a minus if we have a negative number, change a positive to a negative number (without the - of course), and then use the neg_int_to_string() function to get the digits. When we are done, the int_to_string() function has the position behind the last digit, and it terminates the string by putting '\0' there:

```c
#include <stdio.h>
#include <math.h>

char *neg_int_to_string(int n, char *s)
{
  assert(n < 0);
  char const *digits = "0123456789";
  if (n <= -10) {
    s = neg_int_to_string(n / 10, s);
  }
  *s = digits[-(n % 10)];
  return s + 1;
}

void int_to_string(int n, char *s)
{
  if (n == 0) {
    s[0] = '0'; s[1] = '\0';
    return;
  }

  if (n < 0) *s++ = '-';
  if (n > 0) n = -n;
  s = neg_int_to_string(n, s);
  *s = '\0';
}

int main(void)
{
  int n = 11;
  int digits = log10(n) + 1;
  char buf[digits];
```

```
  for (int i = -n; i < n; i++) {
    int_to_string(i, buf);
    printf("%d = '%s'\n", i, buf);
  }

  return 0;
}
```

If you don't want the recursion to return the next pointer, you can update it in the calls instead; you just need to pass a pointer to the string pointer so you can change it.

```
void neg_int_to_string(int n, char **s)
{
  assert(n < 0);
  char const *digits = "0123456789";
  if (n <= -10) {
    neg_int_to_string(n / 10, s);
  }
  *(*s)++ = digits[-(n % 10)];
}

void int_to_string(int n, char *s)
{
  if (n == 0) {
    s[0] = '0'; s[1] = '\0';
    return;
  }

  if (n < 0) *s++ = '-';
  if (n > 0) n = -n;
  neg_int_to_string(n, &s);
  *s = '\0';
}
```

We started out with a relatively simple function that constructs a string in reverse order and then got another approach that inserted the digits from left to right. But we did not end up with a repeat of the examples in the two previous sections. Rather, we saw how we can recursively move the destination pointer when we have an algorithm that works from right to left, but we have to implement it going from the left to the right. The recursive calls move the pointer along, so we have the right location when we need it.

There is nothing here that you couldn't do with indices as well. You would have to provide both the string and an index to the recursive functions and update the index as you move through the string. Besides that, the solution is exactly the same. I find the pointer solution more elegant myself, though, and we only need one function argument to keep track of the string and where we should insert digits.

Run-Length Encoding

In this section, we will write a program for run-length encoding. Run-length encoding has its origin in lossless compression and is the simple idea that if you have a sequence with long runs of the same data, then you can replace the run with a number that tells you the length of the run and then one instance of the data object. For strings, the run-length encoding of

"aaaabbbbbbbaabbbcbbccccc"

would be

"4a7b2a3b1c2b5c"

The original string starts with four a's, then it has seven b's, then two a's again, and so on.

It is not always the best of ideas to compress a string with run-length encoding. If you have no runs of more than one repetition, you are adding one digit in front of every single input character, and you end up with a string that is twice as long as you started with. But that is something for compression people to worry about; we are focusing on pointers, and we can use char pointers to get a simple and efficient implementation of a run-length encoding algorithm. The following program is all it takes:

```
#include <stdio.h>
#include <string.h>
#include <assert.h>

char const *skip(char const *x)
{
  assert(*x != '\0');
  char c = *x;
  while (*x == c) x++;
```

```c
    return x;
}

void runlength_encode(char const * restrict input,
                      char * restrict output)
{
  while (*input) {
    char c = *input;
    char const *next = skip(input);
    int length = next - input;
    output += sprintf(output, "%d%c", length, c);
    input = next;
  }
}

int main(void)
{
  char const *x = "aaaabbbbbbbaabbbcbbccccc";
  char buffer[2 * strlen(x) + 1];

  runlength_encode(x, buffer);
  printf("%s\n", buffer);

  return 0;
}
```

The function `skip()` returns the pointer beyond the input x, where we can find a character different from *x (or x[0]). We are not allowed to call it when x points at the last character in the string, identifiable by x pointing to the zero char. If we did, the function would start looking at bytes beyond the string, and there is no way to know how the runtime system will react to that. So we `assert()` that the first character is not '\0', and then we move x along until we see the first character that is different from the previous. We will always find one if the input is zero-terminated, so eventually the loop ends, and we return the new position.

If we call `skip()` on a string, x, we get a pointer at some offset beyond x. That offset is the number of repeats of x[0] at the beginning of x. So for the run-length encoding, the repeat count is `skip(x)` - x. The difference between the two pointers is the number of characters between them.

In the `runlength_encode()` function, we use two pointers, one pointing into the input at where the next run of character is found and one pointing into the output at where we should write the next encoding. These *must not* point to overlapping buffers. You cannot encode a string into itself because the encoding can get longer than the string itself. If you try to run the function with the same string as both input and output, you risk overwriting your input before you need it. I have tried making that explicit by qualifying the pointers as `restrict`, but the compiler will not check that for you. If you call the function with overlapping buffers, you could be in trouble.

We get the character for the next run from *input, and then we use `skip()` to figure out how long the next run is:

```
char c = *input;
char const *next = skip(input);
int length = next - input;
```

We write the encoding to output, and here we use the `sprintf()` function from `stdio.h`. This function works like `printf()` but writes the formatting text to a buffer. That buffer is our output—that is where we want the encoding to go. `sprintf()` returns the number of characters excluding the zero terminal (it does terminate the string, but the return value is excluding it). That is what we want. We want to put the next encoded run right after the previous, and we do not need to zero-terminate the output until we have written the entire encoding. We need to move output past the encoded run, however, and here we exploit that `sprintf()` will return the number of characters it wrote into the buffer. If we increase output by this amount, it points at the first character past the ones we just wrote.

```
output += sprintf(output, "%d%c", length, c);
```

Now we have written the encoding of the repeat of the character that input points at and moved output to the next location where we can write an encoding, so what remains is to move input to the next run of characters. That is where next points after we skipped, so the last step in the loop is

```
input = next;
```

Once we have looped through the entire input, the output must be zero-terminated, but because `sprintf()` already does this—it just doesn't return the length of that additional character—we are good to return.

If this seemed simple to you, then you have now gotten the hang of how character pointers work to implement strings.

Finding Words

Now imagine that we want to iterate through all the words in a string. For simplicity, define a word to be anything that starts with a letter and consists only of letters. The function isalpha() in C's standard library (you included it with the header <ctype. h>) checks if a character is a letter. We can define these two functions to skip through a word—that is a sequence of letters—and to find the next word from where we currently are, that is, search until you find the next letter.

```c
char *skip_word(char *x)
{
  while (*x && isalpha(*x))
    x++;
  return x;
}

char *find_word(char *x)
{
  while (*x && !isalpha(*x))
    x++;
  return x;
}
```

We want to iterate through all the words in a string, and we can do this by repeatedly calling the two functions.

```c
#include <stdio.h>
#include <ctype.h>

char *skip_word(char *x)
{
  while (*x && isalpha(*x))
    x++;
  return x;
}
```

```
char *find_word(char *x)
{
  while (*x && !isalpha(*x))
    x++;
  return x;
}

int main(void)
{
  char const *words = "\tfoo! bar\n\tbaz qux\n";

  char *x = find_word((char *)words);
  while (*x) {
    printf("Current position: '%s'\n", x);
    x = find_word(skip_word(x));
  }

  return 0;
}
```

I define words to be char const *, but the functions work with char *. I did not do this merely to confuse the reader. I want the functions to work with char * because a user of them might want to modify the string they search for words in. If they return a char const *, the user would need to cast the type every time the user calls them. If we return char * but take a char const * as input, then we would need to cast the return type, and we would be violating the promise we make when we say that we do not allow the input to be modified. That is why I don't want the two search functions to work on constant strings. Why then do I define word to be constant? I don't have to; I could define it as char *. C would allow me to, but it isn't safe, and that is the second point I want to make now.

If you modify a literal string—one you define inside your program by putting a string in double quotes—anything can happen. The C standard allows you to assign them to non-constant char pointers for historical reasons, but you should always consider them constants. Your literal strings are compiled into your program, and most operating systems will not allow you to modify the area of memory where your program sits when you run it. You can check what your operating system will do if you modify a literal string by running this program:

#include <stdio.h>

```
int main(void)
{
  char *string = "foo";
  string[1] = 'O'; // Changing foo to fOo?
  printf("Succes! string is now '%s'\n", string);
  return 0;
}
```

Even if you get away with it, though, you shouldn't rely on mutable literal strings. On other platforms, trying to change one will likely crash the program.

Literal strings are consecutive bytes terminated by zero, just as any other string, but you should always consider them const. And as for any other const type, modify them at your own risk. Unfortunately, C considers them non-const when it type-checks, but that is how it is. Just because C does this doesn't mean that you should. Declare them const. If you need to modify a string you define in your program, then you need to make a copy first.

Do not worry about strings you define as char arrays and copy into. What we did with the preceding string_copy() examples is always safe. It is only literal strings you have to worry about and only because the type-checker doesn't enforce that they are constants. If you always declare them char const *—and don't cast when you shouldn't—then you are safe. Yes, I know we cast the string in the preceding program, so we could iterate through the words, but in this particular case, it is okay; we don't modify the string, and that is what matters. If you are careful, you are sometimes allowed to cheat the type-checker.

We have a fine program for iterating through the words in a string, but I think we can improve on it slightly. When we need to iterate over something, I prefer to use the *iterator design pattern*. This pattern suggests that we should have some representation of the iteration that we can use as an object to get through the elements. Typically, it means that we need to set up the object, initializing the iterator, we have a way to ask for the next element, and we have a way of recognizing that we have seen all the elements. In some cases, we also need to free resources held by the iterator object after we are done with it. We don't need the full pattern for this small example, but I would like to have at least the part where I set up an iterator and where I ask for the next word. Calling find_word(skip_word(x)) to get the next word doesn't exactly scream that we are asking for the next word in a sequence—we need to understand what those two functions do before we know that. And checking *x to see if there are more words is not an explicit test for iteration termination either.

179

I would prefer something that looks like this:

```c
for (char *iter = first_word((char *)words);
     iter != WORD_ITER_END;
     iter = next_word(iter)) {
  printf("Current position: '%s'\n", iter);
}
```

This is how the iterator design pattern is implemented in the C++ standard library, and it matches C well—not entirely because we do not have destructors to help us deallocate resources, but frequently enough that it is worthwhile to look to C++ for ideas. If we implement a function that gives us the first word, `first_word()`, and then one that provides us with the `next_word()` later, we can get the words. With for-loops, we typically terminate once we are one past the last element, so if we can make the iterator return an object that indicates this, `WORD_ITER_END` here, then we know when to terminate the loop. We cannot always get it this way—we cannot overload comparisons in C, but we can often get *something* we can use.

The iterator will be a `char *` pointer, and we will terminate when it is the NULL pointer. We can compare a `char *` to NULL, and since a valid word is never the NULL pointer, it is not something we can confuse for a real word. If the iterator isn't NULL, it should point at the next word. All we need to do to implement the design pattern is to find the first word when we initialize the iterator:

```c
// NULL pointer instead of pointer to zero terminal
#define NULLIFY(x) ((*x) ? (x) : 0)
#define WORD_ITER_END 0

char *first_word(char *x)
{
  return NULLIFY(find_word(x));
}
```

and when we ask for the next word, we skip the current word and find the next—same as we did explicitly in the previous version.

```c
char *next_word(char *x)
{
  return NULLIFY(find_word(skip_word(x)));
}
```

The macro NULLIFY() turns a pointer to the zero char into a NULL pointer, so we can recognize when we have moved past the last word.

Whether you find it worthwhile to add design patterns to such a tiny program is mostly a matter of taste. I probably wouldn't if this was all I needed to do with the code. But I think you will agree that it didn't take much extra code to make it explicit in the code that we start from the first word and continue taking the next word until we are done. I don't think find_word(skip_word(x)) is quite as obvious; at least I do not think it would be as obvious six months later when I need to debug my code.

The full program, with the iterator, now looks like this:

```c
#include <stdio.h>
#include <ctype.h>

char *skip_word(char *x)
{
  while (*x && isalpha(*x))
    x++;
  return x;
}

char *find_word(char *x)
{
  while (*x && !isalpha(*x))
    x++;
  return x;
}

// NULL pointer instead of
// pointer to zero terminal
#define NULLIFY(x) ((*x) ? x : 0)
#define WORD_ITER_END 0

char *first_word(char *x)
{
  return NULLIFY(find_word(x));
}
```

```
char *next_word(char *x)
{
  return NULLIFY(find_word(skip_word(x)));
}

int main(void)
{
  char const *words = "\tfoo! bar\n\tbaz qux\n";
  for (char *iter = first_word((char *)words);
       iter != WORD_ITER_END;
       iter = next_word(iter)) {
    printf("Current position: '%s'\n", iter);
  }

  return 0;
}
```

Straying away from the main topic, pointers, we can expand on the iterator pattern a little here. Our word iterator works through two functions, one that finds the beginning of a word and one that finds the end of a word. The iterator interface is a "first" function and a "next" function. Writing the iterator functions if we have the find and skip function is trivial. If we wanted to iterate over integers in a string, we could implement it like this:

```
char *find_integer(char *x)
{
  while (*x && !isnumber(*x))
    x++;
  return x;
}

char *skip_integer(char *x)
{
  while (*x && isnumber(*x))
    x++;
  return x;
}

char *first_integer(char *x)
```

```
{
  return NULLIFY(find_integer(x));
}

char *next_integer(char *x)
{
  return NULLIFY(find_integer(skip_integer(x)));
}
```

#define INTEGER_ITER_END 0

The isnumber() function, also from <ctype.h>, checks if a character is a digit (plus additional characters that should be interpreted that way in the local configuration). The only difference between the two iterators is the names we give the functions and the function we use to recognize the character class, so we could generate the code using templates. If we already have a find and skip function, we could use this macro:

```
#define GEN_FIND_SKIP_ITER(name, find, skip)     \
char *first_##name(char *x)                       \
{                                                 \
  return NULLIFY((find)(x));                       \
}                                                 \
char *next_##name(char *x)                         \
{                                                 \
  return NULLIFY((find)((skip)(x)));               \
}
```

You would then generate the word iterator this way:

```
GEN_FIND_SKIP_ITER(word, find_word, skip_word)
```

We can equally easy create the find and skip functions:

```
#define GEN_FIND_SKIP(name, type)     \
char *skip_##name(char *x)             \
{                                     \
  while (*x && (type)(*x))             \
    x++;                              \
  return x;                           \
}                                     \
```

```
char *find_##name(char *x)              \
{                                       \
  while (*x && !(type)(*x))             \
    x++;                                \
  return x;                             \
}                                       \
```

where we could generate the integer find and skip like this:

```
GEN_FIND_SKIP(integer, isnumber)
```

Getting all the functions in one go can be done with this macro:

```
#define GEN_ITER(name, type)                            \
GEN_FIND_SKIP(name, type)                                \
GEN_FIND_SKIP_ITER(name, find_##name, skip_##name)
```

It makes sense to have both GEN_ITER() and GEN_FIND_SKIP_ITER() since we might have more complex find and skip functions than those we generate with GEN_FIND_SKIP(). Still, with the GEN_ITER() macro, we can easily create iterators for various types. For example, if we want an iterative over words, those identified by isalpha(), then we write

```
GEN_ITER(word, isalpha)
```

and if we want an integer iterator, we write

```
GEN_ITER(integer, isnumber)
```

Where we used the preceding word iterator, we had WORD_ITER_END to indicate when we had reached the end. Generally, we need an indicator that depends on what we iterate through, but since our iterator code will always give us a NULL pointer when there are no more elements, we can just check for that. There is nothing wrong with that solution. So iterating through both words and numbers is quickly done, with the same design pattern code:

```
#include <stdio.h>
#include <ctype.h>

// NULL pointer instead of pointer to zero terminal
#define NULLIFY(x) ((*x) ? x : 0)
```

```
#define GEN_FIND_SKIP_ITER(name, find, skip)             \
char *first_##name(char *x)                               \
{                                                         \
  return NULLIFY((find)(x));                              \
}                                                         \
char *next_##name(char *x)                                \
{                                                         \
  return NULLIFY((find)((skip)(x)));                      \
}                                                         \

#define GEN_FIND_SKIP(name, type)                         \
char *skip_##name(char *x)                                \
{                                                         \
  while (*x && (type)(*x))                                \
    x++;                                                  \
  return x;                                               \
}                                                         \
char *find_##name(char *x)                                \
{                                                         \
  while (*x && !(type)(*x))                               \
    x++;                                                  \
  return x;                                               \
}

#define GEN_ITER(name, type)                              \
GEN_FIND_SKIP(name, type)                                 \
GEN_FIND_SKIP_ITER(name, find_##name, skip_##name)

GEN_ITER(word, isalpha)
GEN_ITER(integer, isnumber)

int main(void)
{
  char const *x = "\tfoo! 1231 bar\n\tbaz qux12\n";

  for (char *iter = first_word((char *)x);
       iter;
```

```
      iter = next_word(iter)) {
    printf("Current position: '%s'\n", iter);
  }

  for (char *iter = first_integer((char *)x);
       iter;
       iter = next_integer(iter)) {
    printf("Current position: '%s'\n", iter);
  }

  return 0;
}
```

Compacting Words

We can take another approach to get the words in a string, where we do not extract them one by one, but rather rewrite the string, so we have the words separated by a single space. It doesn't give us an easier way to iterate through them, but it gives us an excuse to explore strings and pointers a little more.

So, the goal is to take a string such as

```
"\tfoo! bar\n\tbaz qux\n";
```

and turn it into

```
"foo bar baz qux"
```

If we have a pointer to the input, from, and a pointer to where we want the output, to, then we can copy the words, skipping everything else, like this:

```
void copy_words(char *from, char *to)
{
  from = find_word(from);
  while (*from) {
    copy_word(&from, &to);
    from = find_word(from);
    if (*from) *to++ = ' ';
  }
  *to = '\0';
}
```

where find_word() is the function from the previous section and copy_word() is explained in the following. The idea is this: we move from to the start of the first word. Then, as long as there is more input, that is, from doesn't point to the zero byte, we copy the next word into to, and then we advance from to the next word. If there are more words, from will point to a letter—if find_word() doesn't find a letter, the string it returns points to the zero byte (examine the source code for the preceding function if you wonder why that is). In that case, we need a space in the output. When we do *to++ =, we put a space at the position that to points to and then advance it, so the next character we insert in the output goes after the space. When we have exhausted the input, so *from is zero, we must terminate the output string as well, and we do that by putting a zero at the location that to now points to.

The copy_word() function should move a complete word from from to to. We can implement it like this:

```
void copy_word(char **from, char **to)
{
  while (isalpha(**from)) {
    *(*to)++ = *(*from)++;
  }
}
```

The function is short, but it might require some deciphering. The input pointers are pointers to strings, so pointers to pointers to char. It might seem more natural to use pointers to char, but we want to advance both string pointers, so they point past the word we copy, and if we used char * arguments, we could only advance the local variables and not the pointers we call the function with. To advance the from and to pointers in copy_words(), we need to give their addresses to copy_word(), which is what we did. We called the function as copy_word(&from, &to), and it advances both pointers past the next word.

Because from is a pointer to the string we scan through, we must dereference it once to get the string and then again to get the character it points to, so it is **from that is the character we must look at to determine if we have a letter or not; thus, we write isalpha(**from).

When we copy a character, we use `*(*to)++` = `*(*from)++`. We dereference the two arguments, `*to` and `*from`, to get the strings they point to, then do it again to get the characters they point to, `*(*to)` and `*(*from)`. We copy the character at `*(*from)` to `*(*to)`, and then we increment the pointers (`*to`) and (`*from`) using the ++ postfix operator.

I swear that I didn't write the code this way to obfuscate it. You can split the operations into more steps, like this:

```
void copy_word(char **from, char **to)
{
  char *x = *from, *y = *to;
  while (isalpha(*x)) {
    *y = *x; x++; y++;
  }
  *from = x; *to = y;
}
```

but it is debatable how much it helps. There is one operation per statement; we either check a character, make an assignment, or increment a pointer. But there are more steps and more variables to keep track of. For an experienced C programmer, the first version will be easier to read. There is much condensed into a few operations, but they are idioms of the language. You get used to seeing something like `*p++` and understand that you are dereferencing a pointer and then moving it to the next position. Be careful, though. While `*p++` dereferences and then increments the pointer, (`*p)++` increments the object the pointer holds the address of. The increment operation, p++, has lower precedence than the dereferencing, so the implicit parentheses are `*(p++)`. Even if you prefer to write your own code, so it looks like the second function, others will likely write code that looks like the first. It is worthwhile to get used to this notation. Don't overdo it, of course, but incrementing or decrementing pointers, before or after you dereference them, is something you will see all the time.

Back to copying words. The function `copy_words()` does what we want. Give it a string to read the words from and a buffer to put the results in, and you get the words in a space-separated string. But here's the thing: you don't need two strings if the input string is one you are allowed to modify. Your input and output string can be the same. As we scan along with the input, the pointer will never fall behind the output pointer. For a while, the two pointers might point to the same location in the string, but if they do not, then `from` is ahead of `to`. So if we copy from the string into itself, we move bytes toward the beginning when we remove non-letters and copy the words. We can write a function that uses this idea:

```
void compact_words(char *s)
{
  copy_words(s, s);
}
```

If you call it with a string, you turn the string itself into the version with space-separated words, and you do not use any extra memory to do it.

You can try it out with this program:

```
int main(void)
{
  // We modify the string we wordize, so we
  // cannot use a literate string. Those are immutable.
  // This initialises a mutable buffer instead. The
  // string is copied into the buffer, including the zero-
  // terminal, when the buffer is initialised.
  char string[] = "\tfoo! bar\n\tbaz qux\n";
  compact_words(string);
  printf("'%s'\n", string);

  return 0;
}
```

The string is modified when we call `compact_words()`, so I have used a stack-allocated buffer instead of a literal string.

When we have an algorithm that gives us a reduced representation of the input, but puts it in the same memory locations as input, we say that we *compact* the input, thus the name of this section. We did the same thing in one of the examples of Eratosthenes' Sieve in Chapter 6.

Buffer Overflow Errors

Buffer overflow is among the leading causes of software bugs and security holes, and your compiler cannot help you much with warnings or errors. Buffer overflows are a general class of errors where out-of-bounds errors in arrays are a subclass. An out-of-bounds error occurs when you access data outside the memory range of an array. If you define

```
int array[3];
```

then the legal locations you can look in the array are `array[0]`, `array[1]`, and `array[2]`, and you should not try to access entries before zero, `array[-1]`, or after index 2, `array[3]`.

This appears obvious, and it is, yet it happens very often when the indices are not as clear, for example:

```
char buf[n];
buf[n] = '\0';
```

Here, the intent is to define a character buffer and zero-terminate it. It looks correct until you examine it closer. The buffer has length n, so you can index from 0 up to n-1, but *not* index `buf[n]`. The same error happens here, where it might be even less straightforward:

```
char const *s = "foobar";
char buf[strlen(s)];
strcpy(buf, s);
```

We make a buffer and copy s into it. But we forgot that `strlen()` gives us the length of a string up to, but not including, the terminal zero byte. The size of the buffer should be `strlen(s) + 1` to make room for zero. It gets worse, of course, if you want to write an unknown string into a buffer. With `strcpy()`, you will write beyond the buffer if the string is longer than the buffer. You want to use the function `strncpy()` if you want to safely copy strings of unknown length.

You also get into trouble if the string you copy from isn't zero-terminated. Then `strcpy()` will keep reading beyond the end of the input buffer, and then you will again access data outside of the memory block you are allowed to index into.

Buffer overflows often lead to security holes because they might allow an attacker to change the data in a program and thus trick it into doing something it shouldn't. Take a simple example such as this:

```
bool validate_password(char const *password)
{
  bool valid_password = false;
  char buffer[10];

  printf("Password: ");
  gets(buffer);

  if (strcmp(password, buffer) == 0)
    valid_password = true;

  return valid_password;
}
```

We have a buffer that we read a string into, but we do not validate that the input is shorter than the buffer. The buffer can hold 9 characters and the termination byte, but if you type in a password that is 11 characters or longer, the program will write outside the bounds of the buffer. If you are lucky, you access memory that the underlying operating system and hardware know you are not allowed to, or the following `strcmp()` call will read into such memory, and then the program crashes. But what happens if `valid_password` sits right after the ten `chars` in `buffer`? Then their memory locations are inside your program, and the hardware doesn't see anything wrong in you accessing it. If you type in 11 characters, `gets()` puts the first in `buffer`, the next in `valid_password`, and then a terminal byte after that. The 11th character you write is probably not zero, so `valid_password` changes its value from `false` to `true`.

I cannot give you a reproducible example of this. It is up to the compiler where it puts the local variables, and while they are likely to be close to each other—they are both on the stack—they won't necessarily be laid out as I just described. If `valid_password` comes before `buffer`, then overwriting `buffer` will not affect it. The point, however, is that if your program writes outside the memory that you have allocated for an array, you open yourself up for serious bugs, especially if you let a user give you input that you then process without checking.

If you have defined an array, that is, a block of memory, you can only safely access that memory; access beyond it, via indices or pointers, and a whole host of bad things can happen. If you are lucky, the memory outside the array is not yours to look at. The operating system might not have given your program permission to access it, and then if you do, it will immediately terminate your program. That is the best-case scenario. Worse, you can read garbage data because you have expectations about the type of the object you are looking at, and you probably make more assumptions based on that. Those assumptions are not true when you look at an area of memory that could be used for practically anything. The absolutely worst-case scenario is if you write outside the array and your program doesn't crash. Now you have most likely destroyed data that is essential for the program somewhere else. Writing outside a buffer is a common technique for hackers—they make a program overwrite variables and thereby trick the program to change behavior.

Many of the functions from this chapter were vulnerable to these errors because we didn't check overflow. It requires slightly more code to do this, but it is not a major undertaking. For example, to put a limit on how much we should be allowed to copy, we can add a parameter for the length, decrease it for each byte we copy, and bail out if we reach zero. With the run-length encoding example, we could use snprintf() instead of sprintf(). That function takes an argument that tells it the max number of characters to write, so we can ask it to copy up to the buffer length we have left. It returns how much it should have copied (but it never copies too much), so if it returns a number larger than we gave it, we know we are out of space, and we can finish encoding.

```c
#include <stdio.h>
#include <string.h>
#include <stdbool.h>
#include <assert.h>

char const *skip(char const *x)
{
  assert(*x != '\0');
  char c = *x;
  while (*x == c) x++;
  return x;
}
```

```c
bool runlength_encode_n(char const * restrict input,
                        char * restrict output, int n)
{
  while (*input) {
    printf("n == %d\n", n);
    char c = *input;
    char const *next = skip(input);
    int length = next - input;
    int used = snprintf(output, n, "%d%c", length, c);
    output += used; n -= used;
    if (n < 0) return false; // we couldn't write it all
    input = next;
  }
  return true; // Success
}

int main(void)
{
  char const *x = "aaaabbbbbbbaabbbcbbccccc";
  int n = 10;
  char buffer[n + 1];

  bool did_we_make_it = runlength_encode_n(x, buffer, n);
  if (did_we_make_it) {
    printf("We encoded the entire string.\n");
  } else {
    printf("We only got a prefix.\n");
  }
  printf("Encoding: %s\n", buffer);

  return 0;
}
```

For all the functions in the standard library that blindly copy or write strings, some versions limit how much they write. You should, naturally, use those safer functions. And you should write your functions with the same defensive programming in mind.

CHAPTER 8

Substrings Through Ranges

One thing that bothers me with the iterators in Chapter 7 is that when we searched for words or integers, we didn't get the string we matched back. We got a pointer to the position where the match started. We would need to search again for the end of the match if we wanted to know how large the match was. To extract the words, we either have to copy them into another string or need a way to represent substrings. Both are easy to do, but the more interesting one is representing and working with substrings, so in this chapter, we will experiment with a string representation that can handle this. We will not implement a complete library for an alternative string representation, but enough to work as a starting point if it is something you will later wish to do.

The problem with using the zero termination character to define the end of a string is that we cannot terminate a substring within a string. If we add a zero char there, then we have terminated the entire string at that point. The zero termination is a simple solution to strings. It embeds the termination inside the string, so we do not need extra bookkeeping to know where a string ends, even if we start modifying a string from a starting point inside it. But we need an alternative now. Two obvious solutions present themselves. Keep track of where a substring starts and how long it is, or keep track of where it starts and where it ends. The two solutions are equivalent. If we have a pointer to where the string starts, `begin`, and we have its length, `n`, then `begin + n` is a pointer one past the string. Conversely, if we have a pointer to the beginning, `begin`, and one past the end, `end`, then `end - begin` is its length.

© Thomas Mailund 2021
T. Mailund, *Pointers in C Programming*, https://doi.org/10.1007/978-1-4842-6927-5_8

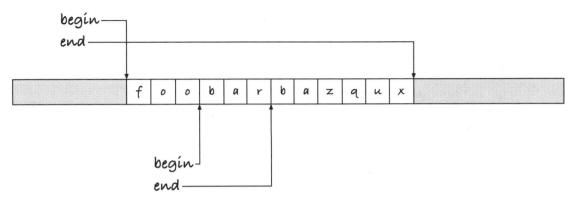

Figure 8-1. *Range representation of substrings*

The choice is arbitrary, but I will go with pointers to the beginning and end of substrings; see Figure 8-1. In the figure, we have two overlapping strings, foobarbazqux and bar, and since there are no termination symbols, you will not be able to see that the bar string sits inside the longer foobarbazqux string unless you examine the pointers. I chose the begin/end, or range, representation because it resembles the way we represented ranges in arrays in Chapters 5 and 6, so it is familiar to us. We can define the data structure like this:

```
struct range {
  char *begin;
  char *end;
};
typedef struct range substr;
```

I named the struct range but the string type substr because I intend to use the range data structure for more than substrings. It will also be part of the iterator design pattern later.

I will let functions that return substr objects or take them as arguments pass them by value. They are tiny objects, only two pointers, and in practically all functions that work with this string representation, we need to pass both pointers to the functions in any case, so we might as well pass them as part of their struct. Using pass by value lets us use expressions that create strings in function arguments. We cannot take the address of an expression; we need a variable for that, so this will not be possible with pass by reference. Returning by value greatly simplifies our code, since we cannot return the address of local variables—they will disappear before the caller can use them—and we haven't learned how to allocate memory on the heap yet.

When we create a substr object, we create a struct with a begin and end field, and we can use this macro to save a few type strokes:

```
#define SUBSTR(b,e) \
  (substr){ .begin = (b), .end = (e) }
```

If you have a zero-terminated C string, we can find the zero terminal and get a pointer to it. That will point one past the last "real" character and will function as the end pointer in our new representation:

```
substr as_substr(char *s)
{
  char *x = s;
  while (*x) x++;
  return SUBSTR(s, x);
}
```

If you have a buffer, s, and you want a substring going from index i to j in it, you can do this:

```
substr slice(char *s, int i, int j)
{
  assert(i <= j);
  return SUBSTR(s + i, s + j);
}
```

As an invariant of the structure, we will require that begin and end always point into the same allocated buffer (with one exception), and we require that begin <= end. The two pointers can be equal, and if they are, we have an empty string. We will not allow end to come before begin, however. Then the length of a string is always end - begin. The special case for the representation is that we will allow begin to be NULL. We can use that to test for special cases in our functions, for example, to indicate that we have searched for a substring and didn't find it, or we can use this NULL substring to indicate iterator termination.

These helper macros make it easier to check for NULL and empty strings and to get their length.

```
#define null_substr(x)  ((x).begin == 0)
#define empty_substr(x) ((x).begin == (x).end)
#define substr_len(x)   ((x).end - (x).begin)
```

To make it easier to return NULL substrings, we define a constant:

```
static substr const NULL_SUBSTR = { .begin = 0 };
```

If we have our string representation but need to translate it into C's representation, one option is to copy the string to a buffer and zero-terminate it. The following function does that. We do not check for buffer overflow in it, but leave that responsibility to the caller. The caller of a function can easily, and efficiently, check if the buffer's length is at least substr_len(x) + 1 long.

```
char *substr_to_buf(char *to, substr from)
{
  while (from.begin != from.end) {
    *to++ = *from.begin++;
  }
  *to = '\0';
  return to;
}
```

The function implicitly assumes that you are not writing into the buffer that from is a range of. If you do, then you might overwrite the string you are copying before you get the copy. The function is not intended to handle such cases, so it doesn't. We will write a copy function later that handles such cases correctly.

When we work with substr objects, we can be more defensive about buffer overflow. If the objects are created, so they point into a valid buffer, then we have a valid range we can write into, and in our code, we can ensure that we never write outside of the bounds of the range.

Since C's I/O functions assume that strings are zero-terminated, we cannot use them with our new representation. But we can easily write our own, of course. I won't write many, but as an example, this function writes a string to standard output:

```
void print_substr(substr s)
{
  while (s.begin != s.end) {
    putchar(*s.begin++);
  }
}
```

We can create the two strings from Figure 8-1 and print them like this:

```
char buf[] = "foobarbaz";
substr string = as_substr(buf);
substr bar = slice(buf, 3, 6);

print_substr(string); printf("\n");
print_substr(bar); printf("\n");
```

If your substr ends at the zero terminal of an underlying C string, then you can, of course, still use functions like printf():

```
printf("my favorite string is \"%s\"\n",
       string.begin);
```

But if not, you would end up printing past the string and on to the next zero terminal—if there even is one, because we do not require that our substr objects point into a C string, only that they have an underlying char buffer.

You can, of course, copy a substring if you want to use it with printf():

```
char tmp[substr_len(bar) + 1];
substr_to_buf(tmp, bar);
printf("my second favorite string is \"%s\"\n",
       tmp);
```

Or, if the underlying buffer is not read-only (like a C literal string), you can insert a zero terminal before you write and restore the character there after. These two functions handle that:

```
char zero_term(substr s)
{
  char c = *s.end;
  *s.end = '\0';
  return c;
}

void restore_term(substr s, char c)
{
  *s.end = c;
}
```

and you can use them like this:

```
char c = zero_term(bar);
printf("%s\n", bar.begin);
restore_term(bar, c);
```

In this example, it works because we used a char array as the underlying buffer. If we had used a literal string for buf earlier, the behavior would be undefined.

In the remainder of the chapter, we will not concern ourselves with converting to and from C's strings and our substr objects. We will explore how to write our own string library—or at least a toy version of one—and we can always write code for dealing with conversion or I/O as needed.

Basic Operations

As warm-up exercises, we can implement a few simple string operations. We have implemented reversal a couple of times so far in the book, so we can start there. It is a familiar function, and nothing much changes when we are reversing substr objects:

```
void substr_rev(substr s)
{
  if (empty_substr(s)) return;
  char * restrict x = s.begin;
  char * restrict y = s.end - 1;
  for (; x < y; x++, y--) {
    char c = *x; *x = *y; *y = c; // swap
  }
}
```

If begin and end point to the same location, y would end up pointing one before y, so we would never enter the for-loop, and all would work as intended. However, subtracting 1 from begin is only guaranteed to give us a valid pointer if that location is within the allocated memory we are working with. It is *highly* unlikely that this could ever be a problem—I cannot imagine which architecture we would have to work on— but to be completely standard compliant, we shouldn't subtract one from a pointer that could point to the beginning of the buffer. It is trivial to avoid the situation, so that is why we have the empty_substr() test at the beginning of the function.

If the string isn't empty, we get a pointer to the first element, x, and a pointer to the last element, y. The last element lies one before end because our data structure says that end should point one past the last character. While we reverse, the two pointers point into the same buffer, but they should not point at the same characters (except where they meet in the middle where it doesn't matter). So we can declare the pointers restrict. It doesn't give us any compiler optimization in this function, because we only fetch a value from each once before we move the pointers. Still, when a pointer is not supposed to be able to read a value written to through another, we might as well declare that. In the future, we might change the ctual fetches, and then there could be optimization benefits. If in the future, it goes the other way, and we need the pointers to access overlapping data, we can always remove restrict again. Here, it works mostly like a comment to the programmer that the data doesn't overlap.

Other than that, the reversal function works the way we have seen before. We move x upward and y downward, swapping chars as we go along, and we stop when they meet at the middle of the string.

A similarly simple operation is swapping two substrings. They could be from the same buffer or from different buffers, but we will require that they do not overlap if they are in the same buffer. It is not well defined what it would mean to swap strings that overlap unless the overlapping part is identical in the two. So we will only swap non-overlapping strings. The code for that is simple, bordering on the trivial:

```
void swap_substr(substr x, substr y)
  char * restrict p = x.begin;
  char * restrict q = y.begin;
  for (; p != x.end && q != y.end; p++, q++) {
    char c = *p; *p = *q; *q = c; // swap
  }
}
```

For a proper swap with this function, the two substrings should have the same length. Otherwise, only parts of the longer string are moved. That check is also something we leave to the caller, but we still make sure that we do not write outside of either substring. We wouldn't want buffer overflow, even if the caller didn't check if the swap was appropriate. When we have all the necessary information to avoid buffer overflow, which we do with our representation, unlike C's plain buffers, then we should use it to write defensive code.

A more useful function than those earlier is a general copy function. Here, we should also consider if substrings can overlap. The strcpy() function says that it is undefined what happens if the input and output overlap, so the function we wrote in Chapter 7 implicitly assumed that they didn't. It would work if the strings overlap but the destination was at a lower address than the source, but it would fail if it was the other way around. We can do better than that.

The issue is that if the source and the destination of a copy overlap, then we risk overwriting part of the source before we copy it. Consider Figure 8-2 where we have overlapping strings x and y. If we want to write x into y, and we start from the left, we first copy f into the first position in y. That is the first letter in the overlapping range, however, and now the b in bar is gone. When we reach it in the copy, we will have replaced bar with foo, and we will end up with y being foofoo. However, if we started from the right instead, we would have written bar into the non-overlapping part of y before we got to the overlap, and we would end up with the correct foobar. If we copied in the other direction instead, from y to x, then copying from the left would work—we would have copied the overlapping bar into the beginning of x before we started writing in it, but now copying from the right doesn't work. We have to choose the direction of the copy based on where the two substrings sit if they overlap. If the destination sits to the left, then we can copy from the left, but if it sits to the right, then we must copy from the right.

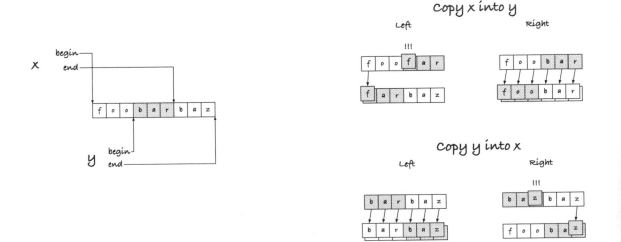

Figure 8-2. *Copying overlapping substrings*

We shouldn't copy a longer string into a shorter one. We risk writing outside of the buffer that way. Our data structure tells us that we can write to the end of a substring, but we do not know if there is any valid memory to write to beyond it. However, there is nothing wrong with writing a shorter string into a longer. That is often useful, for example, if we wish to concatenate several strings. So we will write as much as we can from the source string into the destination, stopping if we reach the destination end. If we finish copying before we reach the end of the destination, we want the caller to know how much we wrote. We can do this, among other ways, by returning a new substr that begins at the next free character in the destination string and goes to the end of the destination.

Such a copy function can look like this:

```c
#define MIN(a,b) (((a)<(b)) ? (a) : (b))

substr copy_substr(substr to, substr from)
{
  size_t n = MIN(substr_len(to), substr_len(from));
  // copy right cannot handle empty strings,
  // so bail out here
  if (n == 0) return to;

  if (to.begin < from.begin) { // copy left
      char * restrict y = to.begin;
      char * restrict x = from.begin,
           * xend = from.begin + n;
      while (x < xend) {
        *y++ = *x++;
      }
  } else { // copy right
    char * restrict y = to.begin + n;
    char * restrict x = from.begin + n,
         * xbeg = from.begin;
    do {
      *(--y) = *(--x);
    } while (x > xbeg);
  }

  return SUBSTR(to.begin + n, to.end);
}
```

We take the shortest string length to compute the actual intervals we should work with. It is the easiest way to place the pointers before we copy in both directions. When we copy from the right, we decrement and assign before we test if we have reached the beginning of the interval. Intervals are asymmetric when it comes to the beginning and end because the end pointer refers to the address one past the last character, while the beginning points to the first character. Because of the difference, the code for copying from the right doesn't work if we start with an empty string, so we explicitly bail out at the beginning if this is the case.

We use the two `begin` pointers to determine if we should copy from the left or from the right. We don't test if they actually overlap, because we can copy them either way. Technically, it is undefined behavior to compare the `begin` pointers if they are not pointing into the same allocated buffer. Still, if they don't, then they don't overlap, and then we do not care about the result of the comparison—the copying will still work, regardless of the test.

For comparing strings, we can also write our own function. In fact, we must, because C's `strcmp()` will only work on zero-terminated strings. It is fairly straightforward to implement `strcmp()`, because you just compare the strings character by character until you see a difference, breaking out of the loop if you see a zero character. We can do almost the same with a `substr` string, but we have to handle the case where we make it through the entirety of one or both of the strings differently.

When we use zero-terminated strings, unless we are comparing two identical strings, we will eventually see a difference; if nothing else, we will see a zero character when we reach the end of one of them. If one string is a prefix of another, they are identical to that point, and the ordering on strings says that the shorter should be smaller. If we break when we see a character that differs between the two strings, we also catch that one is a prefix of another. We correctly identify the shorter as the lexicographically smaller string, because it is the one that has the zero character. With our new string representation, we can still determine the order when we see different characters, but otherwise we must continue until the end of the shortest string and then determine which of the two strings were the shorter. An implementation can look like this:

```
int substr_cmp(substr x, substr y)
{
  while (x.begin != x.end && y.begin != y.end) {
    if (*x.begin < *y.begin) return -1;
    if (*x.begin > *y.begin) return +1;
```

```
    x.begin++; y.begin++;
  }
  // We've reached the end of one of the substrings.
  // If they had the same length, they are equal,
  // otherwise, the shorter string is the smallest
  if (x.begin < x.end) return +1;   // x is longer
  if (y.begin < y.end) return -1; // y is longer
  return 0; // the strings are equal
}
```

We cannot directly use this function with a qsort(), because we have given it the same interface as strcmp(), but with a wrapper you can now sort substr objects:

```
#include <stdio.h>
#include <stdlib.h>
#include <string.h>
#include "substr.h"

int cmp_func(void const *x, void const *y)
{
  substr const *a = x;
  substr const *b = y;
  return substr_cmp(*a, *b);
}

int main(void)
{
  char const *x = "foobarbaz";
  int n = strlen(x);

  substr suffixes[n];
  for (int i = 0; i < n; ++i) {
    suffixes[i] = slice((char *)x, i, n);
  }
```

```
qsort(suffixes, n, sizeof *suffixes, cmp_func);
for (int i = 0; i < n; ++i) {
  print_substr(suffixes[i]); putchar('\n');
}

return 0;
}
```

In the program, assume that

```
#include "substr.h"
```

gives you the definition of the substr functions we have written.

We could go on for a while implementing functions that operate on our substr string representation, but before we continue, I think it is time to look at the iterator problem that motivated the new representation in the first place.

Revisiting Word Iterators

In Chapter 7, we used the function find_word():

```
char *find_word(char *x)
{
  while (*x && !isalpha(*x))
    x++;
  return x;
}
```

to find the first character in a word—or what we defined to be a word—and we used the function skip_word():

```
char *skip_word(char *x)
{
  while (*x && isalpha(*x))
    x++;
  return x;
}
```

to move to the first character past a word. We combined these two to give us an iterator that identified the positions in a string where a word occurred, but the iterator did not give us the actual word. We would need to combine the iterator with a call to skip_word() to get it. Now that we have a representation of strings where we can represent substrings, we can update the iterator to get the actual words.

Returning the word we find is simple. We can return a substr from the iterator function. We used the word we found as the iterator itself, searching for the next occurrence from the end of the previous, and we can do that again. To try something else, however, I will add an explicit iterator object this time. We initialize an iterator object before we loop through the words, and we repeatedly call the function that gives us the next word with the same iterator until we have exhausted the words in the string. We will still search for the next word from the end of the previous—or from the beginning of the string for the first word—but with the explicit iterator, we separate the responsibility of the token we return from the responsibility of iterating. It also gives us a place to save information about the full string, so we stop iterating before we move outside of the buffer. The word we return from the iterator only contains the substring containing the word, so we need the extra information for iterating in any case.

The iterator object doesn't have to be complicated. We are searching for the first/next occurrence in a substr, so a natural representation is simply a substr. We will define a separate type for iterators, however, to make the intent of such objects clear.

```
typedef substr substr_iter;
```

An iterator function should take an iterator object, find the next occurrence, return it, and update the iterator, so it is ready for the next call. Because we must update the iterator, we pass it by reference, that is, as a pointer. To indicate that there are no more words to iterate over, we must return a special object that we can recognize as meaning this, and we were foresighted enough to define such an object. If we return NULL_SUBSTR, a substr where begin is a NULL pointer, then we have signalled that no more words are coming.

The word iterator looks like this:

```
substr next_word(substr_iter *iter)
{
  char *begin = find_word(iter->begin);
  if (*begin == '\0') {
    // no more words
```

```
    return NULL_SUBSTR;
  }
  char *end = skip_word(begin);
  iter->begin = end;
  return SUBSTR(begin, end);
}
```

The iterator contains the interval we should search in, so we search for the beginning of a word with find_word() starting at iter->begin. If we do not find a word, then we should stop iterating, so we return NULL_SUBSTR. Otherwise, we find where the word ends; the search starts from the beginning of the identified word, and we return what we find as a substr.

You can use the iterator like this (where you get the relevant functions from the substr.h header):

```
#include <stdio.h>
#include "substr.h"

int main(void)
{
  char const *x = "\tfoo    bar123baz\nqux321";
  substr_iter iter = as_substr((char *)x);
  for (substr word = next_word(&iter);
       !null_substr(word);
       word = next_word(&iter)) {

    print_substr(word); printf("\n");
  }

  return 0;
}
```

It will print

```
foo
bar
baz
qux
```

We start with setting the iterator to the entire string, then we repeatedly call next_ word(&iter) (pass by reference) until we see a null substring.

We can also rewrite our function from Chapter 7 for copying words to using the word iterator. Then we need to combine it with the copy_substr() function from the previous section. We can iterate through a string and get all the words, and then we must copy them into the destination string. The copy function returns a substr containing the remainder of the string we have copied into, so we can repeatedly copy to it. If we have implemented copy_substr() correctly, and I think we have, then we do not need to worry about buffer overflow or such when we use it. We can keep writing to the output string, even when we have filled it completely, because copy_substr() will not write beyond the bounds of its input, which in that case will be an empty string. We do not need any checks for how far we have written; we can keep writing words as long as we get some from the iterator.

We need to separate the words in the output with space. This is also easy to handle with a working copy_substr(). If we have a separator substr, we can safely write it to the output string between the words. There is a special case with either the first or the last word. If we write a separator after each word, we have written one too many when we are done, because we shouldn't write it after the last word. We could go back one character after the loop, but then we must be sure that we have entered the loop, to begin with; we don't want to remove a character if we never wrote any words. Similarly, if we write a separator before each word, we have written one too many before the first. An easy solution is to change the separator along the way. We start with an empty string, which we can safely write before the first word, and after the first word, we change it to a space. That solution looks like this:

```
substr copy_words(substr to, substr from)
{
  // remember where we started
  char *begin = to.begin;

  // sep is used to put spaces between
  // words but not before the first word
  substr sep = as_substr("");
  // empty string substr_iter iter = from;

  for (substr word = next_word(&iter);
       !null_substr(word);
```

```
      word = next_word(&iter)) {
    to = copy_substr(to, sep);
    to = copy_substr(to, word);

    // after the first iteration, sep should always
    // be space
    sep = as_substr(" ");
  }

  return SUBSTR(begin, to.begin);
}
```

At the beginning of the function, we remember where the output string started. We want to return the string that contains all the words, but to in the function moves every time we write to it. When we are done with the iterator, `to.begin` points to the first character after the words, so we want to return the substring that goes from the original beginning to that position.

If you want a compacting version, you can do what we did in the previous chapter and call `copy_words()` with the same string as input and output.

```
substr compact_words(substr s)
{
  return copy_words(s, s);
}
```

As we copy words, we do not modify any part of the input that we need to read later, so this is safe.

Other iterators are equally simple to implement. Let us not repeat the code with an iterator that finds integers again, but try something new. How about an iterator that finds all occurrences of a string?

We can search for the first occurrence of one string in another like this:

```
substr find_occurrence(substr x, substr y)
{
  int n = substr_len(x);
  int m = substr_len(y);
  if (m > n) return NULL_SUBSTR;
    char *s = x.begin, *end = x.end - m;
```

```
  for (; s < end; s++) {
    if (strncmp(s, y.begin, m) == 0) {
      return SUBSTR(s, s + m);
    }
  }
  return NULL_SUBSTR;
}
```

The function searches for an occurrence of y in the string x. First, we get the length of the strings, n for x and m for y. If the string we are searching for is longer than the string we search in, we cannot find an occurrence, so we return the null substring to indicate that. Otherwise, the address x.end - m is no further left than x.begin, so we are allowed to point there, and it is the last position where we could potentially have a match—to the right of that position, y is too long to match.

From here on, we go position by position and compare the string we point to with s to the substring in y. We use the standard library's strncmp() function. It compares the strings character by character, but only up to m characters, so not beyond the bounds of the shorter string. This is not the fastest way to search for a string, but it is fast enough for our purposes here, and I will refer you to books on string algorithms for better approaches.

If we locate a match, then s points to the beginning of the match, and we know that the match is m characters long, so we return SUBSTR(s, s + m). If we do not find a match in the loop, we return a null substring to indicate that.

For the iterator, we must first search for an occurrence. If we find one, we should update the iterator. Here, we have a choice between an iterator over all occurrences or over only the non-overlapping occurrences. If we want to find all occurrences, we should move the iterator to one past the occurrence we just found. If we only want non-overlapping occurrences, we should move the iterator to the end of the occurrence we just found. We can make this choice an option for the iterator.

```
substr next_occurrence(substr_iter *iter,
                       substr s,
                       int overlaps)
{
  substr occ = find_occurrence(*iter, s);
  if (!null_substr(occ)) {
```

```
    iter->begin = overlaps ? occ.begin + 1 : occ.end;
  }
  return occ;
}
```

In the following example program, the first search that doesn't include overlapping matches will report matches at index 0 and 4, but the one that includes overlaps will also include matches at index 2 and 6.

```
#include <stdio.h>
#include "substr.h"

int main(void)
{
  substr x = as_substr("xaxaxaxaxaxa");
  substr y = as_substr("xaxa");
  substr_iter iter = x;
  printf("searching for %s in %s\n", y.begin, x.begin);
  for (substr occ = next_occurrence(&iter, y, 0);
       !null_substr(occ);
       occ = next_occurrence(&iter, y, 0)) {
    printf("Found an occurrence at index %d\n",
           (int)(occ.begin - x.begin));
  }

  iter = x;
  printf("searching for %s in %s\n", y.begin, x.begin);
  for (substr occ = next_occurrence(&iter, y, 1);
       !null_substr(occ);
       occ = next_occurrence(&iter, y, 1)) {
    printf("Found an occurrence at index %d\n",
           (int)(occ.begin - x.begin));
  }

  return 0;
}
```

The occurrence itself, as returned by the iterator, is not interesting as a substring. We know what we are searching for, and if we get anything but the null substring, we get that string back. But we can use the pointers in the substr object to identify the locations where we have matches.

Replacing Strings

To finish the chapter, we will look at one more operation, and two related functions, that will illustrate a problem with our current string representation and act as motivation for the following chapter, where we get to allocate memory from the heap. We will look at replacing one substring with another and then deleting and inserting substrings as special cases of that.

If we have a string, z, containing a substring x (that we require that the caller ensures is contained in z), and we want to replace x with another string, y, then an easy case is if we can write the result to another string, out. This is a simple matter of copying substrings. First, we copy the part of z that comes before x into out, then we copy y, and then we copy the bit that comes after x in z. We can return the substring of out that we wrote to. See Figure 8-3.

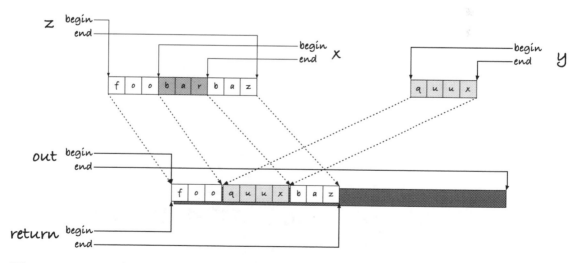

Figure 8-3. *Replacing one substring with another*

For this to work, we also have to require that y isn't contained in the part of out that we write to before we copy y. That is also something we leave to the caller to ensure. If we do all the copying with copy_substr(), then we do not need to worry about writing outside of the bounds of out. In this implementation

```
substr replace_substr(substr out,
                      substr z, substr x,
                      substr y)
{
  substr tmp = out;
  tmp = copy_substr(tmp, SUBSTR(z.begin, x.begin));
  tmp = copy_substr(tmp, y);
  tmp = copy_substr(tmp, SUBSTR(x.end, z.end));
  return SUBSTR(out.begin, tmp.begin);
}
```

we use a temporary substr, tmp, for copying. It starts out as the full out string, and since we assign each copy to it, its begin moves forward for each copy. After we have copied the last bit of z, its begin points at the first character after the last character we copied, so it should be the end of the substr that we return.

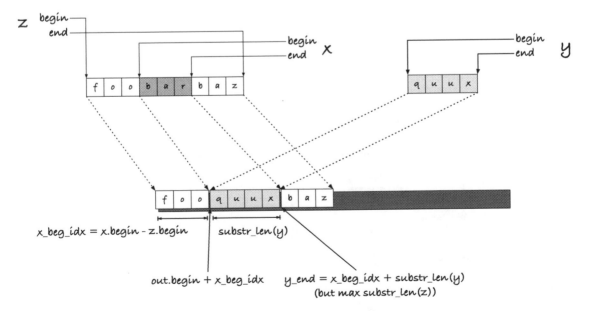

Figure 8-4. *Replacement capable of handling in-place substitution*

If you call this function with z equal to out (or just contained in the first part of out), the function might fail. If the replacement string y is longer than x, we would overwrite the last part of z before we copied it. We can fix this by copying the part of z to the right of x before we copy in y. It just requires a little bit of calculation to work out the indices that this string should be copied to. We can work out the offset into out that x would sit at if we didn't remove it; it is the distance from the beginning of z and to x, so x.begin - z.begin. That is where y will be inserted. To that, we must add the length of y to get where the remainder of z should be copied. If y is too long, blindly adding the length might give us a pointer outside of out, so we must use the minimum of that index and the end of out. See Figure 8-4 for where the offsets will sit.

In code, we can create substrings for the three substrings to copy, z up to x, z after x, and y (which we already have). Using the calculations we just did, we can similarly compute the destinations for the three strings. After that, we copy, remembering to copy y after we have moved the last part of z. We don't need to remember the substrings we get in return from the substr_copy() calls, except the begin pointer when we move the last substring of z. We need that for the return value, which should still use this pointer as its end value.

```
substr replace_substr(substr out,
                      substr z, substr x,
                      substr y)
{
  substr z_before    = SUBSTR(z.begin, x.begin);
  substr z_after     = SUBSTR(x.end, z.end);

  size_t ylen        = substr_len(y);
  size_t outlen      = substr_len(out);
  size_t x_beg_idx   = x.begin - z.begin;
  size_t y_end_idx   = MIN(x_beg_idx + ylen, outlen);
  substr out_before  = SUBSTR(out.begin, out.begin + x_beg_idx);
  substr out_after   = SUBSTR(out.begin + y_end_idx, out.end);
  substr out_y       = SUBSTR(out.begin + x_beg_idx,
                             out.begin + y_end_idx);
```

```
  copy_substr(out_before, z_before);
  char *ret_end = copy_substr(out_after, z_after).begin;
  copy_substr(out_y, y);

  return SUBSTR(out.begin, ret_end);
}
```

If you know that you *are* doing an in-place replacement, rather than just allowing for one, you can simplify the code slightly. You don't need to copy the first part of z—it is already where it is supposed to be—and you can avoid computing some of the offsets because you have them as pointers from x already. It is not a lot you save, though.

```
substr replace_substr_inplace(substr z, substr x,
                              substr y)
{
  size_t zlen = substr_len(z);
  size_t ylen = substr_len(y);
  size_t x_beg_idx = x.begin - z.begin;
  size_t y_end_idx = MIN(x_beg_idx + ylen, zlen);
  char *y_end = z.begin + y_end_idx;

  substr in_after  = SUBSTR(x.end, z.end);
  substr out_after = SUBSTR(y_end, z.end);
  substr out_y     = SUBSTR(x.begin, y_end);

  char *ret_end = copy_substr(out_after, in_after).begin;
  copy_substr(out_y, y);

  return SUBSTR(z.begin, ret_end);
}
```

If you can replace a string, then you can also delete it. You can replace it with an empty string:

```
substr delete_substr(substr out, substr x, substr y)
{
  return replace_substr(out, x, y, as_substr(""));
}
```

```
substr delete_substr_inplace(substr x, substr y)
{
  return replace_substr_inplace(x, y, as_substr(""));
}
```

Again, here it will be up to the caller to ensure that the string, y, is contained in x.

You can also insert strings. Here, we need an index into the original string, and we will demand that the caller ensures that it is a valid index. We can `assert()` it in the code, but that assertion is only tested if the code is compiled with the assertion flag enabled, and it will crash the program if the requirement isn't met, so it doesn't change the contract with the caller.

Usually, a valid index into a string has to be between zero and the length of the string, the latter not included. That is where there is a valid character. When we insert, however, we might want to append to a string, so we should also allow an index that points one past the end of the string.

```
substr insert_substr(substr out, substr x, size_t index, substr y)

{
  assert(index <= substr_len(x));
  char *p = x.begin + index;
  return replace_substr(out, x, SUBSTR(p, p), y);
}
```

For the in-place version, it doesn't make sense to make the index point past the string (but we can allow it to point one past just for consistency). The string will not be added, because it would have to go beyond the bounds of the string we insert into, and we cannot do that with our current framework.

```
substr insert_substr_inplace(substr x, size_t index, substr y)

{
  assert(index <= substr_len(x));
  char *p = x.begin + index;
  return replace_substr_inplace(x, SUBSTR(p, p), y);
}
```

There is the general pattern with our modification functions: when we make the resulting string shorter—we delete a string or replace a string with a shorter string—then we get what we want. If we make the string longer, then we might get the full result if we write to a larger buffer, but otherwise we lose characters that fall off to the right when we copy.

We have to implement the functions this way because we are bounded by the buffers they get as input. We cannot create larger buffers inside the functions to contain the result, because the memory we allocate that way goes on the stack, and it will be deallocated as soon as the functions return. To move beyond that limitation, we must allocate memory on the heap, and that is the topic for the next chapter.

CHAPTER 9

Dynamic Memory Management

So far, we have managed to write programs that only use global and local variables. In C-speak, these are called *static* and *automatic* memory allocation, and static memory allocation lasts the lifetime of the program. In contrast, automatic variables are deleted when you return from the function you defined them in. In practice, automatic means stack allocated, although the C standard doesn't require there to be a stack. The third type of memory is *dynamic* memory, which is the memory you allocate on the heap in the idealized memory model we saw in Chapter 2. This is the memory you explicitly have to ask to get allocated, and you are also responsible for freeing it again once you are done with it. The concept is simple; the functions you use to allocate and free memory are simple, but do not let that trick you. Keeping track of allocated memory is far from easy. If you forget to free memory you are no longer using, your programming is leaking memory, and if it goes on too long, you run out, and your program will likely crash. If you free memory that you still use, you are in the same situation as if you have a pointer to a stack-allocated object that is no longer live. You access it at your peril.

© Thomas Mailund 2021
T. Mailund, *Pointers in C Programming*, https://doi.org/10.1007/978-1-4842-6927-5_9

Only in the most straightforward programs is it easy to track how allocated memory moves through the code, and it would stress my credulity to believe that any large system written in C is entirely free of dynamic memory–related errors. When you work with dynamic memory, you must be constantly vigilant to ensure that when you allocate memory, it will be freed at a later point, and not too soon. It is not an easy task, and even the best programmers fail. There is a reason that most high-level programming languages do not let the programmer allocate and deallocate memory in this way, but deal with memory management through automatic garbage collection. That is not something we have in C,[1] so we must structure our programs in ways that make it easier to handle ourselves.

In this chapter, I will describe the four functions you get from C for dynamic memory management, and I will show you their use in three examples. Then in Chapters 11 to 12, you will see how we use memory management to implement data structures, and in Chapters 16 and 15, I will show two techniques that alleviate the trouble of memory management slightly.

Functions for Dynamic Memory Allocation

Your platform likely has several functions for allocating memory, most operating systems do, but the C standard only has four since the C11 standard and three before then. They all give you a block of memory if they can allocate it, and a NULL pointer if they cannot, and you are then responsible for freeing that memory later. There is a single function for freeing memory that handles deallocation for all three of the allocation functions.

malloc()

The malloc() function is the simplest of the allocation functions. It takes a single argument, which is the size of the block you want to allocate, and it returns a newly allocated memory block of that size. You can use sizeof() to get the correct size of the memory block you want. The return type is void *, and you do not need to explicitly cast it to another type. You can assign a void pointer to any other data pointer type without cast.

---

[1]There are third-party garbage collectors for C; see, e.g., www.hboehm.info/gc/. It is not part of the standard, though, so we won't discuss them here.

For example, if we allocate a block of size `sizeof(int)`, we get a block of memory large enough to hold an integer:

```
int *ip = malloc(sizeof(int));
```

If we use `sizeof(double)`, we get a block that can hold a `double`:

```
double *dp = malloc(sizeof(double));
```

or if we want a block to hold a `struct`, we can use `sizeof()` of the `struct`'s type:

```
struct S { int i; double d; };
struct S *sp = malloc(sizeof(struct S));
```

If you use the `sizeof()` a type to allocate memory, however, you need to be careful if you change the type of an object later. Since `malloc()` doesn't know or care about types, it only cares about sizes, it will give you a block of memory of the size you specify. If you change the type of a variable, but forget to change the type in the call to `malloc()`, you might get the wrong size of memory. An idiom to avoid this problem is to use a variable to get the size. If you have a pointer of type `T *`, and you want to allocate memory to hold an object of type `T`, then you can do this:

```
T *p = malloc(sizeof *p);
```

Don't worry about dereferencing p here. You are not going to look at any memory you are not supposed to. The variable p doesn't even exist in this code; we are still in the process of defining it. The `sizeof` operator gets the type from p, so it gets the size of what p is a pointer to, and that is all. Now, regardless of how you change the type for p, you get a memory block that can hold the type it points at.

Size is one thing, of course, but it is not all when it comes to storing objects. We discussed alignment in Chapter 2, and that is also relevant for using memory addresses to store values. However, `malloc()` is guaranteed to give you an address where *all* types can be aligned. If you get a memory address from `malloc()`, then you can place any object there that can fit into that memory block. The functions `calloc()` and `realloc()` described later give you the same guarantee, while `aligned_alloc()` takes an argument that specifies how the allocated memory should be aligned.

If you want to allocate an array, you need to explicitly calculate the size of the array. That, however, is simple: you multiply the size of one element with the number of elements you want. To get an integer array of length 10, you could allocate memory like this:

```
int *arr = malloc(10 * sizeof *arr);
```

What you get is a pointer to the first element in the memory block and not an array as such. You can use the memory the way you use an array argument to a function; think of it as an array that has degraded to a pointer. You cannot get an actual array; you only get those by defining them, and then you cannot assign to them. Except for the type, however, there is no difference. You have the same information and guarantees about an array allocated this way, as you do for a function argument array.

If malloc() cannot allocate the memory you want, for example, if there isn't sufficient memory in the process' memory space (or for whatever other reasons), it will return a NULL pointer. For example, if we try to allocate a block of size SIZE_MAX, a macro defined in <stdlib.h> that specifies the largest size an object can have, then we will probably not succeed.

```
char *x = malloc(SIZE_MAX);
if (x) {
  printf("success???\n");
} else {
  printf("couldn't allocate %zu bytes.\n", SIZE_MAX);
}
```

We should always check the return value of the allocation functions before we use the address they return. We will always get all or nothing, but we need to check if we succeeded before we continue our program under the assumption that all went well.

The memory you have allocated with malloc(), or any of the other allocation functions described in this section, should be freed again. You do that with the function free() described later. If you allocate, you free

```
int *ip = malloc(sizeof(int));
// use ip for what you need it for
free(ip);
```

It is implementation dependent what happens if you call malloc() with size zero. You either get a NULL pointer in return or get a minimal allocated object (that you cannot do anything with, without entering undefined behavior). But you are allowed to do it, and you do get a pointer back—just not a pointer you can do anything with. If it isn't a NULL pointer, however, you must still free() it.

calloc()

Like malloc(), calloc() gives you a new chunk of memory, but the functions differ in two ways. Whereas malloc() takes one argument, the size of the memory block you want, calloc() takes two arguments, the size of the elements you want to allocate plus how many elements you want. So, to allocate an array of 10 integers and an array of 20 doubles, you could write

```
int *ip = calloc(10, sizeof *ip);
double *dp = calloc(20, sizeof *dp);
```

Remember to free the memory after use.

```
free(ip);
free(dp);
```

With calloc(), you can avoid some overflow issues when allocating arrays. If you want to allocate an array of n elements of type T, you need to allocate n * sizeof(T) memory. But n * sizeof(T) might be larger than SIZE_MAX. With malloc(), you need to check if this is a problem yourself because malloc() only sees the argument you give it, and by that point, you already have an overflow. You need to check before you call malloc().

```
if (SIZE_MAX / sizeof(T) < n) {
  // not enough memory
}
```

With calloc(), you give the function n and sizeof(T), and it will check for overflow. If there is one, you get a NULL pointer back, the same as if allocation failed.

Of course, this isn't as helpful as it might sound because you still have a logical error in your program that you need to deal with if you want to allocate more space than what is possible. Still, it is better to get an explicit error, a NULL pointer, than a subtle overflow that can hide for a very long time.

The alignment guarantees you get from `calloc()` are the same as for `malloc()`. You can put any element at the first address, and if you use it as an array, the way `sizeof()` works guarantees you that you can do that as well for both allocation functions. That `calloc()` works with a number of elements, and the size of each element, doesn't mean that it works differently if you use it to allocate an array. The two functions behave the same.

The second way in which `malloc()` and `calloc()` differ is in memory initialization. The memory that `malloc()` gives you is not initialized. You can make no assumptions about what the memory contains; you get undefined behavior if you read it before you have written to it. With `calloc()`, you get memory that is initialized to all zero-bits. There are times when this is useful, but be careful. All zero bits might not mean what you think it means. The C standard guarantees you that for integral types, integers and characters basically, all zero bits mean zero (or *a* zero; integers are allowed to have both positive and negative zero). If you want an array of an integral type, then you get an array that is initialized to zero. If you want an array of `double` that is initialized to zero, or if you want an array of pointers initialized as NULL pointers, then you are out of luck. A zero double, or a NULL pointer, *might* be represented as all zero bits, but you are not given such a guarantee by the C standard. It might be the case on the computer you write your program, but not on the server or embedded device it will run on in two years. In most cases, if you want an initialized array, you have to initialize it yourself, and then you can save some time by getting the memory from `malloc()` instead of letting `calloc()` set the memory to zero first.

Suppose you do have an integral type, and you want it initialized to zero. In that case, there can be some advantages to using `calloc()` over getting memory with `malloc()` and then initializing it with `memset()` or a similar function. The underlying operating system might provide a `calloc()` function that doesn't give you the initialized memory right away, but allocates the virtual memory for it. Then it can map that virtual memory to actual memory that is set to zero. As long as you read from memory, all the elements in the array are seen as zero.

When you write, you get a real chunk of memory for parts of the array, and you can change that, while most of the zero entries still map to the same real memory. This, however, is not something that the C standard gives any promises about, but it is a frequent implementation.

I rarely find `calloc()` useful because I rarely want to allocate integral arrays initialized to zero, and it is the only case where I can see any benefit to it. If I need to allocate memory that I need to initialize myself anyway, I prefer to use malloc() and save the extra initialization time. If there is a risk of overflow in the size of the block I have to allocate, I prefer to check that up front and deal with it rather than treat it as an allocation error. If I cannot treat it in any better way, I can always default to the handling I would do if I got a NULL pointer back from the malloc() call.

   If you do not want to handle overflow separately from allocation errors, you can use these macros:

```
#define size_check(n,type)                   \
  ((SIZE_MAX / sizeof(type)) >= (n))
#define checked_malloc(n,type)               \
  (size_check((n),(type)) ?                  \
    malloc((n) * sizeof(type)) : 0)
```

   Then, to allocate an array of n elements of type T:

```
T *p = malloc(n * sizeof *p);
```

   you can use

```
T *p = checked_malloc(n, *p);
```

realloc()

If you need to resize a chunk of memory that you have allocated using one of the other functions, then you go to realloc(). You call it with two arguments, a pointer to the memory you want to resize and the new size you want. For example, if you have an integer array with 10 elements:

```
int *ip = malloc(10 * sizeof *ip);
if (!ip) {
  // handle error
}
```

and you want to grow it to 100 elements, you can use realloc() like this:

```
int *new_ip = realloc(ip, 100 * sizeof *new_ip);
if (!new_ip) {
  // handle error
```

```
}
ip = new_ip;
```

You can use `realloc()` both to grow and shrink memory, so you can go down to 25 elements again later with

```
new_ip = realloc(ip, 25 * sizeof *new_ip);
if (!new_ip) {
  // handle error
}
ip = new_ip;
```

Three different things can happen with a call to `realloc()`, and one of them is the reason I didn't write

```
ip = realloc(ip, 25 * sizeof *new_ip);
```

even though we end up assigning the new memory to the `ip` pointer. In the case that `realloc()` cannot allocate the required memory, it returns a NULL pointer, but it does not free its first argument. If we assigned the call directly to `ip`, we would no longer have a reference to the memory it pointed at, and we would have a memory leak. This mistake is so common that some systems have a `reallocf()` function that does free the first argument in case of an allocation failure, but that function is not part of the C standard. If you use `realloc()`, test the return value before you assign it to the pointer you are resizing.

That was the behavior with failure. If the function succeeds, there are two cases: it managed to extend the memory you already had, or it needed to allocate memory elsewhere. Maybe there is unused memory after the block you already have, and in that case, `realloc()` will give you permission to use it and return the pointer you gave it. If there isn't, then `realloc()` will allocate a new block of memory of the desired size, copy the data you already have to the new block, free the old block, and give you a pointer to the new memory address.

It corresponds roughly to this, except that there is error handling:

```
// ip = realloc(ip, new_size)
new_ip = malloc(new_size);
memmove(new_ip, ip, old_size);
free(ip);
```

```
ip = new_ip;
```

The runtime system knows how large allocated objects are, so `realloc()` will know how much memory to copy.

You shouldn't implement reallocation yourself in this way, of course. You get it for free with `realloc()`, and if `realloc()` can allocate more memory at the location you already have, you can save the copying.

If `realloc()` succeeds, you should never deallocate the old pointer you gave it as an argument. It is either the same as the memory you got back from the call, or it was freed in the call. Assign it to the old pointer if you want, but do not call `free()` on the old pointer. If it was already freed, you are not allowed to do it.

```
new_ip = realloc(ip, new_size);
free(ip); // BIG NO NO!!!
```

The usual pattern is to check the return value and then write it to the old pointer:

```
new_ip = realloc(ip, new_size);
if (!new_ip) { /* handle error */ }
ip = new_ip; // now ip has the new memory chunk
```

If you do this, then you shouldn't free the temporary variable `new_ip`. That would also free the memory that `ip` points to, and you don't want to do that prematurely.

If the first argument to `realloc()` is a NULL pointer, the function works the same as `malloc()`, and you get a memory allocation of the given size or a NULL pointer if the allocation failed.

If you want to check the allocation size before you call `realloc()`, and not consider an overflow different from an allocation error, you can use a macro similar to the one for `malloc()`:

```
#define checked_realloc(p,n,type)         \
  (size_check((n),(type)) ?               \
    realloc((p), (n) * sizeof(type)) : 0)
```

You are allowed to call `realloc()` with size zero, `realloc(p,0)`, but you should *never* do so. The problem is that the standard is unclear on what will happen. In the C89 standard, such a call would free the memory pointed to by p, and that was clear enough. With C99, however, that requirement was removed. If you call `realloc(p,0)`, it is allowed to return a value pointer the way `malloc(0)` does—either a NULL pointer or a valid pointer you can free(), which indicates zero bytes. But what happens to the data that p points to? If realloc() returns NULL because of an error, it hasn't deleted p, but if realloc() succeeds, it should free() the data. If you call realloc(p,0) and get NULL back, was it a failure, so p isn't freed, or was it a failure so it was? You don't know, and what happens depends on your runtime system and which standard it conforms to. If you free(p) because you got NULL, you might be freeing an object that was already deallocated, but if you don't, then you might leak memory. It is a mess, but a compromise in the current standard because different implementations already rely on different behavior. With all undefined behavior, though, you are best off avoiding it.

The preceding macro does not check if we attempt to allocate zero bytes. If you end up in that situation, you probably want to handle it differently than an allocation error. Most likely, you want to replace realloc(p,0) with something like

```
free(p);
p = 0;
```

or such, but this is not what the macro is intended for. It should allocate or indicate an allocation failure, not an allocation success for zero bytes.

aligned_alloc()

The aligned_alloc() function is a newcomer to the C standard, and it allows you to put alignment restrictions on allocated memory. It takes two arguments, the alignment information and the size of the memory you want to allocate. Except for the alignment information, it works like malloc(), so you have to free() memory you get from it.

```
int *ip = aligned_alloc(alignof(int), sizeof(*ip));
double *dp = aligned_alloc(alignof(double), sizeof(*dp));
// use pointers...

free(ip);
free(dp);
```

The alignment argument doesn't have to be the alignment requirement of the type you allocate for (but you are in trouble if it is more relaxed and you try to put something of that type there later). The size must be a multiple of the alignment, though.

Unless you are writing very specialized code, you do not need to use this function. The other allocation functions will give you memory where you can allocate *any* type of object, and this gives you memory where you can only place types that satisfy the alignment constraints. More memory addresses are open to `aligned_alloc()` because it doesn't have to give you memory available for all types, but it is unlikely to be worth it to try to optimize on this.

free()

If you allocate memory on the heap, you must free it again. Local variables go out of scope and are automatically deleted, global variables never are, but dynamic memory is something you must explicitly deallocate when you are done using it. The function the C standard gives you for that is `free()`. It takes one argument: a pointer to the memory you wish to free.

```
free(p);
```

Do not call `free()` with the same value twice (unless you accidentally got the same memory address back from a subsequent allocation). You should free memory once, and only once, and calling `free()` twice with the same address is undefined behavior.

Do not free memory that wasn't allocated with one of the four functions listed earlier unless your platform's documentation explicitly says that you can. Operating system–specific allocation functions will usually have their separate deallocation functions as well.

The standard says that you can call `free()` with a NULL pointer, and it will do nothing. Still, in much code, you see explicit tests for NULL before calling `free()`. This is mostly anachronism from old systems where `free()` didn't check for NULL. If you use a standard-compliant compiler and runtime system, then you can safely call `free()` with a NULL pointer.

A call to `free()` cannot fail, at least officially, so if it does, you are in deeper trouble than we can do anything about. You have to assume that once you call `free()`, you have deallocated the memory; you will not get a return value that tells you if you succeeded.

String Operations

Without memory allocation, we couldn't write functions that returned longer strings in Chapter 8. We could shorten strings, but the input buffers for our functions gave us an upper bound on how long the result of the operations could be. This was a problem when we tried to replace a shorter string with a longer. Now we have the functionality to deal with this, so let us try to write a new replace function.

All the functions will create new strings from input strings, and while we know that none of the input strings have a size greater than SIZE_MAX, we do not know that the new string won't have. To be good citizens when allocating memory, we should check that we do not have an overflow when we compute the size of the new buffer we allocate. Unfortunately, checking code, and often code that handles errors, tend to get as long as the code that does the actual job, so I prefer to hide it away a little. I will use these two macros to check if I can add a size to a variable without exceeding the limit, and if so, do it. Otherwise, I will jump to an error label to handle that. I know that goto has a bad reputation, but in some cases it is unjust. If used in a structured way, such as moving error handling code to somewhere else in your function, it makes the code cleaner and not harder to read. There isn't much error handling in the functions we write here—if we cannot allocate the memory we need, we will return a NULL pointer—but I use the goto anyway. If you prefer, replace goto error with return 0. The effect is the same. In a more complicated function, there is more error handling, and then the goto is a better choice.

The first macro tests if we can add a value, x, to var:

```
#define size_check_inc(var,x)        \
  { if (SIZE_MAX - (var) < (x))      \
      goto error;                    \
    (var) += (x);                    \
  }
```

The second checks if we can add a product. Here, of course, we cannot check if the product, x * y, exceeds the limit, because if it does, the damage is already done, so we need to divide by x and check if we then have room for y. If x is zero, we cannot divide by it, but in that case, there is room for the product; it is zero, after all, so we only jump to error handling mode if x is greater than zero, and there isn't room for the product.

```
#define size_check_inc_prod(var,x,y)              \
  { if ((x) > 0 &&                                \
        (SIZE_MAX - (var)) / (x) < (y))           \
      goto error;                                 \
    (var) += (x) * (y);                           \
  }
```

I will write a version that works on C's zero-terminated strings, but it is equally simple to write a function that works on the substr data structure from Chapter 8. You can try and modify with version to do that as an exercise.

The following function takes as input a string x and indices i and j that the caller is responsible for guaranteeing satisfy 0 <= i <= j < strlen(x). The substring of x from index i to (but not including) j should be replaced with the string y, and the function should return a new string as its result.

```
char *replace_string(char const *x, int i, int j, char const *y)
{
  size_t xlen = strlen(x);
  size_t ylen = strlen(y);
  size_t len = xlen - (j - i) + 1; // 1 for zero terminal
  size_check_inc(len, ylen);

  char *new_buf = malloc(len);
  if (!new_buf) goto error;

  strncpy(new_buf, x, i);
  strcpy(new_buf + i, y);
  strcpy(new_buf + i + ylen, x + j);

  return new_buf;

error:
  return 0;
}
```

The first task is to work out the length of the output—we need to know how much memory to allocate before we can do anything else. If x has length xlen, then x excluding the substring we remove has length xlen - (j - i). That is the part we get from x. On top of that, we get the characters in y, and if the length of y is ylen, the total length of the output is len = xlen - (j - i) + ylen + 1 where the last + 1 is to make room for the zero terminal as well. We start by setting len to xlen - (j - i) + 1. We know that this cannot exceed SIZE_MAX, assuming i and j are valid input, because x has at least that size. The buffer that holds x is xlen + 1 (xlen is the string length and x also has the zero terminal). We might not be able to add ylen to this, so this assignment we need to check. If it fails, we jump to error and return a NULL pointer.

Otherwise, we have the new length, and so we allocate a new buffer and jump to the error handling if the allocation failed. This again means that we return a NULL pointer to the caller. It would leave it up to the caller to deal with allocation errors—if we continued as if nothing had happened, the program would likely crash if tried to copy into a NULL pointer. It is undefined behavior, and we certainly do not want that. Better to let the caller handle it. If you have a way to let them know what went wrong, then the error handling location is where to do it. You could, for example, set the global variable errno to something appropriate. On UNIX-compliant systems, malloc() will set it to ENOMEM, but if it is a size overflow, ERANGE might be more appropriate. The latter is from the C standard and used to indicate that you have used a value outside the range of a type. Unfortunately, there is not much standard compliant you can do with general error handling. It is up to the platform you write your code for or conventions in your program. I am not doing anything with my error handling here, except returning NULL. That is good enough for this book; whether it is good enough for your programs, I leave to your discretion.

If the allocation was successful, we start copying. We need to copy the characters in x up to (but not including) index i. The string we replace starts at index i, so x[i] should not be copied. We cannot use strcpy() because x[i] is not necessarily the zero terminal, but strncpy() will do what we want. If we want to copy the characters up to index i, we want to copy i characters, so we copy i characters from x into new_buf. It is undefined behavior if we use strcpy() or strncpy() on overlapping strings, but since we are copying into a freshly allocated buffer, there is no risk of that. The next two copies are simple strcpy() calls. The y string is zero-terminated, and since x is zero-terminated, and j < xlen (the caller should guarantee this), x + j is a zero-terminated string.

Blindly copying with strcpy() opens up for buffer overflows, but we are in the fortunate position of having guaranteed that the buffer we write to can contain the string. When we used strlen() to compute the length of the strings, we got a guarantee that we would find a zero termination character in the strings. If the input strings are corrupted and strlen() was reading beyond allocated memory, that is a problem. Still, the length we got is the one we took into consideration when allocating new_buf, so if the allocation was successful, then we have space to write the characters that strcpy() sees, no matter what the strings look like. Of course, in a multithreaded environment, the strings can change between calling strlen() and strcpy(), and this is more likely to happen if the buffers are corrupted, but there is a limit to how much checking we can do in one function. The strings could also be deallocated between getting their length and copying them. Thread-safe code is beyond the scope of this book, and I will assume that our thread is the only one looking at these buffers. Then the function is safe.

When you call the function, you either get a NULL pointer in return, indicating an allocation error, or you get a freshly allocated string, which you must free() when you are done with it.

```
char const *x = "foobarbaz";
char *y = replace_string(x, 3, 6, "");
if (y) {
  assert(strcmp(y, "foobaz") == 0);
  free(y);
} else {
  // Handle allocation error
}
```

As we saw in Chapter 8, if we have a replace function, we can also get an insertion and deletion function for free:

```
char *insert_string(char const *x,
                    int i,
                    char const *y)
{
  return replace_string(x, i, i, y);
}

char *delete_string(char const *x, int i, int j)
```

```
{
  return replace_string(x, i, j, "");
}
```

For a more complicated example, consider a function that takes an array of strings as input and joins them into a single string with a separator between them. For example, with strings "foo", "bar", and "baz" and separator ":", we want the string "foo:bar:baz". Python's join() method on strings is the inspiration for this function. In code, we could use it like this:

```
char const *strings[] = {
  "foo", "bar", "baz"
};
size_t n = sizeof strings / sizeof *strings;
char *z = join_strings(":", n, strings);
if (!z) {
  perror("Error joining string");
  exit(1); // Just bail now...
}
printf("z = %s\n", z);
free(z);
```

The implementation looks like this, and I will describe it as follows:

```
char *join_strings(char const *sep,
                   int n, char const *strings[n])
{
  size_t len = 1; // 1 for zero terminal
  size_t sep_len = strlen(sep);
  size_t reps = (n > 1) ? (n - 1) : 0;
  size_check_inc_prod(len, sep_len, reps);

  for (int i = 0; i < n; i++) {
    size_t string_len = strlen(strings[i]);
    size_check_inc(len, string_len);
  }
```

```
  char *new_buf = malloc(len);
  if (!new_buf) goto error;

#define append_string(src) \
    { for (char const *p = src; *p; p++) *dst++ = *p; }
  char *dst = new_buf;
  char const *xsep = "";
  for (int i = 0; i < n; i++) {
    append_string(xsep);
    append_string(strings[i]);
    xsep = sep;
  }
  *dst = '\0';
#undef append_string

  return new_buf;

error:
  return 0;
}
```

As with the previous function, our first task is to work out how much memory we need to allocate. We need at least the memory it takes to store all the input strings, and then we need space for the separators. We compute the latter first because it is easier to know how much memory we have to work with when checking if we get a size overflow that way.

We start out with a length of one to store the terminal character. Then we get the length of the separator and how many of them we need. If there is more than one string, then we need (n - 1) repeats. We add seplen * reps to len if it doesn't cause an overflow. Then we start iterating through the strings. For each string, we check if we can add it without overflow, bailing to error if we can, of course, and if there is room, add it to the total length. Once we have computed the total length, then we can allocate a new buffer. If the allocation fails, we bail to error once more.

Then we copy all the strings and separators. We use the variable xsep to handle the special case of the first string. We write a separator before all strings—otherwise, we would have to deal with a special case with the last string—but the first time we write the separator, it is an empty string. After that, it is the function argument for the separator.

I use the macro

```
#define append_string(src) \
{ for (char const *p = src; *p; p++) *dst++ = *p; }
```

for copying into the new buffer. It copies src until it reaches the zero terminal, and it updates the dst pointer for each copy. We start with dst pointing to the first character in new_buf, and we will finish with it pointing at the last, where we insert the zero terminal. The macro is only relevant in this block of code, so I undefined it after all the copying. It refers to a variable inside the function, so it won't work elsewhere anyway. If you do not like using a macro like that, you can replace it with a function, but then you must update dst after the function call. If you use one of the string_copy() functions from Chapter 7 you could write

```
dst = string_copy(dst, src);
```

for each of the copies.

As a last example, we will implement a function that does a search and replace (and delete all occurrences if you replace a string with the empty string). We should be able to use it like this:

```
x = "foobarbazbax";
z = replace_all_occurrences(x, "ba", "");
if (z) {
  printf("z == %s\n", z); // foorzx
  free(z);
} else {
  perror("Error replacing occurrences");
}
```

We will use the string representation we implemented in Chapter 8 and the iterator we made for finding all occurrences of a string. The function is a little longer than the one earlier, but the flow of the code is much the same. First, we figure out how long the new string should be, and then we copy the bits of pieces to it. This is the code, and I will explain it as follows:

```
char *replace_all_occurrences(char const *z,
                              char const *x,
                              char const *y)
{
  substr ssz = as_substr((char *)z);
```

```
  substr ssx = as_substr((char *)x);
  substr ssy = as_substr((char *)y);
  size_t zlen = substr_len(ssz);
  size_t xlen = substr_len(ssx);
  size_t ylen = substr_len(ssy);

  // Compute the new string's length
  size_t len = zlen + 1; // + 1 for terminal
  substr_iter iter = ssz;
  for (substr occ = next_occurrence(&iter, ssx, 0);
       !null_substr(occ);
       occ = next_occurrence(&iter, ssx, 0)) {
    len -= xlen;
    size_check_inc(len, ylen);
  }
  char *new_buf = malloc(len);
  if (!new_buf) goto error;

#define copy_range(b, e) \
{ for (char const *p = (b); p != (e); p++) *dst++ = *p; }
  char const *src = z;
  char *dst = new_buf;
  iter = ssz;
  for (substr occ = next_occurrence(&iter, ssx, 0);
       !null_substr(occ);
       occ = next_occurrence(&iter, ssx, 0)) {
    copy_range(src, occ.begin);
    copy_range(ssy.begin, ssy.end);
    src = occ.end;
  }
  copy_range(src, z + zlen);
  *dst = '\0';
#undef copy_range

  return new_buf;

error:
  return 0;
}
```

We want to replace all occurrences of x in the string z with the string y. We will use the next_occurrence() iterator from Chapter 8, so we need a substr representation of both z and x for that. We won't necessarily need one for y, but if we copy substrings later, and substrings of z are represented as ranges, we might as well represent y as a range. So the first thing we do is get the range representations of the three strings.

Next, we get the length of the new string. We need to remove all the x occurrences and replace them with y, and since we only have the iterator to give us all the occurrences, we must iterate through it. At each step, we update the length of the output. We start with a length that is zlen plus one for the terminal zero; if there are no occurrences, then the return value should be a copy of z. It must be a copy because it should be a new string we know that we can free without interfering with z. But we do not know that we should return a copy yet because it depends on whether there are any occurrences. If there is an occurrence, then we should remove xlen characters and add ylen. Before we do this, however, we should check if we risk an overflow.

The natural thing might be to write

```
size_check_inc(len, ylen - xlen);
```

here because it is the difference between ylen and xlen we need to add. This will work if ylen is larger than xlen. Incidentally, it will also work if ylen < xlen, and we only wrote

```
len += ylen - xlen;
```

because arithmetic with unsigned integers are guaranteed to work as arithmetic modulus the largest number, in this case, SIZE_MAX. That means that len + (ylen - xlen) is equal to (len - xlen) + ylen, even though the ylen - xlen might overflow. (The C standard, incidentally, makes no such promises about *signed* arithmetic, where it leaves under- and overflow as undefined behavior). However, because we test if we can add ylen - xlen to len with the comparison SIZE_MAX - len < ylen - xlen, we will have a problem if there is an overflow. If ylen < xlen, there is obviously room for updating the string, but ylen - xlen becomes a large number, and the test will determine that there isn't. That is why we remove xlen from len before we check. The two-line check is not as pretty as I would like, but I am not going to write a separate macro just for this case.

When we have successfully computed the new size, without overflow, we allocate the new buffer, bailing to `error` if the allocation fails. Then we start copying. We use a pointer, `src`, that initially points to the beginning of z and after that points one past the previous occurrence we found. The string from `src` to the beginning of the current occurrence is a part of z we should copy. After copying that, we should copy y into the buffer. Then we update `src` to the end of the occurrence, so it is ready for the next. When we are done iterating, `src` points one past the last occurrence, or the beginning of z if there were none, and the characters from `src` to the last byte in z, `ssz.end`, are the terminal part of z that we should copy. Then all that remains is to zero-terminate the new buffer, and we can return it.

Dynamic Arrays

The string operations create new buffers of the correct size, as we need them, but sometimes we need to adjust the size of objects to adapt to the data a program progresses. With dynamic memory allocation, we can allocate new blocks as needed, but it often requires that we copy our data to a new location.

Take something as simple as an array. We allocate it, fill it up, then we need to add one more element. To handle that, we allocate an array that is one larger and put the element there. But now we need to add one more, so we do the whole thing again, copying all the existing elements to a new location before we can add the new element. After inserting n elements, you might have copied $1+2+3+ \ldots + (n - 2) + (n - 1)$ elements, a sum that grows as n squared. The *dynamic array* data structure gives you better performance, as long as you only extend the array by appending to it. The number of copies it takes to append n elements grows linearly instead of quadratically. You still get the same constant-time performance for accessing and updating existing elements.

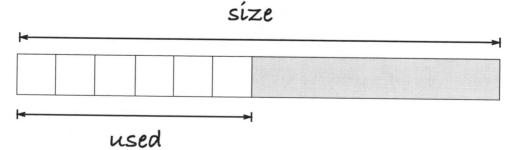

Figure 9-1. *Dynamic arrays*

The data structure is simple. We have an allocated array of memory, and we keep track of how much we have allocated and how much we have used; see Figure 9-1. An integer dynamic array could be implemented like the following struct:

```
struct dynarray {
  size_t size;
  size_t used;
  int *data;
};
```

We can get and update elements in the data memory as we can with any other array, and to make it easier, we can provide a macro to access the i'th element:

```
#define da_at(da,i)    (da)->data[(i)]
```

If you want to know the length of the array (the used part), we can provide a macro for that as well:

```
#define da_len(da)    (da)->used
```

As should be obvious from the macros, if we access the used part of the array, we access it as any other C array, and we get similar performance. I say similar because we do have to look up the address of the array through a pointer, but the difference is hardly noticeable.

When implementing the dynamic array, I will not handle overflow as different from allocation errors, so I will use the checking macros from earlier in the chapter:

```
#define size_check(n,type)                  \
  ((SIZE_MAX / sizeof(type)) >= (n))
#define checked_malloc(n,type)              \
  (size_check((n),(type)) ?                 \
    malloc((n) * sizeof(type)) : 0)
#define checked_realloc(p,n,type)           \
  (size_check((n),(type)) ?                 \
    realloc((p), (n) * sizeof(type)) : 0)
```

If we grow to a size where this is an issue, I really don't know how to handle it, and I expect that allocation failure is an issue long before. So, I might as well treat them as the same thing.

The struct itself doesn't take up much space, so it is something I expect we allocate on the stack. The data buffer, however, is something we must allocate on the heap. The following function can handle that for us. It takes a dynamic array as its first argument, passed as a pointer, so we can modify it, and then the initial used and size numbers. You could argue that with an array that we haven't put anything into, we haven't "used" anything yet, and of course, you are right. I have added that parameter to give us something that we can also use as a normal array. With a normal array, we allocate it with a certain size, and we can access the elements in it from the get-go. They are not initialized until we write to them, but they are there. If you initialize a dynamic array of size n, with n "used" entries, then you get what you would get with a C array of length n. If you allocate it larger than the used part, you give it some room to grow with when we append to it. We require that the caller ensure that the used part of the array is not larger than the total size of the array.

We will require that an array always has size at least one. It prevents problems with realloc() and zero size, and when we grow the array later, in the append operation, we don't have to worry about special cases when doubling zero-sized arrays.

```
#define MAX(a,b) (((a) > (b)) ? (a) : (b))
#define MIN_ARRAY_SIZE 1
```

The initialization code looks like this:

```
bool da_init(struct dynarray *da,
             size_t init_size,
             size_t init_used)
{
  assert(init_size >= init_used);
  init_size = MAX(init_size, MIN_ARRAY_SIZE);
  da->data = checked_malloc(init_size, *da->data);
  da->size = (da->data) ? init_size : 0;
  da->used = (da->data) ? init_used : 0;
  return !!da->data;
}
```

We allocate data of the given size and write it into the `struct`'s `data` field. This might fail, but if you call `da_init()`, then `da` shouldn't hold anything important in that field, to begin with. We will return a false value if the allocation failed. First, however, we also set the `size` and `used` fields. We could set them to the function's input, which is what we want the fields to hold if the allocation succeeded.

The caller is supposed to check if the allocation worked, so any value we put there would be fine if it didn't. However, as a defensive programming measure, we set the values to zero if the allocation failed. It makes it slightly less likely that we confuse uninitialized data as valid (although only slightly, since we do not check the array size when we access items by index, similar to C's arrays). If the caller forgets to check if the allocation worked, but checks the array's length, they will see that they have an empty array (and if they append to it later, they might succeed instead of entering undefined behavior).

The expression `!!da->data` might look odd to the untrained eye. Still, it is a C idiom. `da->data` is a pointer, so it evaluates to false if the pointer is NULL and true otherwise. We want to return true if the allocation succeeded. Hence, it is the truth value of `da->data` we wish to return. However, the return value of the function is `bool` (defined in `<stdbool.h>`) and `da->data` is `int *`. We could change the return type to `int *` and use it as a truth value, but that could be confusing for the reader of the code. We could cast `da->data` to `bool`, but that is even worse. We don't know if that cast is meaningful because the casting rules do not guarantee that a NULL pointer gives us the value that `bool` considers false. We do know, however, that if we use the `!` operator, then NULL becomes true and non-NULL becomes false. So now we have a truth value that `bool` can understand; we just need to flip it, so NULL becomes false again, and non-NULL becomes true—thus, the `!!`. Returning `(da->data != NULL)` would also work, but `!!` is the common idiom.

If you allocate memory, you should also deallocate it. If you write a function that initializes a structure for you, you also ought to write a function to clean it up later. It puts the responsibility for correctly freeing resources on the programmer that writes the data structure rather than the user, and it leaves a single place to update if the data structure changes rather than every place the data structure is used. The only resource we allocate with a dynamic array is the `data` field, but I still think it is appropriate to have a function for deallocating an array. It could look like this:

```
void da_dealloc(struct dynarray *da)
{
  free(da->data);
```

```
    da->data = 0;
    da->size = da->used = 0;
}
```

We free the allocated memory, which is the primary purpose of the function. If the allocation failed when we initialized the array, the function will still work because da->data would then be NULL, and we are allowed to free that. After we free the memory, we set da->data to NULL, making it safe to call da_dealloc() on it again. We are not supposed to, but if it happens accidentally, we have prevented any harm that could come from this. We also set the size and used integers to zero to indicate that we no longer have an array. If, accidentally, the user tries to append to a deallocated array, without reinitializing it again first, setting the entries this way will also make that safe. When we append, we check size and used to see if we should reallocate, and we will use realloc() there, which can handle a NULL pointer. The user is not supposed to do this, but there is no harm done in making it a little safer for them making mistakes.

The way that appending works is this: if there is room behind the last element, when used < size, then we put the new element there and increment used. If not, then we allocate more memory and copy the existing elements (if necessary), and since there now is extra space, we put the new element behind the previous last and increment used. Consider Figure 9-2. Here, we start with a dynamic array of size two, with no used entries. We can append to it twice before we run out of memory, but by the third append, we must allocate a new memory buffer. We allocate one that is twice as big, copy the two elements we have, and then insert the third. There is one free slot for the next append, but after that, we once again have to allocate more memory and then copy the now four elements. We allocated an array of size eight this time, so after copying and inserting one element, we have three empty slots for appending. Once those are used, we have eight elements that we need to copy when we allocate more memory.

Suppose we, as in the figure, double the size of the dynamic array every time we run out of memory. In that case, we can argue that if we append n elements to an array, then we do not copy more than $2n$ elements, and thus that we do not spend an excessive amount of time copying (unlike if we grow the array by one element every time). You reason like this: every time you append an element, you put two "copies" in the bank for later. These will pay for later copying. In the figure, we insert two elements before the first copy (but you can start with any size and do the same reasoning). That means that we have four "copies" in the bank when we resize the array to size four. We only copy two elements, so we have two "copies" left. That is fine; it is always good to have some savings, and we are only arguing that we do not copy more than we have in the bank. When we resize again, we have inserted two more elements. That added four "copies" to the two we already had, so we have six "copies" in the bank. Four of them pay for the copying we do when we resize to length 8. It leaves our savings at two, once again. We have appended four more items before we resize again, which means that we have eight new "copies" from the appending we did. Those eight can pay for copying the now eight elements when we resize to length 16 (and we still have two left).

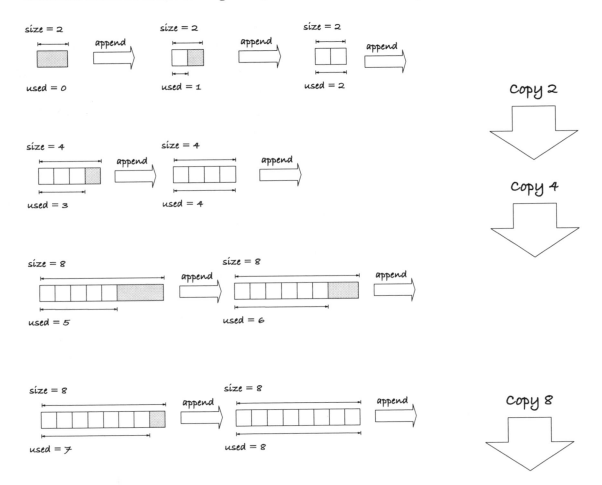

Figure 9-2. *Appending to a dynamic array*

The reasoning works as we continue, and every time we resize, we have saved up enough to copy (with the two original "copies" in the bank after we have copied). The two at the beginning is a consequence of the size we started with; the larger the initial size, the more we have leftover, but we always have at least n "copies" in the bank when we need to copy *n* elements. The argument will also work if you do not double the size every time, but grow it by any fixed factor greater than one. If it is smaller than two, you have to put a little more in the bank, and if it is larger, you can save up a little less with each append.

We need to write the code for resizing a dynamic array. While the preceding reasoning only works if we resize when we append, we might as well write a general resize function, so the user can explicitly grow or shrink the array. We obviously want to use realloc() for resizing. It will automatically copy the objects if necessary, and we might avoid copying altogether if the runtime system can give us more (or less) memory without copying.

A resize function can look like this:

```
#define MIN(a,b) ((a) < (b)) ? (a) : (b)
bool da_resize(struct dynarray *da,
               size_t new_size)
{
  size_t alloc_size = MAX(new_size, MIN_ARRAY_SIZE);
  int *new_data =
    checked_realloc(da->data, alloc_size, *da->data);
  // If we cannot allocate, leave everything
  // as it is, but report an error
  if (!new_data) return false;
  da->data = new_data;
  da->size = alloc_size;
  da->used = MIN(da->used, new_size);
  return true; // success
}
```

We first make sure that we do not attempt to realloc() a zero-sized array. It will be valid for the user to resize an array to size zero, it is one way to reset it, so subsequent append operations add to an empty array, but we do not want the actual memory to be an empty array. So, we make sure that we have at least MIN_ARRAY_SIZE before we allocate.

245

Having a minimal array size means that we do not have to worry about reallocating zero bytes, but we still need to check for overflow of the size, so we use the checked_ realloc() macro to call realloc(). We save the result in a new_data pointer because we need to check if the reallocation was successful before we save the pointer in the dynamic array structure. If the allocation didn't succeed, we will leave the array as it is. All the data in it is still valid, and the caller might be able to salvage the situation. If we freed the memory and cleaned up the array, the data would be lost. So, we abort and inform the caller that there is work to do, and leave it at that.

If the allocation succeeded, we update the data pointer (the old data will no longer be valid if the realloc() call gave us a new memory block), and we update the size and used values. The MIN() expression is there to allow a caller to resize an array to shorter than the used part. We give size the alloc_size value, which we know is at least MIN_ARRAY_SIZE, because that is how much memory we have allocated. We give used the new_size value instead of alloc_size, so it is possible to resize the array to length zero from the user's perspective.

When we append, we need to check if there are more free addresses, so we compare used and size. If they are equal, we need to allocate more memory before we can append. Since we already have da_resize(), the only interesting bit is computing the new size. We want to double the size, but this might not be possible. Two things could happen: first, we could get a value that is larger than SIZE_MAX, in which case we would get an overflow. The da_resize() function will catch if we try to allocate more integers than we can get, but if we already have the overflow before we call that function, it cannot help us. At a minimum, we must give it a new_size that hasn't overflown, and 2 * da->size could do that. Second, we might not be able to allocate twice as much memory as we currently have, but still be able to allocate *some*. If we haven't reached SIZE_MAX yet, or SIZE_MAX / sizeof(*da->data) integers, we should still attempt a resize, even if we cannot get all the memory we want.

We can use this macro to determine the maximum length an array of a given type can have:

```
#define max_array_len(type)       \
  (SIZE_MAX / sizeof(type))
```

It only serves the purpose of explaining what the expression SIZE_MAX / sizeof(type) means, nothing more. Still, giving expressions names is useful for making the code more readable. The current size cannot exceed this if the array is correctly initialized. Neither `da_init()` nor `da_resize()` would let us allocate the data for this, with their checked allocation macros.

We can add another macro to test if we are already at our maximum:

```
#define at_max_len(n,type)           \
  ((n) == max_array_len(type))
```

If we allow our array to get to this maximum, we need to check if we are there before we attempt to grow it in an append operation. Because if we are at max capacity, then append should always fail.

This macro will check if we can double the current memory, and if so, do it, and otherwise give us the maximum we could get:

```
#define capped_dbl_size(n,type)           \
  (((n) < max_array_len(type) / 2)        \
    ? (2 * (n)) : max_array_len(type))
```

Of course, it isn't perfect because there are sizes in between the max and double the current. Still, I expect that such a situation is exceedingly rare, and there is no need to complicate the code further to deal with it. Not merely giving up if we cannot double the memory is already being generous.

While less obvious, this is also a place where we use that dynamic arrays have size at least one. We could have allowed zero-sized arrays (dealing with `realloc()` explicitly), but then growing the size by a factor two might give us a size of zero back. Our code assumes that when we grow the size by a factor of two, we have new, unused slots available afterward. For that to work, two times the size of the array must be larger than the array. It is, as long as the size isn't zero.

So, before we append, we check if it is necessary to grow the array. If it is, we check if we are at maximum already, in which case we fail. Otherwise, we grow it to twice the size (or the possible maximum if that is too much). That can also fail, in which case the append failed, but if we managed, we add the new value at the end of the array. That part, fortunately, is simple. You put the new value at index `da->used` and increment the used counter.

```
bool da_append(struct dynarray *da, int val)
{
  if (da->used == da->size) {
    if (at_max_len(da->size, *da->data)) return false;
```

```
    size_t new_size = capped_dbl(da->size, *da->data);
    bool resize_success = da_resize(da, new_size);
    if (!resize_success) return false;
  }
  da->data[da->used++] = val;
  return true; // success
}
```

To use a dynamic array, put a `struct dynarray` variable on the stack (or allocate it on the heap with `malloc()`; you already know how to) and initialize it. After that, you are allowed to access and update the elements between index zero and `used`, and if you want, you can append to it, growing it along the way. Remember that appending can fail, so you should check the return value. The array doesn't break because append fails. You keep the existing values (and you should still explicitly deallocate it later, even if you encountered a failed operation). When you are done with the array, you must deallocate it again by calling `da_dealloc()`.

```
int main(void)
{
  struct dynarray da;

  int success = da_init(&da, 4, 4);
  if (!success) {
    printf("allocation error\n");
    exit(1);
  }

  for (int i = 0; i < da_len(&da); i++) {
    da_at(&da, i) = i;
  }
  for (int i = 0; i < da_len(&da); i++) {
    printf("%d ", da_at(&da, i));
  }
  printf("\n");
```

```
printf("current length %zu\n", da_len(&da));
for (int i = 0; i < 10; i++) {
  if (!da_append(&da, 10 * (i + 1))) {
    printf("allocation error");
    // we cannot append any more, but
    // the array is still in a valid state
    break;
  }
}
printf("current length %zu\n", da_len(&da));
for (int i = 0; i < da_len(&da); i++) {
  printf("%d ", da_at(&da, i));
}
printf("\n");

da_dealloc(&da);

  return 0;
}
```

You can shrink a dynamic array as well as grow it if you add an operation that removes the last used element. In that case, you should not shrink it when it hits half the size. You could risk that you shrink it down to a size such that it now has the maximum capacity, and the next operation is appending. In that case, you would need to allocate new memory and move all the array data. Then you might remove the last element again, shrink, and copy all the elements once more. You could end up moving back and forth that way, copying more than the analysis we did earlier allows us to. If, however, you wait with shrinking to half the size until only a quarter of the array is in use, then you can analyze the performance similarly and show that you still put a limit on how often you copy. I will not implement this for dynamic arrays, but we will see shrinking in the data structure we cover next.

Gapped Buffers

Allocating new strings instead of modifying existing ones has its uses, and in many applications, it makes it easier to work with strings. We can allocate exactly the memory we need when we modify a string, and if all functions return freshly allocated memory, we know that we should always free it. However, if you implement something like an editor, then it is not a viable approach. Copying the entire content of a string every time you add or remove a character will be hopelessly slow.

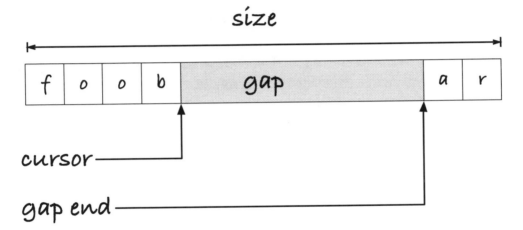

Figure 9-3. *A gapped buffer*

Imagine that we want to implement an editor, where we need each change to the text to be fast. We don't know the final size of the text, so we must dynamically resize the buffer we work with as we edit. If we only appended characters to a string, then something like the dynamic arrays would be efficient, but that is rarely the case. We need a data structure where we can edit in the middle of a text efficiently. A simple structure for this is the *gapped buffer*.

Just as we leave extra space behind the used part of a dynamic array, we leave extra space in a gapped buffer, but since we need to insert characters anywhere in a buffer, we do not necessarily leave it at the end. Instead, we represent a text buffer in three parts—the string that is before the cursor and the string that comes after it and in between a gap of free memory we can add to; see Figure 9-3.

When we insert a character, it goes at the position where the cursor sits, which, as luck will have it, is where we have extra room (and when we do not have a gap, we will allocate memory, so we get a gap by doubling the buffer size, as we did for dynamic arrays). If we need to move the cursor, we can simultaneously move a character from before the gap to after it, if we move the cursor left, or the other way if we move it right. If we delete a character, that is, if we delete to the right of the cursor, we can grow the gap one to the right. If we press backspace, we can grow the gap one character to the right (by moving the cursor one to the left). See Figure 9-4 for an example.

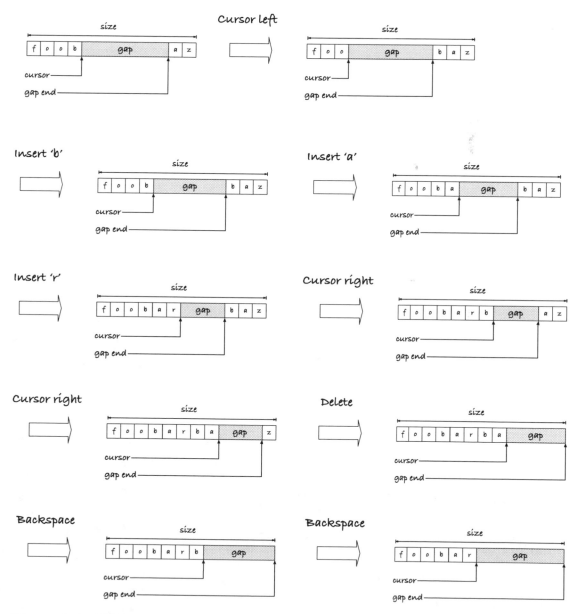

Figure 9-4. *Editing in a gapped buffer*

We grow the buffer when we run out of gap space, and if the gap takes up too much space, we can shrink the buffer as well to reduce our memory usage.

We can implement the data structure like this:

```
struct gap_buf {
  size_t size;
  size_t cursor;
  size_t gap_end;
  char *buffer;
};
```

The cursor and the end of the gap are offsets into buffer rather than pointers. If we reallocate buffer, the two values could point into memory that is no longer ours to work with, so we would need to compute offsets into new memory in any case. We might as well use offsets in the first place.

We use the following macros to get the size of the text before and after the cursor and the total number of used characters:

```
#define gb_front(buf)   ((buf)->cursor)
#define gb_back(buf)    ((buf)->size - (buf)->gap_end)
#define gb_used(buf)    (gb_front(buf) + gb_back(buf))
```

This time, I will write a function that allocates a full buffer, rather than just the data, as we did with dynamic arrays. There is no good reason for this other than to show you that. There would be nothing wrong with putting the buffer on the stack (as long as the actual data is allocated on the heap).

The allocation function looks like this:

```
#define MAX(a,b) (((a) > (b)) ? (a) : (b))
#define MIN_BUF_SIZE 1024

struct gap_buf *new_buffer(size_t init_size)
{
  struct gap_buf *buf = malloc(sizeof *buf);
  if (!buf) return 0;
  buf->buffer = malloc(MAX(init_size, MIN_BUF_SIZE));
  if (!buf->buffer) {
    free(buf);
```

```
    return 0;
  }
  buf->size = init_size;
  buf->cursor = 0;
  buf->gap_end = init_size;
  return buf;
}
```

We first allocate the struct. If that doesn't work, we give up; there is nothing else for us to try. If we can get the struct, we allocate the buffer. We have a minimum buffer size of one kibibyte. We don't want to waste time on tiny allocations on buffers that are too small to matter anyway, and putting a minimal non-zero size on buffers means that we do not need to worry about realloc()'ing zero bytes.

If the second allocation fails, we also will report a failure, but we have allocated data now that we haven't freed, the struct in buf. If we return now, that memory is unreachable of our program, and we can never free it. So, we must free() it before we return. If all succeed, however, we can initialize the gapped buffer. We set the size, naturally, and put the cursor at the front of the buffer, and since the buffer is empty, the end of the gap goes at the end of the buffer, init_size.

When we free the gapped buffer, we must first free the underlying buffer. The two were allocated separately, so they must be freed separately.

```
void free_buffer(struct gap_buf *buf)
{
  if (!buf) return;
  free(buf->buffer);
  free(buf);
}
```

The if-statement at the top is there to avoid problems if a user calls free_buffer() with NULL. They are not supposed to, but it doesn't cost us anything to play it safe. The order of the two free() calls is important. After free(buf), you have no guarantee that you can get buf->buffer; it requires that you look up a value in memory that is no longer yours. So we must free the memory in this order.

We leave the allocation code for last, as that is the most interesting, and implement the other operations first. Moving the cursor is the simplest. We need to move a character from the beginning to the end, or vice versa, and update the cursor position:

```c
void cursor_left(struct gap_buf *buf)
{
  if (buf->cursor > 0) {
    buf->buffer[--buf->gap_end] =
        buf->buffer[--buf->cursor];
  }
}

void cursor_right(struct gap_buf *buf)
{
  if (buf->gap_end < buf->size) {
    buf->buffer[buf->cursor++] =
        buf->buffer[buf->gap_end++];
  }
}
```

The cursor index points to the first empty place in the gap, and the gap_end index points to the first used character at the back of the buffer.

So when we move left, we need to decrement the indices before we move a character (the character should move from the position before the cursor to the position before the current end of the gap). When we move right, we need to increment after we copy the character.

When we delete a character, we move the cursor to the left or the gap end to the right, depending on the type of delete. In either case, we will resize the buffer to half its size if we end up with less than a quarter used. The reason for that cutoff, I explained at the end of the previous section.

```c
void backspace(struct gap_buf *buf)
{
  if (buf->cursor > 0)
    buf->cursor--;
  if (gb_used(buf) < buf->size / 4)
    shrink_buffer(buf, buf->size / 2);
}

void delete(struct gap_buf *buf)
{
```

```
if (buf->gap_end < buf->size)
  buf->gap_end++;
if (gb_used(buf) < buf->size / 4)
  shrink_buffer(buf, buf->size / 2);
}
```

Even though `shrink_buffer()` will involve a reallocation, we will implement it such that it cannot fail. We get to that later.

For inserting a character, however, we can fail if the buffer is full, and we cannot grow it, so there we need to return a value we can check. The function looks like this:

```
#define capped_dbl_size(s) \
  ((s) < SIZE_MAX / 2) ? (2 * (s)) : SIZE_MAX

bool insert_character(struct gap_buf *buf,
                      char c)
{
  if (buf->cursor == buf->gap_end) {
    size_t new_size = capped_dbl_size(buf->size);
    bool grow_success = grow_buffer(buf, new_size);
    if (!grow_success) return false;
  }

  buf->buffer[buf->cursor++] = c;
  return true;
}
```

If the cursor is at the same index as `gap_end`, the gap is empty, so we need to grow the buffer. We double the size, except that we stop at `SIZE_MAX` if it isn't possible. The following `grow_buffer()` function will deal with attempts to grow a buffer to its current size, so we do not explicitly test for that here. If growing the buffer fails, we report that, and we do not insert the character—there is no place to insert it, after all. Otherwise, we are in the situation we would be in if we didn't have to grow in the first place. We put the character at the current cursor position and move the cursor one forward.

When we resize a gapped array, we need to treat growing and shrinking differently. We can use `realloc()` for both, but we need to move the part of the buffer after the gap to its new location when we resize, and here growing and shrinking are asymmetric. If we grow the buffer, we need to move some text to the end of the new memory we get, and we cannot do that before we get that memory. If we shrink, however, we need to move it before we resize; if the buffer shrinks, then the memory after the new size is no longer ours to use. It might still be there if the address we got back is the same, but we are not allowed to use it. If we get a new address, then the last part of the original data was not moved to that location. We have to move the data before we call `realloc()`; only if we do that, we have it after resizing the buffer.

For both functions, however, we need to do the same memory copy. We need to move the data from `gap_end` to the end of the old buffer to the position that is `gb_back()` from the end of the new buffer:

```
void move_back(struct gap_buf *buf,
               char *new_buf, size_t new_size)
{
  memmove(new_buf + new_size - gb_back(buf),
          buf->buffer + buf->gap_end,
          gb_back(buf));
}
```

The growth function will check that we are allocating more space and give us an error otherwise. It prevents, among other things, that we try to grow the maximal size of a buffer. Otherwise, it is similar to what we saw for dynamic arrays. We allocate a new buffer, and if it fails, we report an error. Otherwise, we update the gapped buffer. First, we move the data at the end of the buffer to the new position, and then we update the size and `gap_end` position. We do it in the opposite order, though, because the `gb_back()` macro we use to get the number of characters after the gap depends on the size, so we cannot update the size first.

```
bool grow_buffer(struct gap_buf *buf, size_t new_size)
{
  // We cannot grow to a smaller (or equal) size
  if (buf->size >= new_size) return false;

  // Allocate a larger buffer
  new_size = MAX(new_size, MIN_BUF_SIZE);
  char *new_buf = realloc(buf->buffer, new_size);
  if (!new_buf) return false;
```

```
// Move the segment to the right of the cursor
move_back(buf, new_buf, new_size);

// Update struct -- set end before updating
// the size or gb_back(buf) will be wrong
buf->buffer = new_buf;
buf->gap_end = new_size - gb_back(buf);
buf->size = new_size;

return true;
}
```

When we shrink, we move the data and update all the meta-information before we attempt to reallocate the buffer. If the reallocation worked, then the data is automatically moved to the correct location, and all is well. If it didn't, then no damage is done, as long as the cursor, size, and gap end are placed correctly.

```
void shrink_buffer(struct gap_buf *buf,
                   size_t new_size)
{
  // We do not resize if we lose data!
  if (new_size < gb_used(buf)) return;

  // Move the segment to the right of the cursor
  move_back(buf, buf->buffer, new_size);

  // Update struct -- set end before updating
  // the size or gb_back(buf) will be wrong
  buf->gap_end = new_size - gb_back(buf);
  buf->size = new_size;

  // Allocate a smaller buffer
  new_size = MAX(new_size, MIN_BUF_SIZE);
  char *new_buf = realloc(buf->buffer, new_size);
  if (new_buf) buf->buffer = new_buf;
}
```

If `realloc()` failed, we will still be using the old buffer, but nothing will break. We still have a buffer to work with. True, we are using more memory than we think we are, and it would be better to shrink it, but if we try to grow or shrink later, `realloc()` will still work, and maybe we get the right size at that time. If we tried to move the data back and restore the full gap that we have room for when a `realloc()` failed, on the other hand, we could damage the runtime performance of the gapped buffer. We would copy all the elements before attempting to shrink, then move them back, and the very next operation could be another delete where we did the same thing. Each operation could involve copying all the remaining elements twice. Compared to that, leaving a little extra memory that will be freed later anyway, if we remember to deallocate our buffer, is preferable.

In `move_back()`, I used the `memmove()` function from `<string.h>` rather than `strncpy()`. It does the same thing, except that it won't stop at zero terminals, and it can handle overlapping memory. The former is not a major issue. The gapped buffer can contain zero characters, without considering its terminal symbols, but it wouldn't be a problem if we didn't allow that. As for overlapping data, we don't expect to see that, unless we reach the upper limit of buffer size. When we shrink the buffer, the gap takes up three-quarters of the buffer, so when we move the data to the right of the gap forward, we do not write into overlapping memory. When we grow the size, if we double the buffer length, then we cannot write into overlapping memory either, *unless* we hit the upper limit of `SIZE_MAX`. Regardless of that, however, I do not consider the buffer content a C string, which is what `strncpy()` is made for, but rather a chunk of memory that I need to move, and then I prefer to use `memmove()`. You are unlikely to get into trouble if you use `strncpy()` instead.

CHAPTER 10

Generic Dynamic Arrays

Before we move on to the next topic, recursive data structures, I would like to take a short intermezzo and look at dynamic arrays once more. We implemented dynamic arrays for integers, but in this chapter, we will explore techniques to implement *generic* dynamic arrays, that is, dynamic arrays that will work with any data type. Some of the methods relate to pointers, so it is not entirely outside of this book's scope, but not all. Still, I feel I would be neglecting an essential topic if I introduced dynamic arrays and not say a few words about how you can generalize the code to work with more than one type. I will touch upon generic code in later chapters as well, but not in the level of details as I will in this chapter. I will trust that you can generalize what you see here to other cases.

C has limited support for generic code, bordering on nonexistent. We do not have a template mechanism like C++ or generics as in Java. There is *one* data type we can consider generic, `void *`, and that is only if we are feeling generous. We can assign any pointer to a `void` pointer and get it back again, and that is as far as `void` pointers take us. It is enough for our first attempt at a generic dynamic array, however, and in many cases, this suffices. If we are willing to do a little more work, we can map all types of objects into buffers indexed by character pointers. If the objects are correctly aligned, this is a valid way to store objects and get pointers to them. That will be our second attempt.

An alternative approach to `void *`/`char *` representations is to generate code using macros. The C preprocessor is a primitive programming language, with little more than simple text replacement functionality. Still, it is enough that we can write template code that we can then instantiate with the types we need. We will explore two different approaches using this in our third and fourth attempts.

None of the approaches is superior to the others; rather, they have different strengths and weaknesses, so you would choose between them, or mix them at times, based on your applications. When you need generic code, however, it is typically a variant of these four you use.

© Thomas Mailund 2021
T. Mailund, *Pointers in C Programming*, https://doi.org/10.1007/978-1-4842-6927-5_10

Void Pointers

We can use void pointers as a generic type because we are allowed to store any data pointer type in them.[1] Using void * for our data is the simplest way to implement a generic data structure. For dynamic arrays, we only require minimal changes. We used *da->data every time we needed the size of the underlying data, for testing size overflow and computing array sizes, so we have already done most of the work to deal with alternative types. We need to update int to void in a few places (I have highlighted where in the following code listing), but most of our code remains the same:

```
struct dynarray {
   size_t size;
  size_t used;
  // Update int * => void **
  void **data;
};

#define da_at(da,i) (da)->data[(i)]
#define da_len(da)  (da)->used

bool da_init(struct dynarray *da,
             size_t init_size,
             size_t init_used)
{
  assert(init_size >= init_used);
  init_size = MAX(init_size, MIN_ARRAY_SIZE);
  da->data = checked_malloc(init_size, *da->data);
  da->size = (da->data) ? init_size : 0;
  da->used = (da->data) ? init_used : 0;
  return !!da->data;
}
```

---

[1] I write "data" pointer explicitly, because the C standard does not guarantee that we can store function pointers in them, but that isn't important here. Any pointer to data can be assigned to void *, and you can safely get the pointer value back. You don't even need casts to do so.

```
void da_dealloc(struct dynarray *da)
{
  free(da->data);
  da->data = 0;
  da->size = da->used = 0;
}

bool da_resize(struct dynarray *da,
               size_t new_size)
{
  size_t alloc_size = MAX(new_size, MIN_ARRAY_SIZE);
  // Updated int * => void **
  void **new_data =
    checked_realloc(da->data, alloc_size, *da->data);
  if (!new_data) return false;

  da->data = new_data;
  da->size = alloc_size;
  da->used = MIN(da->used, new_size);
  return true;
}

// Update val type int => void *
bool da_append(struct dynarray *da, void *val)
{
  if (da->used == da->size) {
    if (at_max_len(da->size, *da->data)) return false;
    size_t new_size = capped_dbl(da->size, *da->data);
    int resize_success = da_resize(da, new_size);
    if (!resize_success) return false;
  }
  da->data[da->used++] = val;
  return true;
}
```

I didn't include the various macros we used for size checking and allocation, since they do not change. They got the sizes from da->data, and they will automatically work with the new type.

You can define and initialize a dynamic array as before:

```
struct dynarray da;
bool success = da_init(&da, 0, 0);
if (!success) {
  printf("allocation error\n");
}
```

but if you want to use it for a type such as int, you cannot use a literal value any longer. You cannot write

```
da_append(&da, 42);
```

for example, because while you can store all *pointer* values in a void *, you cannot store all *values*, and 42 is an int and not a pointer. You cannot take an address of a value either, so this will not work:

```
da_append(&da, &42);
```

If you want to insert an integer (or any other non-pointer type), you need a variable you can take the address of:

```
int i = 13;
da_append(&da, &i);
```

or you need a compound initializer:

```
da_append(&da, &(int){42});
```

In both cases, you create local (stack-allocated) variables and use their addresses. This is not in itself a problem. We designed the dynamic array to be something we would stack allocate, so it might not be a problem to stack allocate the values either. Still, often, we do not want to put too much memory on the stack because it is a limited resource, so it is not ideal. Worse than that, however, is how easily we can get into trouble with storing local variables if we really intend to store their values. You might think that this would insert values zero to four into a dynamic array:

```
for (int i = 0; i < 5; ++i) {
  da_append(&da, &i);
}
```

but you are, obviously, inserting the same address five times, and when the loop
terminates, the integer at that address has value 5, and that is what the five "values"
in the dynamic array have. Worse, once the loop ends, the variable goes out of scope,
and its memory can be reused by the compiler for something else. If you turn on
optimization, most likely the i in these two loops will use the same memory:

```
for (int i = 0; i < 5; ++i) {
  da_append(&da, &i);
}
for (int i = 10; i < 15; ++i) {
  printf("%p %d\n", (void *)&i, i);
}
```

(you need something like the printf() call to prevent the compiler from optimizing
the second loop away entirely). When I test this code, the array contains five times 15
afterward.

Using literal compounds won't help you either. You get one location in memory for
where they sit, so even if you write code like this:

```
for (int i = 0; i < 5; ++i) {
  da_append(&da, &(int){i});
}
```

you do not get what you want. It will insert five times 4 in the array (and like all stack
memory, it will be reclaimed later; we are not copying the value but storing a stack
location).

If you want to store values in this void * dynamic array, you should dynamically
allocate it to avoid all these issues.

```
for (int i = 0; i < 5; ++i) {
  int *p = malloc(sizeof *p);
  if (!p) continue;
  *p = i;
  da_append(&da, p);
}
```

Then, of course, you have to remember to deallocate it again later:

```
for (int i = 0; i < da_len(&da); i++) {
  free(da_at(&da, i));
}
da_dealloc(&da);
```

Then may the gods have mercy on your soul if you happened to put a local variable in the array as well; trying to free stack variables only leads to tears and misery.

Furthermore, of course, getting values back as integers does not give us pretty code because we need to both cast and dereference the values:

```
for (int i = 0; i < da_len(&da); i++) {
  printf("%d ", *(int *)da_at(&da, i));
}
```

This, however, can be fixed with a macro:

#define da_at_as(da,i,type) *(type *)da_at(da,i)

and then

```
for (int i = 0; i < da_len(&da); i++) {
  printf("%d ", da_at_as(&da, i, int));
}
```

I know that it now looks like this is a poor solution to generic dynamic arrays, but it isn't all that bad. All the problems we see are because we want to store non-pointer types in the array. If your application works with heap-allocated objects, then this dynamic array implementation is ideal. It is simple and efficient code; it handles your objects without issues, as they are already pointers (and you have to free the objects anyway), so it does not give you extra work. In many applications, this solution is the optimal choice. It just isn't ideal when what you want to store is not pointers.

The only thing you lose with this solution if you are working with heap-allocated objects anyway is type-checking. Since you can assign between any pointer type and void * without explicit casts, you can write code such as

```
double *dp = malloc(sizeof *dp);
if (!dp) { /* deal with error */ }
*dp = 3.14;
```

```
da_at(&da, i) = dp;
// do some processing
int *ip = da_at(&da, i);
// now ip points to a double, and that is
// probably a bad thing
```

Here, ip *may* point to a double, if the index i didn't change. We are not even guaranteed that because we are only guaranteed that we get the original value back when we assign the value in a void * back to the correct pointer type. But even if we have the right address, we should not attempt to treat the data at this address as an int if it was a double when we assigned to it. We cannot mix types that way.

I would say that this small breach of type safety is worth what we get for a simple and efficient dynamic array for pointers, though.

Generic Memory Buffer

If we want to store objects other than pointers in a dynamic array, we can also do that in a generic way. We can allocate memory that fits the kind of objects we want to store in the array, compute indices into it based on the object size, and copy data into it when we add elements to the array.

We will not tailor the dynamic array to a specific type, but store the object size in it. Because of that, we must update all our overflow and size computation macros, so they work with an object size value instead of a type. Everywhere there was a type before, we make the parameter an object size, obj_size:

```
#define size_check(n,obj_size)                 \
  ((SIZE_MAX / (obj_size)) >= (n))

// Use object size instead of type
#define checked_malloc(n,obj_size)             \
  (size_check((n),(obj_size)) ?                \
    malloc((n) * (obj_size)) : 0)

#define checked_realloc(p,n,obj_size)          \
  (size_check((n),(obj_size)) ?                \
    realloc((p), (n) * (obj_size)) : 0)
```

```
#define max_array_len(obj_size)                    \
  (SIZE_MAX / obj_size)

#define at_max_len(n,obj_size)                     \
  ((n) == max_array_len(obj_size))

#define capped_dbl(n,obj_size)                     \
  (((n) < max_array_len(obj_size) / 2)             \
    ? (2 * (n)) : max_array_len(obj_size))
```

Otherwise, the macros stay the same. The only difference is how we get the size of an individual object.

In the dynarray struct, we add an obj_size, and we change the type of data to char *. We can access all memory with character pointers, so it is a pointer type of choice for what we will do.

```
struct dynarray {
  size_t size;
  size_t used;
  // Added size of objects
  size_t obj_size;
  // Update int * => char *
  char *data;
};
```

When we access elements in the array, we need to compute their offset. If the type of data matches the size of the objects, C will do it for us when we do pointer arithmetic. In an integer array, data[i] is the i'th integer. When we have a char * buffer for our data, and the objects have size obj_size, we must do the computation ourselves. To get the i'th item, we have to multiply i with obj_size:

```
#define da_get(da,i) \
  (void *)((da)->data + (i) * (da)->obj_size)
```

The void * cast is there, so we can assign the address to a pointer of the right type without explicit casting if we so wish.

With this macro, we still work with pointers, although we intend to store any kind of value in the dynamic array. There is no way around that. When we don't know which type we are implementing the array for, we only have raw memory to work with. If the user can tell us the type, however, we can of course cast and dereference values, so we can supply a macro for that:

```
#define da_at_as(da,i,type) *(type *)da_at(da,i)
```

With this macro, we can write code such as

```
// get i'th element as int
int i = da_at_as(da, i, int);
// add i to j'th element (as int)
da_at_as(da, j, int) += i;
```

and mostly treat the items as values. We cannot get C to automatically infer the type, however. It is not that smart.

With da_at_as(), we can both read and write to values in the array, by providing the type—but be careful here because if the type doesn't match the obj_size in the array, you are heading for disaster. The previous solution was polymorphic, in the sense that you could store any pointer type in the same dynamic array, but this solution is not. The array expects to store one type of objects—or at least store objects of the exact same size—so do not let the polymorphic nature of da_at_as() fool you.

Initializing the array only changes slightly. We take the size of objects as a parameter, use it in the allocation computations, and store it in the struct:

```
bool da_init(struct dynarray *da,
             size_t init_size,
             size_t init_used,
             size_t obj_size)
{
  assert(init_size >= init_used);
  init_size = MAX(init_size, MIN_ARRAY_SIZE);
  // Use obj_size for the size parameter
  da->data = checked_malloc(init_size, obj_size);
  da->size = (da->data) ? init_size : 0;
  da->used = (da->data) ? init_used : 0;
  // Remember the object size
```

```
  da->obj_size = obj_size;
  return !!da->data;
}
```

We do not need to update da_dealloc() because it didn't rely on the underlying type to begin with.

```
void da_dealloc(struct dynarray *da)
{
  free(da->data);
  da->data = 0;
  da->size = da->used = 0;
}
```

When we resize, we need to change the type of the new buffer—it was int * in the previous chapter, but we need it to be char * now—and we need to use the obj_size instead of type for the allocation computations.

```
bool da_resize(struct dynarray *da,
               size_t new_size)
{
  size_t alloc_size = MAX(new_size, MIN_ARRAY_SIZE);
  // Updated int * => char * and use obj_size
  char *new_data =
    checked_realloc(da->data, alloc_size, da->obj_size);
  if (!new_data) return false;

  da->data = new_data;
  da->size = alloc_size;
  da->used = MIN(da->used, new_size);
  return true;
}
```

Append cannot use the type of the items to assign to the next free position because it doesn't know the type. This means that, to append an element to the dynamic array, we must move the bytes of objects, for which we need addresses, that is, pointers. A void pointer will work for the data argument, and since we already know the object size, we know how much to copy.

```
// val has type void * instead of int
bool da_append(struct dynarray *da, void *val)
{
  if (da->used == da->size) {
    if (at_max_len(da->size, da->obj_size)) return false;
    size_t new_size = capped_dbl(da->size, da->obj_size);
    int resize_success = da_resize(da, new_size);
    if (!resize_success) return false;
  }
  // copy memory...
  memcpy(da->data + da->used * da->obj_size,
         val, da->obj_size);
  da->used++;
  return true;
}
```

This means that we cannot append values, but only objects we can get the address of. You cannot, for example, append an integer:

```
da_append(&da, 13);
```

but you can append a compound expression:

```
da_append(&da, &(int){ 13 });
```

The values are copied into the array, however, so

```
for (int i = 0; i < 5; ++i) {
  da_append(&da, &i);
}
```

will add the numbers zero to four to the array, and changing i after we have appended its value doesn't change the item in the array.

There are cases where a solution such as this is useful, where we administrate an array of objects of a type where we only know the size. We do not need to worry about heap-allocating all objects we put into the array. However, the type-checking is more of an issue here than in the previous solution. The da_at_as() macro is particularly problematic since we cast raw memory and interpret it as a type that may or may not match the objects in the array. With the void pointer solution, at least we knew that we were accessing pointers, but here we could easily get buffer overflows if we supplied the wrong type when we access the element in an array. This solution requires that we are ultra-careful about using arrays correctly, only accessing them using the correct type.

The next solution gives us type-checking back, by generating code for each type we use dynamic arrays for.

Code Generating Macros

We can use macros to generate type-specific dynamic array code. That way, we get type-safe code, and without implementing separate structures for each type, we want to put in our array. The only real drawback is that the executable will have to contain separate functions for each code as well, so the size of your program grows. This is rarely a problem, unless you write programs for small embedded systems, though, so not something that should detract of this approach.

We need to parameterize the dynamic array type, with the underlying type of objects, so we need a macro to generate the struct type. It can look like this:

```
#define GEN_DYNARRAY_TYPE(TYPE)      \
  typedef struct {                   \
    size_t size;                     \
    size_t used;                     \
    TYPE *data;                      \
  } TYPE##_dynarray;
```

We use a typedef here to name the new type. We could equally well have defined the name of the struct:

```
#define GEN_DYNARRAY_TYPE(TYPE)      \
  struct TYPE##_dynarray {           \
    size_t size;                     \
    size_t used;                     \
    TYPE *data;                      \
  };
```

but if we are defining a type, we might as well typedef. The name of the type will be <type>_dynarray where <type> is the type we generate it for, so writing

```
GEN_DYNARRAY_TYPE(int)
```

will generate a type called int_dynarray whose data will be of type int. Likewise

```
GEN_DYNARRAY_TYPE(double)
```

will generate a type called double_dynarray with a double pointer for data.

Because we generate a name from the type parameter, there are some restrictions on what we can use. If the parameter has spaces in it, for example:

```
GEN_DYNARRAY_TYPE(long long)
```

or

```
struct point { double x, y; };
GEN_DYNARRAY_TYPE(struct point)
```

the compiler will complain. All is not lost, however, because we can always typedef such types, so we *can* generate a name. This will work fine for creating a dynamic array of points:

```
typedef struct { double x, y; } point;
GEN_DYNARRAY_TYPE(point)
```

This restriction on type names is the only limitation the macro has. The code generating macros we see later have the same restriction, for the same reason. We cannot get around it when we use macros to generate names.

The macro for accessing objects by index doesn't have to change, but it is type-safe now because it accesses the right type of objects. Getting the length (or the used number of objects) is the same as before as well.

```
#define da_at(da,i)    (da)->data[(i)]
#define da_len(da)     (da)->used
```

To get the array functions, we can take the code for the integer dynamic array from the previous chapter and replace int with TYPE the relevant places, which are a few places since we used *da->data in all the macros that worked on the array's size. We need to set the correct type of dynamic arrays from the function arguments, TYPE##_dynarray, in the resize function new_data should have type TYPE *, and in the append function, the parameter val should have type TYPE. That is all.

271

```
#define GEN_DYNARRAY_FUNCTIONS(TYPE)                      \
bool TYPE##_da_init(TYPE##_dynarray *da,                  \
                    size_t init_size,                     \
                    size_t init_used)                     \
{                                                         \
  assert(init_size >= init_used);                         \
  init_size = MAX(init_size, MIN_ARRAY_SIZE);             \
  da->data =                                              \
    checked_malloc(init_size, *da->data);                 \
  da->size = (da->data) ? init_size : 0;                  \
  da->used = (da->data) ? init_used : 0;                  \
  return !!da->data;                                      \
}                                                         \
                                                          \
void TYPE##_da_dealloc(TYPE##_dynarray *da)               \
{                                                         \
  free(da->data);                                         \
  da->data = 0;                                           \
  da->size = da->used = 0;                                \
}                                                         \
                                                          \
bool TYPE##_da_resize(TYPE##_dynarray *da,                \
                      size_t new_size)                    \
{                                                         \
  size_t alloc_size =                                     \
    MAX(new_size, MIN_ARRAY_SIZE);                        \
  TYPE *new_data =                                        \
    checked_realloc(da->data,                             \
      alloc_size, *da->data);                             \
  if (!new_data) return false;                            \
  da->data = new_data;                                    \
  da->size = alloc_size;                                  \
  da->used = MIN(da->used, new_size);                     \
  return true;                                            \
}                                                         \
```

CHAPTER 10   GENERIC DYNAMIC ARRAYS

```
                                                     \
bool TYPE##_da_append(TYPE##_dynarray *da,           \
                      TYPE val)                      \
{                                                    \
  if (da->used == da->size) {                        \
    if (at_max_len(da->size, *da->data))             \
      return false;                                  \
    size_t new_size =                                \
      capped_dbl(da->size, *da->data);               \
      int resize_success =                           \
        TYPE##_da_resize(da, new_size);              \
      if (!resize_success) return false;             \
  }                                                  \
  da->data[da->used++] = val;                        \
  return true;                                       \
}
```

That macro generates all the functions, so we get a complete implementation of a dynamic array of type T by invoking

```
GEN_DYNARRAY_TYPE(T)
GEN_DYNARRAY_FUNCTIONS(T)
```

If we want to use the same type of dynamic array in more than one place in our code, however, we must be careful. We cannot generate the functions with the same name more than once, or we will get problems with the linker. It is hardly a problem, though, since we can add a macro that generates the prototypes for the functions:

```
#define GEN_DYNARRAY_PROTOTYPES(TYPE)                \
bool TYPE##_da_init    (TYPE##_dynarray *da,         \
                        size_t init_size,            \
                        size_t init_used);           \
void TYPE##_da_dealloc(TYPE##_dynarray *da);         \
bool TYPE##_da_resize (TYPE##_dynarray *da,          \
                       size_t new_size);             \
bool TYPE##_da_append (TYPE##_dynarray *da,          \
                       TYPE val);
```

Then, to get a dynamic array of, say, int objects, you can put

```
GEN_DYNARRAY_TYPE(int)
GEN_DYNARRAY_PROTOTYPES(int)
```

in a header file, say int_dynarray.h, and

```
GEN_DYNARRAY_FUNCTIONS(int)
```

in an implementation file, int_dynarray.c.

That is it! That is all there is to generating the code for a dynamic array using macros. If you have a type, and the preceding macros, you can automatically generate the code to work on a dynamic array of that type:

```
typedef struct { double x, y; } point;
GEN_DYNARRAY_TYPE(point)
GEN_DYNARRAY_FUNCTIONS(point)
```

We use a generated dynamic array the same way as we used the int array in the previous section, and since all the functions know the type, our code is checked by the type-checker.

```
int main(void)
{
  point_dynarray pda;
  bool success = point_da_init(&pda, 0, 0);
  if (!success) exit(1); // bail out

  for (int i = 0; i < 5; i++) {
    success = point_da_append(
        &pda, (point){ .x = i, .y = i }
    );
    if (!success) break;
  }

  for (int i = 0; i < da_len(&pda); i++) {
    point *p = &da_at(&pda, i);
    printf("<%.1f, %.1f>\n", p->x, p->y);
  }

  point_da_dealloc(&pda);

  return 0;
}
```

Inlining Macros

If you are okay with generating code for each type we need a dynamic array of, then maybe you are okay with generating code for each operation as well. We can write macros that inline the operation code each place we use them. We get the same type safety as we get with the generated functions because the generated code knows the type of each dynamic array we operate on. Inlining code can be faster than calling functions (at the cost of slightly larger programs, since the same code is repeated everywhere we do an operation on a dynamic array).

If we inline all the code, we don't have to muck about with extra files for the generated functions, but it comes with two drawbacks. First, error handling, as we shall see, is slightly more complicated—if you are brave enough to ignore it, you get simpler code, but you probably shouldn't ignore errors. Second, if you have a programming error, the response you get from the compiler is harder to understand. It will refer to code expanded from a macro, which means you need to understand that to fix the problem. With functions, we never have to worry about the implementation and only the interface; with inlined macro code, we are not so lucky.

But let's get to it. First, the macros for getting an item in an array and for getting the length of an array: They will not change much, but now that we do not use functions that take pointer arguments, there is no reason to work with the addresses of arrays, so we make the macro work directly with the array object and not a pointer to it (we use . instead of ->):

```
#define da_at(da,i)  ((da).data[(i)])
#define da_len(da)   ((da).used)
```

This means that we will be calling them as da_at(da,i) and da_len(da) instead of da_at(&da,i) and da_len(&da) and still have a consistent calling convention for all the operations.

We need a macro for defining the dynamic array struct, but this time we will not use one that creates a type definition. Instead, we will write a macro that gives us an anonymous struct with the right elements:

```
#define dynarray(TYPE)          \
struct {                        \
  size_t size;                  \
  size_t used;                  \
  TYPE *data;                   \
}
```

Notice that there is not a semicolon at the end. The intended use for the macro is to define dynamic array objects with syntax such as

```
dynarray(int) int_da;        // a dynamic array of int
dynarray(double) double_da; // a dynamic array of double
```

Since we are not generating a name, we do not have the issue with what type names we can use, so you can also declare a dynamic array of points like this:

```
struct point { double x, y; };
dynarray(struct point) point_da;
```

We need an operation for initializing an array. With the function solution that we have used so far, we would get a status value back to see if the allocation was successful. As a first attempt, we can try to do the same with a macro expansion. In C, you cannot make a general sequence of statements into an expression you can get a value from, so while it would be nice if we could simply take the function body from the previous code and turn into an expression, it might not be possible. There are compiler extensions that allow it. For example, in GCC and Clang you can use so-called *statement expressions* and write

```
#define da_init(da, init_size, init_used)            \
({(da).data =                                         \
    checked_malloc(MAX(init_size, MIN_ARRAY_SIZE),    \
                   *(da).data);                       \
  (da).size = (da).data ? init_size : 0;              \
  (da).used = (da).data ? init_used : 0;              \
  !!da.data;})
```

We enclose the code in curly brackets and then parentheses, and we get code that returns a value. We could use this macro like

```
dynarray(int) int_da;
bool success = da_init(da, 0, 0);
```

This isn't portable C, however, and if you switch to another compiler, it likely won't work. If all the statements are expressions, and not variable definitions or control structures like if, for, and such, then we can achieve the same with the *comma operator*. If you put commas between expressions, you evaluate them in turn, and the result is the result of the last expression. We only have simple statements in the initialization code, so we could replace all the semicolons with commas, put them in parentheses, and get what we want:

```
#define da_init(da, init_size, init_used)                \
((da).data =                                             \
   checked_malloc(MAX(init_size, MIN_ARRAY_SIZE),        \
                    *(da).data),                         \
 (da).size = (da).data ? init_size : 0,                  \
 (da).used = (da).data ? init_used : 0,                  \
 !!da.data)
```

With resize and append, however, we both need if-statements and need to define a variable to hold freshly allocated memory, so we don't overwrite the array's data if the realloc() failed. We might be able to handle if-statements with the ?: operator, but defining variables will be a problem. We will need another solution for those operations, so to keep the code consistent, we should go with an initialization operation that can also work for the other two. One option, which we will take, is to require that the user provide a variable that we can write the status to:

```
#define da_init(da, status, init_size, init_used)        \
do {                                                     \
  (da).data =                                            \
    checked_malloc(MAX(init_size, MIN_ARRAY_SIZE),       \
                    *(da).data);                         \
  (da).size = (da).data ? init_size : 0;                 \
  (da).used = (da).data ? init_used : 0;                 \
  status = !!da.data;                                    \
} while (0)
```

The second argument to the macro must be a variable that we can write to, and it is that variable that the caller must check to see if the allocation was successful. The caller cannot test on a return value; they must provide a variable. Still, if we are serious about testing that an allocation worked (and we should be), then it is not a high price to pay for consistency—and we will need it later anyway.

The `status` variable is the second argument, and I would like to say it is second only to the dynamic array because it is so important to test for success, but the honest answer is that I would have preferred it to be last because it functions like a return value. However, the append operation, for reasons that I will explain later, cannot have the `status` parameter last, and as we seek consistency, the initialization won't get it either, then.

If you are puzzled by the `do-while` around the code, I can briefly explain. It is a C idiom that lets you use a macro expansion as a statement. Imagine that we define the macro

```
#define FOOBAR(x) foo(x) ; bar(x)
```

and use it in some code as

```
FOOBAR(42);
```

That is fine; it expands to two function calls:

```
foo(42) ; bar(42);
```

Now put it in an `if`-statement:

```
if (x > 0)
  FOOBAR(x);
```

and it expands to

```
if (x > 0)
  foo(x) ; bar(x);
```

where `bar(x)` will be called regardless of the value of `x`, since only `foo(x)` is in the body of the `if`-statement. This is probably not what the caller intended. You could complain that the user should have written

```
if (x > 0) {
  FOOBAR(x);
}
```

but the fact is that the curly braces are not necessary in C, if the if body only has a single statement. We should write our macros such that they cause the least confusion, especially if the user invokes them in what would be valid C if we had a function instead of a macro.

You could try to fix it with curly brackets:

```
#define FOOBAR(x) { foo(x) ; bar(x); }
```

Then the expansion of

```
if (x > 0)
  FOOBAR(x);
```

becomes

```
if (x > 0)
  { foo(x) ; bar(x); };
```

which will work. However

```
if (x > 0)
  FOOBAR(x);
else
  baz(x);
```

becomes

```
if (x > 0)
  { foo(x); bar(x); };
else
  baz(x);
```

and the semicolon after the macro expansion, before else, is a syntax error. If you use brackets like this, you have to leave out the semicolon in FOOBAR(x):

```
if (x > 0)
  FOOBAR(x)
else
  baz(x);
```

which then would break again if we changed the macro definition to something that is a single expression.

A do-while loop is a single statement, in which we can group as many statements as we like. When we write while(0), we will only execute the loop body once, so the effect is the same as if we had grouped a sequence of statements.[2] It has the added benefit that we can use a break statement to leave the sequence of expanded statements, something we will exploit shortly.

In the da_resize() function, we used the type of the array when we allocated new_data. One way to get it into the macro is to make it an argument, like we did for defining the dynamic array structure.

```
#define da_resize(da, status, type, new_size)          \
do {                                                    \
  size_t alloc_size =                                   \
    MAX(new_size, MIN_ARRAY_SIZE);                      \
  type new_data =                                       \
    checked_realloc((da).data,                          \
      alloc_size, *(da).data);                          \
  if (!new_data) { status = false; break; }             \
  (da).data = new_data;                                 \
  (da).size = alloc_size;                               \
  (da).used = MIN((da).used, new_size);                 \
  status = true;                                        \
} while (0)
```

or we could use compiler extensions like GCC and Clang's __typeof__ macro to get it from the struct:

```
#define da_resize(da, status, new_size)                \
do {                                                   \
  size_t alloc_size =                                  \
    MAX(new_size, MIN_ARRAY_SIZE);                     \
  __typeof__(da.data) new_data =                       \
    checked_realloc((da).data,                         \
        alloc_size, *(da).data);                       \
  if (!new_data) { status = false; break; }            \
```

---

[2]An optimizing compiler can easily see that we will never run the body more than once, and simplify the code, so there is no overhead to it.

```
    (da).data = new_data;                          \
    (da).size = alloc_size;                        \
    (da).used = MIN((da).used, new_size);          \
    status = true;                                 \
} while (0)
```

However, that would be compiler specific and not portable. Luckily, as it turns out, we do not *need* to know the type of data we allocate. It is, after all, just a chunk of memory until we assign it to the struct's data field. So, we can leave it as a void pointer, which is what we get from realloc() in the first place.

```
#define da_resize(da, status, new_size)            \
do {                                               \
  size_t alloc_size =                              \
    MAX(new_size, MIN_ARRAY_SIZE);                 \
  void *new_data = checked_realloc((da).data,      \
        alloc_size, *(da).data);                   \
  if (!new_data) { status = false; break; }        \
  (da).data = new_data;                            \
  (da).size = alloc_size;                          \
  (da).used = MIN((da).used, new_size);            \
  status = true;                                   \
} while (0)
```

We once again have the status parameter that we use for reporting allocation errors, and if we couldn't allocate, we use break to bail out of the rest of the code. We can use break because we put the code in a do-while body.

As a stylistic issue, some object to macros that declare variables, as we do here with alloc_size and new_data. The macro declares variables that the user cannot directly see when using the macro. The statements are in their own block, so we will not get name clashes or overwrite existing variables, but if a macro declares a variable, it can shadow another variable.

281

Shadowing variables is often a source of errors. For example, in

```
int i;
// some code
for (int i = 0; i < n; i++) {
  // more code
  foo(i);
}
```

did we intend to call foo(i) with the first i or the iteration variable? Generally, we should avoid overshadowing. In the macro, the variables we introduce only live for the duration of the array operation, and we cannot accidentally use the values they hold in our code. So, why is it a problem? It is a problem because some compilers will, with the right compilation flags, warn you about shadowing variables or even turn them into errors. This is a good thing, as it can help you avoid errors, but it will not work if you use macros such as the one we just wrote—at least if they accidentally generate a variable that shadows another.

For the size variable, we can easily replace it with the expression we used to compute it. It is a value that we can compute without needing a variable. We cannot get rid of new_data as easily, however, as we need a place to store the allocated memory until we can assign it into the dynamic array. We cannot recompute it. If we check the call of one realloc() to see if it was a success and then assign the result of a second call into the array, then the second call could fail. That would leak memory, and we would have a NULL pointer in a dynamic array that thinks it has data. With the way that we implement dynamic arrays in this section, we need to declare variables in the macro expansion. If we accept that we can lose our data (though not leak memory) when an allocation fails, we can avoid them. I will show you an example in the next section. For now, however, you will have to live with this potential issue.

Append looks much like the function version, except that we use break instead of return when resizing isn't possible, or failed, and we use the status argument to report errors.

```
#define da_append(da, status, val)              \
do {                                            \
  if ((da).used == (da).size) {                 \
    if (at_max_len((da).size, *(da).data))      \
      { status = false; break; }                \
```

```
    size_t new_size =                              \
      capped_dbl((da).size, *(da).data);           \
    da_resize(da, status, new_size);               \
    if (!status) break;                            \
  }                                                \
  (da).data[(da).used++] = val;                    \
  status = true;                                   \
} while (0)
```

There is an issue here that is not obvious at first glance. We want to be able to append arbitrary expressions (that evaluate to the correct type), so we would expect code like this to work:

```
// MACRO CODE HERE

struct point { double x, y; };

int main(void)
{
  bool success = true;
  dynarray(struct point) pda;
  da_init(pda, success, 0, 0);
  if (!success) goto error;

  for (int i = 0; i < 5; i++) {
    // APPENDING A POINT...THIS WILL FAIL
    da_append(
      pda, success,
      (struct point){ .x = i, .y = -i }
    );
    if (!success) goto error;
  }

  for (int i = 0; i < da_len(pda); i++) {
    printf("<%.1f,%.1f> ",
      da_at(pda, i).x,
      da_at(pda, i).y
    );
  }
```

```
  printf("\n");

  da_dealloc(pda);
  return 0;

error:

  da_dealloc(pda);
  return 1;
}
```

You will find that the expression

```
da_append(
  pda, success,
  (struct point){ .x = i, .y = -i }
);
```

fails, however. The problem is that macros are pretty dumb. The C preprocessor doesn't understand C, and it doesn't see (struct point){ .x = i, .y = -i } as a single argument. There is a comma in it, so it sees two arguments, (struct point){ .x = i and .y = -i }. The preprocessor works with raw strings and not C expressions, and it doesn't care that you intended the argument to be C expressions; if you have a comma, you have more than one argument.

Since C99, the preprocessor has had so-called *variadic macros*, that is, macros that take a variable number of arguments. The standard gives you very little to work with on those; you can specify that a macro takes a variable number of arguments and then insert all of them into the generated code, and that is all. Luckily, it is all we need.

You specify that your macro takes a variable number of arguments using three dots, ..., and you get what the caller provided with the variable __VA_ARGS__. In da_append(), we can write a variadic macro like this:

```
#define da_append(da, status, ...)                    \
do {                                                   \
  if ((da).used == (da).size) {                        \
    if (at_max_len((da).size, *(da).data))             \
      { status = false; break; }                       \
    size_t new_size =                                  \
```

```
      capped_dbl((da).size, *(da).data);           \
    da_resize(da, status, new_size);               \
     if (!status) break;                            \
  }                                                 \
  (da).data[(da).used++] = __VA_ARGS__;             \
  status = true;                                    \
} while (0)
```

We cannot put the `status` variable after the three dots, which is why we put it as the second argument to all the operations. With this definition of `da_append()`, the preceding code will run.

This implementation is intended for having dynamic arrays stack allocated—except for the data—and is intended for working with them locally in one function. Passing dynamic arrays along in function calls was not the intended use, but, of course, someone will eventually come along and want to do that. Here, we have to be careful. You always have to pass them as references. If you pass a dynamic array by value, you get two different `structs`, with separate `size` and `used` data, but sharing the same data buffer. If a function resizes an array, for example, by appending to it, the instance of the array at the caller doesn't change, but the `data` field might no longer be valid. It could be freed in the resizing operation. So, always pass by a pointer.

Is all well if we do that, though? Not completely. If we write a function such as this:

```
bool add_origin(dynarray(struct point) *da)
{
  bool status;
  da_append(
    *da, status,
    (struct point){ .x = 0, .y = 0 }
  );
  return status;
}
```

and we want to call it elsewhere:

```
dynarray(struct point) da;
bool success = 0;
da_init(da, success, 0, 0);
if (!success) goto error;
success = add_origin(&da); // <- type error
```

we get a type error. The dynarray() macro creates an anonymous struct, and two anonymous structs, even with exactly the same definition, are not the same type. If you want to use dynamic arrays as function parameters, then you must typedef them. You can define the same function as

```
typedef dynarray(struct point) point_array;
bool add_origin(point_array *da)
{
  bool status;
  da_append(
    *da, status,
    (struct point){ .x = 0, .y = 0 }
  );
  return status;
}
```

and call it as

```
point_array da;
bool success = 0;
da_init(da, success, 0, 0);
if (!success) goto error;
success = add_origin(&da); // <- correct type
```

Heap-Allocated Inlined Array

The variables we defined in the macros in the previous section are necessary (at least some of them) because we want to preserve the data if realloc() fails, so we need to store the result of a call in a temporary variable. If we can accept that we lose all our data if we cannot append to an array, then we can simplify the code and get rid of the variables. We might be willing to lose everything if we cannot append, for example, if we are using a dynamic array in an algorithm where we really cannot continue if we cannot append. In such a situation, we would need to abort anyway.

This is a relatively simple change. We can write a function that replaces realloc() that will free() its input if it cannot allocate. It could look something like this:

```
void *free_realloc(void *p, size_t size)
```

```
{
  void *new_p = realloc(p, size);
  if (!new_p) free(p);
  return new_p;
}
```

Your system might already have such a function. On BSD-based systems such as macOS, but also on many Linux systems, it is called reallocf().

With that, we can assign to the dynamic array's data pointer directly. Imagine that we have a checked_free_realloc() that works like checked_realloc() but with free_realloc(), then resizing could now look like this:

```
#define da_resize(da, new_size)                       \
do {                                                  \
  (da).data =                                         \
    checked_free_realloc((da).data,                   \
    MAX(new_size, MIN_ARRAY_SIZE),                    \
    *(da).data);                                      \
  (da).size =                                         \
    ((da).data) ? MAX(new_size, MIN_ARRAY_SIZE)       \
              : 0;                                    \
  (da).used =                                         \
    ((da).data) ? MIN((da).used, new_size)            \
              : 0;                                    \
} while (0)
```

I got rid of alloc_size and substituted in MAX(new_size, MIN_ARRAY_SIZE) the two places we use it, and I reset the size and used numbers if the allocation failed. I also got rid of the status variable because now we can test if da.data is NULL after resizing and get the status that way.

```
da_resize(da, 1024);
if (!da.data) { /* handle error */ }
```

This change is too small to warrant an entire section, so I will add a little more to show you something new about dynamic memory allocation and structures. We will allocate the entire array on the heap and put both the size/used information and then data in the same allocation. It is not a better solution than what we already have, but it gives me an excuse to teach you about *flexible array members* of structures and nesting generic meta-information in a struct.

The meta-information we need for a dynamic array is size and used, and we can define a struct for them:

```
struct da_meta {
  size_t size;
  size_t used;
};
```

We will put such a struct at the top of type-specific structures like this:

```
#define dynarr(TYPE)          \
struct {                      \
  struct da_meta meta;        \
  TYPE data[];                \
}
```

We will only use heap-allocated dynamic arrays, so you are supposed to declare arrays of type T as

```
dynarr(T) *da = /* initialise */ ;
```

I will get to the data array there shortly. By putting the meta-information at the top of the type-specific struct, we know that the memory for the meta-information sits at the first address of such structures. If we cast a dynarr(T) pointer to a da_meta pointer, we can treat the memory as if it was the meta-information struct. This means that we can write generic functions that only know about the meta-information and the size of objects, and not the various types we need. For example, we can write a function that reallocates memory for dynamic arrays like this:

```
void *realloc_dynarray_mem(struct da_meta *p,
                           size_t meta_size,
                           size_t obj_size,
                           size_t new_len)
{
  // Is there a size overflow?
  if (((SIZE_MAX - meta_size) / obj_size < new_len))
    goto fail;
```

```
  struct da_meta *new_da =
    realloc(p, meta_size + obj_size * new_len);
  if (!new_da)
    goto fail;

  new_da->size = new_len;
  new_da->used = MIN(new_da->used, new_len);

  return new_da;


fail:
  free(p);
  return 0;
}
```

The meta_size is the size we set aside for meta-information (and I will explain it later), the obj_size is the size of the objects in the array, and, obviously, new_len is the length we want to resize the array to. This function handles overflow checks and allocation errors by freeing the existing pointer, p, and if it manages to allocate the new memory, it sets the new size and used meta-information.

We can use the function for generic versions that create new arrays or grow them to twice their size:

```
void *new_dynarray_mem(size_t meta_size,
                       size_t obj_size,
                       size_t len)
{
  struct da_meta *array =
    realloc_dynarray_mem(0, meta_size, obj_size, len);
  if (array)
    array->used = 0;
  return array;
}

void *grow_dynarray_mem(struct da_meta *p,
                        size_t meta_size,
                        size_t obj_size)
```

```
{
  // Can we double the length?
  size_t used = meta_size + obj_size * p->size;
  size_t adding = MAX(1, p->size);
  if ((SIZE_MAX - used) / obj_size < adding) {
    free(p);
    return 0;
  }

  return realloc_dynarray_mem(
    p, meta_size, obj_size, p->size + adding
  );
}
```

The new_dynarray_mem() function sets used to zero. It is set to the minimum of len and its existing value in the call to realloc_dynarray_mem(), but it is not initialized there, so that value will be rubbish, and we must explicitly set it. The grow_dynarray_mem() function doesn't attempt to get SIZE_MAX if it cannot grow the size to twice the former length. This is only to make the code simpler; you can extend it to work more like the previous versions if you want.

The functions can work with dynamic arrays without knowing the underlying type because we have extracted the meta-information as a separate type and because we treat the pointer to a dynamic array as a pointer to a da_meta structure (and safely so, as long as the meta struct is always the first member in the dynamic array struct).

For concrete dynamic arrays, those we declare with dynarr(T), we provide macros that get the size of objects from the variables we use:

```
#define new_da(da, init_size)                      \
  new_dynarray_mem(sizeof *(da),                   \
                   sizeof *(da)->data,             \
                   (init_size))

#define da_free(da)                                \
  do { free(da); (da) = 0; } while(0)

#define da_at(da,i)    (da->data[(i)])
#define da_len(da)     (da->meta.used)
```

```
#define da_append(da, ...)                        \
do {                                              \
  if ((da)->meta.used == (da)->meta.size) {       \
    (da) = grow_dynarray_mem(                      \
      (struct da_meta *)(da),                      \
      sizeof *(da), sizeof *(da)->data             \
    );                                             \
    if (!(da)) break;                              \
  }                                               \
  (da)->data[(da)->meta.used++] = __VA_ARGS__;    \
} while (0)
```

In the calls to new_dynarray_mem() and grow_dynarray_mem(), the meta_size parameter is the size of the dynamic array type, that is, the dynarr(T) struct. I will beg a little more of your patience, and I promise I will get to why that is.

You can then use, for example, an integer array, like this:

```
int main(void)
{
  dynarr(int) *int_array = new_da(int_array, 0);
  if (!int_array) goto error;
  printf("%zu out of %zu\n",
         int_array->meta.used,
          int_array->meta.size);

  for (int i = 0; i < 5; i++) {
    da_append(int_array, i);
    if (!int_array) goto error;
  }

  for (int i = 0; i < da_len(int_array); i++) {
    printf("%d ", da_at(int_array, i));
  }
```

```
    printf("\n");

    da_free(int_array);

    return 0;

error:
    return 1;
}
```

The new_da() macro gives us a new dynamic array, of the correct type, and all the other operations will either leave us with a valid dynamic array or set their argument to NULL. This includes da_free(). It will set the pointer to NULL to indicate that it is no longer a valid dynamic array. You should test if the array is NULL after every operation that can fail—here, it is only the initialization and da_append() because we didn't include the resize operation and because free() can never fail. If you use the arrays correctly, that is, you assign a new array to a variable as soon as you declare the pointer, then the array can never be in an invalid state. It is either an array or a NULL pointer.

The initialization takes the variable we declare as input, which might look a little odd. The new_da() macro needs to know the type of the array that we want to be initialized, and it cannot infer where we will assign the result of calling the macro, so we must provide the type. We have two options here, explicitly provide the type:

```
#define new_da(type, init_size)                     \
  new_dynarray_mem(sizeof(dynarr(type)),            \
                   sizeof(type),                    \
                   (init_size))
```

or get the type from a variable, as before. There are two issues with using the type. First, it makes it easier to initialize an array with the wrong type.

```
dynarr(T) *da = new_da(S, 10);
```

Of course, you could argue that it is easy to spot, and it is, but we often make mistakes like

```
int *p = malloc(sizeof(long));
```

when we update types in our programs, which is why we use the idiom

```
int *p = malloc(sizeof *p);
```

and it is the same idiom we use when we provide the variable name to the `new_da()` macro.

The other issue is more subtle and highly unlikely to be a problem. In the macro that takes the type, we write `sizeof(dynarr(type))` to get the size of the array. If we write

```
dynarr(T) *da = new_da(T, n);
```

we would expect that the `dynarr(T)` on the left and the `dynarr(T)` in the macro expansion are the same. And it is, in the sense that it is the same code, and any sane compiler will construct the types with the same padding and thus the same size. However, the C standard does not explicitly require it. I cannot imagine a compiler insane enough to use different paddings for identical `struct` declarations, but when it comes to compiler insanity, it is better to be safe than sorry. Using the variable we declare as the macro input solves both issues, and it isn't far from the idiom we use with `malloc()`, so it is not something that bothers me.

Now finally we come to the `meta_size` arguments and flexible array members of `struct`s. Flexible array members are `struct` members that are empty arrays, that is, arrays defined without a size as our `TYPE data[]` member. They were added to C in the C99 standard, although they have been around as compiler extensions longer (and as various hacks like length-zero arrays `TYPE data[0]` longer than that). Flexible array members have to be the last member of a `struct`, and the reason will be obvious when I explain what they are used for.

Our plan is to declare member such that we have the meta-information first, followed by the objects in the array. A straightforward approach would be to allocate memory as

```
dynarr(T) *p = malloc(sizeof(da_meta) + len * sizeof(T));
```

or something to that effect. It allocates the memory we need for the meta-information and then memory for `len` copies of the underlying type. However, straightforward is too often wrong, and the problem with this approach is alignment. We will allocate enough memory, but we can't necessarily put objects of type T right after the meta-information. If T has alignment constraints that don't fit the size of `da_meta`, we get in trouble.

When we declare a `struct`, C defines the memory layout of the `struct` with the necessary padding to align the members correctly. So, if we define

```
struct S {
  // stuff
  T array[10];
};
```

we get a type, `struct S`, where the member `array` sits at an offset where we can place ten objects of type T. If we instead of `array[10]` write `array[]`, we get an offset for `array` where we can put zero T, but correctly aligned. If we dynamically allocate memory, and `array` is the last member, it doesn't matter that we didn't declare the `struct` so it has space for the T objects. We still get an offset where we can place them. And if we allocate sufficient memory, then we *can* put objects there. Thus, with

```
struct S {
  // stuff
  T array[];
};
```

we can allocate memory as

```
struct S *p = malloc(sizeof *p + n * sizeof *(p->array));
```

and get space for the "stuff" first in the structure and then additionally room for n objects of type T. If we access them through the `array` member, they have the right alignment. That is what the empty array gives us.

Consider a `struct` like this:

```
struct S {
  char c[2];
  int array[];
};
```

If we left out the array, the size would be two. That is because char always has size two and can align at any offset. If we allocated space for the char array and then tried to put integers after it, however, we would get an error if integers cannot sit at alignment two (which they cannot on my machine; they want alignment four). Including the empty array makes the size of `struct S` four (again, on my machine) because the `array` member must sit at an offset where I can place an integer. If I allocate

```
struct S *p = malloc(sizeof(struct S) + 10 * sizeof(int));
```

I will get the member for the struct plus 10 int, and I can put the integers starting at the offset where array is found. You can get the offset of a struct member using the macro offsetof() from the <stddef.h> header, so you can examine what C says on your own machine with

```
printf("%zu %zu\n", sizeof(struct S),
        offsetof(struct S, array));
```

If the array was of a different type, for example, char, the alignment might change. With

```
struct T {
  char c[2];
  char array[];
};
```

and

```
printf("%zu %zu\n", sizeof(struct U),
        offsetof(struct U, array));
```

it tells me that the size of the struct is two, and so is the offset of array. The size is two because we need to store the char array of length 2, and right after that we have an offset where we can place array, but we do not need to allocate any memory for it—the array is empty, and it doesn't count. The padding is needed to give us a valid offset, but we don't add memory just to store the flexible array member. When array is a char array, it can go after the other member without padding, so the size of the struct is the same as the array c.

This doesn't mean that the flexible array member goes at the last address of the struct, however. Its offset is not always equal to the size of the struct. Consider

```
struct U {
  void *p; int i;
  char array[];
};
```

On my machine, pointers have to align on offsets multiples of eight, integers multiples of four, and chars of course anywhere. The size of p and i take up 8 bytes for the pointer and 4 for the integer, so 12 bytes. Since array is of char, it can align right after i, and its offset when I check it with

```
printf("%zu %zu\n", sizeof(struct U),
       offsetof(struct U, array));
```

tells me as much. Still, sizeof(struct U) is 16. What gives? Well, the size of a struct has to be such that we can align one copy after another, if the first is correctly aligned. If p sits at a valid alignment, a multiple of eight, and I put two struct U in a row, the second element's p must also sit at a multiple of eight. If the size of struct U was 12, it wouldn't. There is extra padding, after the offset we get for array, to make it possible to align struct U in an array.

Structs with flexible array members are not supposed to go into arrays—we use the array for dynamic memory allocation—but the rule for sizes of structs still applies. If we allocate space for a struct U, with an extra 10 bytes for the array, we can write

```
struct U *u = malloc(sizeof *u + 10 * sizeof *u->data);
```

and we can access u->data as an array with ten chars in it. This is what we do with the preceding dynamic arrays. We allocate space for a struct with a flexible array of the correct type. It guarantees us that we get space for the meta-information and the padding to get the correct alignment for the data member. But if the size of the struct is larger than the offset of the data member, we are wasting some space. We are wasting sizeof(dynarr(T)) - offsetof(dynarr(T), data).

On my machine, this is nothing. My size_t has size 8 and alignment 8; I can put any other type after the meta-information without padding, and there isn't additional padding to align a potential following struct da_meta. I still use the flexible array, though, to make sure that a future setting won't have alignment issues. If I also want to ensure that I am not wasting memory, however little, I can allocate memory for the struct up to the data member offset, and then the elements in the array, but not the potential padding following the data offset. Instead of using sizeof *(da) in the macros—which gives me the size of the struct—I could use the offset of the data array.

If we know the type of the dynamic array, then we can get the offset using the offsetof() macro:

```
offsetof(dynarr(T), data)
```

but our macros use a pointer to an array to get information about the type. Since offsetof() needs a type, we need to get the type of the macro argument. A compiler extension in most compilers is __typeof__ (or __typeof or typeof(); it is not a standard operator so it has different names). It gives you the type of an object, and then we can use it with offsetof(). With GCC or Clang, this macro will give us the data offset of a dynamic array:

```
#define da_data_offset(da) \
  offsetof(__typeof__(*(da)), data)
```

You can replace `sizeof *(da)` with `da_data_offset(da)` in the `new_da()` and `da_append()` macros to use the offset rather than size.

The problem, of course, is that we are relying on a compiler extension. In many cases, since it is a common extension, it isn't a problem. We can pick the compiler-specific notation via preprocessing flags.

However, it is always better to restrict ourselves to the C standard if we can.

How do we compute the offset of a member? A common definition of the macro is a variation of this:

```
#define offsetof(type,member) \
  (size_t)&((type *)0)->member
```

It makes a NULL pointer of the given type and then gets the address of its member. If the pointer is to address zero (which a NULL pointer is on systems that can define `offsetof()` this way), then the member address is the offset from the top of the struct. We can get the same information using a pointer to a `struct` and a pointer to its member:

```
#define offset_pointer(p,member) \
  (size_t)((char *)&(p)->member - (char *)(p))
```

It looks like we dereference the pointer here, when we get `(p)->member`, but we take the address of the member and not what it looks at, so the macro works even if `p` is NULL. As long as it is a valid pointer, we get the offset this way. Thus, we can use that:

```
#define da_data_offset(da) \
  ((char *)&(da)->data - (char *)(da))
```

Unfortunately, we do need it to be a valid pointer, and an uninitialized pointer isn't necessarily that. And in `new_da()`, we have an uninitialized pointer. Even if an uninitialized pointer would work, if you turn on compiler warnings, you would see it complain if we calculated the offset of it with this macro. We are using the value of an uninitialized variable, even though we don't care about the actual value.

You can fix it by setting the pointer to NULL before you create a new dynamic array in new_da():

```
#define new_da(da, init_size)                  \
  ((da) = 0, new_dynarray_mem(                 \
                  da_data_offset(da),          \
                  sizeof *(da)->data,          \
                  (init_size)))
```

We can get away with this because assigning to da and the allocation are both expressions that we can use with the comma operator. We do not need compiler extensions like statement expressions.

It doesn't change the use pattern much, because you are supposed to assign the value of the allocation back into that pointer when you call new_da(). So, it shouldn't hold anything of value in the first place. If you write code such as

```
dynarr(int) *d1 = new_da(d1, 10);
dynarr(int) *d2 = new_da(d1, 10);
```

where you reuse a variable (and lose access to the member it points to), then you are going to get into trouble at a later time anyway (because the type of the two arrays could diverge). Still, if you don't like it, I understand you. Then stick to the typeof () solution, if your compilers support it, or use the size of the struct (you are not wasting many bytes compared to the memory you use for storing objects in any case).

If you want to call functions with dynamic arrays as parameters, you have the same issue with types as in the previous section. If you write a function such as this, for inserting points in an array from their x and y coordinates:

```
struct point { double x, y; };

void add_points(size_t n,
                double xs[n], double ys[n],
                dynarr(struct point) *da)
{
  for (int i = 0; i < n; i++) {
    da_append(da, (struct point){ .x = xs[i], .y = ys[i] });
  }
}
```

you cannot use it as

```
dynarr(struct point) *points = new_da(points, 0);
size_t n = 5;
double xs[5] = { 0.0, 1.0, 2.0, 3.0, 4.0 };
double ys[5] = { 4.0, 3.0, 2.0, 1.0, 0.0 };
add_points(n, xs, ys, points);
```

because the types do not match (even though they are created from the same expanded macro). You must typedef the array type.

```
struct point { double x, y; };
typedef dynarr(struct point) point_array;

void add_points(size_t n,
                double xs[n], double ys[n],
                point_array *da)
{
  for (int i = 0; i < n; i++) {
    da_append(da, (struct point){ .x = xs[i], .y = ys[i] });
  }
}

int main(void)
{
  point_array *points = new_da(points, 0);
  size_t n = 5;
  double xs[5] = { 0.0, 1.0, 2.0, 3.0, 4.0 };
  double ys[5] = { 4.0, 3.0, 2.0, 1.0, 0.0 };
  add_points(n, xs, ys, points);

  return 0;
}
```

You *also* have to call the function with a *reference* to the dynamic array. That is, you have to use a pointer to the array. It looks like we are doing that already, perhaps, because we use a pointer to point_array, but a dynamic array in this implementation is already a pointer. We need a pointer to the array, so a pointer to a pointer. If you run the preceding code and then attempt to access the points array:

```
int main(void)
{
  point_array *points = new_da(points, 0);
  size_t n = 5;
  double xs[5] = { 0.0, 1.0, 2.0, 3.0, 4.0 };
  double ys[5] = { 4.0, 3.0, 2.0, 1.0, 0.0 };
  add_points(n, xs, ys, points);

  for (int i = 0; i < da_len(points); i++) {
    printf("<%.1f,%.1f> ",
           da_at(points, i).x,
           da_at(points, i).y);
  }
  printf("\n");

  da_free(points);
  return 0;
}
```

you will likely get an error. In add_points(), we append to an array that is initialized to have length zero, so we will realloc() it multiple times. We are growing it, so most likely this involves freeing the original data and getting a new address from realloc(). So after the call to add_points(), the points array contains the address of freed memory. We cannot safely use it.

Inside add_points(), the pointer is updated when we grow the array (and we should have checked for allocation errors in the function!). But the updated pointer was never propagated back to the calling code. Changing a function argument does not change the calling variable.

One option, of course, is to return the dynamic array from functions that modify them, and always remember to assign them back to the correct pointer:

```
struct point { double x, y; };
typedef dynarr(struct point) point_array;

point_array *add_points(size_t n,
                        double xs[n], double ys[n],
                        point_array *da)
```

```c
{
  for (int i = 0; i < n; i++) {
    da_append(da, (struct point){ .x = xs[i], .y = ys[i] });
    if (!da) break;
  }
  // Return the dynamic array again
  return da;
}

int main(void)
{
  point_array *points = new_da(points, 0);

  size_t n = 5;
  double xs[5] = { 0.0, 1.0, 2.0, 3.0, 4.0 };
  double ys[5] = { 4.0, 3.0, 2.0, 1.0, 0.0 };
  // Remember to assign back to the array!
  points = add_points(n, xs, ys, points);

  if (!points) goto error;

  for (int i = 0; i < da_len(points); i++) {
    printf("<%.1f,%.1f> ",
           da_at(points, i).x,
           da_at(points, i).y);
  }
  printf("\n");

  da_free(points);
  return 0;
error:
  return 1;
}
```

This, however, only works if functions never take more than one array as input or at least never modify more than one. It is not particularly safe, since it is easy to forget to assign the function return value back to the array. A better solution is to pass pointers to pointers as arguments. If you have a pointer to the dynamic array pointer, then you can use it, dereferenced, as the dynamic array. If the macros update it, they update it in the calling function as well.

```c
// Use a pointer to the dynamic array pointer
void add_points(size_t n,
                double xs[n], double ys[n],
                point_array **da)
{
  for (int i = 0; i < n; i++) {
    da_append(*da, (struct point){ .x = xs[i], .y = ys[i] });
    if (!*da) break;
  }
}

int main(void)
{
  point_array *points = new_da(points, 0);

  size_t   n = 5;
  double  xs[5] = { 0.0,  1.0,  2.0,  3.0,  4.0 };
  double  ys[5] = { 4.0,  3.0,  2.0,  1.0,  0.0 };

  // call by reference
  add_points(n, xs, ys, &points);
  if (!points) goto error;

  for (int i = 0; i < da_len(points); i++) {
    printf("<%.1f,%.1f> ",
           da_at(points, i).x,
           da_at(points, i).y);
  }
  printf("\n");

  da_free(points);
```

```
    return 0;

error:
    return 1;
}
```

It turned out to be a long intermezzo chapter, but we learned a few things along the way. Most of it related to generic code, with void pointers, raw memory, or a lot of macros, but we also learned about flexible array members and how to use those. So all was not lost. In the next chapter, we return to the schedule program, where we will look at a different type of data structures.

CHAPTER 11

Linked Lists

We now change our focus to a different kind of data structures, so-called *recursive data structures*. Those are data structures defined in terms of themselves, and in C, the only way that you can implement them is through pointers. If you pick up a random algorithm book, more than half of the data structures described there will likely be recursive, so we obviously can only scratch the surface of this topic, but in this chapter and the following two, we will see some examples.

A recursive data structure is one that contains members of its own type. In this chapter, we look at linked lists, where a list is defined as follows:

1. A list is empty.

2. Or a list contains an element and a list (the "tail" of the list).

We will modify it slightly in Chapter 4, so a list has a reference to *two* other lists. In Chapter 12, we have a search tree where

1. A tree is empty.

2. Or it contains a value and two subtrees.

In both cases, item 2 is the recursive part.

We could try to implement the list definition like this (notice that this is not valid C and will not compile):

```
struct list; // forward decl.
struct empty_list {};
struct nonempty_list {
  int value;
  struct list tail;
};
struct list {
  enum { EMPTY, NON_EMPTY } tag;
```

© Thomas Mailund 2021
T. Mailund, *Pointers in C Programming*, https://doi.org/10.1007/978-1-4842-6927-5_11

```
union {
  struct empty_list empty;
  struct nonempty_list non_empty;
} list;
};
```

It is a direct translation of the definition. The "or" in the definition is naturally defined as a union, and we have two cases: empty and non-empty. Here, the element that the non-empty list contains is an integer. We need a tag, the enum to tell them apart, and we put that into a list struct. It is not directly recursive, because a struct list doesn't contain a struct list, but it is indirectly recursive as a struct list contains a struct nonempty_list, which in turn contains a struct list.

The definition is overly complicated because we do not need an empty struct for an empty list, so we could also define the list like this, where it is obviously recursive:

```
struct list {
  bool is_empty;
  int value;
  struct list tail;
};
```

There is a flag to indicate whether the list is empty and the values we need if it isn't.

The definition won't work, and it can't work, because to allocate memory for a struct list, we must allocate memory for the embedded struct list, so we would need infinite memory. The recursion has a base case, the empty list, that for any given instance means that we use finite memory, but we have to allocate infinite memory if we define the list this way.

Pointers ride to the rescue. Instead of embedding the tail of the list into the struct, we can use a pointer to a list. The pointer takes up finite memory, regardless of how large the tail is.

Pointers are both necessary and sufficient to implement recursive data structures in C. With recursive data structures such as a list, we (usually) never have to worry about allocation overflow and such, so they are simpler to implement in that regard. Working with recursive data structures is mostly a question of moving pointers around to achieve what we want. That, of course, opens up new issues instead. We need to be careful with setting pointers correctly. Making sure that memory is correctly freed is often also more problematic if objects are connected in complicated ways. So it is a new set of challenges we will now encounter. The data structures we see, linked lists and search trees, are among the simplest, but they illustrate well the kind of programming you need to work with recursive data structures.

Singly Linked Lists

The definition "a list is empty or has an element and a tail" is a so-called *singly linked list*, since the non-empty, recursive, part refers to a single tail. We can implement them like this:

```
struct link {
  int value;
  struct link *next;
};
```

I have named the structure link rather than list. A list will be a pointer to a sequence, or chain, of such links. The pointer is NULL if the list is empty; otherwise, it will point to a link where we can find the first value in the list and a pointer to the next link in the chain. So, the list definition, updated to the pointer/link representation, is

1. An empty list represented as NULL.

2. Or a pointer to a struct link that has a value and a pointer, next, to a list.

We can allocate a link using

```
struct link *new_link(int val, struct link *next)
{
  struct link *link = malloc(sizeof *link);
  if (!link) return 0;
  link->value = val;
  link->next = next;
  return link;
}
```

We get the size of the memory to allocate from `sizeof *link` (when `link` points to a `struct link`, it is the size of the struct). The `sizeof` operator cannot give us overflow—if you can represent a `struct` at all, then you can `malloc()` size for it. So, there is no need to worry about overflow, but of course we can still get an allocation error, so `malloc()` can return NULL, in which case we have to give up. We return a NULL pointer in return, so the user can handle the error. Otherwise, we set the `value` and `next` members.

Ignoring allocation errors, we can construct a list of the numbers 1, 2, and 3 with

```
struct link *list =
  new_link(1, new_link(2, new_link(3, 0)));
```

Since C evaluates the function arguments before it calls a function, we will first evaluate `new_link(3, 0)` which creates a link with `value` 3 and a NULL pointer for next; see the top-right corner of Figure 11-1. Here, I have drawn the NULL pointer as a pointer that ends in a short line. I will generally draw NULL pointers that way or, when figures would otherwise get too messy, leave them out entirely. When illustrating data structures, I will draw the individual `struct`s as boxes and the pointers as arrows.

When we call `new_link(2, - )`, with "-" as the result of `new_link(3, 0)`, we create a new link, the middle of Figure 11-1, where the value is 2, and the `next` pointer refers to the link from the first call. Then, when we call `new_link(1, - )`, bottom left of Figure 11-1, we create a link with value 1 where `next` points to the link from `new_link(2, - )`. You can think of `new_link()` as prepending a value to a list, but we can also make an explicit operation for that:

```
struct link *prepend(struct link *list, int val)
{
  // new_link() returns 0 for allocation error,
  // and we just propagate that.
  return new_link(val, list);
}
```

With

```
struct link *list =
  new_link(1, new_link(2, new_link(3, 0)));
```

we have a problem if any of the allocations fail. If the first allocation, new_link(3, 0), fails, we end up with a list of 1 and 2 instead of 1, 2, and 3. Not what we want, but not as bad as it could be. If one of the other new_link() calls fails, however, it is slightly worse. The failed call will look like an empty list, since the function returns NULL, but the input to the function call is an allocated link. If the function call fails, we lose access to that memory. Our program no longer has a pointer to it, and we have no way of getting one either, and so we cannot free() it. We should probably be more careful.

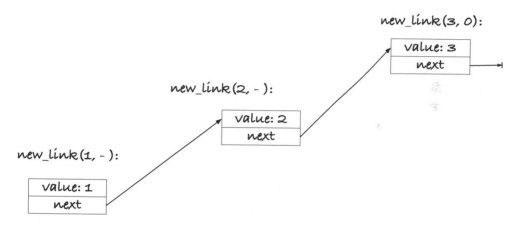

Figure 11-1. *new_link(1, new_link(2, new_link(3, 0)));*

We can write a function that frees an entire list. That means it must free all the links in the list's chain, not just the first link (which we can easily free with free()). It could look like this:

```
void free_list(struct link *list)
{
  while (list) {
    // Remember next, we cannot get it
    // after free(list)
    struct link *next = list->next;
    free(list);
    list = next;
  }
}
```

In the while-loop, list is a pointer that is either NULL (in which case we are done and leave the loop) or it points to a valid link. We need to free the link, but we also need to continue with its next pointer. If we free the link first, then we no longer have a valid pointer to the link, and thus we cannot safely get next, so we extract next first, then we free, and then we continue the loop.

Using a while (list) { ... } construction is typical for running through a list when implemented this way. We exploit that the NULL pointer evaluates to false, and we just need to remember to update list to list->next at the end of the loop body. For example, if you want to print the elements in an integer list, you can write

```
void print_list(struct link *list)
{
  printf("[ ");
  while (list) {
    printf("%d ", list->value);
    list = list->next;
  }
  printf("]\n");
}
```

If you want to determine if a given integer is in a list, you can write

```
bool contains(struct link *list, int val)
{
  while (list) {
    if (list->value == val)
      return true;
    list = list->next;
  }
  return false;
}
```

It is the same pattern, and almost all loops through a list will follow this pattern.

Now that we can free a list, we can handle allocation errors when we attempt to construct one as well. If the construction fails, we can (for example) delete what we have so far and get an empty list instead of an incomplete one, without leaking memory. The following function constructs a list from an array, but if it gets an allocation error, it will clean up and return NULL:

```
struct link *make_list(int n, int array[n])
{
  struct link *list = 0;
  for (int i = n - 1; i >= 0; i--) {
    struct link *link = new_link(array[i], list);
    if (!link) { // Allocation error -- clean up
      free_list(list);
      return 0;
    }
    list = link;
  }
  return list;
}
```

It constructs the list from the array backward. Remember that new_link() prepends the new element to the list, so if we ran through the array from left to right, we would get a list with the elements in reverse. The variable list holds the head of the current list, and we update it to link at the end of the for-loop's body, where we know that the allocation was successful.

Prepending to a list is a fast operation. We allocate a new struct link, and we set a value and a pointer, and that is all. But what about appending? That is both slower and turns out to be more complicated code:

```
struct link *append(struct link *list, int val)
{
  if (!list) return new_link(val, 0);

  struct link *last = list;
  while (last->next) {
    last = last->next;
  }
  last->next = new_link(val, 0);

  // If we didn't set the last link, then we had
  // an allocation error and should return 0.
  // Otherwise we return the new list
  if (!last->next) return 0;
  else return list;
}
```

There is no avoiding having to find the last link in the chain if we want to append. With a singly linked list, we only have direct access to the first link in the chain (but we will fix that later in this chapter with doubly linked lists). So, we need to search through as many links as there are. We cannot use the while (list) pattern now, however, because then when we find the end of the list, list will be NULL, and we are one past the link we want. We must find the last link, which is the link where next is NULL. So, we must use while (list->next) to get that. In the code, I have named the variable last to indicate that it is the last link we are searching for. However, this won't work if we start out with a NULL pointer. Then we would dereference a NULL pointer when we write last->next, and that is undefined behavior (and almost guaranteed to crash our program). We have to handle an empty list as a special case.

If we append to an empty list, we want a list with a single element, so if the input to append() is NULL, we return a new link (with 0 as its next pointer). Otherwise, we can search for the last link, and once we have it, we can allocate a new link and make the next pointer in the last link point to it; see Figure 11-2. In the figure, the original link is the one from Figure 11-1, with three links, 1, 2, and 3, and we append 4 to the list.

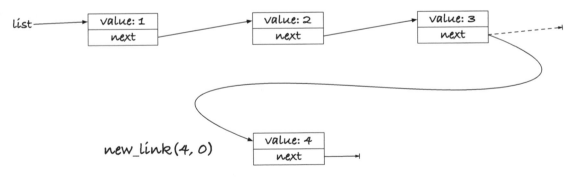

Figure 11-2. *Appending to a singly linked list*

That means that we create a new link for 4, with NULL for its next pointer, and then we change the old next pointer for link 3 (shown as a dashed pointer), so it is no longer NULL but points to the new link.

The allocation, however, can fail. We can still assign the result of the allocation to the last link's next pointer—if the allocation fails, it then remains NULL—but we need to report the error. So if the allocation fails, we will return a NULL pointer. Otherwise, we return the original list. By returning the original list, we get the rule that append() either returns NULL, in case of an allocation failure, or returns the result of appending a value to a list—the list we get by appending the value to the input list. If the input is empty or contains values, we get the same result—the updated list.

It is not a pretty interface, I admit. There are several cases of what can happen. Errors give us NULL, which is fine. But with successful allocations, we modify the input if it isn't NULL, and we return a completely new list if it is NULL. If we always wanted a new list, we could create one by copying the elements in the input. I won't list the code here, but implementing it is a good exercise if you want to test yourself. That leads to a new headache if you don't want to keep different copies of lists around because then you would have to remember to free the input when you do not want it any more. On the other hand, if you *sometimes* get a copy back, and sometimes not, what happens with code such as this:

```
struct link *list1 = make_list(n, array);
struct link *list2 = append(list1, val);
```

The make_list() function can return a NULL pointer, so list1 might be NULL. If it is, then list2 is a completely new list. If it isn't, and append() didn't fail, then list1 and list2 are pointers to the same list. So, should you free() both lists or just one of them? If they are the same, you can only free one. If they are different, you must free both. You can test if they are the same, of course. This isn't the most difficult issue that will come up with memory management in this section—it gets worse, but we will alleviate it with a small change to the code in the next section. Still, it illustrates that we have to worry about assigning the result of an append to a new list.

The problem with freeing memory isn't confined to append(). We have a similar problem with prepend(). Consider this code:

```
struct link *list1 = make_list(n, array);
struct link *list2 = prepend(list, -1);
// some code
free_list(list1);
free_list(list2);
```

If list1 is NULL, everything is fine. We prepend a link to it to get list2, and we can free both the NULL pointer in list1 and the link in list2. But if list1 has a chain of links, then list2 (if the prepend() succeeded) consists of one link and then a list that is shared with list1. When we free list1, we free all the links after the first in list2, so when we call free_list(list2), we can safely free the first link, but all the remaining are already gone. If we try to free() them, we get undefined behavior (and it won't lead anywhere pleasant). Here, the problem isn't that prepend() can sometimes give us a new list and sometimes an old list, but that it will provide us with a list where all but one link is shared with the old list. (Again, we will improve upon it in the next section.) I just want to show you the problems in a straightforward solution first, so you recognize that they exist, and will be careful in the future, and not conclude from a better solution that things are simple and that there is nothing to worry about. There most certainly is.

A more natural way to use prepend() (the wrapper we wrote around new_link()) and append() is like this:

```
list = append(list, 6);
list = prepend(list, 0);
```

We always update a list when we modify it, so we always assign the result back to the list. Unfortunately, this doesn't work. The functions will give us NULL pointers if the allocation fails, and if we assign the result to the list, then we lose access to the allocated memory we already have. We leak. We always need to test the return values before we can update the existing pointer.

```
struct link *new_list = append(list, 6);
if (!list) {
  perror("List error: ");
  exit(1); // Just bail here
}
list = new_list;
new_list = prepend(list, 0);
if (!list) {
  perror("List error: ");
  exit(1); // Just bail here
}
list = new_list;
```

If you don't mind losing the values you have already put into a list, for example, if you cannot handle allocation errors anyway and need to bail if you see them, you can simplify the user's code by deleting the input of the operations:

```
struct link *prepend(struct link *list, int val)
```

```
{
  struct link *new_list = new_link(val, list);
  if (!new_list) free_list(list);
  return new_list;
}

struct link *append(struct link *list, int val)
{
  struct link *val_link = new_link(val, 0);
  if (!val_link) {
    free_list(list);
    return 0;
  }

  if (!list) return val_link;

  struct link *last = list;
  while (last->next) {
      last = last->next;
  }
  last->next = val_link;
  return list;
}
```

In both functions, we allocate the new link early, and if it fails, we free the input and return NULL. Otherwise, we handle the operation without errors. With those operations, you can always assign a list operation back to the list itself and check if it is NULL to see if there were errors.

```
list = append(list, 6);
if (!list) goto error;

list = prepend(list, 0);
if (!list) goto error;
```

But let us leave allocation behind and look at a few operations where we do not add new elements to a list and thus can have no allocation failures. A simple operation is a concatenation. Given two lists, construct a new list that contains all the links from the two lists:

```
struct link *concatenate(struct link *x,
                         struct link *y)
{
  if (!x) return y;
  struct link *last = x;
  while (last->next) {
      last = last->next;
  }
  last->next = y;
  return x;
}
```

We will need to find the last link in the first list to add the second list to it, so we have a special case if x is empty. If it is, we return y. The concatenation of an empty list with another is the links in the second list, so that will work. Otherwise, we find the last link, and by setting its next pointer to point to the first link in y, we have concatenated them.

Since we do not allocate new links, the function cannot fail. You still need to be careful with memory management, though. If you write

```
struct link *list3 = concatenate(list1, list2);
```

you now have three pointers to links, list1, list2, and list3. The list2 list is unchanged. It doesn't matter if it was empty or not; we have not changed any of its links; we have just made the last link in list1 point to it. That is, we have made the last link in list1 point to it, *if* list1 *wasn't empty*. If list1 was empty, then list3 is an alias for list2. If list1 was not empty, then list3 is an alias for (the modified) list1. This, of course, is an issue when we need to free the lists. If we free list2, then we have freed the tailing links in list2 (and list1 if it wasn't empty). If we free list1, and it was empty to begin with, then we haven't freed anything (because free(0) doesn't do anything). But if list1 wasn't empty, we have freed all three lists. We have freed list3 because it is an alias for the modified list1, and we have freed list2 because free_list() will free all the links in the list, and that includes those we got from list2. The only safe option is to free list3 and never list1 and list2 after appending them.

After appending two lists, you are best off by considering the input gone, and never look at it again. The first argument, unless empty, is modified, and the second argument is something you cannot safely free. If you do not want a concatenation operation that, in this way, destroys the input, you should program a version that makes a copy of the two lists instead. To test your understanding of linked lists, this is another good exercise that I recommend that you do.

If you have a concatenate() operation, then you can implement append() in terms of it:

```
struct link *append(struct link *list, int val)
{
  return concatenate(list, new_link(val, 0));
}
```

It is a simple approach to implement the operation, but it is not a particularly good idea. The new_link() allocation can fail, and concatenate() won't notice. So, we simply add allocation errors to the concatenate() function that is problematic enough as it is. It is not a bad idea to implement one operation using another in general, of course, but this particular choice is a poor one.

For a slightly more complex example, here is a function that reverses a list:

```
struct link *reverse(struct link *list)
{
  if (!list) return 0;

  struct link *next = list->next;
  struct link *reversed = list;
  reversed->next = 0;

  while (next) {
      struct link *next_next = next->next;
      next->next = reversed;
      reversed = next;
      next = next_next;
  }
  return reversed;
}
```

Figure 11-3 shows the steps in the function, when run on a list with the values 1, 2, 3, and 4, in that order. The original list, with its four links, is shown in A). In B), we have the pointers we set up before the while-loop. We have a special case if the input list is empty, since we will need to be able to refer to the next link in the list, and there isn't one if it is empty, so we handle that before we get to this point. If the list isn't empty, we get a pointer, next, to the second link in the list, we make reversed point to the first link, and we set the first link's next to NULL. The reversed pointer will hold the reversed list, and the reversed list must end with the first link in the input, which is what it does at this point. An invariant in the loop will be that reversed holds the reversed links of those we have processed so far. The first link's next pointer is set to NULL because reversed should end after that link. The old pointer values are shown as dashed lines and the new and unchanged pointers as solid lines.

Now we start the while-loop in C), and in it we get hold of the next link's next value. We need it to continue the loop later, where we have changed the link that next points to. We only need it for that, so we do not do anything with next_next yet. Now, we get hold of the link that next points at, however, and prepend it to reversed. Prepending it to reversed makes it the first element in the list of reversed links so far, which upholds the invariant. The way we prepend is through updating pointers. The next link's next pointer should point to reversed (changing it here is the reason we needed next_next), and reversed should point to next so that the link is now the front of the reversed list.

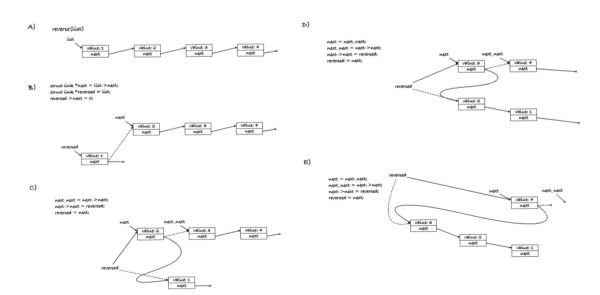

Figure 11-3. *Reversing a singly linked list*

When we move to D), we first update next, so it points to the new next link. We do it at the end of the loop body, but in the figure I have listed it as the first statement in the code since it is a change we make between C) and D). We now do the same operation as we did to get to C). We prepend the current next link to reversed, remembering the next->next link in next_next. After that, reversed holds the values 3, 2, and 1 (if you follow the solid lines from what reversed points to, that should be clear). In E), we handle the last link. Here, next_next becomes NULL, so we terminate the while-loop when we are done, and reversed holds the reversed list.

Manipulating pointers like this is an integral part of working with recursive data structures. The example is the most complex we will see in this chapter, but it is not unusually so. If you need to manipulate a data structure in a nontrivial way, it helps to draw how you want to rearrange the pointers, like in the figure. It can get complicated, but drawings help immensely.

The last operation we will consider is deleting all links with a given value. The implementation can look like this:

```
struct link *delete_value(struct link *list,
                          int val)
{
  if (!list) return 0;
  if (list->value == val) {
      struct link *next = list->next;
      free(list);
      return delete_value(next, val);
  } else {
      list->next = delete_value(list->next, val);
      return list;
  }
}
```

It is a recursive solution that says that deleting all occurrences of val in an empty list is the empty list (what else would it be?). If the first link's value is val, then the result is what we get from deleting val from the rest of the list, and finally if the first value is not val, then the result is the current value followed by the result of deleting val from the rest of the list. Here, "followed by" is handled by assigning the result of the recursive call to the current link's next pointer. In the case where we delete a link, we get its next pointer before we free(), since otherwise we would need to dereference to a deleted link, which is undefined behavior.

The function cannot fail; we do not attempt to allocate any new memory, but of course that doesn't mean that we are entirely safe from memory management issues. If you write

```
delete_value(list, 42);
```

then is list now a valid pointer? That depends. If the first link in list had the value 42, we have deleted that link, but list still points to it. It points to a deallocated chunk of memory, so it is not valid. If list was empty, or didn't have 42 in its first link, then list now holds the updated list where all occurrences of 42 are deleted.

With this function, however, the solution is easy. It is always safe to write this:

```
list = delete_value(list, 42);
```

because you get the updated list back. It might be the same address as the input, when we do not delete the first link, but if we do get a different address back, it is the list without 42, which is what we want.

To sum up, in this section, we have seen how we can implement a recursive data structure, a singly linked list, using a struct with a member that is a pointer to the same struct's type. We have also seen how we can implement various operations on the type. Although the data structure is simple, we have learned that there are many potential pitfalls with memory management. We have to deal with allocation errors, but that is the least of our worries. The real problem is freeing memory correctly once allocated.

Correctly freeing memory is practically always a concern with recursive data structures. The problem is that they tend to create aliases for the same memory. Here, when we concatenate, for example, we end up with one reference to the tail part of another list. If we delete the list through the tail reference, then the chain of links from the front will eventually run into freed memory, and we cannot handle that. If we free from the front, then the original reference to the second list will point to freed memory.

While such aliasing is sometimes unavoidable, we can often alleviate it with a better interface to the operations, and we will do that in the next section. The interface we have implemented here is horrible when it comes to safe memory management, I admit. But I wanted to show you a lousy solution before I showed you a good one, so you would be aware of the problems and appreciate the solution.

The solution in the next chapter involves a (very) slight change to how we represent lists, and naturally given the topic of the book, it involves a pointer. Then practically all our problems go away. In Chapter 15, we will see another approach to dealing with aliasing between recursive data structures.

Adding a Level of Indirection

The leading cause of our troubles with memory management was that our operations returned new lists that potentially referred to links the input also referred to. We can change the implementation such that we modify the input instead of returning new lists. We won't have to create new copies for each list that we return, but we will implement the operations such that we do not create more than one list with a pointer to the same link. When we prepend or append, we update the existing list; when we concatenate, we move the links from one list to another, so the second list no longer holds them. This isn't possible with the representation we used so far for lists—a pointer to a link—for two reasons. We cannot modify the calling variables, so they no longer point to a function's input, and we cannot modify an empty list, represented as a NULL pointer. The solution to both is one level of indirection: a list will no longer be a pointer to a link, but a pointer to *a pointer to* a link.

Adding a level of indirection in this way comes in handy in many applications. It is a case of calling functions by reference all over again. If we have to modify the variables the caller has, we need to get pointers to them, so we have to work with pointers to pointers to links. If we do that, then empty lists are no longer NULL pointers—that we cannot modify—but rather they point to a NULL pointer. We can modify such a list by changing the value it points to. We can use the same definition of links and the allocation function for them with the new lists:

```c
struct link {
  int value;
  struct link *next;
};

struct link *new_link(int val, struct link *next)
{
  struct link *link = malloc(sizeof *link);
  if (!link) return 0;
  link->value = val;
  link->next = next;
  return link;
}
```

I will rename the deallocation function to have one function for freeing link memory and another for lists. The function for freeing a chain of links is the same as before, but we call it free_links():

```
void free_links(struct link *list)
{
  while (list) {
    struct link *next = list->next;
    free(list);
    list = next;
  }
}
```

Now we define a list to be a pointer to pointer to struct link and provide a macro to test if it represents an empty list—in which case it points to a pointer to NULL. For convenience, and to make the code more readable, we also provide a macro to get the links in a list:

```
typedef struct link ** list;
#define is_list_empty(x)  (*(x) == 0)
#define list_links(x)       *(x)
```

We can still heap-allocate lists. They have a different type, but we can heap-allocate any type we can get the size of (which we can, of course, with sizeof). If the allocation is successful, a good initial value for a list is the empty list, so the pointer it points to should be NULL:

```
list new_list(void)
{
  list x = malloc(sizeof *x);
  if (x) *x = 0;
  return x;
}
```

When we free a list, we should free the links it points to and then the list itself:

```
void free_list(list x)
{
  free_links(list_links(x));
  free(x);
}
```

In many cases, the new representation doesn't change anything. If we have a function that merely iterates through links, like print_list() or contains(), the only change is that we should get the links from the list using list_links():

```
void print_list(list x)
{
  printf("[ ");
  struct link *link = list_links(x);
  while (link) {
      printf("%d ", link->value);
      link = link->next;
  }
  printf("]\n");
}

bool contains(list x, int val)
{
  struct link *links = list_links(x);
  while (links) {
      if (links->value == val)
          return true;
      links = links->next;
  }
  return false;
}
```

Where we see changes is when we create or modify lists, and in most cases, the code will still look the same; we just get some benefits practically for free. Take the make_list() function from earlier. It looks mostly like before, but by creating a list instead of a link pointer, we get some benefits.

```
list make_list(int n, int array[n])
{
  list x = new_list();
  if (!x) return 0;

  for (int i = n - 1; i >= 0; i--) {
    struct link *link =
```

```
      new_link(array[i], list_links(x));
    if (!link) { // Allocation error -- clean up
      free_list(x);
      return 0;
    }
    list_links(x) = link;
  }

  return x;
}
```

We allocate a list at the beginning, to get that over with. If the allocation fails, we will have to report an error, so we might as well do that up front. After that, we can use the list's links as we used the link pointer in the previous version. It is initially the empty list, and as we update it, we add the links to the list. The code is exactly as before, except that we have to free the entire list if we get an allocation failure. We call free_list() to do that. We also called free_list() in the previous version, but that function only deleted links—we had no distinction between lists and links there—but you cannot use the free_links() function here.

If we successfully allocate all the links, we return the list, and here we have improved upon the interface of the previous function. With the make_list() from the last section, we could not distinguish between a failure and an empty list. We could, of course, check n before we called the function and that way determine if we expected to get an empty list back, but both empty lists and errors would give us NULL pointers. With our new representation, NULL is not an empty list and vice versa. An empty list is a pointer to a NULL pointer, and that is different from a NULL pointer. The new make_list() function gives us NULL if we have an error, and a list otherwise, and an empty list cannot be confused for NULL.

The prepend() function looks much like before as well. We create a link, and if that fails, we return an error. If not, the new link's next pointer is the input list. Before, we returned the new link, and we could now have two aliases to the input string: a reference to it in the calling code and the next pointer in the new link. Now, we change the input list, so it points to the new link. Because of our new representation, we can modify the input list.

```
int prepend(list x, int val)
{
```

```
  struct link *link =
    new_link(val, list_links(x));
  if (!link) return 0;
  list_links(x) = link;
  return 1;
}
```

For the append() and concatenate() functions, I will write a helper function that gives us the last link in a chain, when a list is not empty. It looks like the while-loops that did this in the previous section:

```
// Only call this with non-NULL links
struct link *last_link(struct link *x)
{
  // When we start from x, there is always
  // a link where we can get the next
  struct link *prev = x;
  while (prev->next) {
    prev = prev->next;
  }
  return prev;
}
```

Now, to append, we have two cases. If the input list is empty, we do not have a last link, so we should put the new link we created as the (entire) link chain in the list. Otherwise, we need to get the last link in the link chain and put the new link as its next.

```
int append(list x, int val)
{
  struct link *val_link = new_link(val, 0);
  if (!val_link) return 0;

  if (is_list_empty(x)) {
    list_links(x) = val_link;
  } else {
    last_link(list_links(x))->next = val_link;
  }
  return 1;
}
```

Concatenate works similarly. We have two cases, one where x is empty, in which case we should set its link chain to the links in y, or it has links, in which case we should find the last and set the last link's next to the links from y. In either case, we should remove the links from y so we do not have two lists containing the same links, so we do that before we return.

```
void concatenate(list x, list y)
{
  if (is_list_empty(x)) {
    list_links(x) = list_links(y);
  } else {
    last_link(list_links(x))->next =
      list_links(y);
  }
  // remove alias to the old y links
  *y = 0;
}
```

If you want a function that copies elements from one list to another, you can implement it using concatenate(). Free the existing links, then concatenate the links into the list (removing them from the second list in the process).

```
void copy_list(list x, list y)
{
  free_links(list_links(x));
  concatenate(x, y);
}
```

The two cases, empty and not, and the code that sets a link pointer, in append() and concatenate(), look very similar. If we take the append() case

```
if (is_list_empty(x)) {
  list_links(x) = val_link;
} else {
  last_link(list_links(x))->next = val_link;
```

we could imagine an operation last_next() that would give us

```
last_next(x) => *x
```

if x is empty, and

```
last_next(x) => last_link(*x)->next
```

otherwise. If we had such an operation, we could simplify the two cases into one:

```
last_next(x) = val_link;
```

Could we get such an operation? Not quite, but very close.

We need an address to write val_link into—either *x or the next value in the last link. If we write a function that gives us that:

```
struct link **last_next(struct link **x)
{
  if (*x == 0) return x;

  struct link *prev = *x;
  while (prev->next) {
    prev = prev->next;
  }
  return &prev->next;
}
```

we can write the two functions as

```
int append(list x, int val)
{
  struct link *val_link = new_link(val, 0);
  if (!val_link) return 0;
  *last_next(x) = val_link;
  return 1;
}

void concatenate(list x, list y)
{
  *last_next(x) = list_links(y);
  *y = 0;
}
```

Since last_next() gives us the address where we should write val_link or y's links, we need to dereference before we assign, thus the *last_next(x) expression.

If you want to put lists on the stack, instead of allocating them on the heap with new_list() and then freeing them again with free_list(), you can do that as well. What you then need is memory to store the link pointer that a list contains. So, the easiest solution is to put a link pointer on the stack and work with its address. To make our code easier to read, we can give it a different name. We can define the type stack_list as a list we have allocated on the stack, like this:

```
typedef struct link * stack_list;
```

You cannot free such a list because you didn't allocate it on the stack, but you should still free its links. A macro that frees the links, and set the pointer to NULL to make it an empty list after we free it, can look like this:

```
#define free_stack_list(x) \
  do { free_links(x); x = 0; } while(0)
```

To get a list from it, you take its address, but if you want a more informative operation, you can again use a macro:

```
#define stack_to_list(x) (&x)
```

You can use it as a list, for example, as the destination for a copy, with code like this:

```
x = make_list(n, array);
stack_list z = 0;
copy_list(stack_to_list(z), x);
free_list(x);
free_stack_list(z);
```

If you now want to test yourself, you can try to implement other operations. They work the same way as the first list implementations; you should just remember to update the input instead of returning new lists.

```
void delete_value(list x, int val)
{
  // We can use the previous implementation, but update
  // x...
}
```

```
void reverse(list x)
{
  // We can use the previous implementation, but update
  // x...
}
```

I will wait with implementing these two functions again until the next section, though. There, we try a slightly different representation, and I can cut off a line or two in the implementation because of that. It is a very minor change, however, so if you are up for it, you should give the functions a go now, before you read on.

Adding a Dummy Element

Adding a level of indirection solves many problems, but a related trick in my experience solves many more. If you have a data structure where you need to deal with special cases, such as empty lists represented by NULL pointers, more often than not, the special cases go away if you add one or more "dummy" elements to the structure. If you write code where you need to test that one or more pointers are NULL or not, quite often you can make the code simpler by assuring that they are *not* NULL. Add objects to the data structure that do not represent real data, but are there as dummies.

Singly linked lists are simple, so we won't gain much from trying them here—we got most of the benefits in the previous section where we changed lists from pointers to links to pointers to pointers to links—we got rid of NULL as the representation of empty lists. So, the approach might underwhelm you in its usefulness. We gain a little more in the next chapter, but you will have to take my word for it when I say that for complex data structures, you can often gain a lot. We won't have room for sufficiently interesting data structures in this book for me to show you. In any case, even if we only gain a little, you will see that with a simple dummy element at the beginning of each list, we gain all the benefits we got in the previous section, and in a few places, we write slightly simpler code.

Well, on with it. A list is once again a pointer to links, but we will never accept that a list is NULL, unless it is to return an error from a function. Instead, a list consists of one element that we do not consider part of the data it holds. It is a "head" or a "dummy" link. If you allocate a list, you allocate a link. If you put a list on the stack, you put a link on the stack (and then work with its address as the list). But the first link is not part of the real data.

So, a list is little more than a typedef, and we can define some macros to wrap calls to link allocation and deallocation:

```
typedef struct link * list;

#define new_list()    new_link(0, 0)
#define free_list(x) free_links(x)
```

The make_list() function looks much like in the previous section. We allocate a list, and if that went well, we allocate the links. The only difference is that we write x->next instead of list_links(x) in the code.

```
list make_list(int n, int array[n])
{
  list x = new_list();
  if (!x) return 0;

  for (int i = n - 1; i >= 0; i--) {
    struct link *link = new_link(array[i], x->next);
    if (!link) { // Allocation error -- clean up
      free_list(x);
      return 0;
    }
    x->next = link;
  }
  return x;
}
```

If you are not modifying the list, you also treat it as before, but when you iterate through the links, you start at x->next. The first link is not real data.

```
void print_list(list x)
{
  printf("[ ");
  struct link *link = x->next;
  while (link) {
    printf("%d ", link->value);
    link = link->next;
  }
```

```
    printf("]\n");
}

bool contains(list x, int val)
{
    struct link *link = x->next;
    while (link) {
        if (link->value == val)
            return true;
        link = link->next;
    }
    return false;
}
```

There is nothing surprising in prepend() either:

```
int prepend(list x, int val)
{
    struct link *link = new_link(val, x->next);
    if (!link) return 0;
    x->next = link;
    return 1;
}
```

but with append() and concatenate(), we get slightly more readable code. At least, more readable if you found

```
*last_next(x) = val_link;
```

hard to read. Because a list always has at least one link, there is always a last link. We do not need the last_next() trick to get a link to append to. We can find the last link, it always exists, and then we can write to its next member.

```
struct link *last_link(list x)
{
    struct link *prev = x;
    while (prev->next) {
        prev = prev->next;
    }
```

```
  return prev;
}

int append(list x, int val)
{
  struct link *link = new_link(val, 0);
  if (!link) return 0;
  last_link(x)->next = link;
  return 1;
}

void concatenate(list x, list y)
{
  last_link(x)->next = y->next;
  y->next = 0;
}
```

Here, we didn't gain much over the second list representation, but I find this code more readable, and it is a step up compared to the first implementation we made. If we had gone directly to the dummy link solution, you would probably agree that we gained something going here.

With delete_value(), we gain a little as well. Because the input list always has a link, we can do this: imagine that we split the list in two, the links up to a link we will call front where all the elements we need to delete are gone and then the rest, from front->next, where we still need to delete. We can start by setting front to the list. The value in the dummy element doesn't count, so everything up to and including front doesn't have the value. Now we repeatedly look at front->next. If front->next has the value, we remove it (we set front->next to front->next->next and free()). Otherwise, we can move front to front->next because that link does not have the value, and then we can continue from that link. This idea can be implemented like this:

```
void delete_value(list x, int val)
{
  struct link *front = x, *next = 0;
  while (front) {
    while ( (next = front->next) &&
            next->value == val ) {
```

332

```
        front->next = next->next;
        free(next);
    }
    front = next;
  }
}
```

We could also have used this algorithm without the dummy element (I left implementing `delete_value()` as an exercise in the previous section, and you can try implementing this solution). Without the dummy element, however, it is harder to set the first `front` pointer.

In `reverse()`, we avoid a special case when the list is empty. It is not a terrible burden to handle an empty list, of course, since the reverse of an empty list is just the empty list, but it goes away. We will always have a `next` pointer when we begin. We can use the list itself for the `reversed` pointer we needed earlier. Once we have a pointer to the list's `next` link, we don't need to remember it in the input any longer, which means that we can use the input's `next` for `reversed`, and when we are done with reversing, we already have the reversed links stored there.

```
void reverse(list x)
{
  struct link *next = x->next;
  x->next = 0;
  while (next) {
    struct link *next_next = next->next;
    next->next = x->next;
    x->next = next;
    next = next_next;
  }
}
```

We started out with simple code for a linked list, but with various issues related to memory management. We resolved those issues by adding a level of indirection, so lists became more than pointers to links. That first step helped us remove aliases between links that could potentially be disastrous when freeing memory. If we are careful with how we write functions, we can avoid them, as long as we can modify our input lists. Adding a dummy element to the beginning of each list didn't add much on top of that, yet still I will suggest that you always reach for a dummy element when you need a level of indirection. You get the indirection for free—you already have all the code needed to work with real elements, and you can reuse it for dummy elements—and you usually avoid a few special cases for free when you take that approach.

We got rid of memory management issues by removing the chance of aliases through different references, but this is, of course, only an option when we do not need different variables to share data. If you cannot avoid that multiple variables or structures refer to the same allocated data, you must have a strategy for how to delete it. The right strategy can be highly application dependent, but we will see some general approaches later in the book. For now, as long as our functions do not leak memory and leave the input and output in a consistent state that the user can rely on, we will be satisfied.

Doubly Linked Lists

With singly linked lists, we have immediate access to the first link in the chain, and we have to search through the list to access others. If we need to delete a link, we need to have a pointer to the link that goes before it and the link that goes after it, so we can connect those. We have access to the next link through the next pointer, but the previous one is something we must keep track of as we search through the list, or we must find it by searching from the beginning. Inserting a new link y after another, x, is easy. We simply need to point y->next = x->next and then x->next = y. But inserting y *before* x requires that we have access to the link before x (so we can insert after that link), which again requires that we have a pointer to it from whatever algorithm we are implementing, or that we search for it. With *doubly linked* lists, we keep track of both the link before and after any given link. We have two pointers, prev for the previous link and next for the next link.

Figure 11-4. *A doubly linked list with elements 1, 2, and 3 and dummy links at the beginning and end*

```
struct link {
  int value;
  struct link *prev;
```

```
  struct link *next;
};
struct link *new_link(int val,
                        struct link *prev,
                        struct link *next)
{
  struct link *link = malloc(sizeof *link);
  if (!link) return 0;

  link->value = val;
  link->prev = prev;
  link->next = next;

  return link;
}
```

With two pointers, we have more special cases to worry about. Either or both of the pointers can be NULL, so a straightforward implementation leaves a lot of case checking. However, as I hinted in the previous section, adding dummy elements can greatly reduce the need for special cases. If we add a dummy link at the beginning and end of each list (see Figure 11-4), all the real links *always* have non-NULL prev and next pointers, and that makes it very easy to manipulate lists.

As long as a link pointer isn't NULL, its prev and next pointers aren't NULL either. That means that we can access the data in neighboring links, and as long as those aren't dummy links, their prev and next pointers aren't NULL either.

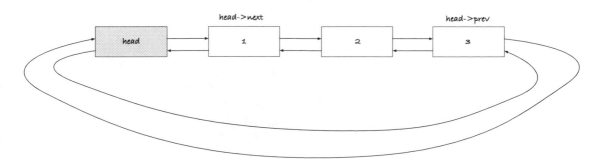

Figure 11-5. *A circular list with a dummy head*

This isn't perfect, though. We don't have to check if a link's prev and next are NULL, if it is a real and not a dummy link, but there are cases where we need a link's neighbors to also have non-NULL prev and next links. That means that we have to check if the neighbors are dummies, which leaves almost as many special cases to check for. Our code will get simpler if we can ensure that even the dummy links have neighbors, but what should we make them point to?

A simple solution is the so-called *circular list*. We will use one dummy link per list, called *head*. Its next is the first real link in the list, and its prev is the last real link in the list. If the list is empty, the head's two pointers point to the head itself; see Figure 11-5. With this representation, all links have neighbors.

A circular list doesn't have to have a dummy element as its head, and some algorithms and data structures depend on circular lists where any link can function as the head (so we can move the head to adapt to data we process). For our purposes, however, having a dummy is easier, as it gives us a representation of empty lists that isn't a NULL pointer.

To give ourselves informative names, we can typedef a list head to be a link.

```
typedef struct link list_head;
```

We can declare a head on the stack if we want to and use this macro to initialize it to an empty list:

```
#define init_list_head(x) \
  (list_head){ .prev = &(x), .next = &(x) }
```

You can use it as

```
list_head head = init_list_head(head);
```

to create a head for an empty list.

The operations we implement will take heads by reference, so we define a list to be a pointer to a head (which is the same as a pointer to a link, of course).

```
typedef list_head *list;
```

To heap-allocate a list, we must allocate a link (which we can do with the new_link() function from earlier). The head is a dummy, so it doesn't matter what value we put in it. We cannot set the pointers in the call to new_link() because we do not have the address for the head before we allocate it, but we can use init_list_head():

```
list new_list(void)
{
  struct link *head = new_link(0, 0, 0);
  if (!head) return 0;
  *head = init_list_head(*head);
  return head;
}
```

To use a head as a list, get its address. To get the first or last "real" element in a list, we can use these macros:

```
#define front(x)    (x)->next
#define last(x)     (x)->prev
```

They will give you the head back if the list is empty, so you can test for an empty list with

```
#define is_empty(x) ((x) == front(x))
```

If you want to set a head to an empty list, you need to reinitialize it:

```
#define clear_head(head) \
  do { (head) = init_list_head(head); } while(0)
```

If you have a list, so a pointer to a head, you can do

```
#define clear_list(x) clear_head(*(x))
```

This doesn't free the links it holds, however, so we need code to do that first, if we need it.

To free the links, we must iterate through them. In the last section, we would iterate as long as the current link isn't NULL, but now links will never be NULL when we follow a chain of next pointers. Instead, we must iterate until we get back to the head. Other than that, there is nothing new. The free_links() function deletes all the (real) links in a list:

```
void free_links(list_head *head)
{
  struct link *link = front(head);
  while (link != head) {
```

```
        struct link *next = link->next;
        free(link);
        link = next;
    }
    clear_list(head);
}
```

It also clears the head, that is, sets it to an empty list, so we don't risk accessing deallocated links after we have freed them.

The free_list() frees a heap-allocated list as well.

```
#define free_list(x) \
    do { free_links(x); free(x); x = 0; } while(0)
```

This is a macro, so we can set the list pointer to NULL after we have freed it. That can make the code safer at times, but of course only if x is the only reference to the list. But it should be, if we free it, so greater problems are present if that isn't the case.

Use free_links() if you have a stack-allocated head, but free_list() if you have allocated the list on the heap.

Link Operations

A simple operation on links is to connect them. If we have links x and y, and we want y to follow x, then we can connect them by setting x's next to y and y's prev to x.

```
static inline
void connect(struct link *x, struct link *y)
{
    x->next = y;
    y->prev = x;
}
```

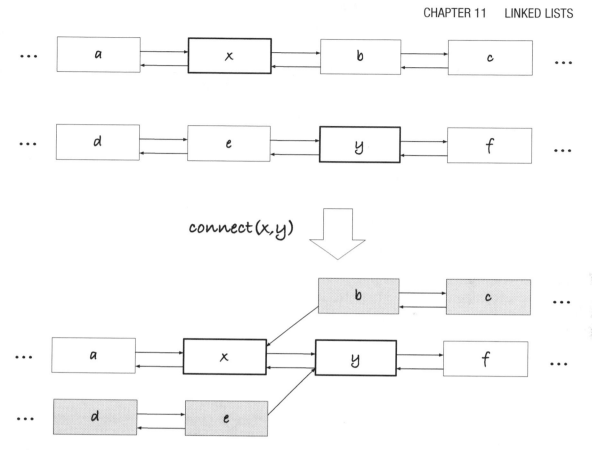

Figure 11-6. *Connecting two links*

When we connect x and y, we move the next pointer in x to y, and we lose access to the links that followed x; see Figure 11-6. Likewise, we lose access to the links preceding y when we point y->prev to x. The link before y still points to y with its next, and the link after x still points to x with its prev, but unless we have access to those links from somewhere else, they are lost to us (which means we would leak memory if we didn't handle this correctly). As the figure also illustrates, it is quite possible to put links in an inconsistent state, where for a link x, x->prev->next != x or x->next->prev != x. This is something we should avoid doing in our code, but intermediate states in an update often look like this.

I have written the operation as an inline function because it is short and best inlined. Since C99, the language has had the inline keyword, which works as a compiler hint to suggest that the function should be inlined if that gets us more efficient code.

```
inline
void connect(struct link *x, struct link *y)
{
  x->next = y;
  y->prev = x;
}
```

I would like to use `inline`, but it requires extra work. It is not enough to define an inline function; you must also provide a linker symbol for it, if the compiler decides not to inline. If you do not provide that, you will likely get a linker error. You can specify that you want to generate an external linkage function from the definition, of course.

```
extern inline
void connect(struct link *x, struct link *y)
{
  x->next = y;
  y->prev = x;
}
```

But now you get a copy of that in any compilation unit that includes the definition, including the linkage symbol, and that will certainly give you linker errors!

Instead, and this is the standard solution, you can declare an `inline` function `static`, as I have done. If so, if the function isn't inlined, the compiler will generate a function, but it will only be visible from within the compilation unit, so you don't get linker errors. However, you do get duplicated code for everything that the compiler doesn't inline. It isn't perfect, and you can set up your compilation environment to do better, but it suffices for us here.

If we have a link x and want to make sure that its `prev` and `next` links point back to itself, we can use this operation:

```
static inline
void connect_neighbours(struct link *x)
{
  x->next->prev = x;
  x->prev->next = (x);
}
```

It ensures that x at least is in a consistent state with respect to its neighbors.

Now say we want to insert a link, y, after another, x; see Figure 11-7. We can do this by connecting y's prev pointer to x and its next pointer to x->next, so it has the right neighbors, and then we connect the neighbors, so x->next will point to y and y->next will point back to y. In code, the operation can look like this:

```
static inline
void link_after(struct link *x, struct link *y)
{
  y->prev = x;
  y->next = x->next;
  connect_neighbours(y);
}
```

This code exploits that x has a next link that we can update. If next or prev pointers could be NULL, we would have to handle special cases. Because we have a dummy head, this is not an issue.

If you want to insert a link before another instead of after, we can do this:

```
#define link_before(x, y)     \
  link_after((x)->prev, y)
```

This assumes that x has a prev link, which is a valid link, but this is also guaranteed by the dummy link. Of course, both x and x->prev might be the dummy, but the code doesn't look at the value we store in the links, so it doesn't care. A link is a link, as far as this code is concerned.

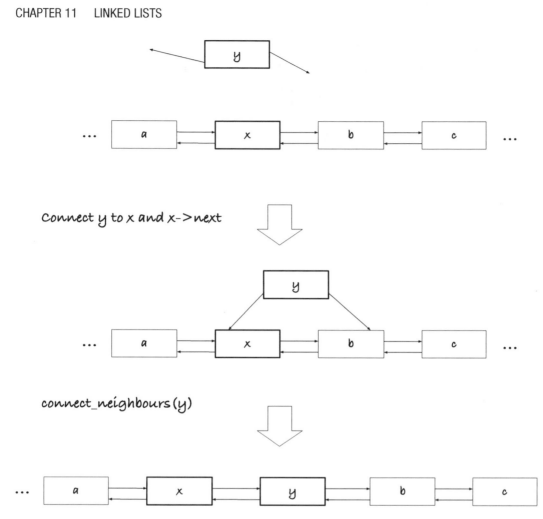

Figure 11-7. *Insert link y after link x*

If we want to insert values, which we obviously do, we need to allocate links to hold them. There are cases where we would want to leave allocation to the caller; see, for example, Chapter 14. Then they can deal with allocation errors, and our code doesn't have to worry about it. But for now, we can provide a function that inserts a value before a link:

```
int insert_val_after(struct link *after, int val)
{
  struct link *link =
    new_link(val, after, after->next);
  if (!link) return 0;
  connect_neighbours(link);
  return 1;
}
```

The time we could gain from inlining is small compared to the overhead there is in allocating memory, so there would be little gain in inlining here.

Except for allocating a new link, there isn't much new here. We use `connect_neighbours()` instead of `insert_after()` because we have already set the new link's neighbors in the allocation, but we could just as easily have called `insert_after()`.

If you want to insert a value before a link, we can use a macro:

```
#define insert_val_before(before, val) \
  insert_val_after((before)->prev, val)
```

This is just a wrapper around `insert_val_after()` where we get the `prev` link from `before`. There is no need for a function here.

If we want to remove a link from a list, we should make its previous and next links point past it; the previous link's `next` should point to the link's `next`, and the next link's `prev` should point to the link's `prev` (see Figure 11-8).

The operation is fairly straightforward to implement:

```
static inline
void unlink(struct link *x)
{
  x->next->prev = x->prev;
  x->prev->next = x->next;
}
```

We will leave the link's pointers alone, so they still point to the original previous and next link. After we have unlinked it, it might still be useful to have access to them, even though the link is no longer part of the list.

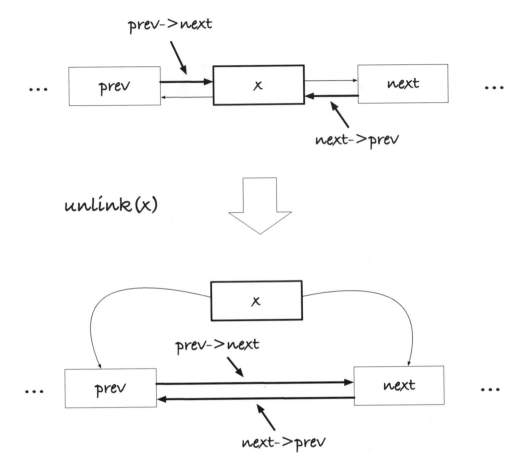

Figure 11-8. *Unlinking x*

If you want to delete a link, you should free it as well as unlink it. The following function does that:

```
static inline
void delete_link(struct link *x)
{
  unlink(x); free(x);
}
```

List Operations

Given a list, we might want to prepend and append to it. We have two versions of both operations: the first where we already have a link we wish to prepend or append, in which case we can use the link_after() or link_before() operations, and the second where we have a value and need to allocate a link, where we can use the insert_val_after() and insert_val_before() operations. Turning the existing operations into prepend/append operations is only a question of giving them new names:

```
#define prepend_link link_after
#define append_link  link_before
#define prepend      insert_val_after
#define append       insert_val_before
```

We didn't have to define these macros, of course. We could equally well have used the existing. But giving them alternative names can make the intent of our code more explicit. A drawback is, of course, that compiler errors might get harder to read, as the compiler will have to explain the expansion of macros when it encounters an error. So it is a question of taste which you prefer.

The make_list() function looks much the same, but it is a little simpler than the singly linked list case. With a circular list, we have immediate access to the last element in the list, so append() is a fast operation. That means that we do not need to run through the array from the back to the front to prepend. We can run through the array from the beginning and forward and append.

```
list make_list(int n, int array[n])
{
  list x = new_list();
  if (!x) return 0;
  for (int i = 0; i < n; i++) {
    if (!append(x, array[i])) {
      free_list(x);
      return 0;
    }
  }

  return x;
}
```

We allocate the head as the first operation (and report an error if we couldn't). After that, we append the array elements one by one. If there is an allocation error in the `append()` operation, we free the list and return NULL. Otherwise, we have successfully created the list and can return it.

When we have to run through all the links in a list, things are a little different. We start with the head of the list, as we did when we introduced a dummy for the singly linked lists. That doesn't change. We can get the first link we need to look at using the `front()` macro that gives us the next link in the head. But where we earlier continued iterating through next pointers until we hit NULL, we need a different termination condition. With a circular list, we *never* reach NULL. When we are done with all the links, we will have returned to the head of the list. That is what we must compare each link against.

The `print_list()` function looks like this:

```
void print_list(list x)
{
  printf("[ ");
  struct link *link = front(x);
  while (link != x) {
    printf("%d ", link->value);
    link = link->next;
  }
  printf("]\n");
}
```

We get the first `link` with `front(x)`. If the list is empty, we will get the head back, so it is possible that `link == x`. When that happens, we never enter the loop, which is what we want. If there are no elements in the list, then we shouldn't print any. If `link` is not x, we iterate. We print the current value and move `link` to the next link. Once `link` progresses all the way back to the head, the loop condition `link != x` is false, and we terminate.

The rule is this: you start with `front(x)`, you iterate as long as `link != x`, and in each iteration you increment `link = link->next`. As a for-loop, where the three steps are made explicit, the function would look like this:

```
void print_list(list x)
{
  printf("[ ");
```

```
  for (struct link *link = front(x);
       link != x;
       link = link->next) {
    printf("%d ", link->value);
  }
  printf("]\n");
}
```

The contains() function, which also has to iterate through the list, follows the same pattern:

```
bool contains(list x, int val)
{
  for (struct link *link = front(x);
       link != x;
       link = link->next) {
    if (link->value == val)
      return true;

  }
  return false;
}
```

To concatenate two lists, x and y, putting the result in x, we must connect the last element in x, last(x), to the first in y, front(y), and then connect the last link in y, last(y), to x; see Figure 11-9. In A), we have the two lists before the operations. When we connect last(x) to front(y), we go to B). Both x and y are in inconsistent states because their last(x) and front(y) links do not point back to them, but that is fine. We don't need consistency yet. We connect last(y) to x, C), and now x->prev points to last(y), and if we follow the links from x along the circle, we go through all the links from x and y and end up in x when we have seen them all.

This leaves x with all the links and y in an inconsistent state—it points to links that do not point back to it—so we should clear it when we are done to avoid future problems. In code, it looks like this:

```
void concatenate(list x, list y)
{
  connect(last(x), front(y));
  connect(last(y), x);
  clear_list(y);
}
```

Getting the last elements is faster with circular lists than with the singly linked lists we had in the previous section. There, getting the last link in a list took time proportional to the number of links in the list, but here it takes constant time. Concatenate is thus a constant time operation with our current lists, whereas it was a linear time operation before.

A)

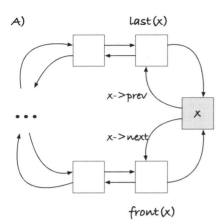

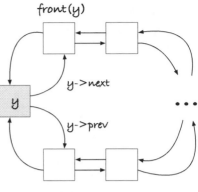

B)

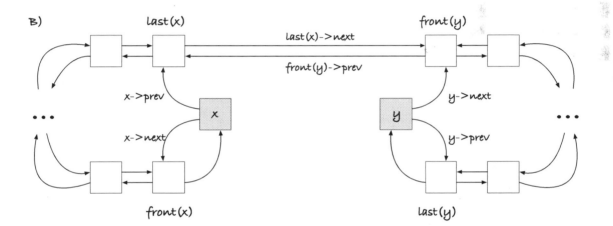

C)

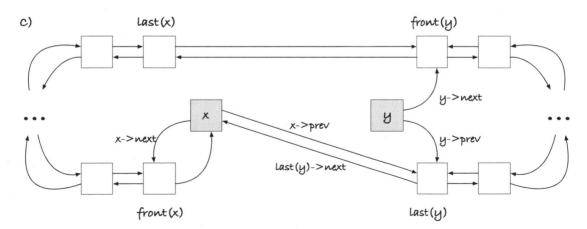

Figure 11-9. *Concatenating x and y, general case*

We don't delete y, but we empty it. The caller must free it if they no longer need it. We could free it here that just changes the API. It is a design choice.

This process looks like something that would have special cases if x, y, or both are empty, since then there is overlap between the various front(), back(), and head links. By luck more than design, this isn't the case. The same procedure works when one or both lists are empty. Consider the case where x is empty, and thus x = back(x); see Figure 11-10. When we connect back(x) with front(y), we move x->prev so it points at front(y), and front(y)->prev points to x. This doesn't change back(y), and when we connect back(y) to x, x->prev becomes back(y), and once again we have a circle of all the links starting and ending in x (and an inconsistent y that we clear at the end).

If y is empty (see Figure 11-11), y = front(y) = last(y). We connect last(x) to front(y) = y and get the case in B), where last(x)->next points to y and y->prev points to last(x), which makes last(x)=last(y) (remember that last(y) is the link that y->prev points to). Then, when we connect last(y) to x in C), we point last(x) back to x (x->prev to last(y) which it was pointing to already). The y list is broken, which is always the case after concatenation, but x is back in its original state, which is what we want when we concatenate it with an empty list.

If both lists are empty, Figure 11-12 A), connecting last(x) to front(y) means pointing x->next to y and y->prev to x, B). That makes back(y) = x, so when we connect back(y) to x, we set x->next back to x, and we are back where we started with respect to x. We once again broke y, but who cares about y?

Cases where either list consists of one element do not need special treatment either. If front(x)=last(x) or front(y)=last(y), we only touch one of their pointers in the connect() operations, and the concatenation works as if they were different links.

Deleting all occurrences of a value is similar to the singly linked case, except that we do not need to keep track of the previous link, so we can remove one. Each link already has a pointer to the previous link, and unlinking and deleting individual links is easy. You still need to get the current link's next pointer before you delete it, though, because once you have freed a link, you cannot get their content.

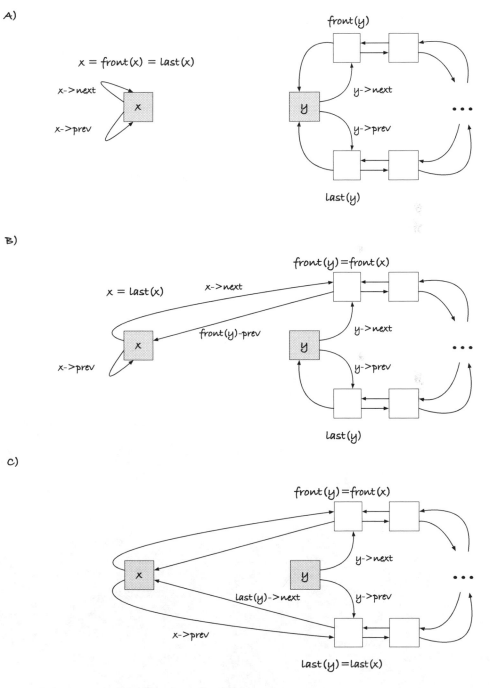

Figure 11-10. *Concatenating x and y when x is empty*

A)

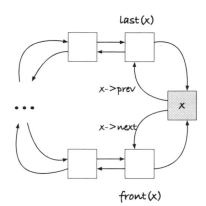
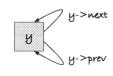

B)

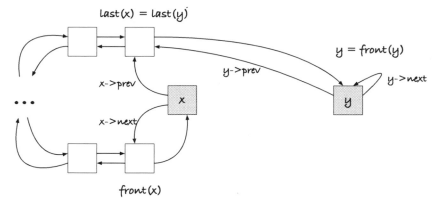

C)

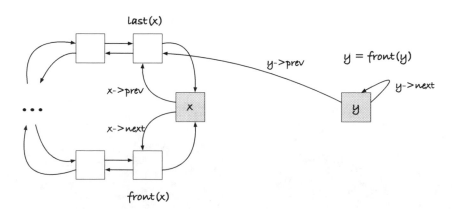

Figure 11-11. *Concatenating x and y when y is empty*

A)

$$x = front(x) = last(x) \qquad\qquad y = front(y) = last(y)$$

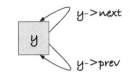

B)

$$x = last(x) = last(y) \qquad\qquad y = front(y) = last(x)$$

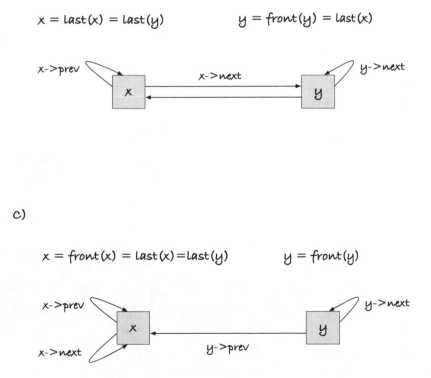

C)

$$x = front(x) = last(x) = last(y) \qquad\qquad y = front(y)$$

Figure 11-12. *Concatenating x and y when both lists are empty*

```
void delete_value(list x, int val)
{
  struct link *link = front(x);
  while (link != x) {
    struct link *next = link->next;
    if (link->value == val)
      delete_link(link);
    link = next;
  }
}
```

Reversal is easier than for singly linked lists. You have direct access to both the beginning and end of circular doubly linked lists, so you can reverse them the way we did with arrays in Chapter 6. Start with pointers to both ends, swap the values, then move the pointers forward/backward, and stop when they meet.

```
#define swap_int(x,y) \
  do { int tmp = (x); (x) = (y); (y) = tmp; } while(0)

void reverse(list x)
{
  struct link *left = front(x);
  struct link *right = last(x);
  while (left != right) {
    swap_int(left->value, right->value);
    left = left->next; right = right->prev;
  }
}
```

This, of course, will only be fast if the values we store in links are small. Here, we have integers, and they are quick to swap, but nothing prevents us from implementing lists where each link holds massive amounts of data. For that matter, we might be writing generic code that doesn't know what the links hold; see Chapter 14. Luckily, there is an even simpler way to reverse a doubly linked list that is just as fast. We can swap the pointers in each link.

```
#define swap_p(x,y) \
  do { struct link *tmp = (x); (x) = (y); (y) = tmp; } while(0)
```

```
void reverse(list x)
{
  struct link *p = x;
  do {
    swap_p(p->prev, p->next);
    p = p->prev;
  } while (p != x);
}
```

When we swap the prev and next pointers in a link, we leave the list in an inconsistent state. The link's neighbors do not point back at it. However, if we swap all the way around the list, we will have a consistent, reversed, list. Consider the example in Figure 11-13 where we reverse a list containing elements 1, 2, and 3. The next pointers are drawn as solid lines and the prev pointers as dashed lines. To read the links in order, you follow the solid arrows from front(x) and back to x. In A), before we reverse the list, you get 1, 2, and 3. Now, when reversing, we start by pointing p at x, A), and flip its prev/next to go to B). The flipped pointers are shown as thicker lines. To get to the next link, we cannot use p->next—it would take us to last(x) and not front(x)—but we can take p->prev to get to its previous next. It will take us to the link containing 1, and we are in the state in B). At this point, the list is not in a consistent state. From p, we can follow next pointers around the links we haven't processed until we get to x, but the link x doesn't match its neighbors. We will fix that as we process the links.

A)

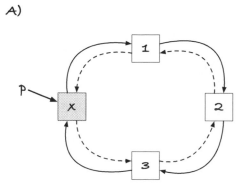

B)

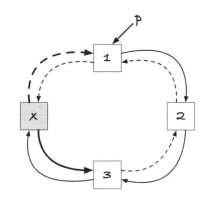

C)

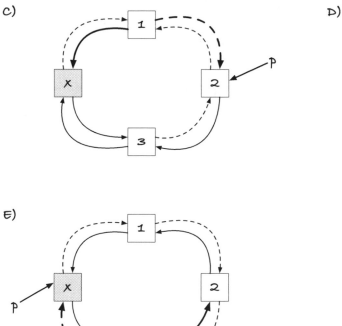

D)

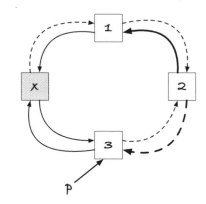

E)

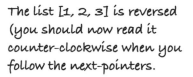

The list [1, 2, 3] is reversed (you should now read it counter-clockwise when you follow the next-pointers.

Figure 11-13. *Reversing a list by swapping next/prev pointers*

Once again, we switch p->next and p->prev, and we end up in C). We still have the unprocessed links in front of us—good because we need to process them—and the links x and 1 are correctly wired; 1 is last(x), which it should be in the reversed list, and 1's next pointer connects it to x. The links between 1 and 2 are not wired correctly, but when we move on to D, they will be. Generally, from p->prev, we can follow next pointers back to x, and get the processed links, in reverse order from where we started. The links following p, i.e., the links we visit if we follow next pointers starting at p, gives us the unprocessed links in the original order. As we move on, and in the example that is the last step, we flip the pointers in link 3 to go to E), and now we have a consistent list. For all links q, q == q->prev->next and q == q->next->prev, and from x, we can run around the circle to get all the links. But since all the links were swapped, we run around the circle counterclockwise, and we get the links in reversed order.

If we start with an empty list, we still swap x's prev and next pointers, since we use a do-while loop rather than the usual while loop. We use the do-while because we do not want to terminate at the first link, which will be x. This, however, is not a problem. If x is empty, then swapping prev and next gives us the original (empty) list back.

What if you wanted to make a copy of a list? You cannot simply point a list's head at the links of another list because then we would not have a consistent list. If we want two lists with the same elements, they need to have separate links, which means we need to copy all the values from one list into new links for the copy. Luckily, this is fairly straightforward. We can iterate through the first list, get the values, and append them to the second.

```
list copy_list(list x)
{
  list res = new_list();
  if (!res) return 0;

  for (struct link *p = front(x);
    p != x; p = p->next) {
    if (!append(res, p->value)) {
      free_list(res);
      return 0;
    }
  }

  return res;
}
```

The only complication with copying is that we need to deal with allocation errors. That means that we need to check if the head is successfully allocated, and we need to check the status of each append(). If we see an error from append(), we must free the list we have already created before we return NULL, so we do not leak memory.

What about comparing two lists to determine if they are equal, that is, that they hold the same values and in the same order? Here, we need a loop that goes through the links in both lists. If we iterate through the links, pair by pair, we can determine that the lists are not equal if we see different values. If not, we will terminate when we reach the end of at least one of the lists. Should we reach the end of both lists at the same time, then the lists were equal, but if we only reached the end of one of the lists, they were clearly not—one is longer than the other, after all.

```
bool equal(list x, list y)
{
  struct link *p = front(x);
  struct link *q = front(y);
  while ( (p != x) && (q != y) ) {
    if (p->value != q->value)
      return false;
    p = p->next; q = q->next;
  }
  return (p == x) && (q == y);
}
```

The test (p == x) && (q == y) is true if we reached the end of both x and y, and false otherwise.

Sorting Doubly Linked Lists

There is nothing particularly special about sorting doubly linked lists, so this section is not here to teach you anything new about sorting. But sorting linked lists involves moving pointers around, and so it serves as an excellent excuse to learn more about that. With linked lists, we cannot access elements in constant time, as we can in an array, so we cannot use every algorithm for sorting, but many of the classical algorithms still work, and we will see some of those.

Incidentally, if you want to check if the elements in a list are sorted, you can do it like this:

```
bool is_sorted(list x)
{
  struct link *p = front(x);
  while (p->next != x) {
    if (p->value > p->next->value)
      return false;
    p = p->next;
  }
  return true;
}
```

We iterate until p->next hits x. Usually, we stop when p reaches back to x, but in this case, we want to compare two consecutive links, and we do not want to compare a value with the dummy head, so we stop one link early. In the iteration, we check if the current value is larger than the next. If it is, those two links at least are out of order, and the list isn't sorted. If all links are smaller or equal to the next, then the list is sorted.

Selection Sort

Selection sort works as follows: you scan through the list, collecting a sorted list behind you, and in each iteration, you identify a minimal value among the remaining links and append it to the sorted list. If you always take a minimal value, and your sorted list starts out empty, then you end up with a sorted list when you are done. If you implement selection sort on an array, you move the minimal element by swapping with the next unsorted element, but with linked lists, we can move links without swapping. We can unlink the minimal element from the unsorted list and append it to the end of the sorted list by setting the prev and next pointers correctly.

The main function looks like this, and I will explain the two helper functions, get_smallest() and move_links(), as follows:

```
void selection_sort(list x)
{
  list_head sorted = init_list_head(sorted);
  while (!is_empty(x)) {
```

```
    struct link *next = get_smallest(x);
    unlink(next);
    append_link(&sorted, next);
  }
  move_links(x, &sorted);
}
```

We use a stack-allocated list head for the sorted list. There is no need to heap-allocate this list since we only use it while we sort. Then we iteratively identify a minimal element, unlink it from the existing list (making x one element shorter), and append it to sorted. Since we remove a link from x in each iteration, it will eventually be empty, at which point all the links are in sorted. At that point, the while-loop terminates. All that remains is to move the links back to x, so it now contains the sorted links.

Finding a minimal link involves searching through x's remaining links.

```
struct link *get_smallest(list x)
{
  assert(!is_empty(x));
  struct link *p = front(x);
  struct link *res = p;
  while (p != x) {
    if (p->value < res->value)
      res = p;
    p = p->next;
  }
  return res;
}
```

The function assumes that the input list is not empty (which it won't be in selection_sort()), which means that we have a value in front(x). Of the links we have seen so far, the front must be the one with the smallest value, so we get a reference to it, res (for result). Now we iterate through the links, and if we see a link with a smaller value than the one we have, we update res so it points to the new link. When we are done with the loop, we have seen all the links in x, and res points to one with a minimal value.

When we are done sorting, the sorted list sits in sorted and x is empty. We need to move the links back to x, so the caller gets the sorted list; sorted is a local variable and will be lost as soon as the function returns. To get the links back, we need to connect them such that x->next points to the first link in sorted and x->prev points to the last. We should only do this if sorted is not empty because otherwise we would make x's prev and next point to a variable that is soon to be deallocated. The function for moving the links back to x could look like this:

```
void move_links(list x, list y)
{
  if (!is_empty(y)) {
    connect(x, front(y));
    connect(last(y), x);
  }
}
```

If x wasn't empty when we called the function, the links would be lost, except if y was empty, in which case x would be unchanged. For our selection_sort() function, this isn't an issue. We will always have an empty x, so if y is also empty, we still get the right result. If you want a version that will always work, we can free x's links first. This ensures that we will not leak memory when we change x's links, and since free_links() sets the input to the empty list, we are guaranteed that x is empty after that. Such a version could look like this:

```
void move_links(list x, list y)
{
  free_links(x);
  if (!is_empty(y)) {
    connect(x, front(y));
    connect(last(y), x);
    clear_list(y);
  }
}
```

Here, we also clear y, to not leave it pointing to links that now belong to x. For selection_sort(), where sorted goes out of scope after we move the links, this isn't an issue, but for a more general case, we should leave y in a state where it doesn't refer to links that are no longer its.

An alternative implementation could look like this:

```
void move_links(list x, list y)
```

```
{
  free_links(x);
  if (!is_empty(y)) {
    *x = *y;
    connect_neighbours(x);
    clear_list(y);
  }
}
```

Here, we assign the full content of y into x, which includes the prev and next pointers. This is likely faster than two invocations of connect() and one of each of front() and last(). It sets x's pointers correctly, but we still need to point the beginning and end links back to x, which is what connect_neighbours() does.

This version is faster than the previous if it is fast to copy the full content of a struct link from one address to another. When links consist of two points and an integer, that will be the case. If you pack more data into links, the trade-off might change. If you work with generic lists (Chapter 14), where links carry more data than captured by the struct link structure, you will only copy parts of the link (see Chapter 14 for details). When the links are the heads of lists, however, this will not be an issue.

Insertion Sort

The insertion sort algorithm works by scanning through the list, keeping a sorted list behind the current value, and in each iteration, taking the next value and inserting it at its correct, sorted, position behind the current index. If we sort arrays, we insert the next value by swapping elements toward the left, until we find the correct location, but with a linked list, we can simply unlink the next value and insert it into the sorted sequence.

```
void insertion_sort(list x)
{
  list_head sorted = init_list_head(sorted);
  struct link *p = front(x);
  while (p != x) {
    struct link *next = p->next;
    unlink(p);
    insert_sorted(&sorted, p);
```

```
    p = next;
  }
  move_links(x, &sorted);
}
```

In this implementation, p runs through the list, and we unlink the values one by one to insert into the sorted list that we then move back into x when we are done. This is close to how we would implement it in an array, but since we are unlinking from x, we can simplify the code slightly. We can iteratively remove the head of the list, which is what p will be in any case when we keep unlinking it. Then the code looks like this:

```
void insertion_sort(list x)
{
  list_head sorted = init_list_head(sorted);
  while (!is_empty(x)) {
    struct link *p = front(x);
    unlink(p);
    insert_sorted(&sorted, p);
  }
  move_links(x, &sorted);
}
```

Given a sorted list and a link, it is straightforward to insert the link at the correct position. Run through the list until we find the first link with a value larger than the one we are inserting, and then insert the new link before it.

```
void insert_sorted(list x, struct link *link)
{
  struct link *p = front(x);
  while (p != x && p->value < link->value)
    p = p->next;
  link_before(p, link);
}
```

There is the possibility that the new link has a value larger than all the links in the list (if nothing else, it will happen when we have an empty list). However, with our circular lists, we handle this situation the same as for other links if we test for termination before we test the current link's value, p->value, in the loop condition. If we reach the end of the list before we see a link with a larger value, then the new link should go at the end of the list, but that means putting it before the list's head, which is what we do.

This insert_sorted() function searches from the left and stops when it finds a larger value. It does what it is supposed to do, but it is from the opposite direction as the traditional array version of insertion sort. Links with the same value will be reversed if we sort with this insertion; in algorithmic terms, the implementation is "unstable." If we want to preserve the order of links with the same value, we should put new links behind, not in front of, the existing links with that value. This is trivial to fix, though. Insert from the right instead of the left.

```
void insert_sorted(list x, struct link *link)
{
  struct link *p = last(x);
  while (p != x && p->value > link->value)
    p = p->prev;
  link_after(p, link);
}
```

Merge Sort

Merge sort is a divide and conquer algorithm, which means that we are looking at a recursive solution to sorting. The idea is this: split the list into two parts, sort them recursively, and then merge the result. The base case for the recursion is if the list is empty or has length 1, in which case it is already sorted.

```
void merge_sort(list x)
{
  if (is_empty(x) || front(x)->next == x)
    return; // length zero or one lists are sorted

  list_head y = init_list_head(y);
  split_list(x, &y);
  merge_sort(x); merge_sort(&y);
  merge(x, &y);
}
```

The list y goes on the stack, as there is no need to heap-allocate it.

In the array version of merge sort, splitting usually means that we take the first half of the elements and put in the first list and the second half of the elements and put them in the second list. This is easy in an array, where we identify sequences by indices, and getting the middle index is a simple matter of dividing the sequence length by two. With linked lists, however, we would have to run through all the links to count up the length and then back through the list to find the link where we should break the list in two. An easier solution is to run through the list and take every second link and move to the other list.

```c
void split_list(list x, list y)
{
  assert(is_empty(y));
  struct link *p = front(x);
  while (p != x) {
    struct link *q = p->next;
    unlink(p); append_link(y, p);
    if (q == x) return;
    p = q->next;
  }
}
```

We run p through the list and point q to the link after p. We unlink p to move it into the other list, and then we update p, so we skip q, leaving that link in the list. If q is the head of the list, we shouldn't skip past it—that would take us back to the beginning again—so we break the iteration and return from the function if/when that happens.

Merging two sorted lists means moving through them, in each iteration taking the smallest front of the two and putting it in the output list. We can implement it like this:

```c
void merge(list x, list y)
{
  list_head merged = init_list_head(merged);
  struct link *p = front(x), *q = front(y);

  while( (p != x) && (q != y) ) {
    struct link *smallest;
    if (p->value < q->value) {
```

```
    unlink(p);
    smallest = p; p = p->next;
  } else {
    unlink(q);
    smallest = q; q = q->next;
  }
  append_link(&merged, smallest);
}

concatenate(&merged, x);
concatenate(&merged, y);
move_links(x, &merged);
}
```

We point p and q into the lists, starting at the front. Then we continue as long as we haven't reached the end of either list, where we identify the smallest value of the two and unlink it (and move the corresponding pointer to the next link). We can still get p->next and q->next after we have unlinked them because we left a link's pointers alone in the unlink operation. Of course, they will point somewhere else when we have appended the link, but we do that after we update the pointers. We append the smallest link to the output. When we have reached the end of either list, we are done in the loop. The other list will have elements left unless we started with two empty lists, but we know that these are larger than those we have in the result so far, so we can simply concatenate them into the result. We do not have to test which of the lists is empty, because if we concatenate both of them, one is empty and that operation will not break anything. We return the result through x, so the final step is moving the merged links there. It is a design choice to return through x, but by returning through one of the input lists, we avoid heap-allocating a result list. In any case, the input lists are destroyed in the process; we have moved all the links from them.

Since we remove the links from the lists when we merge them, we can simplify the code slightly. If we had copied results into the result, the original lists would be unchanged, and we would have to run variables p and q through them. So, if you want a merge() function that doesn't destroy the input, it is a small change to the preceding function. Given that we do destroy the input, however, we might as well exploit it. Instead of using variables p and q, we can get the fronts of the lists directly and unlink the smallest in each iteration. Such an implementation could look like this:

```
void merge(list x, list y)
{
  list_head merged = init_list_head(merged);
  while( !is_empty(x) && !is_empty(y) ) {
    struct link *smallest =
      (front(x)->value < front(y)->value)
      ? front(x) : front(y);
    unlink(smallest);
    append_link(&merged, smallest);
  }
  concatenate(&merged, x);
  concatenate(&merged, y);
  move_links(x, &merged);
}
```

Here, we again loop as long as both lists have more links, but we pick the smallest link directly from the fronts. We unlink and append, and the unlink() operation will make smallest->next the new front of its lists, so we still have access to it. Otherwise, the function works as the previous version.

Quicksort

The quicksort algorithm gets its name from the low overhead of its operations. Its expected theoretical running time is not better than merge sort, but moving objects around involves fewer and simpler operations—on arrays, at least. If we quicksort a linked list, the operations are not that much simpler. Still, we can implement it to see how this algorithm can work on lists.

Quicksort is also a divide and conquer algorithm, with a recursion where the base case is the same as for merge sort—an empty list or a list with one element is already sorted. The recursive case splits the list into two parts as well, but with a different strategy. We pick a value, the *pivot*, from the list, and then we split the list into the elements smaller or equal to the pivot and then elements larger than the pivot. We sort the two parts. Now, because all the elements in one part are smaller than all the elements in the other, and because the parts are sorted, we get the sorted list from concatenating the two.

The dangerous part is doing exactly what I described because you could end up with one of the parts empty. If the pivot is the largest element in the list, for example, all the elements are less than or equal to it. Then we would recurse on the original data, entering an infinite recursion. To avoid this, we set the pivot aside in the recursion and put it back between the two sorted lists when we are done. It has to be larger than or equal to all the elements in the first list—because we constructed the list that way—so we will still get a sorted list.

The full algorithm, excluding the partition, looks like this:

```
void quick_sort(list x)
{
  if (is_empty(x) || front(x)->next == x)
    return; // length zero or one lists are sorted

  // Remove the pivot, to make sure that we reduce
  // the problem size each recursion
  struct link *first = front(x); unlink(first);
  int pivot = first->value;

  list_head y = init_list_head(y);
  partition(x, &y, pivot);
  quick_sort(x); quick_sort(&y);
  append_link(x, first); // Get first back into the list
  concatenate(x, &y);
}
```

The partitioning looks like many of the functions we have seen before. Run through the links, and when you have a link with a value larger than the pivot, unlink it and put it in the second list:

```
void partition(list x, list y, int pivot)
{
  assert(is_empty(y));
  struct link *p = front(x);
  while (p != x) {
    struct link *next = p->next;
    if (p->value > pivot) {
      unlink(p); append_link(y, p);
```

```
    }
    p = next;
  }
}
```

I think that by now you have gotten the hang of doubly linked circular lists. Most algorithms that work on them will look like something we have already seen by now, and all involve updating the prev and next pointers—because that is all that links really have—and typically, it involves simple linking and unlinking. Have fun with experimenting with lists; we will move on to the next topic.

CHAPTER 12

Search Trees

Search trees, or in this chapter specifically binary search trees, are also recursively defined. A binary search tree is either an *empty tree* or a *node* containing a value and two trees, a left and a right subtree. Furthermore, we require that the value in a node is larger than all the values in its left subtree and smaller than all the values in its right subtree. It is the last property that makes search trees interesting for many algorithms. If we know that the smaller values are to the left, and the larger values are to the right, we can efficiently search in a tree, as we shall see.

Figure 12-1 shows three different search trees containing the integers 1, 3, 6, and 8. I have shown empty trees as "ground" symbols, but traditionally we do not show them in figures, and in the following figures, I will leave them out. In A), the root holds the value 1, it has an empty left tree, and its right tree's root holds the value 3. In B), the root holds 6 and has both a left and a right subtree. On the left, the subtree's root holds the value 3, and on the right, it holds 8. All the trees in C) have empty right subtrees. As should be evidently clear, the tree representation for a set of values is not unique, as there are many ways you can organize the values such that they satisfy the properties. The organization affects performance when we search, though. When you want to find the node (if any) that holds the value v, you start in the root of the tree. If the value there is v, you are done and can return that node. If not, you determine whether v is smaller than the value in the root, in which case you should search in the left subtree (where the smaller values are). If on the other hand v is larger, you search in the right subtree. If you reach an empty tree, the value wasn't in the tree.

© Thomas Mailund 2021
T. Mailund, *Pointers in C Programming*, https://doi.org/10.1007/978-1-4842-6927-5_12

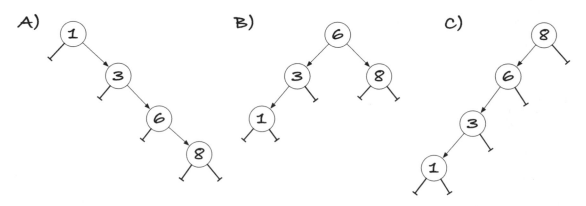

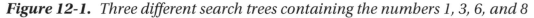

Figure 12-1. *Three different search trees containing the numbers 1, 3, 6, and 8*

The time this search takes is proportional to the height of the tree, which can be proportional to the number of elements the tree holds (as is the case in the trees in A) and C) in Figure 12-1). If the tree is balanced, so the depth of the left and right subtrees is roughly the same for all the nodes, then the depth is logarithmic in the number of elements. There are many strategies for keeping a search tree balanced, but I will refer you to a textbook on algorithms and data structures to explore that. In this chapter, we will only look at strategies for implementing the data structure. For simplicity, we will only consider trees that hold integers and without duplications.

Tree Operations

We want to implement the following operations:

1. Determine if a value is in a tree

2. Insert a new element in a tree

3. Delete a value from a tree

and of course we should have code for freeing a tree once we are done with it.

Contains

If we search for a value v in a tree t, then

1. If t is empty, we report that v is not in it.

2. If the value in t is v, then we report that it is.

3. Otherwise, if v is smaller than the value in t, we look in t's left subtree, and if it is larger, we look in t's right subtree.

It is a recursive operation, where we have two base cases: t is empty or it holds the value we are looking for. The recursive case involves searching a subtree, where we can determine which subtree to search from the value in the root of t.

Insert

If we want to insert a value, v, in a tree t, then

1. If t is empty, we should create a tree with a single leaf, a node that holds the value v and has empty left and right subtrees.

2. If t has a value, and it is v, then we leave t as it is. It already has the value, and the order property from the definition prevents a search tree from holding more than one of the same value.

3. Otherwise, if v is smaller than the value in t, insert it into t's left subtree, and if v is greater, insert it into t's right subtree.

Again, we have a recursive operation. The base cases are again an empty tree or a tree with v in its root, and the recursive cases are insertions into the left or right subtree.

Delete

Deletion is the most complex of the operations. The overall procedure is this:

1. If t is empty, we are done.

2. If t's value is v, then delete t and replace it with a subtree (see the following).

3. Otherwise, delete v from the left or right subtree, depending on whether v is smaller than or greater than the value in v.

Step 2 is where the operation is more complicated than the others. To delete the value in the root of a tree, we need to construct a tree that still has all the remaining values. There are two cases here. One, when t has at most one non-empty subtree, we can immediately replace it, and two, if both its subtrees are non-empty, we replace the value in t with the largest value in its left subtree and then remove that value from the left subtree.

Consider case one, where t has at least one empty subtree, and consider Figure 12-2. In the figure, t is the tree rooted in the black node, and the gray triangle represents the (possible) non-empty tree. If we replace t with its non-empty subtree, we have deleted the value, since any value appears at most once in a tree. All values in t's subtree are smaller than the value in t's parent, if t is a left subtree, or greater than the value in t's parent, if t is a right subtree. So replacing t with its subtree will satisfy the order property of search trees.

If both of t's subtrees are non-empty, we cannot replace t by one of them, but we can do this: find the largest value in the entire tree smaller than v. Since it must be smaller than v, that value must be in t's left subtree, and since it should be the largest, it must sit in the rightmost node in that subtree; see Figure 12-3. To get this value, we go to t's left subtree, and then we run down the tree as long as there is a non-empty right subtree. When we reach a node with an empty right subtree, we have what we are looking for. We take that value, and we update t's value to that. Now we have deleted v from the tree, but we have two copies of the same value, the value in the rightmost node. We need to get rid of one of them. However, the rightmost node has, by definition, an empty right subtree, so we can delete that node following the previous case. So, we delete t's new value from t's left subtree, and then we are done.

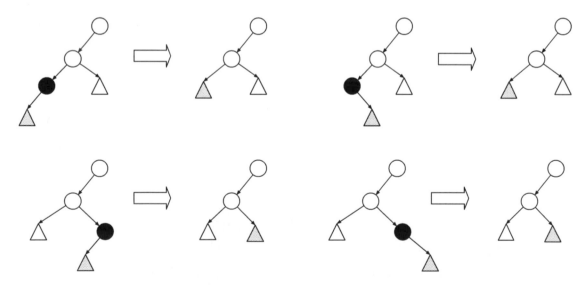

Figure 12-2. *Deleting in a tree with at most one non-empty subtree*

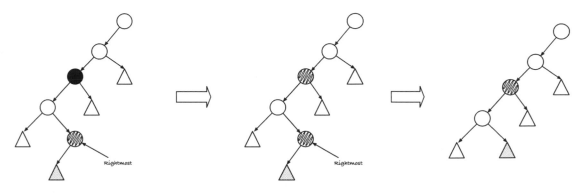

Figure 12-3. *Deleting a value in a tree with two non-empty subtrees*

The procedure works just as well by getting the leftmost value in the right subtree, but we chose the rightmost in the left more by tradition than anything else.

Free

When we free the memory held in a tree:

1. To free an empty tree, do nothing—it is already freed.

2. Otherwise, free the left and the right subtree, and then free the tree.

Recursive Data Structures and Recursive Functions

We didn't talk about it when we implemented lists because lists are particularly simple to work with. Still, when it comes to recursive data structures, it is often useful to think about operations on them as well in terms of recursion. Recursive solutions are usually much more straightforward than corresponding iterative solutions, as they closely match the data structure. However, they come at a cost. If we solve a problem recursively, the recursive calls can fill the call stack, which will crash our program, if we are lucky, or corrupt our memory. With search trees, this is usually not an issue. If we keep a search tree balanced, then the recursion depth is logarithmic in the number of nodes in the tree. That means that we can double the number of nodes and only have to go one recursive call deeper. Unfortunately, we are not writing balanced trees in this chapter, so that will do us no good. And even if we did have balanced trees, there is some overhead in function calls that we can avoid if we do not use recursion.

So, what can we do when the best solution, from a programming perspective, is clean recursive code, but where execution constraints prevent us from recursion? We will explore this with the operations we need on trees in this chapter, but the short answer is that, sometimes, recursion isn't a problem, and you can safely use recursive functions. This is the case with so-called *tail recursion*. If a function calls itself but immediately returns the result of the recursive call—so it doesn't do any further processing with the result of the recursive call, it just returns it—the function is said to be tail-recursive. Then recursion isn't necessary at all. Most compilers, if you turn on optimization, will translate such functions into loops, and calling them involves a single stack frame only. You do not risk filling the stack, and you do not get any function call overhead beyond the first call. If your compiler doesn't do this for you, it is also trivial to rewrite such a function yourself. We will see several examples of such recursions.

We cannot always get tail-recursive solutions.[1] In a tree, if we need to recurse on both subtrees of a node, for example, to free memory, then at most one of the recursive calls can be the result of the function itself. When you are in this situation, you might have to allocate an explicit stack on the heap. There is more available memory on the heap than on the stack, so this alleviates the problem with exceeding the stack space. It isn't always trivial to replace a call stack with an explicit stack, however. Call stacks do more than pushing new calls on the stack; when you are done with a recursive call, you also need to return to the correct position in the calling function. You must emulate function calls in your own code, and while sometimes easy, it can get complicated. We will see a few examples of using explicit stacks and discuss why it isn't advisable in the cases where we need them for our trees.

If we consider using an explicit stack for something like freeing the nodes in a tree, there is another issue. If the stack requires that we allocate heap memory—which it must, if we should be able to handle arbitrarily large trees—then the operation can fail. Should malloc() return NULL, we have an error. We have to deal with that, but if we need the memory to complete the recursive tree traversal, then we are in trouble. Something like freeing memory should never fail—*must* never fail—because it is practically impossible to recover from. And even if we can recover from a failure, we likely will leak memory. It is far better to have a solution where we can reuse memory we already have to solve the problem. There is, of course, not a general solution for this. What memory

---

[1]At least not in C. In languages with closures, it is possible to use so-called continuation passing style programming. But that comes with an overhead in itself, and we cannot implement it without allocating extra memory.

we might be able to reuse and how we can arrange existing memory depend on the data structure we have. There is usually a solution if you work at it a little bit. We will see a way to modify search trees that lets us traverse and delete trees without using recursion, an explicit stack, or any additional memory.

There is much to cover, so read on.

Direct Implementation

We start by implementing a direct translation of the operations into C. It will have some issues, in particular with error handling and efficiency, but we will soon fix those.

The data structure for a tree is what you would expect from the examples with lists. We have a node with a value and two subtrees, and the subtrees must be pointers to the node type's struct. We also define a type stree to be a pointer to a struct node:

```
struct node {
  int value;
  struct node *left;
  struct node *right;
};
typedef struct node *stree;
```

As with lists, we write a function for allocating the fundamental struct. There it was a struct link; now it is a struct node. The function takes the member values as input, but in the insertion function, we will only insert new leaves, so we add a macro for that case.

```
struct node *node(int value, stree left, stree right)
{
  struct node *n = malloc(sizeof *n);
  if (n) *n = (struct node) {
    .value = value, .left = left, .right = right
  };
  return n;
}
#define leaf(V) node(V, 0, 0)
```

The `if`-statement in the function checks if we got a non-NULL value from `malloc()`, and if we did, we assign the values of a `struct node` into n. You could also have implemented the function as

```c
struct node *node(int value, stree left, stree right)
{
  struct node *n = malloc(sizeof *n);
  if (n) {
    n->value = value;
    n->left = left;
    n->right = right
  };
  return n;
}
```

There is no particular good reason to prefer one version over the other; I just happen to like the first one.

A direct translation of the `contains()` operation will look like this:

```c
bool contains(stree t, int val)
{
  if (!t)              return false;
  if (val == t->value) return true;
  if (val < t->value)  return contains(t->left, val);
  else                 return contains(t->right, val);
}
```

This is a good solution for that operation, and there is nothing I would change about it. It is simple, it follows the definition of the operation directly, and it is tail-recursive. In the two recursive cases, the return value of `contains()` is the direct result of the recursive calls to `contains()`. This means that likely your compiler will translate the recursive calls into a loop in the generated code. If you are not afraid to look at assembler code, you can check the generated code using, for example, godbolt.org, where I have put this function at the link `https://godbolt.org/z/3adTr3`. There, you can see what different compilers will generate for this function. If you generate code without optimization, the recursive functions will have one or more `'call'` instructions in them. If you turn on optimization, that `call` disappears and you have loops (in various forms, depending on the compiler). Godbolt.org is an excellent resource if you want to know what code your compiler is generating. To check if a tail-recursive function is translated into a loop, you can generally check if it generates code with a `call` instruction or not. If your compiler isn't supported by godbolt.org, you will have to generate the assembler yourself—the compiler's documentation will tell you how—and then you can check. Compilers generally translate tail-recursive functions into loops. The C standard doesn't require it, but it is usually a safe assumption.

The `insert()` operation looks like this:

```
stree insert(stree t, int val)
{
  if (!t) return leaf(val); // can fail, but we don't handle it
  if (val < t->value) {
    t->left = insert(t->left, val);
  } else {
    t->right = insert(t->right, val);
  }
  return t;
}
```

We return a new leaf with the value if `t` is empty. If `val` is smaller than `t->value`, update `t`'s left subtree with an insertion, and if it is greater, we update `t`'s right subtree with an insertion. If `t->value == val`, we don't do anything; we just return `t` at the end of the function.

This function is more problematic than `contains()`. First, we might have an allocation error in `leaf()`, in which case we return an empty tree that shouldn't be empty. This is easy to capture if we start out with an empty tree since we will probably notice that adding a value to an empty tree shouldn't give us an empty tree back. However, if we insert into a non-empty tree, we call recursively down the tree structure, and somewhere down there, we insert an empty subtree that should have been a leaf. We do not get any information about that back from the call. We get a pointer to the input tree back regardless of whether there was an error or not.

One fix to this problem is allocating the new leaf before we recursively insert it into the tree. That way, we can return NULL in case of an error, and since a successful insertion can never return an empty tree, we can recognize this as an error.

```
stree insert_node(stree t, struct node *n)
{
  if (!t) return n;
  if (n->value == t->value) {
    free(n); // it was already here
  } else if (n->value < t->value) {
    t->left = insert_node(t->left, n);
  } else {
    t->right = insert_node(t->right, n);
  }
  return t;
}

stree insert(stree t, int val)
{
  struct node *n = leaf(val);
  if (!n) return 0;

  return insert_node(t, n);
}
```

Of course, if the value is already in the tree, we have allocated a new node for no reason, but that is the cost of handling allocation errors correctly here. Upfront allocation, even if you risk deleting again, is often an acceptable solution to problems such as these. If you want to avoid an extra allocation, you can always call contains() first (at the cost of an extra search).

Another issue is that the function is not tail-recursive. When we insert val in a subtree, we need to update one of t's subtrees accordingly. When we have more work to do after a recursive call, we cannot get tail recursion. Consequently, there will be function calls here, with the overhead they incur and the risk of exceeding the stack space.

To delete, we need a function for finding the value in the rightmost node in a tree. We can implement a function for that like this:

```
int rightmost_val(stree t)
{
  assert(t);
```

```
  if (!t->right) return t->value;
  else return rightmost_val(t->right);
}
```

We will not call it with an empty tree, so we assert that. Otherwise, t->right would be dereferencing a NULL pointer, which we always want to avoid. We test if there is a right subtree, and if there isn't, we return t's value. Otherwise, we continue searching in t's right subtree. The function is tail-recursive, and with an optimizing compiler, you get an efficient looping function.

Now we can delete():

```
stree delete(stree t, int val)
{
  if (!t) return t;

  if (val == t->value) {
    if (!(t->left && t->right)) {
      stree subtree = t->left ? t->left : t->right;
      free(t);
      return subtree;
    } else {
      t->value = rightmost_val(t->left);
      t->left = delete(t->left, t->value);
    }

  } else if (val < t->value) {
    t->left = delete(t->left, val);
  } else if (val > t->value) {
    t->right = delete(t->right, val);
  }

  return t;
}
```

If we have an empty tree, the result is the tree itself. If t's value is the one we are deleting, we have the two cases discussed earlier. When t doesn't have both subtrees, we remove t and return its subtree. The expression

```
t->left ? t->left : t->right
```

will give us the left subtree if it isn't empty and otherwise give us the right subtree. If both trees are empty, we get the right subtree, but that doesn't matter, since they are both NULL. If t has both subtrees, we get the rightmost value, put it in t->value, and then we delete it from t->left.

Finally, if t->value is greater or smaller than val, we delete recursively, updating the left or right subtree accordingly.

This function, like insert(), is not tail-recursive. Updating the subtrees after the recursive calls prevents this.

When we free a tree, we must free both subtrees as well. The function can look like this:

```
void free_stree(stree t)
{
  if (!t) return;
  free_stree(t->left);
  free_stree(t->right);
  free(t);
}
```

This, obviously, isn't tail-recursive either. We cannot make it tail-recursive because there are two recursive calls involved.

If you want to make a tree from an array, you could write a function such as this:

```
stree make_stree(int n, int array[n])
{
  stree t = 0;
  for (int i = 0; i < n; i++) {
    t = insert(t, array[i]);
  }
  return t;
}
```

We don't have recursion issues here, at least not directly. We iteratively call insert() (which does have recursion issues).

If you want to print a tree, you want to print the left and right subtrees as well, so here we need recursion, and again we cannot get tail recursion because of the two recursive calls:

```
void print_stree(stree t)
{
  if (!t) return;
  putchar('(');
    print_stree(t->left);
    putchar(',');
    printf("%d", t->value);
    putchar(',');
    print_stree(t->right);
  putchar(')');
}
```

Pass by Reference

The problems we have with insertion and deletion are caused by the same design flaw we had in the first list implementation in Chapter 11. We have designed the functions such that they return a new tree instead of modifying an existing one. That means that the recursive calls give us the trees we now need to store in one of t's subtrees. The changes we made to lists will also work here. We want the functions to take a tree that we can update as input. That means that an empty tree cannot be a NULL pointer, but must be something else, or at least that if it is a NULL pointer, it is passed by reference. We can use either of the solutions from the lists, make a pointer to pointers our representation, or use a dummy node. The first solution will work for us here, so that is what we will do.

We will still have the type stree be a pointer to struct node, but change the operations, so they work with pointers to stree instead of stree. So the functions take pointers to pointers to nodes. An empty tree is a pointer to a NULL pointer.

An stree * pointer on the stack will work fine for a tree; we just have to pass it by reference in function calls, but should you want a heap-allocated tree, we can provide a function for that as well:

```
stree *new_stree(void)
{
  stree *t = malloc(sizeof *t);
  if (t) *t = 0;
  return t;
}
```

It allocates an stree * pointer and, if successful, sets the pointed-to value to NULL, making it an empty tree.

If we heap-allocate trees, we should also have a function for freeing them again. So let us change the name of the free_stree() function from before to one that makes it explicit that it is only freeing nodes:

```
void free_nodes(struct node *n)
{
  if (!n) return;
  free_nodes(n->left);
  free_nodes(n->right);
  free(n);
}
```

and provide a second function for freeing a tree as well.

```
static inline
void free_stree(stree *t)
{
  free_nodes(*t);
  free(t);
}
```

Now we make the operations take an stree * argument, which means that we must dereference the argument to get the node. For contains(), the function changes to this:

```
bool contains(stree *tp, int val)
{
  assert(tp);
  stree t = *tp;
  if (!t)              return false;
  if (val == t->value) return true;
  if (val < t->value)  return contains(&t->left, val);
  else                 return contains(&t->right, val);
}
```

To make the code more readable, I cast *tp to an stree so I can refer to the tree with the variable t. Little else changes in the function, but in the recursive calls we must provide an address of a tree, not the tree itself. So, we get the address of t's left or right subtree when we call contains() recursively. We need to call contains() with an address of a struct node pointer, so we call recursively with &t->left (the address of left subtree) or &t->right (the address of the right subtree). The & operator binds such that &t->left means &(t->left), the address of t's left member, not (&t)->left, which would be the left member of whatever structure the address of t is. Since &t isn't a pointer to a structure, it is a pointer to a pointer, and it hasn't got a left member, the expression (&t)->left would give you a type error.

When we use a pointer to a tree in insert(), we will interpret it as the target position where we should insert. If the target points to NULL, we have an empty tree, and if we write a node into the target, we have put a tree there. Thus, we can write insert() as

```
bool insert(stree *target, int val)
{
  assert(target);
  stree t = *target;
  if (!t) {
    return !!(*target = leaf(val));
  }
  if (val < t->value) {
    return insert(&t->left, val);
  } else {
    return insert(&t->right, val);
  }
}
```

We, once again, get the tree that target points to, to make the code more readable. If it is NULL, then target is an address that holds an empty tree, and we want that address to hold a new leaf instead. We, therefore, allocate a leaf and put it in *target. An assignment is also an expression, so (*target = leaf(val)) gives us a value. It is the right-hand side of the assignment, which is the new leaf. If the allocation failed, we get NULL. If we turn a pointer into a truth value (with the !! trick we have seen before), then we turn the assignment into a value that is true if the allocation was successful and false otherwise, which we will return to indicate whether the insertion was successful or not.

The recursive cases didn't change, except that we pass the address of the subtrees along in the call, instead of just the subtrees. That means that we can modify the tree we use in the recursion, so we don't need to update the tree after the call. The function is now tail-recursive.

Be careful when you use an address as a parameter to a function call. You can get into trouble if it is the address of a stack object. There is nothing wrong with it per se. If we put a tree (an `stree` object) on the stack, and use it with our operations, then we have a tree on the stack, and as long as we do not use it after we have returned (which we can't as it is gone by then), then all is well. But if we, for example, took the address of t and passed it along in a recursive call in `insert()`, we could write into the address, but we would be writing into a local variable. What we put there is lost once the call to `insert()` is done. Also, the compiler would see that we use the address of a local variable that presumably should change in recursive calls where we get new memory for local variables, so the tail recursion optimization would not be possible. That, though, is a minor problem, since the function would be broken already if we attempt to pass addresses of local variables along in the call. It is not what we do here, of course. The addresses we pass along in the function calls are addresses in heap-allocated nodes.

The updated `delete()` is also tail-recursive:

```
stree *rightmost(stree *t)
{
  assert(t && *t);
  if (!(*t)->right) return t;
  else return rightmost(&(*t)->right);
}

void delete(stree *target, int val)
{
  assert(target);
  stree t = *target;

  if (!t) return;

  if (val == t->value) {
    if (!(t->left && t->right)) {
      stree subtree = t->left ? t->left : t->right;
      *target = subtree;
      free(t);
    } else {
      stree *rm_ref = rightmost(&t->left);
      stree rm = *rm_ref;
```

```
      t->value = rm->value;
      *rm_ref = rm->left;
      free(rm);
    }

  } else if (val < t->value) {
    delete(&t->left, val);
  } else if (val > t->value) {
    delete(&t->right, val);
  }
}
```

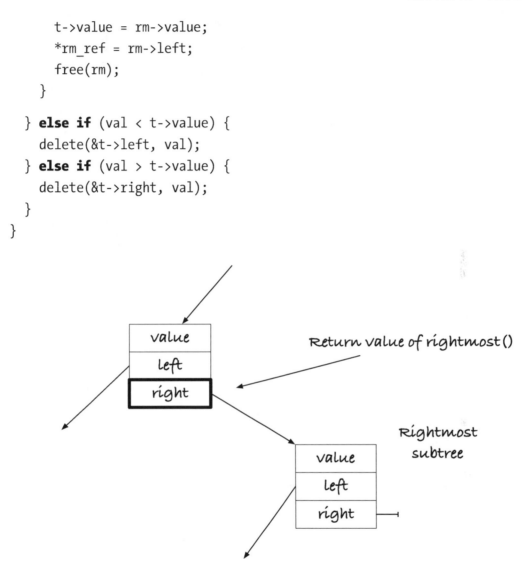

Figure 12-4. *Return value of rightmost()*

Our new `rightmost()` returns the address that holds the pointer to the rightmost tree; see Figure 12-4. We search down a tree's `right` trees until we get to a node where `right` is empty. However, the variable we use in the function is the address that holds the tree, not the tree itself. So, when we reach the rightmost node, the parameter to the `rightmost()` call is the address in the parent node. Dereferencing the result of the `rightmost()` call gives us the rightmost node, and writing into the result changes the right tree in the parent. We exploit this to delete the rightmost value from the left tree. We dereference the rightmost reference to put the value into t, and then we replace the rightmost tree with its left child directly, no second call to delete() this time.

Our remaining functions, make_stree() and print_stree(), do not change much. We will heap-allocate a new tree pointer in make_stree(), and we will pass the tree by reference in print_stree():

```
stree *make_stree(int n, int array[n])
{
  stree *t = new_stree();
  if (!t) return 0;
  for (int i = 0; i < n; i++) {
    if (!insert(t, array[i])) {
      free_stree(t);
      return 0;
    }
  }
  return t;
}

void print_stree(stree *t)
{
  if (!*t) return;
  putchar('(');
    print_stree(&(*t)->left);
    putchar(',');
    printf("%d", (*t)->value);
    putchar(',');
    print_stree(&(*t)->right);
  putchar(')');
}
```

In print_stree(), I didn't bother with a variable that holds the dereferenced value of the parameter. Here, t is the pointer to a tree. That means that I need to dereference t to get a tree, which is why you see expressions such as &(*t)->left. We dereference t to get a tree, *t, then get the left tree in that, (*t)->left, and then we get the address of that tree, &(*t)->left.

Refactoring

The recursive search in contains(), insert(), and delete() (except for rightmost()) is the same, so we can extract it into a separate function and refactor the code. We can write a function, find_loc() (find location), that returns the address that points to the node with a given value or, if the value isn't in the tree, the address where it should sit. It would look like this:

```
stree *find_loc(stree *t, int val)
{
  if (!*t || (*t)->value == val)
    return t;
  else if (val < (*t)->value)
    return find_loc(&(*t)->left, val);
  else
    return find_loc(&(*t)->right, val);
}
```

To see if a tree has a value, find the location, and check if there is a tree there. If there is, the tree contains the value. If there isn't, it doesn't. Since find_loc() returns the address where the tree should be, we must dereference it and turn the pointer into a truth value:

```
bool contains(stree *t, int val)
{
  return !! *find_loc(t, val);
}
```

In insert() and delete(), instead of searching, we call find_loc(), and then we update the tree according to what we find:

```
bool insert(stree *t, int val)
{
  stree *target = find_loc(t, val);
  if (*target) return true; // already there
  else return !!(*target = leaf(val));
}
```

```
void delete(stree *t, int val)
{
  stree *target = find_loc(t, val);
  if (*target) {
    stree t = *target;
    if (!(t->left && t->right)) {
      *target = t->left ? t->left : t->right;
      free(t);
    } else {
      stree *rm_ref = rightmost(&t->left);
      stree rm = *rm_ref;
      t->value = rm->value;
      *rm_ref = rm->left;
      free(rm);
    }
  }
}
```

Iterative Functions

The contains(), insert(), and delete() operations are no longer recursive, but they rely on find_loc() and rightmost() that are. Both of those, however, are tail-recursive, so the code that the compiler generates, when you enable optimization, will not involve function calls. Of course, if you are not comfortable relying on the mercy of your compiler's optimization, you can translate the functions into iterative ones yourself. With tail-recursive functions, that is usually straightforward.

Take find_loc():

```
stree *find_loc(stree *t, int val)
{
  if (!*t || (*t)->value == val)
    return t;
  else if (val < (*t)->value)
    return find_loc(&(*t)->left, val);
```

```
  else
    return find_loc(&(*t)->right, val);
}
```

We want to replace recursion with a loop, so we make a loop condition that should terminate the loop when we would directly return from the recursion's base case. The inversion of the base case condition will usually do.

```
stree *find_loc(stree *t, int val)
{
  while (*t && (*t)->value != val) {
    // loop body
  }
  return t;
}
```

Then, inside the loop body, where you would normally call recursively, you update the function arguments instead. A recursive call will give the parameters new values; we give them those values directly. So

```
find_loc(&(*t)->left, val);
```

would become

```
t = &(*t)->left; val = val;
```

where the assignment to val is obviously not necessary here. The looping version of find_loc() looks like this:

```
stree *find_loc(stree *t, int val)
{
  while (*t && (*t)->value != val) {
    if (val < (*t)->value) {
      t = &(*t)->left;
    } else {
      t = &(*t)->right;
    }
  }
  return t;
}
```

Similarly, the loop version of `rightmost()`, translated using the same procedure, looks like this:

```
stree *rightmost(stree *t)
{
  while ((*t)->right)
    t = &(*t)->right;
  return t;
}
```

Explicit Stacks

Free and print still use recursion. If we want to avoid exceeding the stack space, we can move the recursion from the call stack to an explicit stack. We shall see that it carries its own problems, but let us implement it first.

One way to represent a stack is as a singly linked list. Stack frames hold the information we need for the recursions and then a next pointer to the next stack frame. A stack is empty if it is NULL. For `free_nodes()`, we can implement the stack and stack frames like this:

```
struct free_frame {
  struct node       *node;
  struct free_frame *next;
};

void free_push(struct free_frame **stack, struct node *node)
{
  if (!node) return;
  struct free_frame *frame = malloc(sizeof *frame);
  if (!frame) abort(); // We do not tolerate errors!
  *frame = (struct free_frame){ .node = node, .next = *stack };
  *stack = frame;
}
```

```
struct node *free_pop(struct free_frame **stack)
{
  struct free_frame *top = *stack;
  struct node *node = top->node;
  *stack = top->next;
  free(top);
  return node;
}
```

The push() and pop() functions take the stack by reference, a pointer to a pointer to a stack frame, so they can modify the stack. When we push(), we allocate a new stack frame, initialize it with a node and the top of the stack, and then we point the stack to the new frame so the new frame is now the top of the stack. If the allocation fails, we terminate the program. Freeing data should never fail because we don't know how to handle such a situation—we are probably leaving the program in an inconsistent state, and we will most likely leak memory. We could attempt to recover, so we don't crash the entire program, but here I give up and call abort(). In the following printing code, we will recover slightly more gracefully.

Now the free_nodes() function pushes its input on the stack, and then it loops as long as there are stack frames. It pops the top frame, pushes the two subtrees, and frees the node:

```
void free_nodes(struct node *n)
{
  struct free_frame *stack = 0;
  free_push(&stack, n);
  while (stack) {
    n = free_pop(&stack);
    free_push(&stack, n->left);
    free_push(&stack, n->right);
    free(n);
  }
}
```

When we push the left child first, we process it last, since stacks work in a first-in, first-out fashion. If we wanted to process the left tree first, as we do in the recursion, we would have to push the subtrees in the opposite order. It doesn't matter when we are deleting the nodes, though, so deleting right subtrees before left subtrees is fine.

When we print a tree, we need the left subtree printed before the right subtree, so there we must push the right subtree before the left subtree. However, handling printing is slightly more complicated than that. There are multiple operations we need to do before and after the recursive calls. We must print a left parenthesis before we handle the left subtree. We must print a comma, the node's value, and another comma after the recursive call to the left; only then can we recurse on the right, and once we are done on the right, we must print a right parenthesis. Replacing a call stack with an explicit stack is often complicated if you need to return to different states in your function after the recursive calls. There are different techniques and strategies for dealing with a function's state when we move to an explicit stack. Still, although the printing function is more complex than free_nodes(), it is quite simple, and the solution we implement later just pushes the various operations we do in the function. In our stack frames, we put an operation, which can be LPAR for printing "(", TREE for handling a tree recursively, COMMA for printing a comma, VALUE for printing a node's value, and RPAR for printing ")". For TREE and VALUE, we need an associated node, so we have a struct node pointer in the stack frame as well.

```
enum print_op {
  LPAR, TREE, COMMA, VALUE, RPAR
};
struct print_frame {
  enum print_op op;
  struct node *node;
  struct print_frame *next;
};
```

The stack is a pointer to a frame as well, but I will also put a jmp_buf to handle allocation errors. This is a buffer in which we can store the program's state, which in practice means its registers. If we call the function setjmp(), we store the registers. If we later call longjmp(), we restore them. Restoring means that we reset the stack and instruction pointers, so the program goes to the position on the stack where we called setjmp(), and the instruction pointer starts executing right after the call to setjmp().

The only difference between the call to setjmp() when we stored the registers and when/if we returned to it from a longjmp() is that setjmp() returns zero the first time and a value we give to longjmp() the second time.

The setjmp()/longjmp() functions are a crude version of raising and catching exceptions. We can return to an arbitrary point on the stack, with the program's registers restored, but there is no checking for whether it is a valid state. You can call longjmp() with registers that moves you to a stack frame that is long gone. The mechanism does nothing to clean up resources, and if you lose pointers to heap-allocated memory in a jump, then it is gone. You need to be careful to free resources when you use this mechanism, just as you must be with normal returns from functions. It is highly unsafe, but it will work for our purposes here. We get a way to return to our printing function from nested function calls that push to the stack.

So, we define a stack like this:

```
struct print_stack {
  struct print_frame *frames;
  jmp_buf env;
};
```

and implement push as

```
void print_push(struct print_stack *stack,
                enum print_op op, struct node *node)
{
  struct print_frame *frame = malloc(sizeof *frame);
  if (!frame) longjmp(stack->env, 1); // bail!
  *frame = (struct print_frame){
    .op = op, .node = node, .next = stack->frames
  };
  stack->frames = frame;
}
```

An allocation failure results in a longjmp() which we will catch in the main function. The second argument to longjmp(), here 1, is what setjmp() will have returned in the restored state. As long as it is not zero, we can recognize that we have returned from a longjmp(). We won't implement a pop() operation because we will deal with popping directly in the printing function.

The following two functions push the operations we need to do for one node and execute an operation we have popped from the stack:

```
void schedule_print(struct print_stack *stack,
                    struct node *node)
{
  print_push(stack, RPAR, 0);
  if (node->right) print_push(stack, TREE, node->right);
  print_push(stack, COMMA, 0);
  print_push(stack, VALUE, node);
  print_push(stack, COMMA, 0);
  if (node->left) print_push(stack, TREE, node->left);
  print_push(stack, LPAR, 0);
}

void handle_print_op(enum print_op op, struct node *node,
                     struct print_stack *stack)
{
  switch (op) {
    case LPAR: putchar('('); break;
    case RPAR: putchar(')'); break;
    case COMMA: putchar(','); break;
    case VALUE: printf("%d", node->value); break;
    case TREE: schedule_print(stack, node); break;
  }
}
```

The print function initializes the stack and stores the register states. Then we schedule the first node and iteratively get the top of the stack, take the operation and node from it, and free the top frame before we handle the operation.

```
void print_stree(stree *t)
{
  if (!*t) return;

  enum print_op op;
  struct node *n = 0;
```

```
struct print_stack stack = { .frames = 0 };
if (setjmp(stack.env) != 0) goto error;

schedule_print(&stack, *t);
while (stack.frames) {
  struct print_frame *top = stack.frames;
  op = top->op; n = top->node;
  stack.frames = top->next;
  free(top);

  handle_print_op(op, n, &stack);
}
return;

error:
  while (stack.frames) {
    struct print_frame *top = stack.frames;
    stack.frames = top->next;
    free(top);
  }
}
```

If we get an allocation error, then the push function will call longjmp(), which results in us returning from setjmp() a second time, but now with a non-zero return value. If that happens, we goto the error label and free the stack. In the while-loop, we must free top before we call handle_print_op(). We might not return from handle_print_op—the longjmp() error handling will send us directly to the setjmp()—so we must leave the function in a state where the code in error can clean up all resources. If we free top before we handle the operation, all the stack frames are on the stack, and the error handling code will free them.

Here, we can handle an error, but we cannot undo the damage we have done by writing parts of the tree to output and then bailing. What we print, we cannot undo. And when we use an explicit stack, we can get allocation errors we will have to recover from (unless we give up and abort, as with free_nodes()). There are many cases where we need to dynamically allocate memory for stacks and queues and whatnot when our programs run, but for freeing memory, or for operations that we cannot undo, we should try hard to avoid allocations. This isn't always possible, but for traversing trees, there are tricks.

If you want to traverse a tree, and you don't want to allocate new memory doing it, you have several options. A general option you always have, regardless of whether we consider trees or other objects, is to set aside memory for a stack in your data structures. Add one pointer to the struct node, and you can chain them in a stack if you want to. Pushing and popping works as before, but the stack pointer sits embedded in the struct.

```
struct node {
  int value;
  struct node *left;
  struct node *right;
  struct node *stack;
};

stree node(int value, stree left, stree right)
{
  stree t = malloc(sizeof *t);
  if (t) *t = (struct node){
    .value = value,
    .left = left, .right = right,
    .stack = 0
  };
  return t;
}

void push_node(struct node **stack,
               struct node *node)
{
  if (node) {
    node->stack = *stack;
    *stack = node;
  }
}

struct node *pop_node(struct node **stack)
{
  struct node *top = *stack;
  *stack = top->stack;
```

```
    top->stack = 0;
    return top;
}
```

Then you can free the nodes with

```
void free_nodes(struct node *n)
{
    struct node *stack = 0;
    push_node(&stack, n);
    while (stack) {
        n = pop_node(&stack);
        push_node(&stack, n->left);
        push_node(&stack, n->right);
        free(n);
    }
}
```

For more complex recursions, though, a node must hold all the information necessary for that algorithm, so the structure can grow in complexity beyond what we are willing to accept.

Morris Traversal

Many algorithms can traverse a tree without using an implicit or explicit stack, and we will see one in this section. This algorithm, *Morris traversal*, doesn't require that we add any additional data to the nodes. Instead, it uses a clever way to modify the tree as we traverse it, to simulate recursion, and then restores it to its initial state as the simulated traversal returns.

The algorithm simulates an in-order traversal, that is, one where we first visit all the nodes in the left subtree of a node, then we handle the node, and then we visit all the nodes in the right subtree. Or in C, it simulates this function:

```
void inorder(struct node *n)
{
    if (!n) return;
    inorder(n->left);
```

```
    printf("%d\n", n->value);
    inorder(n->right);
}
```

The Morris traversal algorithm is closely related to so-called *threaded trees* (also invented by Morris). These are search trees with an additional property. If a tree doesn't have a left or a right subtree, that subtree is replaced by a pointer to the node with the next smallest (left) or next highest (right) node in the tree. Figure 12-5 shows an example, where I have only drawn the thread pointers for right subtrees, as those are the only ones we need for the traversal we will implement. The tree holds the values 1, 3, 4, 5, 6, 7, and 8. Node 1 is a leaf, so it does not have left and right subtrees, but it has a pointer to the next value in the tree, 3. Node 4, likewise, doesn't have subtrees, so it has a pointer to the node with value 5. Node 5 does have a left subtree, but not a right subtree, so its (right) thread pointer points to the next value, 6, and so on. Node 8 doesn't have a right subtree, but there is no node with a higher value, so its threaded right pointer is NULL.

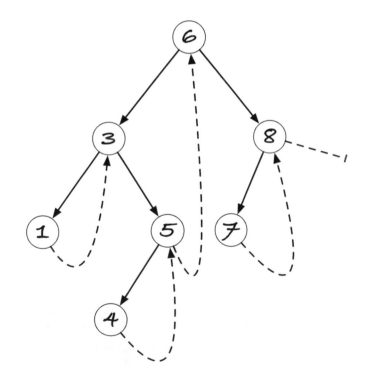

Figure 12-5. *A (right) threaded tree*

Imagine that we need to do an in-order traversal of such a tree. We can recurse by following left pointers as long as we have them, which in the example will take us to node 1. Here, we cannot continue further left, so we visit 1 (we have, trivially, visited all its left children). Now we recurse to the right, that is, we follow its right pointer. Node 1 doesn't have a right child, but we have a "threaded" pointer instead that works like one, so going right from 1 corresponds to returning from the recursion to node 3. When we enter node 3, we would have to recurse to the right, unless we can recognize that we had already been there, so let us, for now, assume that we tag the nodes so we can tell that we have already been to node 3 once. If we can see that, we know that we came back from a left recursion, so we visit node 3 and recurse to the right. In 5, a node we haven't seen before, we recurse to the left, and we get to node 4, where we cannot go further left. We visit 4 and go right. That takes us back to 5, where we realize that we have been before, so we go right instead of left this time, which takes us up to 6. Recognizing that we have been here before, we go right instead of left, to 8, and recurse from here. We have not been here, so we go left, to 7. We cannot continue left, so we go right, back to 8. Since we have been in 8 once before, we visit the node, and then we go right. This time, there is no right child, threaded or otherwise, so the traversal ends.

If we have a threaded tree, the "recursion" works as follows: If we have a node we haven't seen before, we go left. If we have a node that we have seen before, we visit it and go right. "Returning" from the recursion happens whenever a step to the right is along a threaded pointer rather than a real subtree.

How can we get the threaded pointers, and how can we recognize that we are in a node that we have seen before? Notice that if you have a node "n", and another node, m, has a threaded pointer to it, then n is the next value after m in the tree. That means that m is the rightmost node in n's subtree. So we can go from n to m with our `rightmost()` function. Once there, we can, of course, write a pointer to n into the right subtree. So when we enter a node the first time, we can run down and find the node where we should insert a threaded pointer. How do we recognize that we have visited a node before? If we search for the rightmost node in the left subtree, and we encounter the node itself, then we have inserted it the first time we visited the node! So the same rightmost search will tell us if we are seeing a node for the first time or for the second time.

We can modify the `rightmost()` function to get a `rightmost_to()` function that stops early in the recursion if we encounter a given node. If we didn't have that stop condition, we would recurse forever, as following the right subtrees gives us a loop when we make the right subtree point to an ancestor. Such a function can look like this:

```
stree *rightmost_to(stree *t, struct node *n)
{
  if ((*t)->right == 0 || (*t)->right == n) {
    return t;
  } else {
    return rightmost_to(&(*t)->right, n);
  }
}
#define rightmost(t) rightmost_to(t, 0)
```

The `rightmost()` macro is there, so we can use `rightmost()` in deletion, without the weird extra argument.

An in-order traversal that uses right thread pointers now looks like this:

```
void morris(stree *t)
{
  struct node *curr = *t;
  while (curr) {
    if (!curr->left) {
      // Visit
      printf("%d\n", curr->value);
      curr = curr->right;
    } else {
      stree rm = *rightmost_to(&curr->left, curr);
      assert(rm->right == 0 || rm->right == curr);
      if (rm->right == 0) {
        rm->right = curr;
        curr = curr->left;
      } else {
        // Visit
```

```
        printf("%d\n", curr->value);
        rm->right = 0;
        curr = curr->right;
      }
    }
  }
}
```

If you don't have a left subtree, you visit the node and go right. Otherwise, you figure out if you can find yourself as the rightmost node on the left. If not, you update the rightmost node's right subtree to point to the current node, and you recurse to the left. If yes, you restore the right subtree in the rightmost node by setting it to NULL, you visit the current node, and then you go right.

The running time is proportional to the size of the tree. You search for the rightmost node in the left subtree twice in every node (that has a left subtree), but the nodes you run through in such searches do not overlap between different nodes, so each node is maximally visited twice in such searches.

You don't quite get the recursion in print_stree() here, although you visit the nodes in the same order. It is simple to output the left parentheses, the commas, and the node values, but when you return from the recursion by going through a right pointer, you go up a number of recursive calls in one step, and you can't see how many. You can annotate the nodes with depth information and get print_stree() behavior, but I will not bother here. Traversing the nodes in order suffices for most applications, and we rarely need to know the exact tree structure.

Freeing Nodes Without Recursion and Memory Allocation

For freeing the nodes, we can simplify the Morris traversal a bit. If we are deleting the tree anyway, we are allowed to modify it (and we don't need to worry about restoring the tree during the traversal). So, when we process a node with a left subtree, we store a pointer to the node in its rightmost subtree as before. We don't need to check if the rightmost is the node itself because it will never be. It will never be that, since right before we recurse to the left, we remove the left subtree. We can modify the tree, since we are deleting it, and that prevents us from attempting a second recursion to the left.

```
void free_nodes(struct node *n)
{
  struct node *curr = n;
  while (curr) {
    if (!curr->left) {
      struct node *right = curr->right;
      free(curr);
      curr = right;
    } else {
      // Add pointer to rightmost so we can go back
      (*rightmost(&curr->left))->right = curr;
      // Recurse left, but make sure we never go left again
      struct node *left = curr->left; curr->left = 0;
      curr = left;
    }
  }
}
```

It simplifies the algorithm, and we save one rightmost search per node. And we free the tree without using any additional memory, so freeing cannot fail due to stack exhaustion, due to recession, or due to memory allocation errors, if we had used an explicit stack.

Adding a Parent Pointer

A problem with both embedding a stack in the nodes and with Morris traversal is that we can at most run one traversal at a time—because we are using shared memory embedded in the trees. With Morris traversal, we must also complete the traversal before the tree is restored to a consistent state (with the embedded stack, it isn't a problem as we overwrite the stack in a new traversal). Concurrency is out of the question with these strategies (and with many related strategies that rely on modifying trees for traversal).

If we are willing to add a pointer to the parent of each node (with NULL in the root), then we can traverse a tree without modifying it and without dynamically allocating memory while we do it. This does mean extending the node `struct`, of course, but for many of the strategies for balancing trees, a `parent` pointer is necessary in any case, or at least makes the code vastly faster, so it is not a high price to pay.

It is trivial to add the pointer to the struct:

```
typedef struct node *stree;
struct node {
  int value;
  struct node *parent;
  struct node *left;
  struct node *right;
};

int allocated;
stree node(int value, stree parent,
           stree left, stree right)
{
  stree t = malloc(sizeof *t);
  if (t) *t = (struct node){
    .value = value, .parent = parent,
    .left = left, .right = right
  };
  return t;
}
#define leaf(V,P) node(V, P, 0, 0)
```

but then we also need to add it to the operations for modifying the tree. That means that find_loc() must set the parent pointer. We can track the pointer going down the recursion/loop, and if we have a parent pointer argument, passed by reference, we can return it that way:

```
stree *find_loc(stree *t, int val, stree *p)
{
  while (*t && (*t)->value != val) {
    *p = *t;
    if (val < (*t)->value) t = &(*t)->left;
    else                   t = &(*t)->right;
  }
  return t;
}
```

```
bool contains(stree *t, int val)
{
  stree parent = 0;
  return !! *find_loc(t, val, &parent);
}

bool insert(stree *t, int val)
{
  stree parent = 0;
  stree *target = find_loc(t, val, &parent);
  if (*target) return true; // already there
  else return !!(*target = leaf(val, parent));
}
```

We do the same with `rightmost()`, although there we do not set the initial value for p, as we do not always call `rightmost()` with the root.

```
stree *rightmost(stree *t, stree *p)
{
  while ((*t)->right) {
    *p = *t;
    t = &(*t)->right;
  }
  return t;
}
```

When we delete, we get the parent with the first call to `find_loc()`, but if we are in the second case, where the node to delete has both subtrees, we find the rightmost, starting with the tree as the parent (it is the parent of its left child, after all):

```
void delete(stree *t, int val)
{
  stree parent = 0;
  stree *loc = find_loc(t, val, &parent);
```

```
if (*loc) {
  stree t = *loc;
  if (!(t->left && t->right)) {
    *loc = t->left ? t->left : t->right;
    // if there was a subtree, update its parent
    if (*loc) (*loc)->parent = parent;
      free(t);

  } else {

    parent = t; // t is t->left's parent
    stree *rm_ref = rightmost(&t->left, &parent);
    stree rm = *rm_ref;
    t->value = rm->value;
    *rm_ref = rm->left;
    // if there was a subtree, update its parent
    if (*rm_ref) (*rm_ref)->parent = parent;
    free(rm);
  }
 }
}
```

You can avoid the checks for empty children, before you set the parent pointer, by having a dummy node for empty trees. You can share the same node with all empty trees because you will never need to take the parent of an empty tree. You will just need to replace the tests for NULL empty trees with tests for whether a tree points to the dummy.

With parent pointers in place, we can traverse the tree—and this time get a proper "recursion" where we can add the right parentheses for printing the tree structure. We can keep track of which direction we are moving, down or up the tree, and by comparing the parent's left child with a tree itself, we can determine if we are returning from the left or right subtree, to determine whether we should now go right or keep returning.

```
#define left_child(t) \
  ((t)->parent && (t)->parent->left == (t))
```

```c
void parent_traverse(stree t)
{
  enum { DOWN, UP } state = DOWN;
  while (t) {
    switch (state) {
      case DOWN:
        // Recurse as far left as we can...
        while (t->left) { putchar('('); t = t->left; }
        // Emit the leaf we find there
        printf("(,%d,", t->value); // VISIT
        // Then go right, if we can, or up if we can't.
        if (t->right) { t = t->right; }
        else          { putchar(')'); state = UP; }
        break;

      case UP:
        if (!t->parent) return; // back at the root; we're done
        if (left_child(t)) {
          // Returning from a left child, we emit the parent
          t = t->parent;
          printf(",%d,", t->value); // VISIT
          // Then we go right if we can't, or continue up
          // (t is already the parent) if we cannot.
          if (t->right) { t = t->right; state = DOWN; }
          else          { putchar(')'); }
        } else {
          // Returning from a right child just means going up
          putchar(')'); t = t->parent;
        }
        break;
    }
  }
}
```

Freeing the nodes in the same type of traversal is trivial. Do it when you return from a node in the virtual recursion:

```
void parent_free(stree t)
{
  struct node *p;
  enum { DOWN, UP } state = DOWN;
  while (t) {
    switch (state) {
      case DOWN:
        while (t->left) { t = t->left; }
        if (t->right)   { t = t->right; }
        else            { state = UP; }
        break;

      case UP:
        if (!t->parent) { free(t); return; }
        if (left_child(t)) {
          p = t->parent; free(t); t = p;
          if (t->right)
            { t = t->right; state = DOWN; }
        } else {
          p = t->parent; free(t); t = p;
        }
        break;
    }
  }
}
```

There are plenty more algorithms for traversing trees, with or without modifying them, and if you want to get more experience with trees and pointer manipulation, it is a good place to start. For the book, however, it is time to move on to the next topic.

CHAPTER 13

Function Pointers

We now leave data structures for a spell to talk about something new: pointers to functions. Like pointers to data, pointers to functions give us a level of indirection, so we can hold in a variable the address of an object rather than the object itself. Further, with a pointer, the same variable can refer to different objects over time.

When you write a function, you write the return type before the function name, then the parameters after the name, and finally the body. If you declare a function pointer instead, you should put the name in parentheses and put a * before the name. Thus, this defines a function, f, from void to void and a pointer, fp, to functions of that type:

```
void f(void) {}
void (*fp)(void) = f;
```

where, as for all non-const pointers, you can change the value a function pointer points at:

```
void f2(void) {}
fp = f2;
```

For a more complex example, we can define a function, g, that returns double and takes two arguments, the first of type int and the second of type float:

```
double g(int x, float y) { return x + y; }
```

A pointer to the same type looks like this:

```
double (*gp)(int, float) = g;
```

For both fp and gp, we assigned functions, f and g, to them. If we had data pointers, we would have taken the address

```
fp = &f;
gp = &g;
```

© Thomas Mailund 2021

T. Mailund, *Pointers in C Programming*, https://doi.org/10.1007/978-1-4842-6927-5_13

and that is valid syntax as well. Like arrays, if you use an object as a pointer, it becomes a pointer. So, you can assign a function to a function pointer without taking its address— you automatically get its address in that case. Also, as with arrays, this doesn't mean that the address of a pointer to a function is the same as the pointer itself. While you can assign both &f and f to fp, you cannot assign

```
void (*fp2)(void) = &fp;
```

Here, fp is a pointer to a function, and &fp is a pointer to a pointer to a function.

If you need a function pointer type alone, for example, if you are casting one function type to another, you use normal cast notation: you put the type in parentheses. For the function pointer type, you leave out the name after *, so a cast will look like

```
fp = ( void (*)(void) ) g;
```

The notation for function types can make complex expressions hard to read. Consider this function:

```
void (* complex(int x, int (*p)(int)) )(void)
{
  printf("%d\n", p(x));
  return f;
}
```

It is not at all clear that this part

```
void (* /*...*/ )(void)
```

specifies the return type of a function—it returns a void to void function—but that is what it says. The name of the function is complex and

```
(int x, int (*p)(int))
```

are its parameters. The parameter

```
int (*p)(int)
```

is an int to int function pointer. With expressions such as this, typedef is your friend, and to typedef a function type, you put the type name where you would put the pointer name:

```
typedef void (*void_fn)(void);
typedef int  (*int_fn)(int);
```

412

```
void_fn simple(int x, int_fn p)
{
  printf("%d\n", p(x));
  return f;
}
```

The example also shows you how to call the function that a pointer points at: p(x). If you have a function pointer, you use it the same way as if you had a function.

Function pointers are in a different category in the C standard, and there are slightly different rules. Most importantly, you are *not* guaranteed that casting a function pointer to void * and back will work. The POSIX standard does give you this guarantee, but if your setup is merely compliant to standard C, it is not guaranteed. So don't put pointers to functions in data structures that hold void *; it isn't safe. You are, however, ensured that you can convert between any function pointers and back safely, so you can choose any function pointer type to store pointers. If you call a function through a pointer of the wrong type, however, you get undefined behavior.

Function Pointers for High-Order Functions

It is, I think, easiest to learn how to use function pointers through a few examples, and we start with the simplest situation where function pointers are needed: parameterizing behavior in other functions. We use function arguments to parameterize the behavior of a function, but when what we must parameterize is complex, like item comparison in qsort(), we cannot easily do so through data. Rather, again like with qsort(), we can ask the caller to provide a function that handles part of the computation our function must do. The qsort() function doesn't know how to compare elements, so the caller must provide a function that can do that. With such a function in hand, qsort() can sort arrays of any type.

Functions that take function arguments are called *higher-order functions*, and C's support for such functions is rudimentary compared to many modern programming languages. Still, with function pointers, we can implement some basic high-level functions. For the following examples, I will use doubly linked lists from Chapter 11, and to make the code more readable, I will use these two macros:

```
#define abort_append(x,v)          \
  do {                             \
    if (!append((x), (v))) {       \
```

```
      free_list(x); return 0;           \
    }                                    \
  } while(0)

#define for_each(var,x)                  \
  for (struct link *var = front(x);      \
    var != x; var = var->next)
```

The first checks if an append() operation fails, and if it does, it will free the list and return NULL. For all the following functions, that is the appropriate way to handle an allocation error. The second macro just makes it easier to write a loop through a list. It is the for-loop header we use when we want to iterate through all links in a list.

Now to our high-level functions. The first function we will write is map(). It takes a list and a function as arguments, and it creates a new list constructed by evaluating the function on all elements in the input list. So with a function such as this

```
int add2(int x) { return 2 + x; }
```

that adds two to its input, calling

```
y = map(x, add2);
```

will generate a list with all the numbers from x plus 2.

The map() function looks like this:

```
list map(list x, int (*f)(int))
{
  list y = new_list();
  if (!y) return 0;
  for_each(link, x) {
    abort_append(y, f(link->value));
  }
  return y;
}
```

The code is straightforward. We use the function pointer argument f as a function to create new values f(link->value) to append to y.

For the next function, `filter()`, we want a function that takes a list and a predicate—a function that returns a Boolean value—and gives us a new list with all the elements that satisfied the predicate. The function is as simple to write as `map()` and can look like this:

```
list filter(list x, bool (*p)(int))
{
  list y = new_list();
  if (!y) return 0;
  for_each(link, x) {
    if (p(link->value))
      abort_append(y, link->value);
  }
  return y;
}
```

With a function that tells us if a number is even:

```
bool is_even(int i) { return i % 2 == 0; }
```

calling

```
y = filter(x, is_even);
```

will give us the even numbers from x.

The `fold()` function is only slightly more complicated. When we call `fold()` with a list x and function f, we want to iteratively apply f to the elements in x, with the result of one call as the first argument to the next call of f. We need a way to specify what the first argument should be the first time we call f, and we take the easy road and make it a parameter of `fold()`. The implementation looks like this:

```
int fold(list x, int (*f)(int, int), int x0)
{
  list y = new_list();
  if (!y) return 0;
  int res = x0;
  for_each(link, x) {
    res = f(res, link->value);
  }
  return res;
}
```

415

The first call to f will be with f(x0,x1) where x1 is the first value in x. The next call will be f(f(x0,x1),x2) where x2 is the second value in x, and so on.

Using fold(), we can, for example, implement functions for summing and multiplying all elements in a list. We need to give fold() a function for adding two numbers and then sum with an initial value of zero, and we need a function for multiplying two numbers and then take the product with an initial value of one.

```
int add(int x, int y) { return x + y; }
int sum(list x)        { return fold(x, add, 0); }

int mul(int x, int y) { return x * y; }
int prod(list x)       { return fold(x, mul, 1); }
```

These are simple high-order functions, and it can get more involved. However, the way that you use function pointer arguments doesn't get more complicated than this. You take a function pointer as an argument, and you use it as you would any other function. Call it when you need the caller's function to do what you cannot do on your own. There is little beyond that to high-order functions in C.

Callbacks

We use function pointers for much more than high-order functions. In event-driven systems, such as graphical user interfaces, they are frequently used to decouple GUI code from application logic. One design is to hook up GUI elements to so-called *callbacks*, functions that the GUI framework will call when certain events happen.

Imagine a, somewhat simplistic, GUI framework where we have buttons, and buttons can have different events. Without tying our code too much in with the GUI handling, we want to be informed about the events that a given button experiences. The mechanism for this will be a function pointer. Every button holds a function pointer, and they will call that function for each event.

```
enum button_events {
  MOUSEDOWN, MOUSEUP,
  CLICKED, DBLCLICKED,
  // more...
};
struct button;
typedef void (*button_cb)(struct button *,
                          enum button_events);
```

```
struct button {
  char *text; // what the button says
  // lots of gui stuff here
  button_cb cb_func; // <- the callback function
};
```

The application programmer can create a button and install a callback, and after that, the framework will handle the GUI.

```
struct button *but = new_button("my button");
install_button_callback(but, my_callback);
```

In the callback, the application programmer can check which event happened and handle it accordingly:

```
void my_callback(struct button *but,
                 enum button_events event)
{
  switch (event) {
    case CLICKED:
      printf("button %s was clicked\n", but->text);
      break;
    default:
      // nothing
      break;
  }
}
```

In most frameworks, the mechanism is more involved, so events, GUI objects, and callback functions are loosly coupled, but the principle is the same. If you want to be informed about specific events, you install a callback, and that callback is called when the event occurs. Callbacks aren't restricted to GUIs either. In network programming, you might have callbacks to notify you when a package arrives at a port, or in a complicated workflow, you might want to hook in a bit of processing at specific steps in the pipeline.[1]

---

[1]When you have callbacks that manipulate data, rather than just listen to events, they are sometimes called hooks. The way you use them is the same.

Callbacks (and hooks) are mostly used with frameworks, and not with simple programs of the length I can include in this book, so I am sorry, but I cannot give you a more realistic example than the one earlier. You will have to take my word for their usefulness. But in the following examples, I will show you how we combine data and function pointers in various ways with just as interesting results.

Generic String Iterator

In Chapter 7, we wrote two iterators for finding words and integers in a text, and we used macros to separate the generic code from the iterator-specific code. We needed the macros because we had different functions for classifying individual characters as numbers of part of a word, but by far the most of the code was generic, and the macros helped us avoid duplicating it. In the source code, at least, it is, of course, repeated once the macros are expanded.

Now, we are going to solve the same problem, but with function pointers to handle the varying parts of the code. We built our iterators on two functions, one for finding the next character of a class and one for skipping past characters of the class. For words, for example, we had

```
char *find_word(char *x)
{
  while (*x && !isalpha(*x))
    x++;
  return x;
}

char *skip_word(char *x)
{
  while (*x && isalpha(*x))
    x++;
  return x;
}
```

With these two functions, the first instance in a string x would be at y = find_word(x); and the following instances at y = find_word(skip_word(y));. The variable part is the character class, and we used macros to substitute different functions there, otherwise generating the same code.

Now, let us use a function pointer instead. Functions such as isalpha() have type int (*)(int), that is, they are integer to integer functions. We could easily update the preceding functions to take such a function as an argument:

```
char *find(int (*char_class)(int), char *x)
{
  while (*x && !char_class(*x))
    x++;
  return x;
}

char *skip(int (*char_class)(int), char *x)
{
  while (*x && char_class(*x))
    x++;
  return x;
}
```

To get an iterator, we can collect a character class function and a character pointer to the current location in a struct. We can initialize it with a function and a string and return the first occurrence (or NULL if there isn't one).

```
typedef struct {
  char *x;
  int (*char_class)(int);
} find_skip_iter;

#define NULLIFY(x) ((*x) ? (x) : 0)

char *init_iter(find_skip_iter *iter, char *x,
                int (*char_class)(int))
{
  iter->char_class = char_class;
  iter->x = find(iter->char_class, x);
  return NULLIFY(iter->x);
}
```

```
#define init_word_iter(itr, x) \
        init_iter((itr),(x), isalpha)
#define init_int_iter(itr, x) \
        init_iter((itr),(x), isnumber)
```

The macros give us an easy way to initialize an iterator over words and numbers.

Each time we go for the next occurrence, we do a skip followed by a find:

```
char *next(find_skip_iter *iter)
{
  iter->x = skip(iter->char_class, iter->x);
  iter->x = find(iter->char_class, iter->x);
  return NULLIFY(iter->x);
}
```

In action, we can use the iterators like this:

```
int main(void)
{
  char *x = "123 sss 321 xxx 123";

  find_skip_iter itr;
  for (char *y = init_word_iter(&itr, x);
       y; y = next(&itr)) {
    printf("%s\n", y);
  }
  for (char *y = init_int_iter(&itr, x);
       y; y = next(&itr)) {
    printf("%s\n", y);
  }

  return 0;
}
```

The control flow in this example is different from the high-order functions. We do not use a function pointer to parameterize the behavior within one function call. Instead, we parameterize the behavior of an object, the iterator, through function pointers. When we need to get the next item from the iterator, we use the saved function pointers to get there. Other than that, the use of function pointers to parameterize behavior is similar.

Function Pointers for Abstract Data Structures

Abstract data structures are data structures defined by their operations, but not their specific implementation. A stack, for example, is something you can push to and pop from, and you can implement it in various ways. When we develop algorithms, abstract data structures are a conceptual tool we use, but when we implement them, of course, we need a concrete representation. Using a concrete type, however, makes it difficult to change the choice later, if a better implementation comes along. It also makes it hard to experiment with different implementation choices because each change requires that we update all the code that uses the data structure. There are times where we wish to keep the interface to a data structure abstract, and with function pointers, we can do so.

Let us, as an example, take a stack. With some appropriate definition of the type stack, and the elements we put in it, elem, the interface to a stack could look like this:

```
typedef ??? stack;
typedef ??? elem;

stack new_stack  (void);
bool empty_stack (stack);
elem statck_top  (stack);
bool stack_push  (stack, elem);
elem stack_pop   (stack);
void free_stack  (stack);
```

An easy way to hide the underlying implementation is to make stack some opaque type, like a void *, or a pointer to a struct we don't reveal to the user. A stack of integers, for example, could define the types as

```
typedef struct stack *stack;
typedef int           elem;
```

Then, we would be free to implement the struct stack however we want, and the user could only access it through the functions declared through the preceding prototypes. That would work flawlessly if our application only ever needed one implementation of a stack, but it would fail if we used different implementations in different parts of the program. We might have hidden the implementation details, but the stack functions are linker objects, and we can only have one function with any given name at a time.

There are different ways to resolve the problem, but since the chapter is about function pointers, we are going for a solution using pointers. We can wrap the stack operations up in a structure that holds pointers to the different operations. They will operate on an implementation-specific stack, which we might as well represent as a void pointer. Then we are going to wrap everything up in a stack struct that ties the interface and implementation together. The structure of operations, defining a concrete implementation of the stack interface, looks like this:

```
typedef void * impl_stack;
typedef int    elem;

typedef struct {
  impl_stack (*new_stack)   (void);
  bool       (*empty_stack) (impl_stack);
  elem       (*top)         (impl_stack);
  bool       (*push)        (impl_stack, elem);
  elem       (*pop)         (impl_stack);
  void       (*free_stack)  (impl_stack);
} stack_type;
```

It is function pointers with the interface from the original prototypes, except that we use the impl_stack, a void *, as the stack type. A stack is going to be a pointer to a struct that holds a pointer to the implementation stack type and a pointer to the functions that implement the stack:

```
struct stack {
  impl_stack  impl_stack;
  stack_type *type;
};
typedef struct stack * stack;
```

Now, we can implement the original stack interface, operating on a stack type, but where each operation delegates to the function pointed to in the stack_type structure. The only difference to the preceding prototypes is that the new_stack() function takes an argument that is the stack_type:

```
stack new_stack(stack_type *type)
{
  void *impl_stack = type->new_stack();
  stack stack = malloc(sizeof *stack);
```

```
  if (!impl_stack || !stack) goto error;

  stack->impl_stack = impl_stack;
  stack->type = type;
  return stack;

error:
  free(stack);
  if (impl_stack)
    type->free_stack(impl_stack);
  return 0;
}
```

When we create a stack, we create the underlying stack representation using the function from the type, then we wrap up that implementation stack and the type in the stack object.

The remaining functions get the implementation function from the stack_type pointer and call them. It is a simple forwarding call.

```
bool empty_stack(stack stack)
{
  return stack->type->empty_stack(stack->impl_stack);
}

elem stack_top(stack stack)
{
  return stack->type->top(stack->impl_stack);
}

bool stack_push(stack stack, elem elem)
{
  return stack->type->push(stack->impl_stack, elem);
}

elem stack_pop(stack stack)
{
  return stack->type->pop(stack->impl_stack);
}
```

```
void free_stack(stack stack)
{
  stack->type->free_stack(stack->impl_stack);
  free(stack);
}
```

If you want to implement a concrete stack, you must provide each of the functions for the stack_type structure. An implementation using the linked lists from Chapter 11 could look like this:

```
impl_stack list_stack_new(void)
{
  return new_list();
}

bool list_stack_empty(impl_stack stack)
{
  return is_empty((list)stack);
}

elem list_stack_top(impl_stack stack)
{
  return front((list)stack)->value;
}

bool list_stack_push(impl_stack stack, elem elem)
{
  return prepend(stack, elem);
}

elem list_stack_pop(impl_stack stack)
{
  elem elem = front((list)stack)->value;
  delete_link(front((list)stack));
  return elem;
}
```

```
void list_stack_free(impl_stack stack)
{
  free_list(stack);
}

stack_type list_stack = {
  .new_stack    = list_stack_new,
  .empty_stack = list_stack_empty,
  .top          = list_stack_top,
  .push         = list_stack_push,
  .pop          = list_stack_pop,
  .free_stack   = list_stack_free
};
```

If you want to use the dynamic arrays from Chapter 9, you could implement a stack like this:

```
impl_stack da_stack_new(void)
{
  struct dynarray *da = malloc(sizeof *da);
  if (!da) return 0;
  if (!da_init(da, 1, 0)) {
    free(da);
    return 0;
  }
  return da;
}

bool da_stack_empty(impl_stack stack)
{
  return ((struct dynarray *)stack)->used == 0;
}

elem da_stack_top(impl_stack stack)
{
  struct dynarray *da = stack;
  assert(da->used > 0);
  return da->data[da->used - 1];
}
```

```
bool da_stack_push(impl_stack stack, elem elem)
{
  return da_append(stack, elem);
}

elem da_stack_pop(impl_stack stack)
{
  struct dynarray *da = stack;
  assert(da->used > 0);
  return da->data[--(da->used)];
}

void da_stack_free(impl_stack stack)
{
  da_dealloc(stack);
  free(stack);
}

stack_type da_stack = {
  .new_stack    = da_stack_new,
  .empty_stack  = da_stack_empty,
  .top          = da_stack_top,
  .push         = da_stack_push,
  .pop          = da_stack_pop,
  .free_stack   = da_stack_free
};
```

You can use both types of stacks, plus any other implementation you might write, in the same code. Whenever you have an implementation of all the operations, you can collect them in an instance of stack_type and create a new stack from them. After that, any operation you apply to the stack will call the correct function for the concrete implementation. After the stack creation, there isn't any difference in how you use different concrete stacks:

```
int main(void)
{
  // Try with list stack
  stack stack = new_stack(&list_stack);
```

```
  for (int i = 0; i < 5; i++) {
    stack_push(stack, i);
  }
  while (!empty_stack(stack)) {
    int x = stack_pop(stack);
    printf("%d\n", x);
  }
  free_stack(stack);

  // Try with dynamic array
  stack = new_stack(&da_stack);
  for (int i = 0; i < 5; i++) {
    stack_push(stack, i);
  }
  while (!empty_stack(stack)) {
    int x = stack_pop(stack);
    printf("%d\n", x);
  }
  free_stack(stack);

  return 0;
}
```

Function pointers used this way are excellent tools for separating an interface from an implementation. However, if you use them for writing data structures, where runtime performance is important, then you must be careful. It is slower to call a function through a pointer than to call the function directly. There is the obvious overhead of having to load the value of the pointer variable before you can call the function, but that is a small overhead. More critical is that the computer's cache and branch prediction doesn't function well when calling functions at addresses you first need to compute. This can slow down a function call dramatically. For functions you call often, and where performance is critical, you don't want to call indirectly if you can avoid it.

In many cases, calling one operation on an abstract data structure is not time critical. It is important that the operation is efficient, but that relies on the code after we have dispatched the operation to the correct implementation function. The indirect call overhead is not an issue. But in a tight inner loop of an algorithm, you are likely better served with a tighter coupling between the concrete implementation of the data structure and the algorithm, and the corresponding performance gain, than with keeping the data structure abstract. The correct choice, if there is such a beast, is application dependent.

Function Pointers for Polymorphic Data Structures

We can take the idea of combining data and function pointers one step further and use it to implement rudimentary object-oriented programming with dynamic dispatch. It is the same idea as for abstract data structures, but we will need to allow for derived objects to carry more data than the types they inherit from, and we must allow derived classes to have more functions than their base classes. Meanwhile, any object of a derived class must have a form where we can cast it to a base class and use it as such.

To meet these requirements, we can exploit that the C standard guarantees that the first object you put in a struct goes at the first memory address of instances of that struct. If you have a pointer to an instance of the struct, then you can safely cast it to a pointer to the first element. This means that if you nest structs, you can cast your way into the nesting. For example, with

```
struct A {
    int a;
};
struct B {
  struct A a;
  int b;
};
struct C {
  struct B b;
  int c;
};
```

you can access members of a struct C as if they were members of the nested struct B or the nested struct A in the struct B.

```
struct C *x = /* some allocation */;
assert(((B*)x)->b == x->b.b);
assert(((A*)x)->a == x->b.a.a);
```

Anywhere you have a function that works with pointers to struct A or struct B, you can call the function with a pointer to an instance of struct C. (They have to be pointers, of course, because otherwise you copy members, and you will only copy members of the type the function expects).

The C standard promises a little more about the memory layout of structs, and you wouldn't have to nest them here. If the structs share a prefix of members, it also works.

```
struct A {
  int a;
};
struct B {
  int a;
  int b;
};
struct C {
  int a;
  int b;
  int c;
};
```

If you want to use one struct as another, though, it is easier to nest them.

Single Inheritance Objects and Classes

We can use this to create classes and objects (or instances) in an object-oriented programming sense. It is close to how C++ was initially implemented as a preprocessor to C. Use nested structs for objects, so derived objects contain the data their base cases have. For classes, have a struct for virtual functions (or functions with dynamic dispatch, or whatever you want to call them), and use nested structs for derived classes.

Since we need to be able to both extend instances, so objects of derived classes can carry more data than the base classes, and extend classes, so derived classes can have more virtual functions than base classes, we need two parallel hierarchies of nested structs. Obviously, we cannot put both of these at the top of a struct, so the casting trick cannot work that way. Instead, we make objects and classes separate structs. Each object will need to know its class, so objects will have a pointer to their class struct.

This also saves some memory, because each object doesn't have to carry with it all the function pointers; they just need a single pointer through which they can find them. When we need to apply a polymorphic function on an object, we can get the struct of function pointers from the object and call the appropriate function there.

We can define a class pointer as void *, so it can point to any structure, and define the most basic object as something that has such a pointer. I have also defined a macro, basetype(), for the casting, just to make it explicit what we are doing. Then I have a macro, vtbl, that gets the virtual function table, cast to a class type.

```
typedef void * cls;
typedef struct obj { cls *cls; } obj;

#define basetype(x, base) ((base *)x)
#define vtbl(inst, base) \
        basetype(((obj *)inst)->cls, base)
```

You can make the basetype() more type-safe by going into the nested classes rather than casting, but it puts constraints on how the structs must be nested, and if you modify the type hierarchy above a class, you would need to update the code. The cast does what it is supposed to do if you are careful with it.

To call a polymorphic function, f, defined in class A_cls, you need to look it up in an object's vtbl as vtbl(x,A_cls)->f. You will probably want to do that by wrapping the call in a function, for example:

```
int f(A *x, double d) { return vtbl(x,A_cls)->f(d); }
```

Classes must be allocated and initialized before we can use them. There's a function and macro for that:

```
void *alloc_cls(size_t cls_size)
{
  cls *cls = malloc(cls_size);
  if (!cls) abort(); // error handling
  return cls;
}
#define INIT_CLS(p, init)        \
  do {                           \
    if (!p) {                    \
      p = alloc_cls(sizeof *p);  \
```

```
        init(p);                          \
    }                                     \
} while(0)
```

The `INIT_CLS()` gets a pointer to the class, which I expect is a global variable, initially NULL. If the class hasn't been initialized yet, we allocate it and use the `init` function provided to initialize it.

For objects, we can use

```
void *alloc_obj(size_t obj_size, cls cls)
{
  obj *obj = malloc(obj_size);
  if (!obj) abort(); // error handling
  obj->cls = cls;
  return obj;
}
#define NEW_OBJ(p, cls) alloc_obj(sizeof *p, cls)
```

The `NEW_OBJ()` macro creates an object and sets its class. There is not an initialization function here because I expect that initializers will need arguments, so we cannot handle that generically. The same might be true for classes, but if that day arises, we can deal with it then.

```
void print_expr(EXP e)  { vtbl(e, base_expr_cls)->print(e); }
double eval_expr(EXP e) { return vtbl(e, base_expr_cls)->eval(e); }
```

A Hierarchy of Expression Classes

For a concrete example, we can have generic arithmetic expressions. We can define their main interface as having a `print()` and an `eval()` function.

```
// Generic expression type
typedef struct base_expr *EXP;

// Base class, class definition
typedef struct base_expr_cls {
  void    (*print)(EXP);
  double  (*eval) (EXP);
} base_expr_cls;
```

The functions are generic, so the implementation dispatches to the table in the class:

```
void    print(EXP e) { vtbl(e, base_expr_cls)->print(e); }
double eval (EXP e) { return vtbl(e, base_expr_cls)->eval(e); }
```

When we initialize the class, we don't put any methods in there. They are abstract.

```
void init_base_expr_cls(base_expr_cls *cls)
{
  cls->print = 0; // abstract method
  cls->eval  = 0; // abstract method
}
```

There is nothing in instances of the base class (except the nested obj needed for the class pointer).

```
// Base class, object definition
typedef struct base_expr { obj obj; } base_expr;
// Base class, methods (init does nothing)
void init_base_expr(base_expr *inst) {}
```

A concrete expression type is one that merely holds a value. It can look like this:

```
// Value expressions
typedef struct value_expr_cls {
  base_expr_cls base_expr_cls;
} value_expr_cls;
typedef struct value_expr {
  base_expr base_expr;
  double value;
} value_expr;
```

The class struct has the base class struct as its first (and only) member, and the object struct has the base expression object struct as its first member and the value the class should hold.

This is not an abstract class, but one we can instantiate, so we need a place to put the class struct, and we define a pointer for it:

```
// Concrete class, so must have a struct
value_expr_cls *VALUE_EXPR_CLS = 0; // must be initialised
```

We will initialize it later.

The class should define the print() and eval() functions, so we write functions for that, and in the function that initializes the class, we insert them in the nested/base class struct.

```
void value_expr_print(EXP val)
{
  printf("%.3f", ((value_expr *)val)->value);
}

double value_expr_eval(EXP val)
{
  return ((value_expr *)val)->value;
}

void init_value_expr_cls(value_expr_cls *cls)
{
  init_base_expr_cls(basetype(cls, base_expr_cls));
  // override virtual functions
  base_expr_cls *base_expr = basetype(cls, base_expr_cls);
  base_expr->print = value_expr_print;
  base_expr->eval  = value_expr_eval;
}
```

For initializing objects of the type, we need a function that calls the base initializer and sets the value:

```
void init_value_expr(value_expr *val, double value)
{
  init_base_expr(basetype(val, base_expr));
  val->value = value;
}
```

We want a function that creates objects as well, a so-called constructor, and it can look like this:

```
EXP value(double value)
{
  INIT_CLS(VALUE_EXPR_CLS, init_value_expr_cls);
```

```
  value_expr *val = NEW_OBJ(val, VALUE_EXPR_CLS);
  init_value_expr(val, value);
  return (EXP)val;
}
```

It initializes the class, if it isn't already created, then it allocates a new object, initializes it, and returns it.

We want binary operators, and we can define a class for that. I will write one that implements the print() virtual method, but not the eval() method; we will add eval() in subclasses. The implementation can look like this:

```
typedef struct binexpr_cls {
  base_expr_cls base_expr_cls;
} binexpr_cls;
typedef struct binexpr {
  base_expr base_expr;
  char symb; EXP left, right;
} binexpr;

void print_binexpr(EXP exp)
{
  binexpr *binop = (binexpr *)exp;
  putchar('('); print(binop->left); putchar(')');
  putchar(binop->symb);
  putchar('('); print(binop->right); putchar(')');
}

void init_binexpr_cls(binexpr_cls *cls)
{
  init_base_expr_cls(basetype(cls, base_expr_cls));
  base_expr_cls *base_expr = basetype(cls, base_expr_cls);
  base_expr->print = print_binexpr;
}

void init_binexpr(binexpr *binop, char symb,
                  EXP left, EXP right)
{
  init_base_expr(basetype(binop, base_expr));
```

```
  binop->symb = symb;
  binop->left = left;
  binop->right = right;
}
```

It follows the pattern we saw for values, except that we do not have a pointer for the class or a constructor because we are not supposed to create instances of this class. It doesn't define eval(), so our program would crash if we did and then tried to evaluate an expression. In the following, you can read the implementation of an addition and substitution class:

```
// Addition
typedef struct add_expr_cls {
  binexpr_cls binexpr_cls;
} add_expr_cls;
typedef struct add_expr {
  binexpr binexpr;
} add_expr;

add_expr_cls *ADD_EXPR_CLS = 0;

double eval_add_expr(EXP expr)
{
  binexpr *base = basetype(expr, binexpr);
  return eval(base->left) + eval(base->right);
}

void init_add_expr_cls(add_expr_cls *cls)
{
  init_binexpr_cls(basetype(cls, binexpr_cls));
  base_expr_cls *base_expr = basetype(cls, base_expr_cls);
  base_expr->eval = eval_add_expr;
}

void init_add_expr(add_expr *expr, EXP left, EXP right)
{
  init_binexpr(basetype(expr, binexpr), '+', left, right);
}
```

```c
// Constructor
EXP add(EXP left, EXP right)
{
  INIT_CLS(ADD_EXPR_CLS, init_add_expr_cls);
  add_expr *expr = NEW_OBJ(expr, ADD_EXPR_CLS);
  init_add_expr(expr, left, right);
  return (EXP)expr;
}

// Subtraction
typedef struct sub_expr_cls {
  binexpr_cls binexpr_cls;
} sub_expr_cls;
typedef struct sub_expr {
  binexpr binexpr;
} sub_expr;

sub_expr_cls *SUB_EXPR_CLS = 0;

double eval_sub_expr(EXP expr)
{
  binexpr *base = basetype(expr, binexpr);
  return eval(base->left) - eval(base->right);
}

void init_sub_expr_cls(sub_expr_cls *cls)
{
  init_binexpr_cls(basetype(cls, binexpr_cls));
  base_expr_cls *base_expr = basetype(cls, base_expr_cls);
  base_expr->eval = eval_sub_expr;
}

void init_sub_expr(add_expr *expr, EXP left, EXP right)
{
  init_binexpr(basetype(expr, binexpr), '-', left, right);
}

// Constructor
```

```
EXP sub(EXP left, EXP right)
{
  INIT_CLS(SUB_EXPR_CLS, init_sub_expr_cls);
  add_expr *expr = NEW_OBJ(expr, SUB_EXPR_CLS);
  init_sub_expr(expr, left, right);
  return (EXP)expr;
}
```

The code, again, follows the same pattern as we saw for the value_expr class.

The last example I will give is an expression that represents a variable. It is an expression with a named variable, but where we can bind values to the variable and unbind them again. We will make these two operations virtual functions (i.e., functions with a dynamic dispatch through the class) to see how that is done. I cannot think of a situation where we wouldn't use plain old functions for that, but it is an example, so go with it. It is what you are going to get.

The class will have a bind() and an unbind() virtual function, and instances will have the name of the variable and the value we have bound to it.

```
// Variables
typedef struct var_expr *VAR;
typedef struct var_expr_cls {
  base_expr_cls base_expr_cls;
  void (*bind)  (VAR var, EXP val);
  void (*unbind)(VAR var);
} var_expr_cls;
typedef struct var_expr {
  base_expr base_expr;
  char const *name;
  double value;
} var_expr;

// new virtual functions
void bind(VAR var, EXP e) { vtbl(var, var_expr_cls)->bind(var, e); }
void unbind(VAR var)      { vtbl(var, var_expr_cls)->unbind(var); }
```

The implementation we give the bind() function will evaluate the second argument and put it in the value of the first. For unbind(), we set value to NAN (not a number, defined in <math.h>).

```
// implementations of new virtual functions
void var_expr_bind  (VAR var, EXP e) { var->value = eval(e); }
void var_expr_unbind(VAR var)        { var->value = NAN; }
```

From here on, we follow the pattern we have seen already. It is a concrete class, so we have a pointer for it, we have code for initializing the class and the instances, and we have a constructor for the type.

```
var_expr_cls *VAR_EXPR_CLS = 0;

// overriding virtual functions
void var_expr_print(EXP expr)
{
  VAR var = (VAR)expr;
  if (isnan(var->value)) { // isnan from <math.h>
    printf("%s", var->name);
  } else {
    printf("%f", var->value);
  }
}

double var_expr_eval(EXP expr)
{
  VAR var = (VAR)expr;
  return var->value;
}

void init_var_expr_cls(var_expr_cls *cls)
{
  init_base_expr_cls(basetype(cls, base_expr_cls));
  // override virtual functions
  base_expr_cls *base_expr = basetype(cls, base_expr_cls);
  base_expr->print = var_expr_print;
  base_expr->eval  = var_expr_eval;
```

```
  // new virtual functions
  cls->bind        = var_expr_bind;
  cls->unbind      = var_expr_unbind;
}

void init_var_expr(var_expr *var, char const *name)
{
  init_base_expr(basetype(var, base_expr));
  var->name = name;
  var->value = NAN; // NAN from <math.h>
}

// constructor
VAR var(char const *name)
{
  INIT_CLS(VAR_EXPR_CLS, init_var_expr_cls);
  VAR var = NEW_OBJ(var, VAR_EXPR_CLS);
  init_var_expr(var, name);
  return var;
}
```

You can try it out in action with code like this:

```
int main(void)
{
  VAR x = var("x");
  EXP expr = add(value(1.0), sub((EXP)x, value(2.0)));
  // prints 'x' for x and evaluates to nan
  print(expr); putchar('\n');
  printf("evaluates to %f\n", eval(expr));

  // set x to 42
  bind(x, add(value(40.0), value(2.0)));
  // now prints 42 for x ane evaluates to 41
  print(expr); putchar('\n');
  printf("evaluates to %f\n", eval(expr));

  return 0;
}
```

We create one variable, and we keep track of it, so we can bind it. Then we have the expression $1.0 + (x - 2.0)$, written as expressions. If we print it, the output shows x for the variable; if we evaluate it, we get nan because we use a nan from x in the computation. Give x a value, and this changes.

Generating Functions

If we have function pointers, could we point one at a random memory address and start executing the code there? Yes and no. In the good old days, before anyone worried about security, you could write machine code to a buffer, assign the buffer address to a function pointer, and call the function. These days, things are more complicated. That being said, you can usually still do it, although not in any portable way. In this last section of the chapter, I will give you an idea about how you can create and run code, but it will only be a taste of it. There is much more to it, but as we consider architecture and platform-dependent code, I will not dig too deep into the topic.

Typical memory protection in a modern operating system will have *protection bits* on memory locations, which allows you any combination of reading, writing, and executing. The code your compiler generated for you sits in memory that can be read and executed. The memory on our stack and that we allocate from the heap can be read and written to. But a rule of thumb is that you should not have memory that you can both write to and execute (and some operating systems enforce this rule). To generate code, we need memory that we can write to, and to execute it, we must change the protection bits so we can read and execute instead. There will be a system call in your operating system that lets you change the protection bits, but the resolution of protection is not individual bytes. Instead, it is so-called *pages*, of whatever size the hardware and/or operating system specifies. If you have a memory address that falls on the border of a page, a page's memory alignment, you can change the memory protection bit; otherwise, you cannot. With malloc(), we do not necessarily get correctly aligned memory, but we could use aligned_alloc() and implement a function such as this for getting a block of memory we can change permissions for:

```
#include <unistd.h>
void *alloc_code_block(size_t size)
{
  long pagesize = sysconf(_SC_PAGE_SIZE);
```

```
  // with aligned alloc, the size must be a
  // multiple of align size
  size_t pages = (size + pagesize - 1) / pagesize;
  return aligned_alloc(pagesize, pages * pagesize);
}
```

We get the size of a page using the `sysconf()` function (specified in the POSIX standard). Then we round up the memory we need because `aligned_alloc()` requires that we allocate multiples of the alignment value and get an aligned chunk of memory.

Alignment alone might not be enough, though. Various other constraints vary from system to system, so more typical is using the (POSIX) `mmap()` function. It is a POSIX standard function, but it is not so standard that you can get what you want, unfortunately. Some systems have further requirements to what we can change protection bits on, but on macOS and the Linux systems I am familiar with, this function will work for allocation:

```
#include <sys/mman.h>

// Allocate page-aligned memory with mmap()
void *alloc_code_block(size_t size)
{
  // We want a read/write block
  int protection = PROT_READ | PROT_WRITE;
  // MAP_ANONYMOUS not POSIX but necessary on some systems
  // e.g. SELinux
  int flags = MAP_ANONYMOUS | MAP_PRIVATE;
  char *buf = mmap(0, size, protection, flags, -1, 0);
  return (buf != MAP_FAILED) ? buf : 0;
}
```

On a Windows machine, you want to look at the `VirtualAlloc()` function instead.

This gives us a correctly allocated memory block that we can write to. Once we have generated our code, we need to change the protection bits, and we can do that with `mprotect()`, another POSIX function:

```
void *set_exec_prot(void *buf, size_t size)
```

```
{
  // Change to a read/exec block
  int res = mprotect(buf, size, PROT_READ | PROT_EXEC);
  if (res == -1) {
    // munmap can fail, but there is nothing we
    // can do about it here...
    munmap(buf, size);
    return 0;
  }
  return buf;
}
```

The munmap() function is the call we have to use to deallocate memory. We didn't allocate with malloc() or its cousins, so free() is not an option. In any case, we set the protection bits to PROT_READ and PROT_EXEC, so we can now execute code in the buffer.

To free a code buffer, once we are done, we use

```
void free_code_block(void *buf, size_t size)
{
  // munmap can fail, but there is nothing we
  // can do about it here...
  munmap(buf, size);
}
```

On Windows, you want VirtualProtect() to change permissions and VirtualFree() to free the buffer.

With these three functions, we can allocate memory for code, put code in the buffer and make it executable, and free the buffer once we are done with it. You need to generate raw machine code into the buffer, of course, which is tedious, but you can always write a library to help you. A simple example of code generation could look like this:

```
int main(void)
{
  // Adds two to its input and returns
  unsigned char code[] = {
    0x8d, 0x47, 0x02,          // lea eax,[rdi+0x2]
```

```
    0xc3                         // ret
};
/*
Solaris, Linux, FreeBSD and macOS uses the System V AMD64 ABI
where the first integer/pointer argument comes in register rdi.
On windows, it would come in rcx.
If you are there, change "rdi+0x2" to "rcx+0x2".
*/

// Raw memory...
void *code_block = alloc_code_block(sizeof code);
if (!code_block) abort();
memcpy(code_block, code, sizeof code);
code_block = set_exec_prot(code_block, sizeof code);
if (!code_block) abort();

int (*f)(int) = (int (*)(int))code_block;
printf("%d\n", f(3));
free_code_block(code_block, sizeof code);

  return 0;
}
```

The code is for x64 chips and adds 2 to the function's first parameter and returns the result, and it will run on Solaris, Linux, FreeBSD, and macOS (and any system that uses the System V AMD64 ABI calling convention). It will not run on Windows because although Windows run on the same hardware, the convention for where functions get their input differs. On Windows, the input is in register rcx instead of rdi. Sorry, it is hard to write portable code when you write directly to the machine.

There might be another issue between writing your code to memory and executing it, although not on my architecture. The instruction and the data cache/bus might not be the same. So, you could be writing code to memory as data and then executing code at the same addresses, but getting old cached data. If that is the case, you need to flush the caches, and your compiler or system will have ways of doing that—not portable ways, though.

Tagged Pointers

Since we have left any attempts at writing portable code behind us now, I feel that I can show you a trick that isn't exactly portable, but that you can often use anyway. We are writing code for a machine where pointers are simple 64-bit integers, and we can treat them as such. The C standard does not guarantee that, but practically all architectures will let us manipulate pointers as integers, and we can exploit that if we are brave enough.

There is a trick used by virtual machines that exploit this. If we have data that we know has stricter alignment rules than char, that is, that cannot lie on all possible addresses, then we have bits in pointers to them that will always be zero. If integers, for example, align at offset 4, then the two lower bits must always be zero. That means that we can use those bits for something else, as long as we remember to set them back to zero before we use them as pointers. Imagine that we have a virtual machine that represents integers as some structure that can have arbitrary size, perhaps encoded as arrays of int. That means that general integers are int *. But smaller integers can fit into a pointer, so we could put them there if we don't need to put them on the heap. If bit 0 is always 0 for pointers, we could set it to 1 to indicate that we have put the actual integer in the pointer instead. For a small integer, we shift it one bit up and set the lowest bit to one, and that is their representation. For general integers, we have a pointer. To extract an integer, check the lowest bit. If it is 0, dereference; if it is 1, shift the remaining bits down. You get one bit less to represent small integers, but you can save all integers in the same (integer pointer) structure:

```c
#include <stdio.h>

#define smallint(i)      (int *)((i) << 1 | 1)
#define get_smallint(p) ((int)(p) >> 1)
#define is_smallint(p)  ((int)(p) & 1)
#define get_int(p) \
  (is_smallint(p) ? get_smallint(p) : (*(p)))

int main(void)
{
  int *p1 = smallint(1);
  int *p2 = smallint(2);
  printf("%d + %d = %d\n",
```

```
        get_int(p1), get_int(p2),
        get_int(p1) + get_int(p2));

  int i3 = 3;
  p2 = &i3;
  printf("%d + %d = %d\n",
        get_int(p1), get_int(p2),
        get_int(p1) + get_int(p2));

  return 0;
}
```

We could use that to encode the size of the blocks of memory we allocated when we generate code. We can allocate whole pages at a time, which we would have to anyway because the granularity of protection bits is whole pages, and encode how many pages we allocated in the lower bits of pointers. Then we pack those into what I will call a JIT pointer (for just-in-time compilation, the term usually used when we generate code on the fly). If page sizes are 4k (they are on my machine), then we have 12 bits for the size. With appropriate masking, we can pack both the pointer and the size into one pointer. The following jit_ptr() macro packs the size and pointer together, using simple binary or. The jit_pages() macro masks out the lower 12 bits to give us the size, and the jit_func() macro masks away the size bits. The macro uses a compiler extension, __typeof__(), for type-casting. We are no longer writing portable code, so I will use what my compiler provides. If you don't have __typeof__() or something similar, you have to cast where you use the macro.

```
// You can get PAGESIZE from POSIX sysconf(_SC_PAGESIZE);
// from sysconf() from <unistd.h>
#define PAGESIZE 4P96

// You can get the number of free bits from
// POSIX ffs() from <strings.h>  as ffs(page_size) - 1;
#define CODE_SIZE_BITS   12
#define CODE_SIZE_MASK   ((1ull << CODE_SIZE_BITS) - 1)
#define MAX_CODE_PAGES   CODE_SIZE_MASK
#define CODE_PTR_MASK    (~CODE_SIZE_MASK)

#include <stdint.h>
```

```
#define jit_ptr(f,s)      (void *)((uint64_t)f | s)
#define jit_pages(p)      ((uint64_t)p & CODE_SIZE_MASK)
// using compiler extension __typeof__ for cast
#define jit_func(p)       ((__typeof__(p))((uint64_t)p & CODE_PTR_MASK))

void jit_free_void(void *p)
{
  free_code_block((void *)jit_func(p), jit_pages(p));
}
// to avoid function/void pointer warnings
#define jit_free(p) jit_free_void((void*)(p))
```

Here is a function that generates code and returns a pointer, with size encoded:

```
void *create_exec_buf(unsigned char *code, size_t size)
{
  size_t pages = (size + PAGESIZE - 1) / PAGESIZE;
  if (pages > MAX_CODE_PAGES) {
    // Too large for us to store the size
    return 0;
  }
  size_t alloc_size = PAGESIZE * pages;

  char *buf = alloc_code_bock(alloc_size);
  if (!buf) return 0;
  memcpy(buf, code, size);
  buf = set_exec_prot(buf, alloc_size);
  if (!buf) return 0;
  return jit_ptr(buf, pages);
}
```

And you can use it to generate new functions, where you don't need to worry about remembering the allocated size:

```
typedef int (*ii_fn)(int);
ii_fn adder(int j)
{
  unsigned char code[] = {
```

```
  // lea eax,[rdi+<j>] (0x87 because we use 32-bit int now)
  0x8d, 0x87, // j starts at index 2...
              0x00, 0x00, 0x00, 0x00,
  // ret
  0xc3
};
// the int starts at index 2 and goes in the next four
// bytes, little endian...
unsigned char *j_code = code + 2;
for (int offset = 0; offset < 4; offset++) {
  j_code[offset] = (j >> 8 * offset) & 0xff;
}

return (ii_fn)create_exec_buf(code, sizeof code);
}
```

Here, the functions we generated add a number to an integer. Not too exciting, but I don't want too long machine code listings.

You use generated functions like this, where you must remember to `jit_free()` them once you are done:

```
ii_fn add2 = adder(2);
ii_fn add5 = adder(5);
for (int i = 0; i < 5; i++) {
  printf("%d, %d, %d\n", i,
  jit_func(add2)(i), jit_func(add5)(i));
}
jit_free(add2);
jit_free(add5);
```

If you didn't get 12 bits from the page alignment, but something substantially smaller, you could also encode the size in the high bits. On an x64 architecture, pointers are 64 bits, but only 48 of the bits are used. The rest are left for future extensions. Therefore, you have the 16 high bits to play with! The people who specified the machine architecture knew that we would do something like that, so they made rules to prevent it. We are not allowed to set the bits arbitrarily, relying on the system ignoring them.

Instead, all the high bits must be the same as bit 47. If it is set, all the high bits must be set. If it is zero, all the high bits must be zero. It is not exactly hard crypto, so we can easily circumvent the rule they made to prevent us from doing exactly what we are doing.[2] We can put the size in the high 16 bits by shifting up 48 bits. When we want the size back, we shift the size back. When we want to use the pointer as an actual pointer, we remove the size and set the top bits to their canonical form:

```
#define CODE_SIZE_BITS  16
#define MAX_CODE_PAGES  ((1ull << CODE_SIZE_BITS) - 1)
#define CODE_PTR_MASK   ((1ull << 48) - 1)
#define CODE_SIZE_MASK  (~CODE_PTR_MASK)

#include <stdint.h>
#define jit_ptr(f,s) \
  (void *)(((uint64_t)f & CODE_PTR_MASK) | (s << 48))
#define jit_pages(p) \
  (((uint64_t)p & CODE_SIZE_MASK) >> 48)

// upper 16 set if 47 set
#define upper_bits(p) \
  ~(((uint64_t)p & (1ull << 47)) - 1)
#define lower_bits(p) \
  ((uint64_t)p & CODE_PTR_MASK)
#define canonical_ptr(p) \
   (lower_bits(p) | upper_bits(p))

// using compiler extension __typeof__ for cast
#define jit_func(p) \
   ((__typeof__(p))(canonical_ptr(p)))
```

I don't recommend that you use the high bits this way, but you can if you want to. You are in danger when machines are eventually updated to use more bits, but with code this low level, and with code generation, it is a price you might be willing to pay.

---

[2]We probably shouldn't, because the bits could be used in the future. I don't expect our data busses will be larger in the near future, but it is probably still best not to do what I am showing you here!

CHAPTER 14

Generic Lists and Trees

We now return to lists and trees and consider what it will take to make them generic the way we make generic dynamic arrays in Chapter 10. The techniques we used there, working with void pointers or generating code using macros, will also work with lists and trees, but we will take a different approach.

With lists and trees, we are not working with contiguously allocated chunks of memory, so in principle, links and nodes can have any size. A generic data structure needs to know about the bits that define a link or a node, but if we allocate memory to store additional data alongside links and nodes, it will not affect the generic code at all. If we put a link or node structure in a user data structure, the generic code can use those. We have to leave it to the user to allocate all data. If the generic code does not know about user data, it cannot allocate space for it nor can it initialize it—but once the memory exists, it doesn't matter that it was allocated as part of a larger block.

We cannot implement the data structures utterly independent of the user data, however. We need a way to delete links and nodes, for example. Maybe we could unlink links and nodes from the structure and return it to the user for him to free them to get around that. Or we could make the user give us a function pointer to handle deallocation. For search trees, we need to compare nodes, to keep the search tree order, and here we need the user to provide a comparison operator. A function pointer is a natural choice. Generally, there will be functions that the user must supply for various operations. It is a design choice whether they should provide a function when they invoke a data structure operation, or whether we should store the functions with the data structure, and often it will be a mix of the two approaches. It will be a mix in the following sections, where we will add function pointers to lists and trees for the operations we expect to be constant throughout the lifetime of a data structure instance, and where we will add function pointer arguments to operations where we could expect the user to want to use different callbacks.

© Thomas Mailund 2021
T. Mailund, *Pointers in C Programming*, https://doi.org/10.1007/978-1-4842-6927-5_14

Generic Lists

If we remove all user data from a (doubly linked) list, which admittedly was only an integer in our previous implementation, we are left with two pointers to a link.

```
typedef struct link {
  struct link *prev;
  struct link *next;
} link;
```

Most of the operations we had on links didn't look at the data in the link; they only manipulated the pointers, and those functions will work just as well on our reduced structure.

```
static inline
void connect(link *x, link *y)
{ x->next = y; y->prev = x; }

static inline
void connect_neighbours(link *x)
{ x->next->prev = x; x->prev->next = x; }

static inline
void link_after(link *x, link *y)
{
  y->prev = x; y->next = x->next;
  connect_neighbours(y);
}
static inline
void link_before(link *x, link *y)
{
  link_after((x)->prev, y);
}

// This time, unlink will set x's pointers to NULL.
// We don't want to risk the callback function modifying
// the list after the link is removed.
static inline
void unlink(link *x)
```

```
{
  if (!x->prev || !x->next) return;
  x->next->prev = x->prev;
  x->prev->next = x->next;
  x->prev = x->next = 0;
}
```

For links, however, we might want to store function pointers so the user can parameterize them. I will add a function for freeing the memory of a link and for printing a link. The operations you might need will, of course, depend on your applications. You might have no need for printing lists, so you can leave that function out. Your application might hold references to all links you want to delete, so you don't need the list to know about the deallocation function. On the other hand, you might have other operations that you want a list to provide, which will depend on user-provided functions. The code you need to write will be similar regardless of which functions you add to a list.

I will write a structure that contains function pointers and call it a `list_type`. When you create a new list, you must provide its "type" through such a `struct`. A list will contain the functions and the "head" link we use for a circular list.

```
typedef struct list_type {
  void   (*free)(link *);
  void   (*print)(link *);
} list_type;
typedef struct list {
  link head;
  list_type type;
} list;
```

Many of the list operations we had in Chapter 4 need only a slight modification to work with the new `list` structure. We need to work in the `head` member of the `struct` instead of directly on the dummy element in the list. Aside from that, though, there is nothing surprising:

```
static inline
link *head(list *x)  { return &x->head; }
static inline
link *front(list *x) { return head(x)->next; }
```

451

```
static inline
link *back(list *x)  { return head(x)->prev; }
static inline
bool is_empty(list *x) { return head(x) == front(x); }

static inline
void append(list *x, link *link)  { link_before(head(x), link); }
static inline
void prepend(list *x, link *link) { link_after(head(x), link); }
```

To create a list, we need the user to provide a list_type. When can then allocate the list structure, set the pointers in the head member to point to the head, and copy the list pointers into the new struct.

```
list *new_list(list_type type)
{
  list *list = malloc(sizeof *list);
  if (list) {
    *list = (struct list){
      .head = { .next = &list->head,
                .prev = &list->head },
      .type = type
    };
  }
  return list;
}
```

I have chosen to copy the function pointers into the struct rather than have a pointer to a list_type object. This is a somewhat arbitrary choice. It saves the user from having to worry about memory management of a list_type object, but at the cost of having copies of the list_type in every list structure. However, I don't expect there to be many lists of the same type in my imaginary application. There might be many links, so I wouldn't want to put function pointers there if I don't need them—and in any case, the list implementation won't know about what I put in user-defined links—but I am okay with embedding the pointers in the list objects.

To free a list, we must run through the links and free them. We have the embedded free function pointer to help us. We have to make a choice about what happens if the user provided a NULL pointer here, however. We could consider that an error and ignore the issue. It would crash the program if we tried to call the function, but that would be part of the interface if we don't allow NULL pointers. We could also decide to provide a default, for example, free(). That way, if the user doesn't provide a function, we assume that links are heap-allocated objects that we can free(). I will pick a third option and say that if there isn't a free function provided, then we don't free the links.

```
void free_list(list *x)
{
  void (*free_link)(link *) = x->type.free;
  // We can only free if we have a free function.
  // Otherwise, assume that we shouldn't free.
  if (free_link) {
    link *lnk = front(x);
    while (lnk != head(x)) {
        link *next = lnk->next;
        free_link(lnk);
        lnk = next;
    }
  }
  free(x);
}
```

A user might put stack-allocated or global variables in a list. Who knows what users get up to when you aren't looking? As long as they don't provide a free function pointer, we won't free links. If they want the links freed, they must provide a function—otherwise, we might leak memory here. It is a design choice, and you can choose to do it differently.

For printing a list, I will make a different choice. I will provide a default print function that we use if the user doesn't provide one:

```
// Default print function
static void print_link(link *lnk)
{
  printf("<link %p>", (void *)lnk);
}
```

```
void print_list(list *x)
{
  void (*print)(link *) =
    (x->type.print) ? x->type.print : print_link;
    printf("[ ");
  for (link *lnk = front(x);
       lnk != head(x); lnk = lnk->next) {
    print(lnk);
    putchar(' ');
  }
  printf("]\n");
}
```

This is again an arbitrary choice.

For some operations, we might wish to provide a function pointer to the operation itself rather than the list. There are operations where we can imagine we want to parameterize the operation itself, and not expect each invocation of the operation to use a (list) global callback. For example, we could want a function that finds the next link in a chain that satisfies some predicate. The predicate is part of the operation and not a property of the list, and it would give us a way to iterate through a subset of a list. We could implement such a function like this:

```
link *find_link(list *x, link *from, bool (*p)(link *))
{
  for (link *lnk = from;
       lnk != head(x);
       lnk = lnk->next) {
    if (p(lnk)) return lnk;
  }
  return 0;
}
```

Here, we search from the link from and forward to the end of the list, but we will return if we find a link that satisfies the predicate p, a function that takes a link as input and returns a Boolean. We return NULL if we do not find a link; it seems like a good way to indicate that we couldn't find what we were searching for.

If you want to iterate through links, you should start from the front element in the list (the link after the head, or front(x) for a list x) and use the function like this:

```
for (link *lnk = find_link(x, front(x), p);
     lnk;
     lnk = find_link(x, lnk->next, p)) {
   // do something
}
```

How we write a predicate that can look at user data, and how we can get user data out from a link, is covered later. Notice that you have to continue the search from lnk->next in the increment. Otherwise, you get lnk right back because it already satisfies the predicate (unless you change that in "do something").

In Chapter 4, we had a function that would delete all links with a certain value. With a function pointer, we can generalize this and simultaneously have a generic function. Give the function, let us call it delete_if(), a predicate function pointer as argument, and delete the links that satisfy the predicate.

```
void delete_if(list *x, bool (*p)(link *))
{
  void (*free)(link *) = x->type.free;
  link *lnk = front(x);
  while (lnk != head(x)) {
    link *next = lnk->next;
    if (p(lnk)) {
      unlink(lnk);
      if (free) free(lnk);
    }
    lnk = next;
  }
}
```

To delete a link, we, of course, need the free pointer from the type. If it is NULL, we cannot deallocate a link, but we will always unlink() it, so it will still be removed from the list.

These are enough operations for our list, I think. I am convinced that you can work out how to add more functions from the example given. It is time to explore how we can provide user data to links, given that the list implementation doesn't know about that data. Somehow, user data must provide `link` structures to the list, and we should be able to cast between the user structures and the link structures as needed.

Casting to Links

As we saw in Chapter 13, we can implement a form of polymorphism by exploiting that the data you put at the top of a `struct` will, when properly cast, look like that kind of data. If you have a type `T` and we define

```
typedef struct S {
  T t;
  // more here
} S;
```

then we can cast any pointer to an object of type `S` to a `T` pointer and treat the top of the `S` object as a `T` object, and we can cast the pointer back from `T *` to `S *` and get the original object. Be careful here, though. You cannot safely cast any `T *` to `S *`. You obviously can't dereference and access any `T` object as if it were an `S` object—such objects won't have the "more here" data. Depending on how pointers are represented, you might not even be able to represent all pointers to `T` as pointers to `S`, since the structure `S` can have stricter alignment requirements, and that can affect the representation of pointers. But if you stick to pointers to objects of type `S`, you can safely cast them to `T *`, pass those pointers to functions, and get results back, and the `T *` pointers you get—because they really point to `S` objects—can be cast back to `S *`.

For lists, this means that we can define link `struct`s with any data we wish if we put a `link` as the first element in the `struct`. A list's `head` will have type `link`, not the larger link type we define, so you cannot necessarily cast the `head` link to a user type, but you shouldn't be doing that to begin with. It doesn't have any of the user data. The preceding generic list functions do not call user functions with the head of the data, and it is easy enough to avoid if you want to.

As an example, we could want a list of integers, and we could define this struct for links:

```
struct int_link {
  link link;
  int value;
};
typedef struct int_link ilink;

ilink *new_int_link(int value)
{
  ilink *lnk = malloc(sizeof *lnk);
  if (lnk) lnk->value = value;
  return lnk;
}
```

The print and free pointers in a list_type are functions that take link as arguments, but if we only insert pointers to ilink, then we can safely cast from link * to ilink * in functions we intend to use with an integer list, and we can define the type of integer lists as

```
void print_int_link(link *lnk)
{
  printf("%d", ((ilink *)lnk)->value);
}

void free_int_link(link *lnk)
{
  free(lnk); // Nothing special
}

list_type int_list = {
  .free = free_int_link,
  .print = print_int_link
};
```

A predicate we might use for find_link() or delete_if() could check if the value in a link is an even number, but casting the link to the integer link type and checking the value:

```
bool is_even(link *l)
{
  ilink *link = (ilink *)l;
  return link->value % 2 == 0;
}
```

and you could use an integer list as in this small program:

```
int main(void)
{
  list *x = new_list(int_list);
  for (int i = 0; i < 10; i++) {
    ilink *lnk = new_int_link(i);
    if (!lnk) abort();
    append(x, (link *)lnk);
  }
  print_list(x);

  ilink *lnk = (ilink *)find_link(x, front(x), is_even);
  printf("%d\n", lnk->value);

  lnk = (ilink *)find_link(x, lnk->link.next, is_even);
  printf("%d\n", lnk->value);

  for (link *lnk = find_link(x, front(x), is_even);
       lnk;
       lnk = find_link(x, lnk->next, is_even)) {
    printf("%d ", ((ilink *)lnk)->value);
  }
  printf("\n");

  delete_if(x, is_even);
  print_list(x);

  free_list(x);
```

```
// using stack-allocated links
ilink l1 = { .value = 13 };
ilink l2 = { .value = 42 };
struct list_type type = {
  .print = print_int_link,
  .free = 0 // Do not free stack allocated links
};
x = new_list(type);
append(x, (struct link *)&l1);
append(x, (struct link *)&l2);
print_list(x);
free_list(x);

return 0;
}
```

Using Offsets

Putting a link struct at the top of a user-defined link structure works fine until you want to put to use your data with more than one generic data structure. But imagine that you want to put your data into more than one list—or a list and a tree simultaneously. If the generic struct must sit at the top of your struct, then you would need to copy the actual data, so it can go into more than one object. Or put your data somewhere else and only have pointers to it your links and nodes. Having to put the generic struct first in your data structs seems too restrictive, and it is because the generic code will work just fine whether you put the generic data at the top of your structs or not. That code just needs their addresses and doesn't worry about whether those addresses are at offset zero of your struct or not. It is to get your data structs back from the generic code that is the issue. And there is a solution that will let you embed the generic structure—or structures—wherever you want.

Let's imagine that I want to put the same data into two lists, one that lets me run through it in the forward direction and one that lets me run through it in the backward direction. I know that we can already do this with a single doubly linked list, but go along with it; it is only an example. We then need to link the same object into two separate lists, so it needs to contain two link structures. It could look like this:

```
typedef struct double_link {
  link forward_link;
  link backward_link;
  int value;
} dlink;

dlink *new_dlink(int value)
{
  dlink *link = malloc(sizeof *link);
  if (link) link->value = value;
  return link;
}
```

If I give you a link * pointer, and you want to look at the dlink * pointer, how do you get it? In the general case, the answer is that you don't. We don't have a general way of determining if we are pointing to the forward_link or backward_link part of a dlink. There might be some (probably unportable) trickery we can do, but I doubt there is much to be done in entirely portable C. However, we don't just get random link * values thrown at us. We know which list we get a link from. And if it comes from the forward list, our link * must point to a forward_link, and if it comes from the backward list, it must point to a backward_link. And if I know which of the two the link * points to, I can get the address of the dlink structure that contains the link.

The offsetof() macro from <stddef.h> (that we have seen before) tells us at which offset any member sits in a struct. If I call

```
. offsetof(dlist,forward_link)
```

I will get the offset of forward_link in a dlink. That value is how many bytes (technically char) I have to go from the beginning of the dlink to get to forward_link. So, with a pointer p to a dlink, forward_link will sit at

```
(char *)p + offsetof(dlist,forward_link)
```

The (char *) cast is necessary here because offsetof() gives us the number of bytes to go up, but adding to p will move us in jumps of sizeof(dlink). Anyway, if I can go from a pointer to a dlink to its forward_link by adding this offset, I can also go the other way. If I have a pointer to a forward_link, I can subtract

```
offsetof(dlist,forward)
```

and get the dlink it sits in. The following macro will get you the containing struct from a pointer to a member inside it, using that computation:

```
#define struct_ptr(p,type,member) \
  (type *)((char *)p - offsetof(type, member))
```

In the following code, we use this struct_ptr() macro to get the user-defined link from the two generic link structs inside it. Notice that we have to provide different functions to the two list types because the struct_ptr() macro needs to know which member we are using. The callback functions will know which of the embedded links we should use, and it is the only way we can keep track of that in this implementation.

```
void print_dlink(dlink *link)
{
  printf("%d", link->value);
}

void print_forward(link *link)
{
  print_dlink(struct_ptr(link, dlink, forward_link));
}
void print_backward(link *link)
{
  print_dlink(struct_ptr(link, dlink, backward_link));
}

void free_dlink(dlink *link)
{
  // We have to unlink from both lists
  // before we can safely free the link.
  unlink(&link->forward_link);
  unlink(&link->backward_link);
  free(link);
}
void free_forward(link *link)
{
  free_dlink(struct_ptr(link, dlink, forward_link));
}
```

```
void free_backward(link *link)
{
  free_dlink(struct_ptr(link, dlink, backward_link));
}

  list_type forward_type = {
    .free  = free_forward,
    .print = print_forward
  };
  list_type backward_type = {
    .free  = free_backward,
    .print = print_backward
  };

  bool is_forward_even(link *l)
  {
    dlink *link = struct_ptr(l, dlink, forward_link);
    return link->value % 2 == 0;
  }

  int main(void)
  {
    list *forward = new_list(forward_type);
    list *backward = new_list(backward_type);
    if (!forward || !backward) abort(); // error handling

    for (int i = 0; i < 10; i++) {
      dlink *link = new_dlink(i);
      if (!link) abort();
      append(forward, &link->forward_link);
      prepend(backward, &link->backward_link);
    }
    print_list(forward);
    print_list(backward);

  // Try changing the first link in forward...
  dlink *link = struct_ptr(front(forward), dlink, forward_link);
  link->value = 42;
```

```
// Now both lists have changed (because it is the same link)
print_list(forward);
print_list(backward);

// deleting even numbers...
delete_if(forward, is_forward_even);
// removes them from both lists
print_list(forward);
print_list(backward);

free_list(forward);
free_list(backward);

return 0;
}
```

Generic Search Trees

For search trees, we can, not surprisingly, take the same approach as for lists. We can make a generic struct that holds the structure of nodes only and let the user allocate larger objects that contain such a node struct. The node could look like this:

```
typedef struct node {
  struct node *parent;
  struct node *left;
  struct node *right;
} node;
```

I have chosen a node with a parent pointer for this chapter. Most of the operations we will implement do not need the extra pointer, but I want to be able to delete a node from a tree through a pointer to the node. When the data we put in the tree has an existence separate from the tree, which they will if the nodes are merely embedded structs, it can be convenient to be able to remove a node from a tree using just the pointer. If we have a node, but we do not know which tree it sits in, we can still remove the node. If we have a parent pointer, we can do this. Otherwise, we would need to find the node's location in its tree through a search, and we can only do that if we also have a reference to the tree—which we might not have. You will see how we exploit the parent pointer to do this when we implement removal later.

For the tree structure, we need function pointers to handle what we cannot do directly from the generic nodes. I will add a print and free function to the type, as for lists, but we also need something that lets us compare nodes, so we can determine the order of nodes. Here, we could choose to have a comparison function on nodes, but I will split comparisons into two steps. One step is to get a *key* from a node, the relevant data in the node for comparisons, and another that compares keys. This will make it easier to use search trees as tables. If, for example, we want a table from strings to integers, nodes would have to hold both the strings as keys and the integers as values, but when we look up a string in the tree, we do not need to make a node for doing that. We can look up using only the string as a key.

I will implement the function pointer table and the tree struct like this:

```
typedef struct stree_type {
  void const *    (*key) (node *n);
  int             (*cmp) (void const *x,
                          void const *y);
  void            (*print)(node *n);
  void            (*free) (node *n);
} stree_type;
typedef struct stree {
  node root; // dummy node
  stree_type type;
} stree;
```

In the stree structure, we use a dummy node as the tree's root. The purpose of the dummy is the same as for all dummy elements; we can avoid dealing with some special cases. If we have a dummy root of the tree, we can ensure that all "real" nodes have a non-NULL parent pointer. The real tree will start at the root's left child.

This is the interface we will implement:

```
stree    *new_tree(stree_type type);
static inline bool is_empty_tree(stree *tree)
{ return tree->root.left == 0; }

void   insert_node(stree *tree, node *n);
void    print_tree(stree *tree);
void     free_tree(stree *tree);
```

```
node    *find_node(stree *tree, void const *key);
void    remove_node(node *n);
void    delete_node(stree *tree, node *n);

static inline
bool contains(stree *tree, void const *key)
{ return !!find_node(tree, key); }

static inline
void delete_key(stree *tree, void const *key)
{
  node *x = find_node(tree, key);
  if (x) delete_node(tree, x);
}
```

Given a type struct, we can create a tree. We can check if it is empty (which it is if the dummy root's left child is NULL). We can insert nodes, print and free trees, which is self-explanatory. We will have a function that finds a node by key (or return NULL if there is no node with the given key). We can remove a node from the tree—it will remove it from the tree structure but not delete it. This function does not need a tree as input. It is one we can use to decouple a node we have a reference to from the tree it sits in, without having a reference to the tree. We can also delete a node, which will remove it from the structure and then use the stored free function. For that, you need the tree, because the tree holds the free pointer. If you want to check if a key is in the tree, you can get the corresponding node and check if it is NULL. If you want to delete a key, you can also find the node and delete it if it isn't NULL.

Nothing surprises in the function for allocating a tree. We have to require that the key and cmp functions are provided, as they are essential for the workings of a search tree, but other than this, it is a simple initialization function.

```
stree *new_tree(stree_type type)
{
  // key and cmp are always needed. The rest
  // are optional.
  if (!(type.key && type.cmp)) return 0;
  stree *tree = malloc(sizeof *tree);
  if (tree) {
```

```
    *tree = (stree) {
      .root = { .parent = 0, .left = 0, .right = 0 },
      .type = type
    };
  }
  return tree;
}
```

When searching in a tree, we use a modified find_loc() function. It has to use the key and cmp functions from the tree's type for comparisons. Otherwise, it follows the same logic as in Chapter 12.

```
// Find parent and child
node **find_loc(stree *tree, void const *key,
                node **n, node **p)
{
  void const * (*get_key)(node *n) = tree->type.key;
  int (*cmp)(void const *x, void const *y) = tree->type.cmp;

  while (*n) {
    int cmpres = cmp(key, get_key(*n));
    if (cmpres == 0) return n;
    *p = *n;
    if (cmpres < 0) n = &(*n)->left;
    else            n = &(*n)->right;
  }
  return n;
}
```

The function for finding a node is trivial once we have find_loc():

```
node *find_node(stree *tree, void const *key)
{
  node *parent = &tree->root;
  node **real_tree = &parent->left;
  return *find_loc(tree, key, real_tree, &parent);
}
```

When we insert a node, we expect that the user has already allocated and initialized the memory for it, so we cannot have allocation failures. However, we need to deal with what happens if the key in the new node is already in the tree because as we have implemented the tree, we cannot have two nodes with the same key. An easy solution is to get rid of the old node. The semantics is that if we use the tree as a table, we have replaced the old value for the key with the new.

```
void insert_node(stree *tree, node *n)
{
  node *parent = &tree->root;
  node **real_tree = &parent->left;
  void const *key = tree->type.key(n);
  node **target = find_loc(tree, key, real_tree, &parent);

  if (*target) { // remove the old node
    delete_node(tree, *target);
  }

  *target = n;
  n->parent = parent;
  n->left = n->right = 0; // leaf
}
```

In this function, we find the location where we should insert the node, deleting the old node if the key was already there. Then we insert the new node at the right location and connect the node's `parent` pointer to its new parent and set its children to NULL to make it a leaf.

The `remove_node()` function behaves exactly as the delete function we had previously, except that we do not need the initial search for the node. We already have the node and its parent, so we can go right ahead and remove it. We can remove it directly if it has an empty child, and otherwise we have to replace it with its rightmost child.

```
node **rightmost(node **n, node **p)
{
  while ((*n)->right) {
    *p = *n;
    n = &(*n)->right;
  }
```

```
  return n;
}

void remove_node(node *n)
{
  if (!n->parent) {
    // parentless nodes are not in the tree
    // (they have probably been removed before)
    return;
  }

  // Get the location to replace.
  node **loc = (n == n->parent->left)
      ? &n->parent->left : &n->parent->right;

  if (!(n->left && n->right)) {
    // has an empty child...
    *loc = n->left ? n->left : n->right;
    if (*loc) (*loc)->parent = n->parent;
  } else {
    node *rm_parent = n;
    node **rm_ref = rightmost(&n->left, &rm_parent);
    node *rm = *rm_ref;
    *rm_ref = rm->left;
    if (*rm_ref) (*rm_ref)->parent = rm_parent;

    // we cannot simply move the value now, but must
    // reconnect the pointers...
    *loc = rm; // makes *loc point to rm
    *rm = *n;  // copies the struct (i.e. the pointers)
    // When copying the structs like this, we only copy
    // the bits that are in the type they have, so only the
    // three pointers and not whatever else might sit in the
    // actual nodes.
  }

  // now, to make our code safer, we NULL the pointers
  // before we call the free function.
  n->left = n->right = n->parent = 0;
}
```

We set the pointers in the node to NULL before we return from the call. This can be helpful when we call remove_node() in callback function calls, where having NULL pointers here can prevent us from any unnecessary recursion or from accessing data that might have been freed.

The delete_node() function removes the node and uses the stored free function to deallocate it:

```
void delete_node(stree *tree, node *n)
{
  remove_node(n);
  if (tree->type.free)
    tree->type.free(n);
}
```

The functions to print and free a tree need to use the function pointers, but otherwise they do not change. I have listed recursive versions in the following; you are welcome to implement the recursion and stack free variants if you feel for it.

```
// Just recursion this time; the techniques for avoid it
// hasn't changed.
static void default_print(node *n)
{
  printf("<node %p>", (void*)n);
}
void print_node(void (*print)(node *n), node *n)
{
  if (!n) return;
  putchar('(');
    print_node(print, n->left);
    putchar(','); print(n); putchar(',');
    print_node(print, n->right);
  putchar(')');
}
void print_tree(stree *tree)
{
  void (*print)(node *) =
    tree->type.print ? tree->type.print : default_print;
  print_node(print, tree->root.left);
}
```

```
void free_nodes_rec(void (*free)(node *n), node *n)
{
  if (!n) return;
  free_nodes_rec(free, n->left);
  free_nodes_rec(free, n->right);
  if (free) {
    // remove pointers before callback
    n->left = n->right = n->parent = 0;
    free(n);
  }
}
void free_tree(stree *tree)
{
  free_nodes_rec(tree->type.free, tree->root.left);
  free(tree);
}
```

Imagine that we want to put the same data in both a list and a tree—now that we have the option with generic data structures for both. We can use the struct_ptr() macro to get the struct that contains both the link and the node of user data, so that should be straightforward. We could, for example, use that in an application where we want to have strings in some given order, for example, insertion order in a table, and at the same time have efficient lookup to remove strings from the table. A data type that contains nodes, links, and strings could look like this:

```
typedef struct ordered_string {
  node node;
  link link;
  char const *str;
} ostring;

ostring *new_ostring(char const *str)
{
  ostring *n = malloc(sizeof *n);
  if (!n) abort();
  n->str = str;
  return n;
}
```

Print and delete functions could look like this:

```
void print_ordered_string(ostring *str)
{
  printf("\"%s\"", str->str);
}

void free_ordered_string(ostring *str)
{
  // Remove from data structures...
  unlink(&str->link);
  remove_node(&str->node);
  // and then free...
  free(str);
}
```

We can't use those directly with the data structures because they have the wrong type (and with the callbacks, we need to go from nodes/links to ostring using contains()), but they are the functions we can use once we have converted links and nodes. When we free an ostring, we should remove it from both the list and the node, so we use the unlink() and remove_node() functions. Here, where we only have the structure and not the list or tree, it is useful that these functions do not need the list or tree as arguments, but only the link or node.

To get the functions for the search tree, we must adapt the functions to its interface and put them in an stree_type structure:

```
void const *strnode_key(node *n)
  { return struct_ptr(n, ostring, node)->str; }
int strnode_cmp(void const *x, void const *y)
  { return strcmp(x, y); }
void strnode_print(node *n)
  { print_ordered_string(struct_ptr(n, ostring, node)); }
void strnode_free(node *n)
  { free_ordered_string(struct_ptr(n, ostring, node)); }
```

471

```
stree_type strnode_type = {
  .key   = strnode_key,
  .cmp   = strnode_cmp,
  .print = strnode_print,
  .free  = strnode_free
};
```

Likewise for the list interface:

```
void strlink_print(link *lnk)
  { print_ordered_string(struct_ptr(lnk, ostring, link)); }
void strlink_free(link *lnk)
  { free_ordered_string(struct_ptr(lnk, ostring, link)); }

list_type strlink_type = {
  .print = strlink_print,
  .free  = strlink_free
};
```

If we now want a data structure with strings in insertion order, and with a search tree as a map, we can define it like this:

```
typedef struct ordered_strings {
  stree *map; list *order;
} ordered_strings;

ordered_strings *new_ordered_strings(void)
{
  ordered_strings *os = malloc(sizeof *os);
  if (!os) abort(); // handle alloc errors
  os->map = new_tree(strnode_type);
  os->order = new_list(strlink_type);
  if (!os->map || !os->order) abort(); // handle errors
  return os;
}
```

```
void add_string(ordered_strings *os, char const *str)
{
  ostring *ostr = new_ostring(str);
  if (!ostr) abort(); // handle alloc errors
  insert_node(os->map, &ostr->node);
  append(os->order, &ostr->link);
}

void remove_string(ordered_strings *os, char const *str)
{
  node *n = find_node(os->map, str);
  if (n) {
    ostring *x = struct_ptr(n, ostring, node);
    free_ordered_string(x);
  }
}
```

When we add a string, we append it to the list, so we have the insertion order there, and we insert it in the tree, so we can get fast lookup. When we remove a string, we find the data from the tree and remove it, where free_ordered_string() removes it from both the list and the tree.

If you want to remove data by index, in the ordered list, we can implement it like this, where using a negative index will look from the back of the list:

```
link *take_front(list *x, int idx)
{
  for (link *lnk = front(x);
       lnk != head(x); lnk = lnk->next) {
    if (idx-- == 0) return lnk;
  }
  return 0;
}

link *take_back(list *x, int idx)
{
  for (link *lnk = back(x);
       lnk != head(x); lnk = lnk->prev) {
    if (idx-- == 0) return lnk;
  }
```

```
  return 0;
}

void remove_index(ordered_strings *os, int idx)
{
  link *lnk;
  if (idx < 0) {
      lnk = take_back(os->order, -idx - 1);
  } else {
    lnk = take_front(os->order, idx);
  }

  if (!lnk) {
    // report an error...
    return;
  }
  ostring *x = struct_ptr(lnk, ostring, link);
  free_ordered_string(x);
}
```

It is linear time operations, so it might not be optimal for your use, but the functions are there as an example, so I can live with that.

If we free both tree and list, the order will affect the running time. If you delete the list first, you will delete each link, which will call the free function. When the function is called, the link is already unlinked, but there is no harm in unlinking it again—the unlink() function recognizes that there is nothing to unlink and that will be all. You also call remove_node() from the callback deallocator, and this can involve a search for rightmost(). Each deletion might thus trigger a search in the tree. If you delete the tree first, however, the tree deletion code will set the node's pointers to NULL before it calls the callback, so the remove_node() call there will not trigger a search. The unlink() call never triggers a search. So deleting the nodes/links via the tree will be faster than deleting them through the list, so that is what we will do.

```
void free_ordered_strings(ordered_strings *os)
{
  free_tree(os->map);
  free_list(os->order);
  free(os);
}
```

I didn't really have any exciting application in mind with this data structure, but you can see it in use here:

```
int main(void)
{
  ordered_strings *os = new_ordered_strings();

  add_string(os, "foo");
  add_string(os, "bar");
  add_string(os, "baz");
  add_string(os, "qux");
  add_string(os, "qax");

  print_list(os->order);
  print_tree(os->map); printf("\n\n");

  printf("removing 'bar'\n");
  remove_string(os, "bar");
  print_list(os->order);
  print_tree(os->map); printf("\n\n");

  printf("Removing index 1 (baz)\n");
  remove_index(os, 1); // baz
  print_list(os->order);
  print_tree(os->map); printf("\n\n");

  printf("Removing index -3 (foo)\n");
  remove_index(os, -3);
  print_list(os->order);
  print_tree(os->map); printf("\n\n");

  printf("all done\n");
  free_ordered_strings(os);

  return 0;
}
```

As long as we can delegate the allocation of memory to the user of a data structure, it is not hard to implement a generic data structure. We have a minimal `struct` with the information the data structure needs, and this must be embedded in the user's data. Everything else is handled with generic code, supplemented with callback functions provided as function pointers. Lists and trees are not special in this regard; you can do this with any data structure where you can let the user handle memory allocation.

CHAPTER 15

Reference Counting Garbage Collection

Keeping track of when memory should be freed, so we always remember to do it and never call `free()` on the same memory twice, is at times complicated. The scenario where you have a function that allocates some memory, uses it, and then frees it before the function returns is hardly ever problematic. If you have many exit points, that is, you `return` multiple places, you must ensure that you free everything regardless of how you exit the function, but unless it is an incredibly complicated function, it is manageable. However, once you start working with heap-allocated data structures, even as simple as lists and trees, things can get more complicated. The same memory can be referenced from multiple places, and you cannot free it before you remove the last reference (at which point you must).

Consider the first version of singly linked lists from Chapter 11, where we had the `new_link()` function for creating a new link with a `next` pointer to the next link in the list. With that, we could create lists:

```
list x = new_link(11, new_link(12, NULL));
list y = new_link(1, new_link(2, x));
```

where now x is a list with elements 11 and 12, and y is a list with the elements 1, 2, 11, and 12. The two last links in y are shared with x. We cannot free y as long as we need x because we would destroy x's links. We cannot free x while we use y because we would destroy its last two links.

© Thomas Mailund 2021
T. Mailund, *Pointers in C Programming*, https://doi.org/10.1007/978-1-4842-6927-5_15

This is a simple example, and of course we could code our way around deleting the first two, but not the last two links of y if we want to free y, but it should not surprise you to learn that things can get a lot more complicated than this. When we start wiring up data structures with pointers to substructures, keeping track of what memory we have a reference to, and what we can and should free, gets complicated. It is why most modern programming languages have automatic garbage collection to a varying degree. But C does not, so we have to deal with it on our own and implement our own strategies.

One of the simplest approaches to memory management, when we find ourselves in a situation such as this, is *reference counting*. The idea is as trivial as this: you give each object a counter that tracks how many references you have to it. When you add another reference, you increment the counter, and when you remove one, you decrement the counter. If the counter hits zero, you no longer need the object, and you free it.

As a trivial example, imagine that we have heap-allocated integers. We can add a counter to each, as in the following code, and initialize each new object with a count of one—whoever creates the object probably wants a reference to it and will have a pointer to it, so that is the reference we are counting. We can free these objects with free(), since they do not contain anything we must recursively free, but in the example, I have added a function that prints when an object is freed, so it is easier to track. We don't call that function directly; however, we use two other functions for memory management: incref() for adding a reference and decref() for removing one. When you want another pointer to the object, you incref(), and when you want to remove a reference, you use decref():

```c
#include <stdio.h>
#include <stdlib.h>

struct rc_int {
  int refcount;
  int value;
};

struct rc_int *new_rc_int(int i)
{
  struct rc_int *p = malloc(sizeof *p);
  if (p) {
    *p = (struct rc_int){
        .refcount = 1, .value = i
```

```c
      };
    }
  return p;
}

void free_rc_int(struct rc_int *i)
{
  printf("Freeing %d\n", i->value);
  free(i);
}

struct rc_int *incref(struct rc_int *p)
{
  if (p) p->refcount++;
  return p;
}

struct rc_int *decref(struct rc_int *p)
{
  if (p && --p->refcount == 0) {
    free_rc_int(p);
    return 0;
  }
  return p;
}

int main(void)
{
  struct rc_int *i = new_rc_int(42);
  struct rc_int *j = incref(i);
  decref(i); // decrements...
  decref(j); // decrements and deletes...

  return 0;
}
```

In both `incref()` and `decref()`, we allow NULL pointers. When we can get away with it, it is easier to write code where we do not need to treat NULL as a special case, and if we let these two functions return NULL on NULL input, we can write simpler code. In the `main()` function, for example, we don't check for an allocation error because the code will work correctly on NULL pointers as well. In practice, of course, we need non-NULL pointers *somewhere*, but we can defer worrying about that to the point where we have to.

That is the whole idea behind reference counting, but of course there are some practices you need to make it work as well, or the chapter would be finished by now. We are not entirely out of the woods with respect to memory management simply because we add a counter. We still have to know when to increment and decrement the counter. This, however, we can mostly handle on a per-function basis and doesn't require an overview of the entire program and how pointers are connected globally. To demonstrate how we can use reference counting traditionally, I will return to our trusted lists and trees.

Immutable Links with Reference Counting

Imagine that we have an application where we want to work with lists, and we want the lists to be *immutable*, in the sense that if you have a reference to a list, then that list never changes. It will always be the same elements in the same order. Such immutability makes it easy to share data. If we have two lists, and one is a suffix of the other, they can share all the links in the shorter list. Since we cannot change any links, the longer list doesn't have to worry about its suffix changing because we do something to the shorter list. Immutable data structures can reduce our memory usage when different structures can share substructures, they are useful for so-called persistent data structures that have their uses in various algorithms, and they alleviate some problems in concurrent programs. So immutable lists are not an artificial constraint I made up for this chapter; there really are applications where you want them. And if you want them, and you want to share suffixes between them, then reference counting is the ideal strategy for memory management.

We can define an immutable list link like this:

```
struct link {
  int refcount;
  struct link * const next;
  int          const value;
};
```

CHAPTER 15   REFERENCE COUNTING GARBAGE COLLECTION

```
typedef struct link *list;
```

The next pointer and the value are const, so we cannot modify the link's data or the list that follows the link. The refcount is not const, obviously, since even if the list is immutable, we need to keep track of how many references we have to any given link.

The lists are much like the first version of singly linked lists in Chapter 11, and there we had a problem with differentiating between operations that would give us an empty list and operations that would report errors, as both errors and empty lists were represented by a NULL pointer. To avoid this, we can explicitly represent empty lists as a special link. If we have a NULL pointer for a list, it is an error, and if we have an empty list, it is the designated link.

So, a NULL pointer to a list is an error:

```
static inline
bool is_error(struct link *x) { return x == 0; }
```

and we define a special address that we can get through a function get_NIL() to be the empty list:

```
struct link *get_NIL(void);
```

```
static inline
bool is_nil(struct link *x) { return x == get_NIL(); }
```

We can define the special link as a static variable in the get_NIL() function:

```
struct link *get_NIL(void)
{
  static struct link NIL_LINK = { .refcount = 1 };
  return &NIL_LINK;
}
```

That way, we get the same link every time we get the empty list. The initial reference count for the empty list is one, but it should be incremented and decremented like other objects—but never decremented more than incremented, because we obviously do not want to risk deleting it.

To avoid accidentally decrementing the empty list more than we increment it, we can use a macro to access it. The macro will increment the reference each time we use it in an expression.

```
#define NIL incref(get_NIL())
```

We shouldn't use this macro to check if we have an empty list because a test such as NIL == NIL will increment the reference count twice. It isn't really a problem, since as long as we never decrement the counter in an empty list to zero, we are fine. Still, for consistency, we should only increment a reference counter when we are also going to decrement it later. When we use NIL, we increment, so we should only use it in expressions where we will eventually decrement as well. Writing NIL gives us a "new" empty list, and we should think about it as such.

The incref()/decref() and deallocation code look much like the example with reference counted integers. The decref() function will call another function, free_link(), when we need to actually free a link. It is listed later.

```c
struct link *incref(struct link *link)
{
  if (link) link->refcount++;
  return link;
}

void free_link(struct link *link);
struct link *decref(struct link *link)
{
  if (link && --link->refcount == 0) {
    free_link(link);
    return 0;
  }
  return link;
}
```

Now we are almost ready to write list functions, but before we start, we need to lay down the ground rules for how we work with incrementing and decrementing lists. These are the rules that ensure that we increment and decrement correctly, so we always have a valid reference when we need it, and we always decrement references when we no longer need them. Essentially, it boils down to deciding when a function is responsible for incrementing a reference it gets as input and when it is responsible for decrementing a reference that it holds.

Consider as an example a function for computing the length of a list. We will see two versions later, but for now let us just assume that we have a function, length(), that gives us the length, and that new_link() works as in Chapter 11, that is, it creates a new link. Now consider this code:

```
list x = new_link(1, new_link(2, NIL));
int len1 = length(x);
int len2 = length(new_link(1, new_link(2, NIL)));
```

We use NIL for the empty list, so we have separate references to the empty list we create in the two lists we construct, the first when we create x and the second when we create an anonymous list that we immediately call length() on. When we call length(), does it increment/decrement its input? Let us assume that it does neither, and x holds the only reference to the front link it points to. Then, if length() doesn't change anything, we get the length and x remains the same, with the single reference to the list. That would work fine, but then the second call to length() could be problematic. Here, we create a list with the two calls to new_link(), then we call length()—which doesn't increment or decrement anything—and once length() returns, we have lost access to the new list. We have leaked the memory for two links.

On the other hand, if length() decrements its input, so we would free the new list in the third line of the code, then it would also decrement the reference to x in the first line. If x is the only reference to that list, decrementing in length() would free the list, and x would point at freed memory. If length() decrements, and we want to keep x around after the call to length(), we should incref(x) before we call length():

```
int len1 = length(incref(x));
```

Either version of length(), the one that takes ownership of the input and frees it and the one that doesn't, is a fine choice. We just need to be careful, so we always know what kind of function we are using.

I will write functions of both kinds in this section to illustrate how we write both types, but in practice I would recommend choosing one convention and using it for all your functions, or at least all the functions you provide to a user, to minimize confusion. To avoid confusion ourselves in this chapter, I will annotate our functions with two "keywords," borrows and takes, for when a function will leave an input as it is (borrows) or when it takes ownership of the reference (takes) and will decrement the reference. We can add the keywords to our code using preprocessor definitions:

```
#define borrows
#define takes
```

The preprocessor will expand them to empty strings, so they have no semantic meaning in the code, but we can write the keywords together with function arguments. This is not something I will generally recommend that you do in your code—where I, in any case, suggest you only use one of the two approaches—but it is my book, and I say that it is okay in this chapter.[1]

A function that borrows an argument should not decrement the argument, nor should it give the argument to another function that takes it because that amounts to passing on a reference that the borrowing function doesn't own. A function that takes an argument should always decref() the argument or give it to another function that takes ownership of the argument.

To make the "passing of ownership" more explicit in our code, we can use another macro, transfer():

```
#define transfer(x) x
```

The macro doesn't do anything either; the only purpose it serves is to make explicit that we are passing on ownership to someone else. Don't transfer() a reference you do not own. If you have borrowed a reference, and you want to give it away, incref() it first. That gives you your very own reference, and you are allowed to give your own reference away.

Rules for references in arguments are half the strategy. The other is what we expect from pointers that functions return. Do functions return new references that we are responsible for decrementing, or do they give us "borrows" references that we should incref() if we want to keep them? Both approaches are valid, but in this case, for me, the rule that says that functions always give you a reference feels more reasonable. When you get the result of a function call, the function doesn't have a reference any longer—the function call is done, after all—so either it created a reference, which you definitely have to own, or it borrowed a reference and then gave it to you, while it wasn't its to give. I will follow the rule that if a function returns a reference, it is giving the reference to the caller. If it borrowed the reference, it must incref(), so it is allowed to give it away.

---

[1]Should you someday decide to annotate your code using macros in this way, don't pick lowercase short words like this! You are likely to use those for variables or functions as well, and that will break your code. I only use them to make the code here easier to follow. In real code, you should be smarter than this.

With these rules in place, let's write the functions for creating and freeing links:

```
list new_link(int head, takes list tail)
{
  if (is_error(tail)) return tail;

  list link = malloc(sizeof *link);
  if (!link) { decref(tail); return 0; }

  struct link link_data = {
    .refcount = 1,
    .next  = transfer(tail), // gives away the reference
    .value = head
  };
  // explanation below for memcpy()
  memcpy(link, &link_data, sizeof *link);
  return transfer(link);
}
```

When we create a new link, we provide new_link() with a value and a link, and we give the function that link, as we have made clear with the takes keyword before the tail argument. If tail is a NULL pointer, that is, if it is the result of something we consider an error, we won't put it into the new link. We will generally return an error if we get any error lists as input. So, we check for errors first and propagate it if tail is one. Otherwise, we allocate the new link. That can fail, in which case we should return NULL to indicate that we had an error. Before we can return, however, we must decrement tail. The function owns it at this point, and it is responsible for decrementing tail.

If we successfully allocated, we initialize the link. We transfer() the tail to the link, so it now owns the reference. The construction where we first initialize a stack-allocated link and then move the data with memcpy() is to get around the const'ness of value and next and doesn't serve any other purpose. Once the new link is initialized, we give it to the caller. The link is initialized with a reference count of one, and the caller now owns that single reference.

When we need to free a link, when its reference count reaches zero in `decref()`, we call `free_link()`:

```
void free_link(struct link *link)
{
  decref(link->next);
  free(link);
}
```

We must `decref(link->next)` because the link we are deleting has a reference to its next that now disappears.

To warm up for writing list functions, consider first a function for printing a list. A version that borrows a reference could look like this:

```
void print_list(borrows list x)
{
  assert(!is_error(x));
  printf("[ ");
  while (!is_nil(x)) {
    printf("%d[%d] ", x->value, x->refcount);
    x = x->next;
  }
  printf("]\n");
}
```

Since we borrow the list, we don't need to `decref()` it when we are done. If we take the list instead, we would have to

```
void print_list(takes list x)
{
  assert(!is_error(x));
  printf("[ ");
  struct link *l = x; // use separate pointer
  while (!is_nil(l)) {
    printf("%d[%d] ", l->value, l->refcount);
    l = l->next;
  }
  printf("]\n");
  decref(x); // remember to decref a taken list
}
```

We loop through the list, so we need a separate variable for that. Otherwise, we couldn't decref() the correct list when we are done. We don't take ownership of the links that follow x in either function. As long as we have a reference to x, the following links will not be freed—they cannot go away as long as there is a reference to them, and as long as x exists, there will be.

What about the now infamous length() function from earlier? A borrowing version could look like this:

```
int length_rec(borrows list x, int acc)
{
  assert(!is_error(x));
  if (is_nil(x))
    return acc;
  else
    return length_rec(x->next, acc + 1);
}

static inline
int length(borrows list x)
{ return length_rec(x, 0); }
```

I have chosen to implement it as a tail-recursive function for no other reason than to make it a little more interesting when we get to the version that takes its argument. The compiler will turn it into a loop, and we could easily do so as well if we wanted to. The recursive function uses an accumulator, acc, to count the number of links we have run through, and I use another function to give the accumulator a default of zero. With a version that borrows, there is nothing interesting in using reference counting; we run through the list in the recursions as we would with any pointer data structure.

With this function, the code from earlier

```
list x = new_link(1, new_link(2, NIL));
int len1 = length(x);
int len2 = length(new_link(1, new_link(2, NIL)));
```

will leak memory in the second call to length(), where we get a reference that we never decrement. For the second call to work, we need a function that takes its argument, and that could look like this:

```
int length_rec(takes list x, int acc)
{
  assert(!is_error(x));
  if (is_nil(x)) {
    decref(x);
    return acc;

  } else {
    struct link *next = incref(x->next);
    decref(x);
    return length_rec(transfer(next), acc + 1);
  }
}

static inline
int length(takes list x)
{ return length_rec(transfer(x), 0); }
```

There is a little more meat on this one. Because we take the x argument, we are responsible for decrementing it as well, which we have to do in both the base case and the recursive case. It is strictly speaking not essential that we decrement in the base case, where we have an empty list, since we will never free the empty list anyway, but the general rule is to decref() if we take a reference, so that is what we do. In the recursive case, we need x->next, but if decref(x) frees x—it will if we have the only reference to x—then that might free x->next as well. To prevent this, we need to get our own reference to x->next, so we incref(x->next). Even if we weren't worrying about how x->next could disappear when we decref(x), it is only proper that we incref(x->next) in any case. We are going to transfer() it to the recursive call, and it is not ours to give away. It is x that has a reference to x->next, not us, and if we want to give it away, we need our own reference. So based merely on considerations of criminal conduct, we should incref(x->next) before we can call recursively. That we must do it before we decref(x) is because decrementing x's reference counter could free it. Generally, we have to consider decref(x) as analogous to free(x), and with free(x) we know better than to access x->next after we have freed x. It is the same with decref(x). We need to incref(x->next) so we can transfer() it to the recursive call, we need to decref(x) because we have taken it, and we need to do it in the order we do, because we cannot get x->next after calling decref(x).

With this version, when we write

```
list x = new_link(1, new_link(2, NIL));
int len1 = length(x);
int len2 = length(new_link(1, new_link(2, NIL)));
```

the second call to length() works as intended and frees the link we create, so we do not leak memory. The first call, however, is giving x to length(x), so we should either write

```
int len1 = length(transfer(x));
```

to make clear that x is not around after the call, or we should write

```
int len1 = length(incref(x));
```

to keep our own reference after the call.

A borrowing function for reversing a list will look like this:

```
list reverse_rec(borrows list x, borrows list acc)
{
  if (is_error(x) || is_error(acc)) {
    return 0;
  }
  if (is_nil(x)) {
    return transfer(incref(acc));
  } else {
    return reverse_rec(x->next,
                       new_link(x->value,
                                transfer(incref(acc))));
  }
}

static inline
list reverse(borrows list x)
{ return reverse_rec(x, get_NIL()); }
```

We are not actually reversing a list. Lists are immutable, so we can't. We are creating a new list that has the elements in the original list but in reverse order. It is a recursive function with an accumulator once again and with a helper function to give the accumulator a default value. We should start with an empty list, but we can't use NIL here. That creates a new reference to the empty list, and since this function doesn't take ownership of its input, we shouldn't create new references for it. So get_NIL() is what we need.

The function recurses along with the list x, at each level taking the value in x and putting it into a new link, which prepends the new value to the current acc. Once we reach the end of the recursion, where x is empty, acc contains the reversed list. Since acc is a reference that we have borrowed, and since our rule is that functions should return new references to objects, we must incref(acc) when we return the accumulator. In the recursive calls, where we create new links, we should also remember to incref(acc). The new_link() function takes its reference argument, and since we have only borrowed acc, we must get a reference so we can give it away.

A function that takes both arguments would look like this:

```
list reverse_rec(takes list x, takes list acc)
{
  if (is_error(x) || is_error(acc)) {
    decref(x); decref(acc);
    return 0;
  }
  if (is_nil(x)) {
    decref(x);
    return transfer(acc);

  } else {
    int value = x->value;
    struct link *next = incref(x->next);
    decref(x);
    return reverse_rec(transfer(next), new_link(value, transfer(acc)));
  }
}

static inline
list reverse(takes list x)
{ return reverse_rec(x, NIL); }
```

The default argument to the accumulator is now NIL because we want to give the function a new reference to the empty list. If either of the input lists has an error value, we report an error, but because we have ownership of the lists, we must decref() them before we return, also when we have errors, so we do that first. In the base case, we should return acc. We own it, so we can give it away without incref(), but since we also own x, and we do not give it away, we must decref() it. In the recursive case, we need to extract x's value and next before we can decref(x). We need to give x->next to the recursive call, so as with length(), we get a new reference to it before we can call recursively. In the recursive call, we transfer() the accumulator to the recursive call, so we shouldn't decref() that reference.

If you want to concatenate two borrowed lists, you can use this function:

```
list concat(borrows list x, borrows list y)
{
  if (is_error(x) || is_error(y)) {
    return 0;
  }
  if (is_nil(x)) {
    return transfer(incref(y));
  } else {
    return new_link(x->value, concat(x->next, transfer(incref(y))));
  }
}
```

The only reference counting related part of it is remembering that we have only borrowed y, so we cannot give it away. We are giving a reference away when we return it or when we give it to a function that takes the argument, so in both cases, we need to get a reference to y first.

A concatenation function that takes ownership of the lists would look like this:

```
list concat(takes list x, takes list y)
{
  if (is_error(x) || is_error(y)) {
    decref(x); decref(y);
    return 0;
  }
```

```
  if (is_nil(x)) {
    decref(x);
    return transfer(y);
  } else {
    int value = x->value;
    struct link *next = incref(x->next);
    decref(x);
    return new_link(value, concat(transfer(next), transfer(y)));
  }
}
```

Adding a Compiler Extension (Not Portable!)

The code for decref()'ing all arguments that a function "takes," scattered throughout functions, can make the code harder to read. There isn't any way around it if we take ownership of a reference we are responsible for decrementing it unless we give it away. Still, some compilers, at least clang, gcc, and icc that I know of, have an extension that makes it a little easier. This is *not* standard C, but if you are writing code for a specific compiler, and you know that it doesn't have to compile elsewhere, you can exploit it. Very briefly, I will give an example here.

The extension I have in mind is __attribute__((cleanup(f))) that, if you place it where you declare a variable, will tell the compiler to call the function f() with the address of the variable, when the variable goes out of scope. We will use it for lists, so we can define

```
void list_cleanup(struct link **x)
  { decref(*x); }
#define autoclean_list \
  list __attribute__((cleanup(list_cleanup)))
```

The callback function will be called with the address of the variable, and since we are working with lists, which are struct link * pointers, the address will be a pointer to those, so struct link **. When the callback is called, we want to decrement the variable's value, what it points at, since that is the pointer to the link. That is what list_cleanup() does. The autoclean_list macro defines a new type, autoclean_list, that is a list with the callback attribute. Declare a variable as autoclean_list, and the callback will be called when the variable goes out of scope.

The list x here

```
autoclean_list x = new_link(1, new_link(2, NIL));
```

will automatically be decremented (and freed) when x goes out of scope.

The compiler extension doesn't work for function arguments—which would otherwise be nice for our purposes—but it does work for local variables. To use it with function arguments, we can reassign parameters to local variables. A version of new_link() that automatically deletes tail in case of allocation errors could look like this:

```
list new_link(int head, takes list tail_)
{
  autoclean_list tail  = tail_;

  if (is_error(tail)) return 0;
  list new_link = malloc(sizeof *new_link);
  if (new_link) {
    struct link link_data = {
      .refcount = 1,
      .next  = incref(tail),
      .value = head
    };
    memcpy(new_link, &link_data, sizeof *new_link);
  }
  return transfer(new_link);
}
```

We need to incref(tail) when we add it to the link, rather than transfer(tail), since it will be decref()'ed when the function returns.

We don't get much out of it with new_link(), but consider length():

```
int length_rec(takes list x_, int acc)
{
  autoclean_list x = x_;
  if (is_nil(x)) {
    return acc;
  } else {
    return length_rec(incref(x->next), acc + 1);
  }
}
```

Now we get rid of the code for getting x->next before we call recursively, since decref(x) isn't called until x goes out of scope, which doesn't happen until after we have made the function call. So, the recursive case gets more natural code. The same is the case for reverse() and concat():

```
list reverse_rec(takes list x_, takes list acc_)
{
  autoclean_list x = x_, acc = acc_;
  if (is_error(x) || is_error(acc)) return 0;
  if (is_nil(x)) {
    return incref(acc);
  } else {
    return reverse_rec(incref(x->next),
                       new_link(x->value, incref(acc)));
  }
}

list concat(takes list x_, takes list y_)
{
  autoclean_list x = x_, y = y_;
  if (is_error(x) || is_error(y)) return 0;
  if (is_nil(x)) {
    return incref(y);
  } else {
    return new_link(x->value,
                    concat(incref(x->next), incref(y)));
  }
}
```

Simply by assigning the input to local variables of type autoclean_list, we automatically insert decref() at every exit point of the functions. We do not need to worry about accessing links after we have decref()'ed them—that doesn't happen because we do not decref() them as long as they are in scope.

The tail recursion optimization will not be applied, at least not on the compilers I have checked it on, so you will suffer some in speed efficiency if you take this approach, though. Because of that, and because it will no longer be standard-compliant C, this is not an approach I will recommend, but now you know that the possibility exists.

A Generic Reference Counter

With a reference counter for integers and lists under our belts, we might ask ourselves if we could implement generic code for reference counting garbage collection, and the answer, not surprisingly, is yes. All our tricks for generic data structures will work for adding a reference counter to user data. We can embed a counter in our data, and if it is at the top of a struct, we can cast, and if it isn't, we can use the `struct_ptr(p,type,member)` macro from Chapter 14. To learn something new, however, we will take a different approach, where we can also make the reference counter data structure opaque to the user. We will provide the following interface:

```
void *rc_alloc(size_t size, void cleanup(void *, void *));
void *incref(void *p);

// Use this one when decref'ing from a callback
void *decref_ctx(void *p, void *ctx);
// Use this one otherwise

static inline void decref(void *p)
{ decref_ctx(p, 0); }
```

where we only expose reference counted memory through `void` pointers. If you want reference counted memory, you allocate it with `rc_alloc()` that takes a callback for freeing memory as the second argument. That function will be called with the memory you need to free plus a "secret" data structure we use to avoid recursion when freeing cascades to free other objects. The `incref()` and `decref()` functions work as before, but there is a second `decref_ctx()` function for when you decrement from a callback. If you call this version, with the second argument to the callback, you avoid recursion.

To make our code easier to follow, we will still use these macros, but do keep in mind that for a general user interface, we probably want better names.

```
// Annotation macros
#define borrows
#define takes
#define transfer(x) x
```

Those are all the functions and macros we expose in a header file. The rest of the functionality, we hide away in a `.c` file, so we can change it as we see fit.

The data we need to represent a reference counter must reside somewhere in memory, but the addresses we provide the user are theirs to do with as they please, so we cannot put the addresses there. Instead, we will put our bookkeeping information before those addresses. In effect, we are placing reference counters at the top of a structure, except that we do not need a structure. The user doesn't have to use structs but can reference count any data—for example, strings—and we do not need the user to know anything at all about how we handle bookkeeping. We will allocate memory, with malloc(), put our bookkeeping information at the first addresses of the memory we get, and then return a pointer to the memory after that data.

Here, we have to be careful, and I feel that I must stress this because I have seen people forget it countless times. If you do this trick, and you give a user an address higher than the one you got from malloc() yourself, you have to consider alignment. The address we get from malloc() is guaranteed to be such that any data structure can be placed there. That isn't also true for any offset from that address. If we write a function that puts some information at the first addresses and then returns an offset, we must make sure that the user's data can reside at that offset. Otherwise, on some architectures, and for some data, our reference counters will break. Debugging why is going to be hell on Earth.

If your compiler supports C11, and that standard is nine years old at the time of writing so I think it should, it is easy to get right. Then, there is a type, defined in <stddef.h> called max_align_t, that is guaranteed to have the maximum alignment constraints of any type. If a max_align_t can sit at an address, then anything can. We can combine max_align_t with a flexible array member (we used those extensively in Chapter 10 for the same purpose). If we put an empty array with type max_align_t[] after our data, the offset it gets will be valid to return, regardless of what data the user wants reference counted.

If you do not have max_align_t because you are using a compiler for an earlier version of the C standard, then I don't think that there is a portable way to work out what the maximum alignment is from within your program. There is a reason they added the type to the standard, after all. If you cannot get the information out of your system's documentation, a probabilistic approach would be to malloc() a lot of small memory blocks and check how many lower bits are zero. With malloc(), you are guaranteed to get addresses that are maximally aligned, and if it has a non-zero bit somewhere, that is higher than the maximum alignment. This, of course, is not an optimal approach, as you could get unlucky and infer a higher alignment than you need. But I am not aware of anything better that you can do if you don't get the information from the documentation. I will assume that we have a C11 compiler and that we can use max_align_t.

Our reference counter will look like this:

```
struct refcount {
  union { size_t rc; void *stack; };
  void (*cleanup)(void *, void *);
  max_align_t user_data[];
};
```

The rc member is the counter, the cleanup() pointer is for the cleanup callback, and the user_data[] array is there for alignment. The stack pointer is the one we will use to avoid recursing when we delete objects, and I will explain it later. The rc and stack variables are in an anonymous union, since we will never use them both at the same time. We use rc while we have references to the object and stack when we are deleting them. Putting them in a union saves space. On my computer, pointers and size_t are 8 bytes. With rc and stack in a union, the entire struct takes up 16 bytes, which also happens to be the alignment constraint of max_align_t. If you want to know that the maximum alignment is on your machine, you can include <stdalign.h> and use alignof(max_align_t). It might differ from mine, but on my computer, the 16 bytes I use for reference counting is the minimal possible memory I can use if I want to add bookkeeping to general data.

If we put our reference counting data before the user data, we need operations to move back and forth between the addresses. We can use the user_data member to get the user's data, and we can use struct_ptr() to get the reference counting data:

```
#define struct_ptr(p,type,member)                    \
    (type *)((char *)p - offsetof(type, member))
#define refcount_mem(p)                              \
    struct_ptr(p, struct refcount, user_data)
#define user_mem(rc)                                 \
    (void *)(rc->user_data)
```

When we allocate memory, we allocate the number of bytes the user wants plus the size of the reference counter data, initialize the reference counter, and return the user data:

```
void *rc_alloc(size_t size, void (*cleanup)(void *, void *))
```

```
{
    struct refcount *mem = malloc(sizeof *mem + size);
    if (!mem) return 0;

    mem->rc = 1;
    mem->cleanup = cleanup;

    return user_mem(mem);
}
```

With flexible array members, `sizeof` of a struct won't necessarily give us the location of the array, whereas `offsetof()` will, so you could also use

```
#define RCSIZE offsetof(struct refcount, user_data)
void *rc_alloc(size_t size, void (*cleanup)(void *, void *))
{
    struct refcount *mem = malloc(RCSIZE + size);
    if (!mem) return 0;

    mem->rc = 1;
    mem->cleanup = cleanup;

    return user_mem(mem);
}
```

I wouldn't worry about that, however. When there is a difference between `sizeof` and the offset of a flexible array member, it is because of alignment. It happens when the array has lower alignment constraints than the struct itself. That cannot happen with `max_align_t`, so `sizeof(struct refcount)` should be the same as `offsetof(struct refcount, user_data)`. The padding at the end of a structure is there to make alignment work, and it isn't necessary when we explicitly go for alignment to `max_align_t`.

There is nothing new in `incref()`. It works exactly as before, except that we need to adjust the address we get as input to get to the reference counting metadata. We get a pointer to the user's data, and we should return the same, but we need the address of the reference counter to update it.

```
void *incref(void *p)
{
    if (!p) return p;
```

```
  struct refcount *mem = refcount_mem(p);
  mem->rc++;
  return p;
}
```

Because I want to avoid recursion when deleting objects—we don't want to run out of stack space, after all—there is more work in decrementing. Here, the idea is to use the embedded stack variable that we are free to use once we no longer need the counter. If we call decref_ctx(p,x), we use x as a pointer to a stack of objects to be deleted. If x is NULL, we have a top-level deletion, and we will delete the object. If x isn't NULL, we simply put the object on the stack to be deleted later.

We use the function cleanup() for deleting objects:

```
void cleanup(struct refcount *stack)
{
  while (stack) {
    if (stack->cleanup)
      stack->cleanup(user_mem(stack), stack);
    struct refcount *next = stack->stack;
    free(stack);
    stack = next;
  }
}
```

It will iteratively delete objects as long as there are some on the stack, but before it deletes, it calls the user's callback. If the user remembers to use the decref_ctx() function for decrementing, the recursive deletion will go on the stack. Otherwise, the user's objects are still deleted, but with recursive calls to cleanup() via decref().

The decref_ctx() decrements the counter, and if it has to delete, it will do one of two things. If it has a second argument, I call it ctx for "deletion context," it will put the object on the cleanup stack. When that happens, we are already in the process of deleting, and putting the object on the stack schedules it for later deletion. If ctx is NULL, we immediately start a cleanup of the object.

```
void *decref_ctx(void *p, void *ctx)
{
  if (!p) return p; // accept NULL as free() would...

  struct refcount *mem = refcount_mem(p);
  if (--mem->rc == 0) {
    // change the memory for rc/stack to a NULL stack
    mem->stack = 0;
    if (ctx) {
      // Schedule for deletion
      struct refcount *stack = ctx;
      mem->stack = stack->stack;
      stack->stack = mem;
    } else {
      // Start cleanup
      cleanup(mem);
    }
    return 0; // reference is now gone...
  }
  return p;
}
```

Search Trees with Reference Counting

Let us take our fancy new generic reference counter for a spin by implementing
immutable search trees. An immutable tree consists of immutable nodes, and an
immutable node is one where all of the value and the left and the right subtrees are
const:

```
struct node {
  int const val;
  struct node * const left;
  struct node * const right;
};
```

We are going to use reference counting on the nodes, but we do not need to embed any counter information in them when we use the generic reference counting functions.

As with the lists earlier in the chapter, we want to distinguish between "empty" and "error," and we will use NULL pointers to indicate that some allocation error has occurred. This means that we have to use a real object for empty trees, and since all empty trees are alike, we can use a global object for this. However, if we use reference counting on nodes, and we intend to use empty trees as a kind of nodes with no special cases, then the empty tree node must be allocated with the rc_alloc() function. We cannot do this for a global variable, but we can take the approach we did with empty lists and have a function that gives us a special address that represents the empty tree. It will hold a static variable that we cannot initialize where we define it, but we can check if it is NULL, and then initialize it, before we return it.

```
struct node *get_EMPTY(void)
{
  static struct node *empty_node = 0;
  if (!empty_node) empty_node = rc_alloc(sizeof *empty_node, 0);
  if (!empty_node) abort(); // nothing works without it
  return empty_node;
}
```

We can use a macro to get new references to the empty tree and predicates to test if a node is empty or an error, just as we did for lists.

```
#define EMPTY incref(get_EMPTY())

static inline
bool is_empty(borrows struct node *t)
{ return t == get_EMPTY(); }
static inline
bool is_error(borrows struct node *t)
{ return t == 0; }
```

We do not initialize the node part of the empty tree, because we do not intend to use it as a proper node. The purpose of the object is to indicate an empty tree and nothing more. For real nodes, of course, we need initialization, and a function for that can look like this:

```
struct node *new_node(int val,
                        takes struct node *left,
                        takes struct node *right)
{
  struct node *n = 0;
  if (is_error(left) || is_error(right)) goto done;

  n = rc_alloc(sizeof *n, free_node);
  if (!n) goto done;

memcpy(n,
  &(struct node) {
    .val = val, .left = incref(left), .right = incref(right)
  },
  sizeof *n);

done:
  decref(left); decref(right);
  return n;
}
```

The control flow is a little different from what we have seen before, but it is this way, so I only have one exit point from the function, which makes it easier for me to remember to decref() the two tree arguments the function takes. The result will be the node n that we keep NULL until we have passed the points where errors can occur. If either input tree is an error, we jump to the end of the function, at label done, and decref() both trees. At least one of them will be NULL, but decref() can handle that. If we cannot allocate memory for n, we also jump to done, where we decref() the two trees and return NULL (which n will still be). If we make it through the error test and allocation, then we create a node and move the data into the newly allocated memory. Here, we incref() the two trees. If we didn't, we would lose them before we return, when we decref() them. If we didn't incref() them here, we would need a separate exit point for failure and success. It could look something like this:

```
void free_node(void *p, void *ctx); // callback (see below)
struct node *new_node(int val,
                        takes struct node *left,
                        takes struct node *right)
```

```
{
  if (is_error(left) || is_error(right)) goto error;

  struct node *n = rc_alloc(sizeof *n, free_node);
  if (!n) goto error;

  memcpy(n,
    &(struct node) {
      .val   = val,
      .left  = transfer(left),
      .right = transfer(right)
    },
    sizeof *n);

  // success
  return n;

error:
  decref(left); decref(right);
  return 0;
}
```

As long as we remember to decrement the references, or give them away, through any path through the function, we are fine. But you cannot both give them to the new node *and* decref() them. I find the first version easier to read, but your mileage may vary.

The callback for the rc_alloc() function looks like this:

```
void free_node(void *p, void *ctx)
{
  struct node *n = p;
  decref_ctx(n->left, ctx);
  decref_ctx(n->right, ctx);
}
```

When a node reaches reference count zero, we get it here, as a void pointer. It points at a struct node, since we allocated it as such, so we can cast it. To free it, we must decrement the subtrees to release the reference that this node has to them. We use the ctx argument we get when the function is used as a callback, so the reference counting code can avoid recursive calls.

A contains() function on these trees is simple to implement. We can try a borrows version, under the assumption that a user doesn't want us to delete a tree simultaneously with querying it:

```
bool contains(borrows struct node *tree, int val)
{
  assert(!is_error(tree));
  if (is_empty(tree))    return false;
  if (tree->val == val)  return true;
  if (val < tree->val)   return contains(tree->left, val);
  else                   return contains(tree->right, val);
}
```

Because we borrow the reference, there is nothing unusual in the function. There is no incref() or decref() necessary, since we should not decrement borrowed nodes, and we are not returning a node that would have needed a new reference.

The usage pattern of contains() is likely to be something like

```
if (contains(tree, val)) { /* do stuff */ }
```

so borrowing is fine, but with insert() we are more likely to write code such as

```
t = insert(t, val);
```

which tells us that insert() should probably take ownership of its input. We are implementing immutable trees, so we are not getting t back in a modified form. Whatever we get back from the function call is a new tree that holds the elements from the old tree plus val. If we do not get the old tree back, we have lost a reference to it, and we haven't decremented it. We cannot write

```
t = insert(decref(t), val);
```

since that might free t before insert() gets to work with it, so instead we must make insert() handle the decrementing. So, we will implement insert(), so it takes its tree argument:

```
struct node *insert(takes struct node *tree, int val)
{
  if (is_error(tree)) return 0;
  if (is_empty(tree)) {
```

504

```
  decref(tree);
  return new_node(val, EMPTY, EMPTY);
}
if (val == tree->val) return transfer(tree);

int tval = tree->val;
struct node *left = incref(tree->left);
struct node *right = incref(tree->right);
decref(tree);

if (val < tree->val) {
  return new_node(tree->val,
                  insert(transfer(left), val),
                  transfer(right));
} else {
  return new_node(tree->val,
                  transfer(left),
                  insert(transfer(right), val));
}
}
```

The two base cases are error handling, where tree is NULL, and we return NULL, and an empty tree, where we decrement tree and return a new node. Since we decremented the input, we are okay with the ownership, and since new_node() gives us a new reference, we are returning a fresh reference to the user, so we are also fine there. If we find that the value is already in the tree, we can return tree. We own a reference to it, so we can give it to the caller. In the remaining two cases, we will create a new node, with the value we have in tree, one of the existing subtrees, and the result of a recursive call for the remaining tree. Since we intend to give the subtrees to either the new node or the recursive call, we need new references to them. We own a reference to tree, but not its subtrees, so we must incref() them to get our own references. After that, we can safely decref(tree), since the trees we own references to cannot be deallocated. After that, it is a straightforward recursive call in the correct branch.

When removing values, we need to get the rightmost value in the left tree in the general case. We cannot modify the node we find there in any case, so we might as well just get the value in that tree, and for that, we can borrow references:

```
int rightmost_value(borrows struct node *tree)
{
  assert(!is_error(tree) && !is_empty(tree));
  while (!is_empty(tree->right)) tree = tree->right;
  return tree->val;
}
```

For the same reasons as for insert(), we want delete() to take ownership of its input tree. We want to be able to write

```
t = delete(t, val);
```

to "update" an otherwise immutable tree t. The function can look like this:

```
struct node *delete(takes struct node *tree, int val)
{
  if (is_empty(tree)) return transfer(tree);

  int tval = tree->val;
  struct node *left = incref(tree->left);
  struct node *right = incref(tree->right);
  decref(tree);

  if (val < tval) {
    return new_node(tval, delete(transfer(left), val), transfer(right)
  } else if (val > tval) {
    return new_node(tval, transfer(left), delete(transfer(right), val)
  } else {
    if (is_empty(left))  { decref(left);  return transfer(right); }
    if (is_empty(right)) { decref(right); return transfer(left);  }

    int rmval = rightmost_value(left);
    return new_node(rmval, delete(transfer(left), rmval),
                          transfer(right));
  }
}
```

We reply to an error with a NULL pointer, and if we get an empty tree, we give it back. Otherwise, we are going to return a new node where we have modified either the left or right tree, so we need new references to the subtrees and then `decref()` the reference we have to `tree`. Searching left or right to find the node we should delete is straightforward. We create a node that we will hold one of the existing subtrees, which we give to it, and the result of a recursive call, which we give the reference to the other tree. When we have the node we should delete, if either subtree is empty, we decrement that tree and give the other to the caller. Otherwise, we get the value in the rightmost node in the left tree. We are only lending `left` to `rightmost_value(left)`, so we still have the tree after the call. With the `rmval` in hand, we create a new node with that value, we give `left` to a recursive `delete()`, and we give `right` to the new node. The new node is the result.

Circular Structures?

What happens if you have data with a circular structure, for example, circular lists? Can you still use reference counting? The short answer is no. If you want to replace all of your pointers with reference counting pointers, you cannot free memory with cyclic dependencies. Objects that refer to each other in a cyclic structure will never reach count zero—at least not unless you explicitly break the cycle, which is something you probably want to avoid, as that requires the global knowledge of the data structure that we use referencing counting to avoid having.

In many data structures, however, we can have circular dependencies without this issue. There, the trick is to mix reference counting pointers and "raw" or "weak" pointers. For example, if you want to add parent pointers to the nodes in your search trees, you introduce a circular dependency from a node to its children and from the children to the node. But you can use a raw pointer for the parent, for example. Then the reference counter will keep children alive as long as there is a parent that holds a reference to them, but the children will not keep the parent around. If you choose such a strategy, you will have to deal with parents disappearing from children, if that is a problem. If a child can survive longer than a parent, you might, for example, want the deletion callback of a node to set the children's nodes' parent pointers to NULL. It isn't elegant, but it gets the job done.

There are more advanced garbage collection strategies than reference counting and strategies that deal with cyclic dependencies, but they are more complex and beyond the scope of this book. Reference counting gets most of the job done, with little effort and little overhead. It is the method of choice for many applications, including the runtime system of many programming languages. If you find that you need a little extra in terms of memory management, it should be the first strategy you explore.

CHAPTER 16

Allocation Pools

In the last chapter in the book, we will implement our own memory allocation routine. We won't implement the full generality of `malloc()` and friends. There is rarely a need to try to replicate something we already have code for, presumably optimized and thoroughly tested. Instead, we will implement allocation routines optimized for cases where we need to allocate many equally sized objects, and here we can improve upon the performance of the general code that needs to handle the allocation of objects of any size.

There is some overhead to allocating memory, even though `malloc()` is usually very fast. It might involve a system call, and those can be expensive, although with most runtime systems, the allocation and `free()` functions usually have a pool of memory that they can hand out memory from, which alleviates that problem. Still, to keep track of which memory is in use and to correctly handle that you get the right size of memory blocks, and free the right size again, it involves some bookkeeping. A common case, however, is that you have a data structure where you need multiple objects of the same size, like links in a linked list or nodes in a tree. For such an occurrence, we can implement a pool of memory, where we hand out blocks of that size each time we need one. We do not need to search for a block of memory of the right size because all our blocks have the same size, so any free block will do. We need to get memory for the pool of blocks, of course, and for that, we need `malloc()`, but as long as we allocate large chunks of memory, we can minimize the expensive allocations and use the cheap ones most of the time.

If you use such an allocation pool with a data structure, you get another benefit on top of it. When you are done with the data structure and need to free it, you do not need to free all the objects from the pool individually. You don't have to, for example, traverse a tree to free all its nodes, as you would with `free()`. Instead, you can free the allocation pool as a whole and that way free the memory that the tree's nodes use.

So let's dig into implementing an allocation pool.

© Thomas Mailund 2021
T. Mailund, *Pointers in C Programming*, https://doi.org/10.1007/978-1-4842-6927-5_16

A Simple Pool for Tree Nodes

We start with the simplest situation. Assume that we have a struct node that we need a pool for, and assume that we have a cap on how many nodes we will need. If we use nodes in a tree such that we only allocate and never free them—not until we free the entire tree and can free the allocation pool, at least—we can implement an allocation pool similarly to how we implemented the simplest dynamic array in Chapter 9. We allocate a chunk of memory that can hold a fixed number of nodes, and every time we need a new, we get the next free block. The struct for the allocation pool looks like the struct for dynamic arrays:

```
struct node_pool {
  size_t size, used;
  struct node *pool;
};
```

When we allocate a new pool, we allocate memory for this struct and a block of memory for struct node objects:

```
struct node_pool *new_pool(size_t capacity)
{
  struct node_pool *pool = malloc(sizeof *pool);
  if (!pool) return 0;
  pool->pool = malloc(capacity * sizeof *pool->pool);
  if (!pool->pool) { free(pool); return 0; }
  pool->size = capacity;
  pool->used = 0;
  return pool;
}
```

When we free a pool, we need to free the block of memory that holds the nodes and then the struct node_pool itself:

```
void free_pool(struct node_pool *pool)
{
  free(pool->pool);
  free(pool);
}
```

Finally, when we need a node, we get the next free block in the pool:

```
struct node *node_alloc(struct node_pool *pool)
{
  if (pool->used == pool->size) return 0; // Pool is used up
  return &pool->pool[pool->used++];
}
```

If we need more nodes than we allocated memory for, we are out of luck. It is not too bad; there are many applications where we know how many nodes of a tree, or links in a list, that we need a priori. But it is not most of them, so it would be better if we can grow a pool if we need to.

Adding Resizing

The natural instinct when we have to grow an array is to use `realloc()`. Repress that instinct for memory pools. When we hand out nodes from our allocation pools, we are handing out addresses into the array in the pool. If we `realloc()` that array, we have to copy the data to new memory locations. The pointers we have already handed out won't be updated, however. They will still point into the original memory buffer. If you move an object in memory, all the pointers to it have to be updated to its new address. Finding and updating all pointers to an object's address is not for the faint-hearted, and not something I will suggest that you ever attempt. It is, practically, impossible.

We need to grow our memory pool without moving any of the existing objects. That is not really a problem, though, as long as we don't need to store the objects in contiguous memory. We need to do that for arrays, but we don't need memory pools to behave like arrays, after all, so we are not limited in this way. If we need to enlarge the pool, we can allocate a new chunk of memory for more nodes and start to take them from there. That chunk can sit anywhere in memory, as far as we are concerned.

So, we can split a pool into several sub-pools, where each sub-pool is a chunk of contiguous memory, but where the sub-pools are free to be located anywhere. We can chain them together in a linked list to keep track of them that way.

The most straightforward implementation of this idea is to have sub-pools contain a pointer to the next sub-pool and an array of nodes of some constant time:

```
#define SUBPOOL_SIZE 1P24 // an arbitrary number...
struct subpool {
  struct subpool *next;
  struct node nodes[SUBPOOL_SIZE];
};

struct subpool *new_subpool(struct subpool *next)
{
  struct subpool *pool = malloc(sizeof *pool);
  if (pool) pool->next = next;
  return pool;
}
```

We could also use a flexible array member for the nodes in a sub-pool for the data and precede it with a pointer to the next sub-pool and allocate them like this:

```
struct subpool {
  struct subpool *next;
  struct node nodes[];
};

struct subpool *new_subpool(size_t capacity,
                            struct subpool *next)
{
  struct subpool *pool = 0;
  size_t size = offsetof(struct subpool, nodes) +
                (sizeof *pool->nodes) * capacity;
  pool = malloc(size);
  if (pool) pool->next = next;
  return pool;
}
```

With this approach, we can allocate sub-pools of different sizes and perhaps adapt the size of the sub-pools to the algorithm we use them for at runtime. I will assume that we use a constant size for each sub-pool, though.

We still need to keep track of how many empty slots we have in a pool, but there is no need to do this in the sub-pools. We will do the bookkeeping in the pool proper, where we keep track of how many empty slots we have in the top sub-pool:

```
struct node_pool {
  size_t free_slots;
  struct subpool *subpools;
};
```

When we create a pool, we also create the top sub-pool, and then we set the free_slots counter to SUBPOOL_SIZE to indicate that all the slots in the top sub-pool are free for use:

```
struct node_pool *new_pool(void)
{
  struct node_pool *pool = malloc(sizeof *pool);
  if (!pool) return 0;

  struct subpool *subpool = new_subpool(0);
  if (!subpool) { free(pool); return 0; }

  pool->free_slots = SUBPOOL_SIZE;
  return pool;
}
```

When we free a pool, we need to free all the sub-pools. Since we are familiar with how we run through a linked list, there is nothing complicated in that:

```
void free_pool(struct node_pool *pool)
{
  struct subpool *sp = pool->subpools;
  while (sp) {
    struct subpool *next = sp->next;
    free(sp);
    sp = next;
  }
  free(pool);
}
```

It is when we allocate nodes that we need to manage the sub-pools. We will have the invariant that the free slots are all in the top node and that the free slots sit at index free_slots - 1 and down to zero. If we still have free slots left, the next we can give away will thus sit at index free_slots - 1 in the top sub-pool, so we can return the address of that node and decrement the free slots counter. If there are no free slots available, we must allocate a new sub-pool first:

```
struct node *node_alloc(struct node_pool *pool)
{
  if (!pool->free_slots) {
    struct subpool *new_top = new_subpool(pool->subpools);
    if (!new_top) return 0;
    pool->subpools = new_top;
    pool->free_slots = SUBPOOL_SIZE;
  }
  return &pool->subpools->nodes[--(pool->free_slots)];
}
```

Adding Deallocation

Can we also free nodes we have allocated from a pool? We can, of course, free all the memory when we deallocate the entire pool, so the real question is whether we can mark the memory a node occupies as free to be reused by a later allocation. We can do this by chaining free node slots in a linked list, where allocations take the slot at the front of the list, and deallocation prepends a newly freed node to the list.

We do not need to implement such a list of available slots as links containing nodes. Any memory that is used as a node shouldn't be in the free list, and any node in the list shouldn't be used as a node. So, we can embed the list in the same memory as the nodes using a union that is either a linked list pointer or a node:

```
union node_free_list {
  union node_free_list *next_free;
  struct node node;
};
struct subpool {
  struct subpool *next;
  union node_free_list nodes[SUBPOOL_SIZE];
};
```

When we allocate a new sub-pool, it will consist of SUBPOOL_SIZE free nodes, and we should chain these into a free list. If we run through all the slots in the nodes[] array, interpret them as free list pointers in the union, and point them to the address of the next index in the array, we will have chained them. For the last index, we will set next_free to NULL to indicate that it is the last free slot.

```
struct subpool *new_subpool(struct subpool *next)
{
  struct subpool *pool = malloc(sizeof *pool);
  if (!pool) return 0;

  // chain sub-pools
  pool->next = next;

  // chain free node-slots
  for (size_t i = 0; i < SUBPOOL_SIZE - 1; i++)
    pool->nodes[i].next_free = &pool->nodes[i + 1];
  pool->nodes[SUBPOOL_SIZE - 1].next_free = 0;

  return pool;
}
```

The pool proper will have a pointer to the front of the free list, and when we create a new pool, we set the free pointer to the first index in the top sub-pool. That index is the first free slot in the chain we created for the sub-pool.

```
struct node_pool {
  union node_free_list *next_free;
  struct subpool *subpools;
};

struct node_pool *new_pool(void)
{
  struct node_pool *pool = malloc(sizeof *pool);
  if (!pool) return 0;

  struct subpool *subpool = new_subpool(0);
  if (!subpool) { free(pool); return 0; }
```

```
  pool->subpools = subpool;
  pool->next_free = &subpool->nodes[0];
  return pool;
}
```

We do not need to change anything in the function that frees pools. We do not need to iterate through the free list or handle the individual nodes in any way, so freeing a pool is still just a matter of freeing all the sub-pools it contains.

```
void free_pool(struct node_pool *pool)
{
  struct subpool *sp = pool->subpools;
  while (sp) {
    struct subpool *next = sp->next;
    free(sp);
    sp = next;
  }
  free(pool);
}
```

To allocate a node from a pool, we can return the node at the front of the free list and update the free list to point at the next in the chain. If the next_free pointer is NULL, there are no available slots, and we must allocate a new sub-pool. Once we have done that, we have a new list of free nodes that start at the first index in the sub-pool's array.

```
struct node *node_alloc(struct node_pool *pool)
{
  if (pool->next_free == 0) {
    struct subpool *new_top = new_subpool(pool->subpools);
    if (!new_top) return 0;

    // Success, so add new pool to list
    new_top->next = pool->subpools;
    pool->next_free = &new_top->nodes[0];
  }
  struct node *node = &pool->next_free->node;
  pool->next_free = pool->next_free->next_free;
  return node;
}
```

When we want to free a node, we can reinterpret the memory it holds as the union type we use in the pool. It is memory of that type that we have handed to the user, and while they have used it as a `struct node`, we are allowed to cast it back to its true form.[1] If we interpret the memory as the union type, we can write to the `next_free` pointer in it and that way put it at the front of the free list.

```
void free_node(struct node_pool *pool, struct node *node)
{
  union node_free_list *free_list =
                (union node_free_list *)node;
  free_list->next_free = pool->next_free;
  pool->next_free = free_list;
}
```

A Generic Pool

If we can write an allocation pool for `struct node` objects, we can write it for any other type, of course. But as with the other data structures we have considered in the book, it is worthwhile considering one implementation that can handle all types. Can we implement such a generic allocation pool that is oblivious to the concrete types we will allocate memory from?

With the node allocation pools, we never explicitly exploited that the objects in the pools were of any particular type, so it seems as if it should be straightforward to generalize the code. And it is not that difficult. But we did exploit that we knew the underlying type implicitly in a couple of ways, and now we need to handle that without the assistance of the compiler. When we worked with arrays of `struct node` in the sub-pools, the compiler worked out the size of the array for us and made sure that the alignment constraint for nodes was satisfied. That is what we have to handle manually now.

We will handle raw memory, in the form of a buffer we access through a `char *` pointer, in chunks of size `block_size`. We will compute this size, so it satisfies both size and alignment requirements. What that means is the same as `sizeof(T)` means for type T: if we can place an object at an address a, then we can also place one at $a + i *$ `block_size` for all integers i. In sub-pools, we will have a pointer to the next sub-pool and a pointer to raw data:

---

[1]As we know, we cannot always cast any type to any type, but the node from the pool started out as a union, then was cast to the member type, so we are allowed to cast it back.

```
struct subpool {
  char *data;
  struct subpool *next;
};
```

We won't embed the data in the sub-pool this time. We could, but it would have to be at an offset that is a multiple of block_size, so it would require some extra bookkeeping. We wouldn't be able to use a struct member for the data, as we could with the array of nodes. Instead, we would have to allocate memory for both the pointer, SUBPOOL_SIZE * block_size memory for the data, and some extra header, so we could access the data at a multiple of block_size from the beginning of the sub-pool memory. This is not impossible to do, but it is cumbersome. If we use a separate malloc() memory allocation for the data, we know that the first address has maximum alignment and thus that we can place any object there.

Thus, allocating a sub-pool now involves two calls to malloc(): one for allocating the pool and one for allocating the data. The function looks like this:

```
struct subpool *new_subpool(size_t block_size,
                            struct subpool *next)
{
  struct subpool *spool = malloc(sizeof *spool);
  if (!spool) return 0;

  spool->data = malloc(SUBPOOL_SIZE * block_size);
  if (!spool->data) { free(spool); return 0; }

  spool->next = next;
  chain_subpool(spool->data, block_size);

  return spool;
}
```

where the chain_subpool() is responsible for creating a linked list of free blocks.

We do not have a data structure for the blocks and the free pointers, as we are working with raw memory now, but if block_size is large enough—and we will ensure that it is—we can place void pointers in each block and chain them together like that:

```
void chain_subpool(char *data, size_t block_size)
{
  // We need a void ** so we can write a void * into each block.
  void **p = (void **)data + (SUBPOOL_SIZE - 1) * block_size;
```

```
  *p = 0;
  for (size_t i = 0; i < SUBPOOL_SIZE; i++) {
    p = (void **)(data + i * block_size);
    *p = data + (i + 1) * block_size;
  }
}
```

We go through each block and cast its address to void **. If it is a pointer to a void pointer, we can write a void pointer into it. So, we take the address of the next block, computed as data + (i + 1) * block_size. Since data is a char pointer, we are getting addresses block_size apart. It is a char * pointer we get out of this pointer arithmetic, but we can write those into void pointers. If p is the address of a block, interpreted as void **, then *p is a void pointer that we can write to, and that is where we write the address of the next block. The code might be a little hard to decipher, but the result is that for each of the blocks, the first sizeof(void *) of the block_size bytes holds an address. In the last of the blocks, the value is a NULL pointer; we set it in the line *p = 0, and for the remaining blocks, the address is the start of the next block.

The tricky part of making all this work is to have a block_size that will allow you to both embed pointers in the blocks and allow you to place the objects you want the pool to handle. There are two constraints that we must meet. The size of a block must be large enough to both hold void * and the objects, so it must be at least MAX(sizeof(void *), sizeof(T)) if you plan to put objects of type T in the pool. Blocks must also be aligned so you can place both void * and T objects at the beginning of each, so the alignment must be the maximum of the two type's alignment: MAX(alignof(void *), alignof(T)). (Remember that you need to include <stdalign.h> to get alignof().) To satisfy both constraints, block_size must be a multiple of MAX(alignof(void *), alignof(T)) of size at least MAX(sizeof(void *), sizeof(T)), and naturally we want the smallest such multiple. The following function computes such a block size, where the type's size and alignment are in type_size and type_align:

```
#define MAX(a,b) (((a) > (b)) ? (a) : (b))

static inline
size_t aligned_block_size(size_t type_size, size_t type_align)
```

```
{
  // The block size must be a multiple of align of size
  // at least min_size.
  size_t min_size   = MAX(sizeof(void *), type_size);
  size_t align      = MAX(alignof(void *), type_align);
  size_t block_size = ((min_size - 1) / align + 1) * align;
  return block_size;
}
```

To get the block size for objects of type T, you would use `aligned_block_size(sizeof(T),alignof(T)`.

Our plan is to have allocation pools for one type of object only, so we can compute the block size when we create a pool and store it with the pool (together with the sub-pool list and the free list):

```
struct pool {
  struct subpool *top_pool;
  size_t block_size;
  void *next_free;
};
```

We cannot write a function that takes a type as an argument, so we write one that creates a pool based on the size and alignment values instead:

```
struct pool *new_pool_type(size_t type_size, size_t type_align)
{
  size_t block_size = aligned_block_size(type_size, type_align);
  // check size overflow...
  if (SIZE_MAX / SUBPOOL_SIZE < block_size) return 0;

  struct pool *pool = malloc(sizeof *pool);
  if (!pool) return 0;
  pool->top_pool = new_subpool(block_size, 0);
  if (!pool->top_pool) { free(pool); return 0; }

  pool->block_size = block_size;
  pool->next_free = pool->top_pool->data;

  return pool;
}
```

This function looks much like the one from the previous section, except that we need to ensure that we do not have a size overflow when we combine the SUBPOOL_SIZE with the block_size, and we get the first free block in the free list as the address of the sub-pool's data.

It is, of course, more convenient if we can allocate a pool based on a type, and while we cannot write a function that takes a type as an argument, we can write a macro that does it. Therefore, we can write a new_pool() *macro* that takes a type as an argument, get the type's size and alignment specification, and call the new_pool_type() function with those:

```
#define new_pool(type) new_pool_type(sizeof(type), alignof(type))
```

When we free an allocation pool, we must remember to free sub-pools' data as well as the sub-pool, but otherwise that function is straightforward.

```
void free_pool(struct pool *pool)
{
  struct subpool *sp = pool->top_pool;
  while (sp) {
    struct subpool *next = sp->next;
    free(sp->data);
    free(sp);
    sp = next;
  }
  free(pool);
}
```

When we hand out new memory blocks, and when we return them to the free list, the free list is a linked list of void pointers. There is no information about what is at the other end of a void *, so we must cast what we see there to manipulate it. To deliver the next free memory block to the user, we can return the address that pool->next_free points to, but to update the free list, we must also update pool->next_free so it now points at the next block in the list. However, if next_free points at a memory block, that block is free, which means that it should hold data that we can interpret as a pointer in the free list. So we can cast pool->next_free to void ** and read the void * it points at. That will be the address of the next free block, and we should update pool->next_free to point there:

```
void *pool_alloc(struct pool *pool)
{
  if (pool->next_free == 0) {
    struct subpool *new_top =
            new_subpool(pool->block_size, pool->top_pool);

    if (!new_top) return 0;

    pool->top_pool = new_top;
    pool->next_free = new_top->data;
  }
  void *p = pool->next_free;
  pool->next_free = *(void **)pool->next_free;
  return p;
}
```

When we return a block to the pool, we do the same in reverse. We take the memory we are getting back and interpret it as void **. That means that we now consider it as pointing to an address where we can write a pointer to the current free list, after which we can update next_free to point to the now freed block.

```
void pool_free(struct pool *pool, void *p)
{
  void **next_free = (void **)p;
  *next_free = pool->next_free;
  pool->next_free = next_free;
}
```

Manipulating raw memory the way we do with the free lists here means that we have to be super careful. But we made sure that the size and alignment constraints on blocks allow us to put void * data at the beginning of each block, and since we are also careful with casting when we read and write into blocks, we make it work.

We now have a generic allocation pool, from which we can obtain equal-sized blocks of memory and return the blocks to when done using them. If we use the pool in an algorithm, after which we can release all the memory blocks, we can do so as a single operation, and we do not need to free them individually.

We could try to extend our pool so it can handle variable-size memory blocks, but that will add substantially to the bookkeeping, and we would end up implementing our own version of the `malloc()`/`free()` runtime system we already have available. And our solution would likely be inferior to a system that is highly optimized and tested by thousands of users every day.

We could also consider improving the pool, so it deletes sub-pools when they are no longer used. Again, however, I would discourage it. The implementation we currently have doesn't keep track of which sub-pool a block of memory is in, and doing that would incur substantial bookkeeping overhead. Without knowing that, tracking when the last memory block in a sub-pool is released is difficult.

No, I think this is as far as I would take an allocation pool. At least, I have never taken it further, and yet I have managed to implement many data structures with custom allocators for links, nodes, and whatnot. Now you can do so as well.

CHAPTER 17

Conclusions

We have reached the end of the book, and by now, you know everything you need to know to effectively use pointers in your programs. The basic idea behind pointers, seeing them as addresses into memory, where the objects you want to manipulate reside, is a simple one and an elegant solution to many programming issues. You can use pointers to dynamically allocate memory as needed when you only know your needs at runtime. You can use pointers to create recursive data structures—data structures that contain instances of the same structure—such as linked lists and search trees. You can use pointers to code as well, to parameterize your functions with behavior that a function user can provide. You can use indirect references to functions to implement polymorphic data structures, where behavior at runtime is determined by pointers to functions.

Pointers are powerful, and with great power comes great responsibility. You have to treat pointers with respect, or they will punish you. When you use pointers, you are responsible for your own and your program's safety. Misuse them, and you will suffer—and it is so easy to misuse them. You set a pointer up to refer to a vital object in your program. Somewhere else, you release the object because you think you no longer need it. You still have a pointer to it, however, and should you ever be so unfortunate as to access it again—and that easily happens—then destruction will rain down upon you. In any serious C program, you need to use pointers, but you must be careful with them.

It takes experience to safely use pointers, and you will never get to the point where you do not make mistakes. Still, you will make fewer over time and, as a general rule, get better at fixing errors when you do make them. Even the best programmers make mistakes, and programs that have run for decades still contain errors due to incorrect memory usages. They have buffer overflows, memory leaks when the program does not release objects it no longer uses, and dangling pointers referring to memory that is no longer in a sound state. We humans do not appear to be smart enough to write flawless programs, but with experience, we get better at it. We may never achieve perfection,

© Thomas Mailund 2021
T. Mailund, *Pointers in C Programming*, https://doi.org/10.1007/978-1-4842-6927-5_17

but we manage to write useful and (relatively) robust software nevertheless—even in languages such as C.

You now know everything you need to know to effectively use pointers in your programs. You know the conceptual model for pointers—the random access memory model—and you understand the language constructions for creating pointers, manipulating pointers, and accessing the data they point at. You know how we allocate and deallocate memory, how you create data structures using pointers, and how to call functions through pointers. You have seen examples of data structures where we exploit both pointers to data and to functions. The rest is simply more of the same.

This book is too short to cover everything you will run into when you use pointers, but that is okay. In the field where you write your programs, there will be specialized cases, and you will work those out on your own, based on the principles you now know. All it takes, from this point and onward, is experience and applying the techniques that we have covered in new ways. I wish you the best of luck with this.

Index

A

Abstract data structures, 421–428
Actual object, 61, 62
Address, 9–13, 86, 88, 92
aligned_alloc() function, 221, 228, 229,
    440, 441
Alignment, 19–27
alignof(), 21, 519
Allocation functions, 220, 222, 229,
    321, 322, 451
Allocation pools
    adding resizing, 511–514
    deallocation adding, 514–517
    struct node objects, 517
    tree nodes, 510, 511
Arbitrary types, 82–85
Array
    address, 92
    arguments, 105, 123
    bounds, 100
    collections of objects, 91
    const pointers, 91
    declare, 92
    function arguments, 93, 102–105
    function parameters, 102
    index swapping, 126
    integers, 91, 93, 95, 97
    integers/pointers, adding/
        subtracting, 96
    length, 93, 123
    local variable, 124
    memory layout, 15, 22, 94
    memory location, 95
    notations, 96
    parameters, 125
    pointers, 94, 98, 101, 102, 104, 124, 125
    range, 99
    reverse_pointers(), 127
    sizeof(), 92, 98
    struct, 22
    terminal padding, 24
    value, 92
    while-loop solution, 126
Array solution
    compact0() function, 129, 130
    implementation, 128
    non-zero element, 128
    procedure, 128
Assignments
    const and pointers, 59
    pointers to pointers, 60

B

Big-endian/little-endian, 76
Binary search trees, 371
Bit pattern, 50, 69, 76, 144
Bucket sorts, 135
    algorithm, 137
    data structure, 137
    function, 144

© Thomas Mailund 2021
T. Mailund, *Pointers in C Programming*, https://doi.org/10.1007/978-1-4842-6927-5